To Ken O.Connor,
with Best wishes
Ken Shearer

The Investors' and Owners' Guide to Office Building Management

edited by

Kenneth A. Shearer, RPA, CPM

Executive Director
Cushman & Wakefield, Inc.

BUSINESS ONE IRWIN
Homewood, Illinois 60430

This publication is designed to provide accurate and authoritative information in regard to the subject matter covered. It is sold with the understanding that neither the author nor the publisher is engaged in rendering legal, accounting, or other professional service. If legal advice or other expert assistance is required, the services of a competent professional person should be sought.

From a Declaration of Principles jointly adopted by a Committee of the American Bar Association and a Committee of Publishers.

Project editor: Jane Lightell
Production manager: Irene H. Sotiroff
Designer: Laurie Entringer
Compositor: Publication Services, Inc.
Typeface: 11/13 Times Roman
Printer: R. R. Donnelley & Sons Company

Library of Congress Cataloging-in-Publication Data

The Investors' and owners' guide to office building management/
edited by Kenneth A. Shearer.
p.   cm.
ISBN 1-55623-366-3
1. Office buildings—Management. 2. Real estate management.
I. Shearer, Kenneth A.
HD1394.I58 1992
658.2—dc20   91—13120

Printed in the United States of America
1 2 3 4 5 6 7 8 9 0 DOC 8 7 6 5 4 3 2 1

PREFACE

Why another book on property management? In the past few years there have been many changes in the real estate industry. This is a cyclical business, but when a normal cyclical downturn is combined with tax law revisions and overleveraging of developments, the result is reductions in net operating income and, in many instances, foreclosure.

The present real estate market conditions require an emphasis on building management fundamentals. For this reason I have asked respected members of this industry to provide an overview of what they do best in their fields of expertise so that a well-balanced, legally sound collection of articles, each of which is a chapter, could give the reader information and guidance essential to understanding what is required to manage a commercial office building in these changing times.

Each chapter will present its own particular information as an individual source, with no designed interrelationship with other chapters. Obviously, however, the information will intertwine, resulting in a reference work that will supply essential information in a practical way. Because one chapter is not dependent on another, you are encouraged to select the order of each topic according to your own taste, need, or special interest.

Kenneth A. Shearer

ABOUT THE AUTHORS

Kenneth A. Shearer is Executive Director for Corporate Management Services of Cushman & Wakefield, Inc. He is a consultant to all Cushman & Wakefield branch offices Management Services and Project Development Services for building design, operations, systems, and management. He was a marine refrigeration engineer in the U.S. Merchant Marine, where he served from 1942 to 1947. He has been an operating engineer for Rockefeller  Center, then Chief Engineer of a large office and loft complex in Manhattan.

He received his bachelor's degree in Mechanical Engineering from New York University and was an estimator and engineer for five years with a major mechanical contractor in New York City, installing HVAC and plumbing in high-rise buildings. He joined Cushman & Wakefield as an Assistant Property Manager in 1962 and became responsible for the management of more than 70 million square feet of high-rise office building space throughout the country.

He has been involved in the design or start-up of such major projects as Sears Tower, Chicago; Bank of America, San Francisco; Atlantic Richfield Plaza, Los Angeles; Detroit Bank & Trust Building, Detroit; Burroughs Building, Westvaco Building, Burlington Building, Citicorp Center, Pan-Am Building, J.C. Penney Building, Stevens Tower, 1 Astor Plaza, and IBM Headquarters, Manhattan; Champion Paper Headquarters, Stamford, Connecticut; Tampa City Center; Deposit Guaranty National Bank, Jackson, Mississippi; Central National Bank, Cleveland; Dresser Tower, Houston; and Indiana National Bank of Indianapolis Headquarters.

Mr. Shearer is a member of The Building Owners and Managers Association of Greater New York, Inc., and an RPA; he is also a member of the Institute of Real Estate Management and a CPM. In addition, he holds membership in the American Society of Mechanical Engineers, the Real Estate Board of New York, the Board of Directors of the New York Realty Advisory Board on Labor Relations, and the American Arbitration Association Panel of Arbitrators.

Carl Borsari is Senior Vice President for operations at Schulweis Realty Inc. and is responsible for the operation and maintenance of all the office space currently managed by the company. Mr. Borsari is a licensed professional engineer, gaining many years of property management and construction engineering experience at Silverstein Properties, Turner Construction, and Pepsico. He was also an environmental engineering officer in the U.S. Air Force and managed his own development business for more than 10 years. He is a First Vice President of the Building Owners and Managers Association and a Vice Chairman of the management division of the Real Estate Board of New York. Mr. Borsari holds a bachelor's degree in civil engineering from Manhattan College and is a licensed real estate broker in New York.

Calvin Brast is Vice President of Business Development and Modernization for Armor Elevator Company, Inc., a subsidiary of Worldwide Kone Corporation of Finland. In 35 years in the elevator industry, Mr. Brast has held various positions, including Mechanic, Adjustor, Superintendent, Field Engineer, and Chief Engineer. He joined Armor in 1972 and has been very involved in the design and implementation of solid-state SCR drives for Armor and Kone. Mr. Brast also has managed the implementation of the current line of Armor/Kone Products, including microprocessor technology, and has been involved with owners and consultants on many projects worldwide for Armor and Kone.

Joseph C. Canizaro is Chief Executive Officer of Joseph C. Canizaro Interests and is the owner and developer of major projects in the New Orleans area. Over the past 20 years, his firm has completed over 10 million square feet of development including Canal Place, a $500 million, mixed-use development on 23 acres near the French Quarter; the 32-story Texaco Center; a 22-story Crowne Plaza Hotel; buildings for Lykes Steamship Company and Xerox; and the 36-story LL&E Tower, which serves as headquarters for the Louisiana Land & Exploration Company. He is a Trustee and Vice President of programs of the Urban Land Institute and serves on the real estate advisory committee of Harvard University's Graduate School of Design.

Robert O. Castro is a registered professional engineer with more than 30 years experience. As Assistant Chief Engineer for the Rockefeller Center Management Corporation since 1977, he held particular responsibility for energy conservation programs and was involved in the development of local control systems and building automation and operating management information systems. Mr. Castro holds degrees from Brooklyn Polytechnic Institute and Nassau Community College.

James H. Costner is Senior Vice President, National Accounts Services Division, for Willis Corroon, PLC. Mr. Costner is Willis Corroon, PLC's property insurance resource for national accounts. He consults with Willis Corroon, PLC offices and their large clients on matters related to property insurance coverage design, marketing, and loss adjusting. He began his insurance career with Aetna Life and Casualty and later worked for Hobbs Group, a subsidiary of Arkwright Mutual Insurance Company, one of the Factory Mutual Companies.

He is a graduate of Arkansas State University, a CPCU, and ARM. Mr. Costner also has taught risk management at the American University in Washington, D.C. and insurance law at Nashville Tech in Tennessee.

Robert F. Cushman is a partner in the national law firm of Pepper, Hamilton & Scheetz and a recognized specialist and lecturer on all phases of construction and real estate law. He serves as legal counsel to numerous trade associations and construction, development, and bonding companies. Mr. Cushman is editor and coauthor of several books about construction, including the following John Wiley publications: *Construction Litigation; Represent-*
ing the Contractor; Architect and Engineer Liability; Claims Against Design Professionals; Construction Defaults; Rights, Duties, and Liabilities; Construction Failures; and *Construction Bidding Law*. A member of the Pennsylvania bar, he is admitted to practice before the United States Supreme Court and the Court of Appeals for the Federal Circuit. Mr. Cushman served as Executive Vice President and general counsel of the Construction Industry Foundation, as counsel to the American Construction Owners Association, and as regional chairman of the Public Contract Law Section of the American Bar Association. He is permanent chairman of the Andrews Conference Group's Construction Litigation and Hazardous Waste superconferences. Mr. Cushman is a charter member of the American College of Construction lawyers.

Robert De Siena is a Visiting Professor at New York University, Real Estate Institute, and Pratt Institute Graduate School and is Facilities Manager at Ernst and Young's New York headquarters. He is a former Managing Director of Operations and Engineering for Williams Real Estate Company, Inc. and was employed in the property management division of the Irving Trust Company for 23 years. While there he served as Vice President of Fa-
cilities and General Service for 11 years and as a Division Controller of the Real Estate and Administrative Services Division for 8 years.

He is a former President of the Building Owners' and Managers' Association of Greater New York and is currently serving as a Director.

He is also a member of the Executive Committee of the Building Owners and Managers Institute. Mr. De Siena has more than 25 years of experience in finance, accounting, and strategic planning for corporations and full-service real estate agencies. This expertise extends to facilities design, construction management, leasing, maintenance, and security/fire safety in more than 24 million square feet of commercial property throughout the Northeast.

He received his certification in executive development/management from Cornell University in 1981. He also has achieved certifications in Real Property Administration, Facilities Management Administration, and Systems Maintenance Administration from The Building Owners & Managers Institute. Mr. De Siena earned his M.B.A. in finance from St. John's University in 1977 and his B.A. in accounting/finance in 1974 from Pace University.

Steven W. Ford is Vice President of Cushman & Wakefield, Inc. and National Director of the company's Management Services Group. Since joining Cushman & Wakefield in 1976, Mr. Ford has held various staff and management positions. Presently, he is responsible for 100 million square feet in 350 commercial buildings and manages a staff of 53 real estate professionals. He holds a bachelor's degree in accounting and a master's degree in finance from Fairleigh Dickinson University and is pursuing the designation of Real Property Administrator.

Margo C. Grant, an experienced designer for more than 25 years, is Vice President and Managing Principal of the New York office of Gensler and Associates/Architects. In 1973 Miss Grant joined Gensler's Houston office, and since 1979 she has directed the New York office managing a number of outstanding projects for distinguished banking, legal, and corporate clients. Last year she opened the firm's London office, which she oversees as Managing Director. Miss Grant serves on Gensler's management committee and the four-member board of directors. A member of the *Interior Design* magazine Hall of Fame, Miss Grant has had her work published in *The New York Times* and numerous professional design journals.

Kevin F. Haggarty is Executive Director of the Financial Services Group for Cushman & Wakefield, Inc. and is a member of the company's National Management Committee. Mr. Haggarty's expertise includes commercial real estate development, institutional financing, and pension fund and international investment in U.S. real estate. Prior to joining Cushman & Wakefield in 1983, Mr. Haggarty was employed by Salomon Brothers, Inc., where he was re-sponsible for the formation of the commercial real estate group and was in charge of their real estate activities and services from 1980 to 1983. From 1960 to 1980, Mr. Haggarty was associated with the Equitable Life Assurance Society, serving as Manager of the industrial and special purpose properties portfolio, Assistant Vice President and Manager of the office building and hotel portfolio, and Vice President and Officer in Charge of the pension fund separate account. Mr. Haggarty graduated from St. Francis College.

Edward Joyce is a Vice President in the Facilities Management Department of J. P. Morgan and is primarily responsible for the startup and operation of its corporate headquarters building. He has been previously employed as a regional property manager and as a real estate broker for a national commercial real estate firm.

Brad P. Keller is a Manager in the Business Investigation Services Group in the Atlanta office of Coopers & Lybrand. He specializes in providing litigation and reorganization services on real estate and environmental issues. He also has extensive background in providing litigation and management services to troubled financial institutions. Mr. Keller is a member of the American, Oklahoma, and Georgia Bar Associations. He is a 1984 graduate of the St. Louis University School of Law and a 1981 graduate of the University of Missouri with a bachelor of science degree in finance and economics.

Knute P. Kurtz is the partner in charge of the Real Estate Advisory Services Group in the Atlanta office of Coopers & Lybrand. He directs a broad array of services to owners/developers, lenders, and the legal community involved in real estate matters. He is a member of the American Institute of Certified Public Accountants and the Georgia and Louisiana Societies of Certified Public Accountants. He is a contributing author of two books, *Pricing and Proving Construction Claims* and *The Environmental Dispute Handbook*. Mr. Kurtz is a graduate of Nicholls University.

Yee Leung directs the design development and construction documentation for many of Gensler's major corporate and law firm design projects, both in the United States and United Kingdom. Mr. Leung served as Director of architectural design for Gensler's Houston office and later joined the New York office as Director of interior architecture and technical services. He holds a bachelor's degree in architectural engineering from National Cheng Kung University in Taiwan and a master's degree in architecture from Rice University. He has developed systems and procedures to ensure proper coordination between various construction trades and has provided building consultation services for several new corporate headquarters buildings and major office developments in New York City.

Bertram Lewis is an Adjunct Professor of real estate finance and development at the Graduate School of Business at Columbia University and also acts as a consultant. He has been involved in arranging financing for commercial real estate projects since 1965, when he joined the firm of Sonnenblick Goldman Corp. During his 12 years there, he rose to the position of Senior Vice President and was a principal in the company. In 1977, Mr. Lewis organized Sybedon Corporation, a mortgage brokerage and banking firm, and

served as Chairman and principal. In his 25 years of active participation in real estate, Mr. Lewis has been involved with more than $1 billion of financings involving virtually every type of real estate.

Scott C. Liebman is an Associate Director in the financial services group of Cushman & Wakefield Inc., specializing in capital markets. Mr. Liebman's responsibilities include origination, structuring, and placement of real estate transactions and advisory services to corporations, real estate developers, and investors. Prior to joining Cushman & Wakefield, Mr. Liebman was associated with Bankers Trust Company from 1980 to 1984. He graduated from St. Lawrence University with a bachelor of arts degree in 1980.

William O. Lippman, Jr. is President and Chief Executive Officer of Armor Elevator Company, Inc., a subsidiary of Worldwide Kone Corporation of Finland, and Vice President of the board of directors of the National Elevator Industry, Inc. From 1984 to 1987, he served as Vice President of marketing for Armor. Prior to joining Armor, Mr. Lippman worked in the elevator division of Westinghouse Electric Corporation for 24 years, holding various sales and management positions. He graduated from Pennsylvania State University in 1958.

Patrick Lynskey is a principal of Applied Systems and Technologies Inc. (AS&T), an applications engineering systems house founded in 1983 and based in Washington, D.C. AS&T engages in the practical application of emerging computer-based technologies to the day-to-day engineering problems associated with operating and maintaining buildings and plants. Mr. Lynskey is also a principal of two other corporations, both wholly owned by AS&T—Flagship Software Inc., a research, development, and programming operation in Las Vegas, and OASYS, a building systems integration company based in Minneapolis.

Michael J. McCambridge, Senior Vice President of the Rockefeller Center Management Corporation, has operations responsibilities for the 19-building Rockefeller Center complex in New York City. Prior to this position, Mr. McCambridge was affiliated with Cushman & Wakefield, Inc. He joined Cushman & Wakefield in 1970 as an Assistant Vice President in the property management department. He became part of Cushman & Wakefield's De-velopment Consultants Department in 1973 and was elected a Vice President of the firm. In 1982 he was promoted to Director of technical services, with overall technical responsibility for all Cushman & Wakefield projects.

Prior to joining Cushman & Wakefield, Mr. McCambridge was affiliated with Syska & Hennessy, Inc., engineering consultants, serving as project manager for engineering design for the Time & Life Building in Rockefeller Center, among other projects. Mr. McCambridge, a licensed professional engineer, attended the New York Institute of Technology and New York University.

Alfred P. McNulty is President of Applied Project Management Company, a construction management and consulting firm in Cleveland, Ohio. He has developed an effective project control system for medium-sized buildings and has assembled an organization to implement it. His projects have been recognized with significant awards for originality and quality, and for controlled budget and fast schedule. Mr. McNulty is author of *Management of Small* *Construction Projects* (McGraw-Hill, 1981) and numerous articles, and he has taught construction management. After earning a B.S. in Industrial Engineering and an M.S. in Civil Engineering from Princeton and working as a designer, he spent 10 years in field and office roles for Turner Construction, Diesel Construction, and Hunkin Conkey as Vice President before establishing his consulting service. He is a Fellow of the ASCE and is active in community affairs.

Joseph C. Peters is Senior Vice President of Cushman & Wakefield, Inc. and National Director of the company's Development Consultants Group. He is also a member of the company's National Management Committee.

As National Director since 1987, Mr. Peters oversees regional offices where Development Consultants Groups are established. He directs a staff of professionals, including structural, mechanical, and electrical engineers, architects, programmers, auditors, and project managers, who have been the leading consultants to corporate America in analyzing and coordinating the development of headquarters facilities nationwide. He earned his bachelor of science degree in mechanical engineering from the Catholic University of America in 1965 and a master of arts degree from St. Joseph College in 1969.

Jay A. Raphaelson is President of Utility Programs & Metering, Inc. in New York. Prior to establishing the firm in 1977, he was responsible for utility cost allocation at Cushman & Wakefield, Inc. for their commercial properties in New York City. He also held a similar position at Sylvan Lawrence, Inc., a commercial real estate firm in Manhattan.

Mazhar Raslan is President of I.T. Properties in New York and has 17 years of experience in investments, management, and development. He previously was with Banque Indosuez where he raised $90 million of equity capital from Europe and the Middle East for three real estate funds that were invested in commercial properties in the Northeast, on the West Coast, and in Chicago. Prior to joining Banque Indosuez, Mr. Raslan developed and managed properties in Ohio, Florida, and Oman.

Peter G. Riguardi is Executive Vice President of Koeppel Tener Riguardi, Inc. He has handled various leasing activities for Morgan Stanley since 1984 and has represented the following clients in major lease transactions: McGraw-Hill, Standard & Poors, the Swedish Consulate, Tokio Fire & Marine Insurance, First Boston Corporation, and The U.S. Chamber of Commerce. Mr. Riguardi is a graduate of Iona College in New Rochelle, New York.

Kenneth N. Ryan is Executive Vice President and broker with Willis Corroon, PLC in Pasadena, California, and Executive Vice President of their national and international construction industry division. He has been involved with the surety and construction industries since graduating from Gonzaga Law School in 1964 and joining the Travelers Insurance Company claim department. In 1977 he became vice president of the Industrial In-

demnity Surety Department and in 1983 President of Industrial Indemnity Financial Corporation. He is a member of the Associated General Contractors, Construction Financial Management Association, National Association of Security Bond Producers, and Minority Contractors Association.

Stephen B. Siegel is President, Chief Executive Officer, and principal of Chubb Realty, Inc., a real estate investment subsidiary of the Chubb Corporation formed in November 1988. Mr. Siegel has nearly 30 years of experience in the acquisition, development, and leasing of commercial real estate. Prior to joining the Chubb Corporation, he was President, Chief Executive Officer, and Chairman of the Board of Cushman & Wakefield and was instrumental

in its growth as the nation's preeminent commercial brokerage company. In 1987 Mr. Siegel was the leading producer among more than 1,200 Cushman & Wakefield brokers nationwide.

William F. Twomey is Senior Vice President and Director of Property Services for Tishman West Companies. Mr. Twomey graduated with an engineering degree from Pratt Institute in New York City and has more than 25 years of experience in all phases of commercial building property management.

John J. Whalen is General Manager of Fisher Brothers Management Company. He is responsible for supervising the administration and operations of 8 million square feet of commercial office space located on Park Avenue, Avenue of the Americas, and Third Avenue in Manhattan as well as properties in Stamford, Connecticut. He was previously employed by Cushman and Wakefield, Inc., most recently as Vice President and Director of Management

Services, New York Region, where he was responsible for all property management services in New York City, for the coordination of select leasing agencies, and for supervising property management and consulting services in major market cities throughout the United States. Mr. Whalen is a member of the Board of Directors of the Management Division of the Real Estate board of New York, the Building Owners and Managers Association of Greater New York, and the Realty Advisor Board on Labor Relations, Inc. Mr. Whalen is a graduate of S.U.N.Y. at Stony Brook.

AN OVERVIEW OF CUSHMAN & WAKEFIELD

Founded in 1917 as a property management company, Cushman & Wakefield exclusively serves the needs of business in real estate. In addition to management services, its diversified services have grown to include office and industrial/technology sales and leasing, financial and appraisal services, development consulting, and market research. Cushman & Wakefield performs these services in the United States; in Europe, the services are offered through its London-based joint initiative partner, Healey & Baker.

Cushman & Wakefield has been a subsidiary of The Rockefeller Group since 1976. In 1989, Mitsubishi Estate Co. became a major shareholder of The Rockefeller Group.

CUSHMAN & WAKEFIELD'S MANAGEMENT SERVICES

Since its founding, businesses have relied on Cushman & Wakefield's comprehensive management services to translate strategy into results, making the firm America's premier business manager of real estate, with a portfolio in excess of 100 million square feet.

Cushman & Wakefield takes a business-oriented approach, focusing on critical objectives: increasing occupancy, retaining tenants, and achieving positive cash flow or returns on investments.

We are an integrated team of over 1,800 financial, marketing, leasing, managerial, and operational specialists. Our managers are MBAs, certified real estate managers, CPAs, and engineers.

Annually the Management Services Group adds millions of dollars to real estate value and cash flows. Cushman & Wakefield is responsible for a national portfolio, making it the largest nonowner fee manager of business real estate. The portfolio includes mixed-use developments, high- and low-rise office buildings, and industrial parks.

CUSHMAN & WAKEFIELD'S OTHER SERVICES

Commercial Brokerage

Cushman & Wakefield acts as marketing agent for both owners and tenants, and as tenant representative.

As marketing agent, Cushman & Wakefield produces marketing programs to sell, lease, or sublease property quickly and profitably. Action plans include positioning the project in the marketplace, creating effective marketing tools, identifying and qualifying prospective tenants, presenting property features and benefits to prospective tenants, and negotiating favorable rents and terms.

As exclusive tenant representative, Cushman & Wakefield manages each step of the facilities decision process on behalf of the client. This entails understanding what the client needs in terms of facilities, timing, and budget; surveying the market to find the best alternatives available; evaluating the cost of the final choices; and negotiating the most favorable terms possible.

Industrial/Technology Brokerage

Cushman & Wakefield helps businesses identify, evaluate, and negotiate for properties that best satisfy requirements for industrial and high-technology real estate. Cushman & Wakefield has developed a strong nationwide network of brokers to specialize in serving corporate real estate users, investors, developers, and others seeking to acquire, market, or dispose of industrial property.

Appraisal Services

With the largest appraisal organization of any kind in the nation, more than one third of the 180 staff appraisers of Cushman & Wakefield hold the prestigious MAI designation from the Appraisal Institute. Consistent methodology, national coverage, local expertise, accuracy, timeliness, third-party objectivity, and confidentiality are the major reasons why corporate America chooses the Cushman & Wakefield Appraisal Group.

Development Consultants

For 26 years the Development Consultants Group has managed projects totaling over 75 million square feet of office space, ranging from corporate headquarters and major tenant installations to the management of the design and construction of speculative office buildings on behalf of foreign investors.

Financial Services

The Financial Services Group is composed of a multidisciplined, professional staff whose primary business segments are:

- Sales and mortgage of income-producing real property, including office buildings, retail properties, industrial facilities, hotels and other lodging facilities, and multifamily residential projects.
- Negotiation of joint ventures, structuring and placement of participating and convertible mortgages, and securitization of existing commercial mortgages.
- Real estate advisory and consulting services, including analysis and definition of program objectives, real property/portfolio analysis, evaluation/valuation of underutilized properties, and implementation of agreed-upon strategies.

Market Research

Cushman & Wakefield's national research network brings added dimensions of technical expertise, local market knowledge, analytical skills, and creative research techniques to the company's operations. Our research staff lends daily assistance to Cushman & Wakefield brokers and their clients by providing them with the information needed to make informed real estate decisions.

The department prepares specialized local reports and analyses for individual cities and markets. Each local Cushman & Wakefield branch office uses a proprietary database that tracks commercial and industrial properties and availabilities in the respective markets.

The department also provides a wide range of information-gathering, corporate profiling, and location analysis services. The department's professionals provide detailed demographic and economic data for location analysis.

International Capabilities

In May 1990, Cushman & Wakefield moved into the international arena by forming a joint initiative with Healey & Baker, a full-service commercial real estate firm. Healey & Baker maintains 15 offices throughout Europe, including London, Paris, Brussels, and Frankfurt. Through the joint initiative, Cushman & Wakefield provides its services to Healey & Baker clients in the United States. Healey & Baker provides its services to Cushman & Wakefield clients in the United Kingdom and continental Europe.

TABLE OF CONTENTS

PART 1

THE PROPERTY MANAGER

CHAPTER 1

WHAT SERVICES SHOULD THE PROPERTY MANAGER PROVIDE?

William F. Twomey
Tishman West Companies

The basic services that a property manager (or a fee management firm) provides should be consistent regardless of the size or location of the property. The services required may vary depending on the specific needs of the building or its owner. Additional services can be added to the basic services for a fee as required. The manager's goals include

1. Relieving the owner of the day-to-day operation and management of the property.
2. Operating the property to achieve the highest income and the lowest expense *consistent with the goals of the owner.*
3. Preserving and improving the assets of the owner.

Most management contracts provide "standard services," which are defined as manager's or agent's duties. The format varies from contract to contract, and many contracts define the manager's duties in general terms. The "services" usually provided in a "standard" contract are

- Establishing standard operating procedures.
- Setting budgets.
- Accounting.
- Reporting.
- Supervising employees.
- Negotiating utilities and maintenance contracts.

- Obtaining licenses and permits.
- Obtaining insurance.
- Maintenance and repairs.
- Tenant construction.
- Capital improvements.
- General administration.

ESTABLISHING STANDARD OPERATING PROCEDURES

The most basic service the manager provides is establishing a standard operating procedures (SOP) manual. This is the bible that the manager and all his or her employees use in operating the property. This SOP manual should be individualized to meet any unique requirements of the project or of the owner, including any special reporting or accounting requirements.

Depending on the size and complexity of the property, the SOP manual should include an organizational chart that defines and explains the responsibilities and duties of each department and employee category. Job descriptions should include the list of duties required and the reporting expectations for each position.

An effective SOP manual should divide these duties into as many categories as are required to provide reasonable and complete step-by-step instructions. It also should include the appropriate forms and checklists for each category. Sample forms and checklists should be used whenever possible as guides. The manual should include standard forms for every function and job description the manager uses, and it should be updated as changes occur. Some of the categories in the SOP manual include

- An organizational chart.
- Building data.
- General office procedures.
- Accounting.
- A chart of accounts.
- Payroll.
- Reporting.
- Taxes.
- Purchasing.
- Insurance.
- Cleaning.

- Engineering operational procedures.
- Contracted services.
- Life safety procedures.
- Emergency procedures.
- Security requirements.
- Building operations.
- Construction procedures.
- Tenant information.
- Tenant relations information.
- Lease administration policies.
- Advertising and promotion.
- Special events.
- Personnel policies.

There also are many subcategories included under these main headings.

The SOP manual helps provide a consistent level of performance in the administration and operation of the project. It provides the policies and procedures necessary to ensure complete and accurate recordkeeping for the management of the project.

RESPONSIBILITIES OF THE MANAGER

Business Plan

A business plan is normally required for most projects. Usually, owners or asset managers establish a plan for the property that the manager is expected to cooperate with and participate in implementing. If a plan is not available, the manager is responsible for assisting the owner or owner's representative in developing a plan, or if necessary the manager should develop the entire plan for the owner's approval.

The extent of the plan depends on many factors such as age, size, obsolescence, general condition, governmental requirements, market conditions, and the financial condition of the property (i.e., the ability of the property to fund the improvements that may be included in the plan over some agreed-upon time frame.

The plan can be a relatively simple one that covers the operation of the property for a given period of time. (A plan for a new building would usually be less complex than a plan for a older building.) It can include both a short-term and long-term plan for the maintenance and potential improvement of the property, but realistically the plan depends upon the owner's needs and desires. Under usual circumstances this means enhancing the value of the property.

The first step in establishing a business plan is for the manager to communicate with and understand the goals of the owner and, if required, to assist the owner in determining those goals using the manager's overall experience and knowledge of market conditions. If outside brokers are involved in marketing and leasing the property, their experience and recommendations should be included in developing the plan. Information from all pertinent sources should be considered, including code-mandated changes or other rules and regulations of governmental authorities having jurisdiction that could affect the property.

The second step in developing a plan is to prepare a complete report on the condition of the property. This will describe the property's physical, administrative, and financial condition.

The third step is to prepare a written plan for the property, which includes establishing a budget. The budget is usually for a one-year period and generally includes the normal income and expenses that are expected as well as expenses that might be incurred because of obsolescence and/or deferred maintenance discovered during the inspection process. The plan takes into account all the primary functions that are needed for the maintenance and improvement of the property.

The typical plan is divided into four parts: (1) management and building operations, (2) capital improvements, (3) marketing program, and (4) executive summary.

Management and Building Operations
The management and building operations section should include

1. Highlights of inspection results for the physical plant, including mechanical systems, general construction, and so forth. It should also include a prioritized schedule of work that may be required and estimates of the cost to complete such work.
2. Highlights of results of the administrative inspection, including a summary of any pertinent concerns regarding lease administration, reports, accounting information, prior escalation results, arrearage problems, litigation, and so forth. Plans to implement, correct, or improve these areas should be included as well.
3. Present and future staffing requirements and any recommended changes.

4. Contract changes and recommendations on new contracts.
5. Life safety requirements or upgrades, if necessary.
6. Examination of operating costs with recommendations for reductions or increases if required.

Capital Improvements
The capital improvements section should include

1. Recommendations for required capital improvements, including estimates and a time frame for expected completion (these include any capital improvements required by code, major repairs or replacements, general improvements, tenant improvements, etc.).

Marketing Program
The section of the business plan devoted to the marketing program should provide

1. Information on a tenant retention program.
2. A marketing plan for a new space, including budgets for marketing-connected activities such as brochures, fliers, mailings, broker parties, or other activities connected with the marketing effort.
3. A leasing plan, which could include a review of marketing conditions in the immediate area, rates, concessions and vacancies, and historical absorption rates. Recommendations for asking rates, free rent, or other allowances that may be required due to market conditions for renewal, expansion, and vacant space.

Executive Summary
This section should provide

1. A brief overview of the condition of the property and its relative position in the marketplace.
2. A reemphasis of the projected goals set out by the owner and manager and a discussion of the strategies needed to accomplish those goals (particular emphasis on the marketing and leasing plans is important in this section).
3. A restatement of the capital improvements, major repairs, and tenant improvement work needed.
4. Highlights of the financial report and a forecast of expected results, both short term and long term.

Simply put, the plan should address both the short-term and long-term goals of the owner, the process involved in accomplishing those goals, the time frame, the cost, and the expected financial results.

Budget

The budget is a forecast of all anticipated activity affecting the property during the year. It is important that the manager use all available information to provide the owner with a budget that is both useful and accurate. The manager should have a budget format (checklist) that includes the chart of accounts used for the property. This list should show every possible income and expense account that could be used during the calendar and/or fiscal year, including any non-recurring expenses or income. Explanations for all categories of income and expenses should be included in detail. Any potential event that could have an effect on the manager's projections should be explained in advance so that the owner can make appropriate budgetary decisions. Past records, trends, utility company projections, and anticipated increases or decreases due to upcoming negotiations with contractors or employees should all be considered. Expected leasing of all kinds, move-outs, commissions, existing vacancies, capital construction, major maintenance—anything and everything affecting cash flow—should be analyzed.

The budget will forecast annual revenues and expenditures for every account in the manager's or owner's chart of accounts. All budgeted items should be weighted for the 12 months and have narratives and/or schedules as detailed support. An annual budget is weighted by allocating an annual budget amount throughout the 12 months based on when the revenue or expense will be recognized. A weighted budget will identify what, how much, and when an item is to be received or expensed. This is a necessary tool for an owner to analyze the cash flow for the property and to anticipate capital contributions and distributions during the budget period. Every rentable square foot of space in the building should be accounted for in the budgeting of revenues, and all contracts and anticipated expenditures should be considered in the budgeting of expenses.

Utility consumption and *cost* may vary during certain periods of the year, primarily during the summer and winter, and these variations should be considered in calculating the amounts to be included in the weighted budget. Occupancy and its effect on utility and cleaning costs also should be considered. Since utilities and cleaning costs make up a large percentage of operating cost, these charges should be carefully analyzed. Insurance costs and taxes should also be carefully monitored.

The manager is not required to be a tax consultant but is responsible for assuring that the tax bill is accurate and correct. If the manager feels there is a discrepancy, he or she should notify the owner and, if necessary, assist the owner or tax consultant in any appeals process.

Accounting

A manager must maintain an adequate system of records and accounts on a calendar and/or fiscal year basis. These records can be maintained on a cash and/or accrual basis, consistently applied. It is also the manager's responsibility to keep copies of all project records properly filed and under proper security.

The manager must maintain an operating account for the property in a bank or other institution approved by the owner. All cash receipts arising out of the operation of the property will be deposited into this account, and payments of all expenses will be from this account.

Typically, cash receipts are payments of rent and other charges from the tenants of the property. These payments are usually required to be made at the beginning of each month and are in response to a rental invoice supplied to the tenant by the manager. The manager should deposit the payment into the operating account as soon as possible after the cash is received and apply the cash to the tenant's rental account. If the payment is not for the tenant's total outstanding amount, the cash should be applied as specified by the tenant. If not specified, the cash should be applied to the tenant's oldest charges.

Invoices arising out of the operation of the property are matched to purchase orders and delivery receipts; (where applicable) they are coded, approved, and paid. The coding process identifies an invoice as to which cost center will be paying it and which account from the chart of accounts the payment will be charged to. There should be a standard approval process in place to ensure that only proper bills are paid and only the proper amounts are approved. Depending on the amounts to be paid, two or more approvals could be required. Once an invoice is properly coded and approved, it is forwarded for payment. Close control of confirming purchase orders should be maintained, since this is a major cause of duplicate payments.

It is the manager's responsibility to notify the owner of any deficiencies or excess funds in the operating account. Excess funds can be invested in a cash management program approved by the owner, or such funds can be remitted to the owner. Such remittances will usually depend on the operating account balance and anticipated expenditures and collections for the project—for example, accrual of cash for tax or mortgage payments.

It may be necessary for the manager to maintain a separate bank account for the tenant security deposits if required by law or directed by the owner. The owner may wish to have a cash management program applied to the security deposit account.

The manager must supply the owner with monthly accounting reports required under the terms of the management agreement on a timely basis; these are usually included with the monthly report (statement of operations). The monthly accounting report should include a summary of the monthly activity, a listing and explanation of all rental arrears, a statement of occupancy for the project, and a statement of billings, receipts, expenditures, and other financial concerns resulting from the preceding month's operations. A variance report comparing current month and year-to-date profit, loss, and items of income and expense to the budget is also often required as is a forecast of these items for the balance of the year. A building rent roll is also often required.

Rental Arrears are explained as to tenant, amount, description of charges, length of time outstanding, and collection efforts to date.

The *statement of occupancy* should list the percentage and square footage occupied as well as leased. The percentage occupied is used to calculate vacancy credits from the cleaning contract and operating cost adjustments used in calculating escalatable operating costs to be passed on to tenants. However, if rent is being paid on unoccupied space, cleaning and other services must be continued. Otherwise, the tenant may request a rent reduction or cancellation of the lease.

The *rent income statement* details each tenant's prior-period arrears, current billings, total due, total paid, date paid, and arrears forward. There is also a summary page for the property showing total arrears, billing, and collections.

The *expenditures report* lists the current and year-to-date expenditures by account. There should be a brief explanation for every current expenditure.

The *rent roll* is a summary of all current leases at the property. It describes all current billings and all billable charges. It shows lease terms, billing terms, and billing rates. It is preferable for a rent roll to also list leased and vacant (unleased) space at a property. These reports, together with the variance report, give the owner an excellent overview of the current economic status of the project.

At the end of a calendar or fiscal year, an annual accounting report of the project is also required and is included in the manager's annual year-end report. The manager must also cooperate fully with auditors and accountants hired by the owner to perform an annual audit or to prepare tax returns.

Also at the end of a calendar or fiscal year, the manager must compile and prepare schedules of actual and estimated escalatable operating costs and taxes. These costs will be compared to the tenant's base amounts, and the tenant's share of any increases will be calculated. Although there are many different methods employed in the billing of increases in operating costs and taxes to tenants, the intent of all methods is to have the tenants pay their fair share of cost increases caused primarily by inflation and the aging of the building. Typical escalatable operating costs include

- Building payroll.
- Cleaning.
- Security.
- Landscaping and engineering contracts.
- Utilities.
- Building office expenses.
- Building repairs and maintenance.
- Property taxes.
- Insurance.
- Management fees.
- All other costs normally incurred in the operation and maintenance of the building.

Some leases allow the costs of capital improvements to be passed on to the tenant if they are operating cost-saving improvements or improvements required by legislation, e.g., life safety system additions. The costs that can be passed to a tenant are usually specified in the tenant's lease. It is also common to have base and comparative year operating costs adjusted to those that the manager estimates would have been incurred had the building been at a certain, stated occupancy (usually 95 percent). This method provides relative consistency in estimating operating costs from year to year. Adjusting costs to those that would have been incurred at a fixed occupancy will reflect actual increases or decreases in the costs of similar services. Variable operating costs will fluctuate with occupancy, and the intent of these pass-throughs is to compare apples to apples. The manager must check the appropriate tenant lease provisions, compile and adjust operating costs and taxes as called for in the lease, and bill the tenants for their share of any increases.

There are various other formulas used in calculating increases (and sometimes decreases) in rent due to operating costs. One system that is quite common is the use of a *stop clause*. The landlord establishes a flat dollar amount for operating costs and taxes relating to some standard of occupancy (usually 95 percent), and the tenant is responsible for all costs above the stop clause amount agreed upon in the lease. The amount can be stated as a gross amount in total dollars per square foot of leased space. Generally, comparison year's costs are required to be adjusted for occupancy, usually 95 percent. In the event any comparison year's occupancy was less than 95 percent, the estimated costs that would have occurred had the building been 95 percent occupied must be added. The tenant is then billed for any increases in cost over the stop amount.

Some properties use more straightforward formulas based on a labor index, sometimes referred to as the *Penny Formula* or the *Porter Wage Formula*. This method requires increases in rent based on an increase in hourly labor costs, usually on a square-foot basis.

Other forms of calculating rent adjustments are Consumer Price Index (CPI) escalation and percentage rents. *CPI escalation* increases (or decreases) a tenant's base rent in proportion to increases (or decreases) of a particular CPI. *Percentage rent* is additional rent often required of a retail tenant. When sales for a stated period exceed an agreed-upon amount, the tenant must pay the landlord a certain percentage of the overage. This percentage will be stated in the lease.

Regardless of the system used, the manager is responsible for seeing that all items that can be charged to the tenants under the terms of their leases are properly calculated and billed. Other charges that could be billed include

1. Fixed utility charges.
2. After-hours utility charges.

3. Chilled or condenser water for air conditioning supplemental equipment.
4. Operation of air-conditioning equipment after normal operating hours.
5. Tenant charges as sundry billings for miscellaneous extra services.
6. Tenant improvements.
7. Parking charges.

REPORTING

To report to the owner all the activity that occurred during the month, most fee managers use a standard reporting format called a monthly operating report or statement of operations. It includes all the accounting information described previously and all management, leasing and construction information of consequence that occurred during the month. The accounting section should include a current rent roll, rent income statement, arrearage report, expenditure report, variance report, and occupancy report. The variance report compares current income and expenses to the budget and should include explanations of any significant variances from the budget.

The management contract identifies the percentage difference or amounts of variance from the budget that need explanation. This variance report is important because it tells the manager and owner what adjustments need to be made in the management, leasing, and construction of the project for the balance of the year. Such information may also affect decisions for the following year. Major variances could require a reforecasting or a new budget depending on the owner's requirements.

The management section reports on all major activity such as contract changes, employee activity, move-ins, move-outs, insurance claims, tenant issues, litigation, legal issues, maintenance items, and any significant construction activity. The leasing section reports on all current leasing activity, including new leases, renewals, expansions, prospects, marketing activity, and updates on all ongoing negotiations.

The reporting format can vary depending on the owner's requirements, particularly regarding the accounting section. Many owners supply their own reporting format for the managers to use. The report should be designed to provide concise, accurate information that monitors the project's actual performance from month to month.

The manager should provide a year-end report, usually the December statement of operations, which consolidates all the accounting information (income and expenses) for the calendar year and includes a final variance report and other data the owner may need. It should provide a concise, accurate overview of the condition of the project at year end, including trends and reasonable predictions for the coming year.

Employees

The manager is responsible for hiring all direct employees and third-party contractors connected with the operation of the property and is responsible for relieving the owner of liability for the manager's direct employees. The number of direct employees, their type of experience, and their salaries and benefits depend on many factors such as building size, geographic location, experience, number of tenants, building activity, and accounting and reporting requirements of the owner.

The manager's off-site (regional, central office) support may influence employee selection depending on the manager's capability and the support that the regional or central office provides. Central accounting, off-site leasing, engineering, and management support are typical.

To ensure that the most qualified people are hired, the manager should check education and references with former employers and associates. It is also important for the manager to provide proper training for all employees.

It should be understood that usually all employees are the responsibility of the manager and that all payroll costs, compensation insurance, life and health insurance, or any other benefits are the responsibility of the manager. The owner has no liability for these employees, except for the owner's own acts; however, a manager's on-site employees are normally an expense for the owner and are charged to the project as an operating expense. There are also many instances in which a manager may charge the owner a percentage of the fees for off-site employees (e.g., district engineers, part-time managers, district managers, etc.). Generally, this occurs in smaller projects where the size or income from the building does not support full-time personnel. These arrangements should be stipulated in the management agreement.

Utility Contracts

Contracting for utilities such as water, gas, and electricity are straightforward since usually there is only one supplier and one rate for each utility. However, electric companies often have more than one rate for the commercial user. The manager is responsible for substantiating that the rate applied to the project is correct and that any applicable discounts are given. In addition, it is the manager's responsibility to research all business incentive programs developed by the utility companies for either new buildings or for retrofitting existing buildings with energy-efficient equipment or systems.

Maintenance Contracts

The manager is also responsible for assessing the desired level of maintenance service that should be provided to the project. The degree of service can vary depending on such factors as size, location, type of building, type of tenants, and lease commitments. After the service parameters are established, specifications should be developed for each category of service that is required, including janitorial service, window cleaning, trash removal, security, landscaping, elevator maintenance, fire protection, and air conditioning maintenance.

Bid documents should then be prepared for submission to prescreened contractors. Prescreening includes an examination of contractor's capabilities, including analyses of

- Years in business.
- Management staffing.
- Labor force and training methods.
- Quality control measures.
- Affirmative action compliance.
- Insurance capabilities.

The contractor must have sufficient insurance coverage to provide the owner and manager with a level of protection commensurate with the risk associated with the service provided. The bid process identifies the minimum coverage required.

The contract form should include proper indemnification language to protect the owner and manager, and, under most situations, contracts should be cancelable with 30 days notice in writing by manager.

Pricing, while very important, should not be the only consideration in the selection process. Ability, reputation, and insurance and indemnification capacity should also be carefully considered. In certain areas competitive bidding may not be realistic due to the limited availability of contractors; however, logic and good judgment should prevail. In all situations, the owner should be kept informed.

Licenses and Permits

The manager must see that all licenses and permits required by all governmental authorities are current, including any licenses required by the manager and the manager's employees. These may include real estate licenses, business licenses, certificates of occupancy, elevator permits, boiler permits, operator permits, and so forth. Requirements may vary depending on local municipal rules and regulations.

With the exception of those licenses and permits required by the manager to do business, most other requirements are at the expense of the owner and are an operating cost of the project.

Insurance

The manager may be responsible for assisting the owner in obtaining adequate insurance coverage for the project or in securing approval from the owner regarding the insurance coverage and carrier. Reasonable construction replacement cost, adequate rental insurance, and liability coverage are governing factors in determining premium cost. However, it is the responsibility of the owner to set the amounts of adequate coverage.

The manager must do his or her best to ensure that all required certificates of insurance for both tenants and contractors are current. A manager cannot guarantee that every contractor or subcontractor working in the project has adequate insurance, since they may not be made aware of it; however all tenants should be notified of their responsibility to carry the insurance required in their lease and to notify their contractors of the building's insurance requirements. All contractors hired by the manager should provide certificates of insurance with adequate coverage and proper indemnification naming both the manager and the owner as additional named insured.

The property policy should cover all risks, including flood damage, boiler and machinery malfunctions, and general compliance liability in adequate amounts to insure both the owner's and the manager's interest.

The manager may be required to supply a fidelity bond to cover all employees handling money and should obtain adequate liability insurance to cover management operations.

The manager must cooperate with the owner's insurance carriers regarding inspections, recordkeeping, and claims. Claim forms are provided by the carrier, and most large carriers provide an insurance risk manual to be utilized by the manager and his or her employees in handling and processing claims quickly and efficiently. In an emergency situation, the manager may be authorized to expend monies not included in the budget to reduce further losses.

The manager also is responsible for maintaining the risk management program and for implementing inspections for *accident prevention,* which are activities directed at eliminating injury by preventing hazardous situations such as chemical spills, electrical hazards, and fire trap hazards. The risk management manual should include advice and instructions relating to the following:

Industrial Hygiene—activities aimed at reducing and eliminating chronic exposures (e.g., contaminants, carcinogens, toxic substances, etc.).

Safety Training—training for all levels of employees to help reduce risk.

Property Inspections—inspections of tenant, common, and engineering areas and the preparation of reports indicating the conditions observed and any action required.

Emergency Planning—preparation for events such as bomb threats, flood, and fire and preparation of life safety plans where required. Such planning normally requires the preparation of an emergency manual. These potential occurrences vary in different parts of the country (e.g., earthquake, hurricanes, tornadoes, and sandstorms). While fire and flood plans are emphasized, preparation should also be made for short- and long-term power loss.

Maintenance and Repairs

The manager is responsible for the appearance and condition of the project. In addition to determining and communicating what services are expected of the contractor, the manager should provide on-site employees with proper schedules and specifications for all work to be performed on a daily, weekly, monthly, and annual basis. Inspection and reporting procedures should be instituted to ensure that all work is completed satisfactorily and on a timely basis. Inspection reports and checklists should be utilized and should be available to the owner.

While the public areas are most visible and are subject to more scrutiny, the maintenance areas are equally important. Preventive maintenance schedules should be provided for all mechanical systems, including electrical distribution; heating, ventilation, and air conditioning; plumbing and sprinkler (if required), and life safety systems. When a contractor is involved, contract specifications dictate when and what maintenance is required. The manager is responsible for ensuring that the work is properly completed on schedule.

The manager is also responsible for maintaining maintenance records, including life safety system inspections of all alarms, communication systems, and emergency generators. Records should be legible and should be available to the owner, the insurance companies, and other pertinent agencies (e.g., fire prevention departments).

Generally on large properties, the use of personal computers simplifies the tracking and recording of maintenance. In addition, software is available to track budgeted labor hours expended and hours remaining so that productivity or utilization of labor can be managed efficiently.

Tenant Construction and Capital Construction

Depending on the requirements of the management contract, a manager may be responsible for acting as a general contractor, for hiring a general contractor, or for hiring or acting as a construction manager to supervise and/or perform the work.

The manager's primary function is to protect the owner's and tenant's interest. As a minimum, managers must ensure that all building standards are met during the design and construction of all tenant improvement and capital construction and that all code requirements are satisfied.

Building standards vary from structure to structure. For instance, older buildings that have undergone constant renovations may have few or no standards. In this case, the manager and the owner should develop minimum standards to provide guidance to tenants and contractors. Building standards are necessary for visible items such as hardware, doors, locks, ceiling systems, lights, and so forth as well as for the mechanical systems being installed. While the manager is not expected to be a mechanical engineer or to be responsible for the design of these systems, he or she should have a working knowledge of reasonable standards for such systems. The type and number of lighting fixtures, electrical outlets, and special circuits should be examined to prevent overloading of existing circuits. Air conditioning layouts should be examined to ensure building standard design cubic feet/minute (CFM) distribution and to ensure that the building standard required zones and thermostats are included in the design and installation. This examination should apply regardless of whether the landlord or the tenant performs the work.

Most leases require the tenant to obtain the landlord's permission to perform alterations. It's the manager's responsibility to ensure that the process is followed for the protection of both the landlord and the tenant. The manager should provide a tenant alteration approval form for the tenant's signature. This form should reiterate the rules of the building as they relate to alteration and should outline the tenant's and contractor's responsibilities. The form should include insurance and indemnification language for the protection of the manager and owner in addition to the normal building requirements, code requirements, life safety requirements, construction requirements (e.g., protection, noise abatement, hours of operation, and elevator use), and other reasonable regulations. The manager may be required to post a notice of nonresponsibility if the tenant is responsible for doing his or her own work.

The manager should also provide building rules and regulations (including insurance requirements) to the contractors involved before any work begins or any bid process takes place. Some alterations are considered overstandard installations. These could include computer rooms, supplementary air conditioning, additional chilled water or condenser water, steam, domestic hot or cold water, and so forth. If required under the lease, the manager should ensure that appropriate charges are billed as additional rent for these utilities.

Lease Administration

The administration of leases is an extremely important duty of the manager. The information in these *tenant files*, or *legal files*, is used to develop and maintain the plan for operating the project—that is, it is used to determine what rent is to be collected for services provided. In addition to the lease documents, these files include pertinent tenant correspondence files that relate to the leases, including rent increase (or decrease) letters, escalation correspondence, and move-in or move-out notices.

Most managers use a lease summary or lease abstract form to consolidate pertinent lease information for easy access. This form includes information such as basic rentable footage leased, percentage of occupancy to total building rentable rates, term of the lease, renewal options, expansion rights, and other significant information. The abstract form, or the summary, should be used in conjunction with a rental drawing that outlines the leased space.

If a third party is responsible for the leasing of the project, the manager must ensure coordination between all parties (including the owner) in order to provide proper documentation to everyone concerned.

General Administration

While the SOP manual attempts to cover as many administrative functions as possible, it cannot include all the personal services provided by the managers and his or her employees. All these services relieve the owner of the day-to-day operation of the property and are too numerous to include in any manual.

Regardless of the project's size, the personal involvement of the manager and his or her employees is important to the project's financial success. Such personal services include use of questionnaires to determine tenant evaluation of the quality of management (tenant retention program); supervision and personal relations with outside contractors; courtesy to visitors; involvement in the community and organizations for the benefit of the project, tenants, and visitors to the project; public relations and marketing within the brokerage community; and coordination and involvement with municipal authorities (e.g., the fire department on the life safety program and local police for the security program) and other groups.

All activity of the manager should be consistent with the goals of the owner and within the guidelines stipulated in the management agreement and the approved budget. The monthly report is the tool for communicating all the activities of the manager. Such proper written communication will help avoid any confusion in providing the services required.

Above all, management is a service business. Serving the owner, tenants, and visitors is the key to success.

CHAPTER 2

HOW TO SELECT A PROPERTY MANAGEMENT FIRM

Edward Joyce
Morgan Guaranty Bank

Building owners have a variety of reasons for hiring a managing agent as opposed to managing their own property. These reasons may be corporate (e.g., this type of work is not the mainstream of their business), economic (e.g., it is more efficient and less expensive to hire a manager), or geographic (e.g., the property location is remote from their business operations). These underlying reasons will influence the owner's selection of a property management firm.

Most building owners use two general guidelines to identify potential candidates:

1. What firms are doing business in the area?
2. What firms have been retained by other building owners in the area?

The list created by the first question may be further reduced by considering the prospective agents' property portfolios. Some firms specialize in office buildings, while others focus on residential, retail, or industrial properties. Again, this narrowing process is a practical means of identifying potential management candidates.

Some of the potential property management firms may be national firms, while others may maintain a purely regional or local presence. This may or may not be a significant factor in the selection process. The national firm may have an advantage if, for example, the owner has several properties in multiple cities and wants them to be managed by one agent. However, while the national firm may have greater organizational depth, the local management personnel of a national firm may not be as capable as those employed by the preeminent regional or local firm.

A review of the prospective management agents will enable the building owner to identify several firms to be considered for the assignment. In most instances, an owner will want to identify at least three such property management firms and, for major assignments, perhaps six or more managing agents.

After the property management firms have been identified, the owner should invite these firms to submit proposals. While a phone call to each of the property management firms would elicit proposals for property management, a written request for proposal (RFP) is more likely to yield the most useful information. In addition to advising each of the management firms of the owner's interest in retaining a managing agent, the RFP enables the owner to identify the information that it considers most relevant, to provide information to the property management firms regarding the building in a clear and equitable manner, and to maintain an audit trail of the selection process.

Similarly, the receipt of the RFP by the prospective managing agent focuses the agent's efforts. It informs the agent of the building owner's expectations and gives the agent a clear sense of direction. The RFP should accomplish the following:

- Invite the property management firm to submit a proposal.
- Provide the basic information that the property management firm needs to prepare its proposal.
- Require the management firm to confirm its intent to bid.
- Establish a process for the prospective agents to make relevant inquiries, in preparation for the proposal.
- Identify the information that, at a minimum, the owner desires to receive as part of the proposal.
- Establish a benchmark schedule for the proposal process.

At the time the RFP is developed, the building owner should provide information that enables the managing agent to quantify the management task. This includes the type of building, number of floors, gross or rentable area, number of tenants, and construction status. For reasons of confidentiality, certain information such as financing arrangements, rent roll, construction documents, standard lease forms, and current or planned staffing need not and should not be provided. Moreover, it may be in the interest of the building owner to require the managing agent to state in writing that all information received will be considered confidential.

Despite the availability of such information in the RFP, the managing agents will still have questions. Initially, the prospective property managers will want to meet the owner and will want to examine the property. These requests are both productive and necessary.

The most important element of a successful relationship between owner and agent is the "corporate fit" of the two firms. It is essential that the firms share a common approach to property management goals and approach. The dialogue that occurs between the individuals involved in the initial meeting will give an indication of this corporate fit. Nonetheless, this initial meeting should not be considered definitive. In some instances, the initial meeting with some of the prospective agents may yield less than ideal results; however, the better agents will make organizational adjustments to improve the corporate fit.

During the site visit, the owner should keep detailed notes of the meetings with each of the agents. Aside from detailing the inquiries made and the observations offered by the firms, the owner should note the names of the individuals visiting the site, their organizational responsibilities, and background information on each. During the site visits, the owner should try to evaluate each property managers' grasp of the assignment, as well as his or her preparation and intended approach to the assignment. All these elements will enable the owner to make informed business judgments regarding the capabilities of the firms and their resources.

Some owners arrange for all competing management firms to meet simultaneously with the owner to visit the site and request additional information. The advantage of this approach is that all competing firms receive the benefit of all responses to inquiries and no firm enjoys an unfair advantage by eliciting more information from the owner. However, one disadvantage of such an approach is that it can result in a rather large and unwieldy meeting. For a major project, one prospective firm may bring six or more individuals to the meeting; if each firm arrives with a similar entourage, the meeting size can grow rapidly. Furthermore, with multiple competitors at the table, the owner has less opportunity to get a feel for each firm's approach and organizational style.

If separate meetings are held with each prospective property management firm and it is determined from those meetings that significant information was not included in the RFP, the owner should share this information with all the other firms. Such significant information includes any material that is likely to affect the structure of the proposal.

Having had the opportunity to visit the site and review the basic information provided by the owner, the prospective managing agents should be able to generate a well-defined proposal. The RFP should identify the information that the owner considers relevant. This information can differ according to each owner's needs but will probably include

Corporate background—The history of the firm, its current organization, and areas of property management activities.

Financial data—A financial disclosure statement, if available, or an annual report.

Staffing—Both on-site staff and staff from the managing agent's office who will be assigned to the property, identifying which staff are reimbursable (in addition to the management fee) and which are not.

Management fee—A statement of the fee structure, whether quoted as a fixed sum or percentage of rent, including scheduled increases, occupancy credits, reimbursable expenses, and other costs charged to the property by the agent.

Term—A statement of the minimum term required, as well as the suggested contract term and cancellation and/or renewal options.

Current management portfolio—A list of the properties they currently manage, indicating which of these are similar to the proposed assignment.

Again, the information required by the building owner will differ according to the owner's specific business needs and the requirements of the property. Note that the preceding list does not include a request for an operating budget for the property. In most instances, the development of a meaningful budget will require a detailed examination of the property and the disclosure of confidential information by the owner. Moreover, the request for such a budget may be perceived as an invitation to submit a low bid at the expense of the owner. This is to say, the agent may establish an above-average fee for his or her services and offset that cost by reducing maintenance levels or understaffing the building.

While the list of information to be provided by the managing agents may initially appear extensive, the response time to the RFP should be kept to a minimum. For example, the written confirmation of intent to bid should be received within three business days; the site visit should be scheduled within 10 business days; and the written proposal should be due within 15 to 20 business days. Most importantly, the RFP should specify a date and time by which the proposal is due in the office and indicate the number of copies of the proposal to be delivered. Those proposals received after the established deadline should be rejected.

Once the proposal is received by the owner, usually in the presence of two or more individuals for audit purposes, the names of the firms and quoted fee structures should be recorded, dated, and signed. It may also be advisable to record other relevant data, such as recommended building staff and supervisory assignments. Although a more detailed review of the proposals will likely be required to properly evaluate the proposals, this initial recording abstract is important for audit purposes.

In the more detailed review of the proposals, the owner will want to consider a number of factors.

- Does the proposal provide a clear response to the information requested in the RFP?
- Is the proposal assembled in a readable fashion?
- Does the proposal reflect a clear understanding of the owner's business objectives and a grasp of the assignment?
- What is the financial strength of the agent?
- What management resources does the agent intend to devote to the assignment?
- What is the agent's experience with similar assignments?
- What special skills or experience does the agent possess that would benefit the owner?
- What is the total cost to the owner for the services to be provided—that is, the quoted fee plus other reimbursable expenses?

These criteria are not intended to be all-inclusive in providing a basis for comparison, rather they are intended as a guideline for evaluation of the merits of the proposals. Both objective and subjective criteria are used to evaluate the abilities of the competing firms, since a more rigid formula approach would be inappropriate. The selection of the managing agent is best accomplished by good business judgment based on relevant information.

An important consideration in the evaluation process is the actual performance of the managing agent on similar projects in the area. Referring to each agent's portfolio of managed properties, provided in response to the RFP, the owner should be able to obtain information regarding the agent's past performance. Most property management firms are willing to provide contact names and phone numbers for references on their professional performance. These should also be checked. However, remember that businesses do not generally provide contact names for assignments that would not yield a good recommendation. One solution would be to ask the agents to list properties that they have managed previously but currently do not, or the owner can use his or her own resources to identify and contact such project owners. This can often provide more useful insights.

Once the proposals have been reviewed and evaluated, the owner may request a formal presentation by the management firms. While it is entirely appropriate to invite all competing firms to make such presentations, it is generally more practical to invite no more than three firms, based on the evaluation of the written proposals submitted. This approach allows the owner to better focus its efforts. While the other proposals should not be declined at this time, the less attractive prospects should be advised that no further efforts are required of them at this time.

In requesting the invited firms to make a formal presentation, the owner should inform them of the management elements that are of particular interest. These might include

- Introduction of the supervisory personnel who will be responsible for the assignment.
- Introduction of the key on-site personnel who will be provided.
- Review of the management reporting systems to be utilized, both financial and operational.
- Methodology to be used in the development of a formal management plan.
- Explanation of the screening process used by the managing agent in employing the on-site staff.
- On-site staff training programs provided by the managing agent.

Of course, other areas particularly relevant to this project should be identified for more detailed review during the presentation.

All the presentations should be scheduled in close proximity to one another. Further, the managing agents should be given a fixed time, say an hour, in which to complete their presentation. As with the site visit, it will be helpful to keep detailed notes during the presentations and to maintain these notes for audit purposes. These notes will be useful in evaluating the information provided during each of the presentations and in making the final selection of the managing agent.

The two primary criteria employed in making the final selection are (1) the owner's judgment of the potential firm's ability to perform the assignment and (2) the owner's assessment of the individuals to be assigned to the project by the potential managing agent. The first criterion is judged to have been met by the time of the presentation, based on the information provided in response to the RFP. Therefore, it is important during each of the presentations for the owner to initiate a dialogue with the agent's proposed staff. The owner will want to explore each individual's prior work experience, demeanor, and understanding of the assignment.

Once the presentations have been completed, the owner's staff should review and document their judgment of the relative merits of each of the property management firms and select the managing agent they consider most capable.

Once a contract has been negotiated with the successful property management firm, written notice to the other competing firms, declining their respective proposals, should be given. Also it is appropriate to call each of the unsuccessful candidates to thank them for their efforts. In either case, it is not necessary for the owner to provide them with reasons for declining the proposal.

The selection process as outlined here provides a framework for communication and decisions. The preparation of the RFP causes the owner to clearly define the assignment and enables the managing agent to provide all the relevant information. The presentation also enables the prospective management firm to further demonstrate its capabilities and to introduce those individuals who are best able to implement the management plan. Most importantly, the process enables the building owner to make an informed business decision.

CHAPTER 3

DEVELOPING THE OWNER'S OPERATIONAL PLAN

John J. Whalen
Fisher Bros.

Effective property management requires that goals be established to provide benchmarks by which a manager's performance can be measured and that these goals be formalized into a structured plan of operation. The scope of this operational plan should include budget analysis, together with job descriptions and functions of the entire staff, including mechanical, janitorial, and other maintenance personnel. Contract review, lease analysis, market review, and strategies must also be considered. The finished document will provide both the owners and the manager with an effective tool for measuring his or her activity and achievements, as well as an overview of the present state and direction of the property with recommended modifications for future operations.

HISTORY OF THE OPERATIONAL PLAN

The development of an operational plan for the owners of real property is a process that has changed considerably. Twenty to thirty years ago, real estate was seen as a long-term investment for housing the investor's business or as a method of providing income for present and future generations of owners. The expenses relating to the real estate, including real estate taxes and utility costs, were fairly constant. Government was reasonably passive about regulating the property once a building was occupied. Tenants were relatively small organizations and had fairly short-term leases and similar office space. As a result, very little planning effort was required, and the cost of preparing tenant space for occupancy was low. This reduced expense usually resulted in greater profits in cases in which the real estate was an investment.

Eventually, the conditions underlying the development of all operating plans began to change. Inflation and governmental involvement in the form of mandated laws brought significant cost increases. Leases became longer, tenants began to extensively reconstruct the space they occupied, and average tenant size began to increase. The types of real estate owners also began to change as other investors joined the traditional ownerships. Many of these new owners held different attitudes concerning the length of time that real estate should be held prior to its sale. One example was the investor who purchased a property in syndication for tax losses with little concern for a positive net operating income (NOI). The combination of these forces has required the property manager to be more sophisticated and technically proficient in creating operational plans. This was particularly true for tax syndication properties after tax law changes forced owners to focus on improving the economic performance of the real estate. Fortunately, the property manager's tools have improved. Without the technological assistance provided by computers, it would be very difficult to develop and monitor the owners' operational plan.

OWNERSHIP PHILOSOPHY

It is essential for a manager to understand the property owner and his or her philosophy of ownership when developing a plan of operation. There are as many different types of owners as there are types of real estate. The operational plan developed for an owner who expects a short-term hold and a sale or flip that generates significant profit is quite different from the long-term ownership approach adopted by many private investor-developers, insurance company investors, and various foreign investors.

To understand the owner's philosophy, it is important for the manager to interact with the owner as frequently as possible. On one hand, a fee or contract manager may have difficulty understanding the owner's philosophy and intentions, as he or she is often uninvolved until after the property's acquisition. Furthermore, the manager is immediately confronted by many day-to-day items requiring immediate attention. On the other hand, the asset or portfolio manager, when involved, usually has taken part in selecting the property and, in many instances, will have a great effect on the development of ownership philosophy. The in-house manager is in the best position to understand the owner's attitude concerning the investment, because he or she has direct contact with the owners.

Owners may also have a philosophy regarding managerial duties, which may range from responsibility for major expenditures (e.g., cleaning and lighting the property), to the location of the on-site manager's office (i.e., whether it should be in the basement or among the tenants), to the appearance of the lobby and lobby staff. Some of these items may not have enormous economic impact; however, if the property manager understands the owner's wishes, he or she will be able to more easily fulfill the intended responsibilities.

Frequently, the person who best understands the owner's philosophy is not the one charged with the development of the operational plan. Although it should be the responsibility of everyone concerned to ensure that all levels of management understand the owner's philosophy, misunderstandings often occur, and the resulting confusion inhibits the development of a workable plan. Different techniques and strategies must be applied to managing a property, depending upon the nature, attitude, and goals of ownership.

Financial Considerations

The manager's involvement with the total cash flow of the property can also have a significant effect on the development of the operational plan. Property managers are often involved at the NOI level, but they may not have an understanding of the debt service for the project. The property manager who creates an operational plan for real property must start by understanding not only the property's present financial condition but also future plans for financial restructuring. Obviously, the owner must take occupancy into account, as no tenants mean no revenue.

For each tenant lease, the property manager should develop an abstract, or brief outline of the pertinent economic and operational facts. This abstract forms the basis for establishing billing of rent and related charges and provides the manager with an easy way to review lease clauses that relate to the effect of the tenant's occupancy on the operation of the property. Special charges and services—for example, those for overtime or supplemental air conditioning, freight elevator service, utility charge arrangements, and unusual hours of operation on holidays or weekends—would normally be included. Operationally oriented abstracts can frequently circumvent the need to maintain a complete set of leases and lease modification documents on-site.

For a well-managed property, the yearly income generated by tenant leases and identified in the rent roll and lease abstracts can easily be calculated and will make forecasting for the next year a reasonably straightforward process. Rent usually includes operating and tax escalations, rent adjustments, service and utility charges, and any other pass-through expenses. It also provides an accurate identification of income, to the extent that the property is significantly leased. Vacant space (for which rent is not being received) provides the only unknown variable in the analysis of income. The property manager must either estimate an amount for this item or consult others to determine an appropriate projected figure.

With annual income as essentially a fixed amount in a fully occupied property during a given year, the issue of other fixed expenses should be addressed. Debt service and other mortgage expenses, ground rent, rental commissions, and other rent-related expenses such as new-tenant alteration costs and cash contributions (as lease inducements) would be included in this category, as would anticipated lease cancellation costs borne by the owner. Not all property managers have knowledge of all costs of the properties they manage, particularly of expenses related to debt service. This information can be especially important in certain situations—for example, when significant vacancies exist or when the lease for a large area is up for renewal. Such information is vital when major expenditures are being considered for capital projects or extensive repairs, as each of these issues will greatly affect the prospective cash flow for the property.

The Effect of Market Position

The market position of a particular property is a key background element in the development of an operational plan. Market conditions must be considered as part of the process of understanding how a specific property fits into the general marketplace. Other market-related elements must also be taken into account when forecasting both income and expense for future periods, so that the property may be properly positioned within the market. The owner must answer several questions about market positioning, including the following:

- Is the property well-positioned, with an excellent location and an excellent owner reputation?
- Is the property in a secondary location and the owner's reputation less than sterling?
- Does the property have curb appeal?

Different approaches must be considered in each case, and they will be affected by the contents of the leases, particularly where increases in operating expenses are concerned. The market positioning of a property will often have a major influence on the nature and level of expenditures undertaken. Not much can be done about the location of a property, but the potential tenant's perception thereof can be modified if the owner wishes to direct money, effort, and time into neighborhood improvement projects. For instance, the nicest house in a not-so-nice neighborhood is less valuable than a nice house in a nice neighborhood, in most cases. The owner can also undertake a variety of aesthetic improvements, staffing upgrades and service improvements can enhance the market's perception of a property. It is imperative that the property manager comprehend where a property stands in a given market framework and, perhaps even more importantly, to be aware of what the neighbors are doing to improve the property next door, across the street, or down the block. For example, rival property owners may undertake any or all of the following improvements:

- Renovating lobbies.
- Contemplating new facades.
- Modernizing existing elevators or installing new ones.
- Redesigning plazas and landscapes.

Such work, carried out by competing property owners, can have a major effect on a property's market position. Even though they may have similar rental values, the amenities and appearances of adjacent properties can influence a tenant's decision to lease space.

Tenant and Lease Considerations

Before developing an operational plan, the owner, manager, and tenant must all clearly understand the terms of the lease. Service clauses, repair clauses, and additional rent charges—particularly escalation charges and their calculation—also significantly effect the property manager's formulation of an operational plan. The type, length, and specific provisions of tenant leases are also important in establishing an operational plan. As a result, the property manager must thoroughly understand the lease provisions; he or she must be able to answer all of the following questions, among others.

1. Which tenants have net lease obligations for all or part of the operating expenses?
2. How are these net expenses managed?
3. Are they incurred by ownership and passed along to the tenant or dealt with directly by the tenant's facility managers?
4. Are utility charges included in the tenant's rent or billed separately?
5. Are there provisions that permit the tenant to change the original contract; for example, can he or she take responsibility for certain services, or purchase directly from the utility instead of purchasing through the landlord?
6. Which of these changes can the property manager expect during the coming year?

Although most office leases include a pass-through of operating expenses in excess of a base or expense stop amount, other leases use a formula clause to calculate operating expense escalations. Such clauses make use of an index—for example, the consumer price index (CPI) or a salary labor rate for a particular type of worker—to calculate the amount by which operating expenses for each tenant will increase. These index clauses greatly reduce overall operating expenses for a property because, for most of these properties, any economies in the operation of the property improve bottom-line profitability. For leases containing pass-through escalation clauses, it is very important that the property manager understands the history of operating expense calculations so that the tenant's operating expenses do not increase disproportionately. This would make collecting billed escalations difficult.

In addition, the manager should avoid a reduction in operating expenses because such action often raises operating costs in subsequent years beyond reasonable levels. The landlord is then confronted with a situation in which he or she has the responsibility to return excess operating expense profit to the tenant. The tenant generally becomes dissatisfied the following year because the previously deferred operating expenses must now be instated. Unfortunately, this often increases operating costs at a higher rate than the rate of inflation the economy experiences. Expenses in which escalation clauses pass along costs over a base year or a dollar stop amount must also be carefully managed. The levels of occupancy during the operating year as well as during prior years may strongly influence escalation billing because some categories of expenses are directly related to occupancy, although others are fixed. Furthermore, some leases allow adjustments to an assumed occupancy level, commonly 95 percent, while others do not.

Lease language, as it relates to the definition of operating expenses, must receive particular attention. Landlords often incorporate into the lease the ability to pass along operating expenses that might otherwise be considered capital expenses. This generally occurs when capital projects either are the result of a mandate by local law or will result in the reduction of operating expense escalation to the tenant. Such expenses will be passed along as operating expenses on some amortization schedule defined in the lease. This approach, which includes the costs of new local laws as items of escalation, is a defense against municipalities' retroactively changing the rules of the game by initiating costly code modifications, since these costs could not have been considered when the tenants' leases were signed. Contrary to conventional wisdom, landlords generally do not reap huge profits from the initial leasing of their office space and, under certain market conditions, may in fact lease space at a loss. Therefore, when additional expenses are incurred because of a change in building code or other ordinance (particularly if such expenses are significant), the landlord must fund them using these methods; if these expenses had been known before leases were signed, they would have formed an element of the economic negotiation. An amortization of such expense allows the landlord to recover these costs while providing a pass-through to the tenant on an equitable basis.

Another critical tenant-related item of concern the property manager faces while developing an operational plan is the anticipated long-term economy viability of the tenants. The renting market generally trails the economy by 6 to 18 months, and, in softer markets, leases are frequently entered into with less-than-optimum protection in the form of rent guarantees. Therefore, in a down-turning economy the future financial condition of a property's tenants can have important consequences for the development of an operational plan. Curiously, in a strong economic environment, buildings may find themselves tenantless. Tenants will leave because of expansion or consolidation requirements that cannot be met by the present landlord. These vacancies do not present the sudden, often unanticipated, reduction in rent that those noted above cause; however, landlords normally prefer not to have vacant space in their property at any time even though rent is paid, because this creates a negative perception in the marketplace.

FORMALIZING THE PLAN

At this point, we have determined the owner's expectations for the term of ownership of the property, the income for the coming year, the tenants' financial condition, and the level of expense required to maintain the property in its market position. The history of operating cost trends, the subject of pass-throughs in tenants' leases, and the definition of those expenses have also been discussed. The next step is to identify items that fall into the two major budget categories—the capital budget and the operating expense budget—which comprise the greater part of the operational plan. The definition of these terms concerning operating expense escalation may vary from lease to lease; however, generally accepted accounting practice can help to define these categories for the purpose of plan development. The chart of accounts is the list of codes that reflects various types of expenses that a given property is expected to incur. It can be very simple or extremely detailed depending upon the nature and requirements of ownership. A square-footage calculation for the property is useful in determining a cost-per-square-foot factor for each category. This figure makes comparison of properties quite easy, and it is particularly helpful if the owner holds a number of different properties. Furthermore, the total cost per square foot of all expenses, including debt service, reflects the break-even rental income required at full occupancy if an accurate area measurement is used.

Once a square-footage number is established for reference, the major categories of expense may then be examined. Charts of accounts frequently contain many categories that identify virtually every possible classification of work expense; however, it is helpful to reduce the number of categories to a few general classifications, in order to permit ready comparison of costs from year to year and from property to property. Different managers may use different general classification headings for categories, depending upon conditions such as the money spent in a typical year or the particular priorities of the owner. For example, a well-located building with a large amount of ornamental metalwork that seeks to maintain its outstanding appearance may identify metal maintenance as a separate category requiring monitoring. Another property may include this item under a "repairs and maintenance" or "contracts" heading. Exhibits 3–1 and 3–2 show examples of charts of accounts. The first exhibit is a detailed Building Owners and Managers Association (BOMA) International chart of accounts, and the second is a chart of consolidated account titles used by Fisher Brothers Management Company. With some definition of categories established, the actual items of expense can be examined. Once the categories have been selected, the expenses made in each category during the fiscal or calendar year defining the budget period can be determined. This determination provides a reasonable starting point. A clear understanding of past years' trends in operating expenses is essential in projecting an accurate forecast of planned expenses for the upcoming year. For a well-run property, a balance is established between controlling or restricting expenses and adequately maintaining the property's appearance and services to uphold its market position. In supervising this process, the property manager must avoid wide swings in expenses, particularly those that can be passed on to the tenants as additional rent. Planned capital expense programs are typically scheduled to coincide with refinancings, which commonly provide the necessary funding thereof. Without proper coordination, property managers can alienate their employers, their accounting departments, their tenants, and their own employees because required or promised work cannot be adequately funded. This underlies the fact that determining which items—capital expenditures or operating expenses—are included in an operational plan should not begin at budget time—that is, at the time when the numbers for operations in the next year are being assembled—but rather much earlier. In a well managed operation, this can mean that planning, especially for major capital expenditures, takes place years earlier.

To provide adequate maintenance and to allow the property to successfully contend for market share, the on-site manager and his or her staff should continuously identify those items requiring immediate or long-term attention. They must also discuss programs that they can effect in order to deal with trends as or before they develop as standards in the market place. Specific programs and services such as security-related contracts, additional staff and personnel, fire alarms, communication systems, air quality tests, and identification of potential hazardous materials must be examined before they become major issues that affect the landlord's ability to rent the property. The manager must develop a list of such items and regularly review, update,

EXHIBIT 3–1
Building Management Functional Chart of Accounts

Current Assets

Cash

10 000	Petty Cash
100	Operating Accounts
	Payroll Accounts
	Building Operating
	Accounts
200	Money Market Accounts
	Repurchase Agreement
	Money Market Investments
	Money Market Demand
	Accounts
300	Reserves/Escrow
	Real Estate Taxes
	Income Taxes
	Sinking Funds
	Capital Replacement Fund

Accounts Receivable

11 000	Office Rent
	Base Rent
	Pass-Through
	Escrow
100	Retail Rent
	Base Rent
	Overage/Percentage
	Pass-Through
	Escrow
	Merchant Association Dues
200	Parking Income
300	Other Rent
400	Miscellaneous Income
500	Other Receivables
	Advances
	Employees
	Utilities
	Interest Receivable
	Intercompany
	Due From Former
	Tenants
	Joint Venture
	Other

Short-Term Investments
Marketable Securities

12 000	Certificates of Deposit
100	Treasury Bills

200	Acceptance of Deposit
300	Treasury Notes
400	Commercial Paper

Prepaid Expenses

13 000	Utilities
	Electric
	Gas
	Fuel Oil
	Steam
	Chilled Water
	Water/Sewer/Coal
100	Insurance
200	Taxes
	Income
	Real Estate
	Personal Property
300	Ground Rent
400	Professional Fees
500	Merchant Association Fees
600	Leasing Commissions
700	Interest Expense
850	Loan Fees
900	Other

Supplies Inventory

14 000	Operating Supplies
	Office Supplies
	Restroom Supplies
	Floor Cleaning
	Light Bulbs
	Water Treatment Chemicals
	Salts
	Flags and Building
	Decorations
100	Construction Supplies
	Drywall
	Electrical
	Cement Tile
	Plumbing
	Light Fixtures
200	Other

Work in Process

14 300	Building Related
	Project Accounts
400	Tenant Related
	Project Accounts

500 Other
Miscellaneous Active
Inactive

Long-Term (Fixed) Assets

Land

15 000 Building Land
100 Garage/Parking Lot
200 Other

Structures

16 000 Building
Common Area Finishes
HVAC
Elevators/Escalators
Security
Fire and Life Safety
Removable Partitions
Initial Leasing Cost
Initial Interest Cost
Financing Fees
Architectural Fees
Legal Fees
100 Leasehold Improvements
(initial)
200 Building Improvements
(second generation)
300 Tenant Improvements (second
generation)
400 Garage
500 Parking Lot Facilities
600 Other

**Accumulated
Depreciation (Structures)**

17 000 Building
100 Leasehold Improvements
200 Building Improvements
300 Tenant Improvements
400 Garage
500 Parking Lot Facilities
600 Other

Furniture, Fixtures, and Equipment

18 000 Automobiles and Motor
Vehicles
100 Electronic Data Processing

200 Building Operating
Equipment
Vacuums
Floor Machines
Closet Sweepers
Window Washers
Grounds Maintenance
Equipment
300 Office Equipment
Typewriters
Copiers
Desks
Communications
Computers
400 Artwork
450 Other

**Accumulated Depreciation
(Furniture, Fixtures, and Equipment)**

18 500 Automobiles and Motor
Vehicles
600 Electronic Data
Processing
700 Building Operating
Equipment
Vacuums
Floor Machines
Closet Sweepers
Window Washers
Grounds Maintenance
Equipment
800 Office Equipment
Typewriters
Copiers
Desks
Communications
Computers
900 Artwork
950 Other

Long-Term Investments

19 000 Stocks
100 Treasury Bonds
200 Mortgages Held

Deferred Charges (Net)

19 300 Rent Abatements

(continued)

EXHIBIT 3–1 (continued)

400	Lease Costs
	Commissions
	Buyouts
	Design Studies
500	Deferred Project Costs
	Marketing Studies
	Common Area Design
	Studies
	Professional Fees
	Real Estate Tax Zoning and
	so forth
600	Organization Costs
700	Loan Costs
800	Goodwill
900	Other

Current Liabilities

Payables

20 000	Accounts Payable
100	Wages Payable
300	Contract Services Payable
	Various Subaccounts
500	Utilities
	Various Subaccounts
600	Property Taxes Payable
700	Tenant Deposits
800	Unearned Rent
900	Unearned Income
950	Other

Short-Term Debt

21 000	Bank Advances
100	Bank Line of Credit

Long-Term Liabilities

Long-Term Concessions

24 000	Foregone Office Rent
100	Foregone Retail Rent
200	Foregone Parking Income
300	Foregone Other Space Rent

Long-Term Debt

25 000	Mortgages
100	Mortgages: Accumulated
	Amortization
200	Notes Payable
300	Bonds Payable
26 000	**Contingent liabilities**

Equity

Paid-In Capital Stock

29 000	Common
100	Preferred

Additional Paid-In Capital

29 200	Common
300	Preferred

Treasury Stock

29 400	Accounts as Needed

Partner Contributions

29 500	Accounts as Needed

Retained Earnings

29 600	Accounts as Needed
700	Distribution

Revenue/Income

Office Rent

30 000	Base Rent
100	Pass-Throughs
	Operating Expense
	Real Estate Tax
	Business Tax
	Insurance
	Common Area
	Operation
	Operating Expenses
	Taxes
	Other
200	Escalations
	Operating Expense
	Real Estate Tax
	Consumer Price Index
300	Lease Cancellations
400	Rent Abatements

Retail Rent

31 000	Base Rent
050	Overage or Percentage
	Rents
100	Pass-Throughs
	Operating Expense
	Real Estate Tax
	Business Tax
	Insurance

Common Area
Maintenance
Operating Expense
Taxes
Other
200 Escalations
Operating Expense
Real Estate Tax
Consumer Price Index
300 Lease Cancellations
400 Rent Abatements
500 Merchant Association Dues
Income

Parking Income

32 000 Daily/Transient
100 Monthly
200 Annual
300 Other Services

Other Space Rent

33 000 Storage Space
100 Antenna
200 Express Parcel Space Rental
300 Tenant Services
400 Shared Tenant Services
500 Other

Miscellaneous Income

34 000 Vending Machines
100 Telephones
200 Signs
300 Late Charges

Operating Expenses

Cleaning Expenses

40 000 Payroll, Taxes, Fringes
Salaries/Wages
Salaries
Hourly Wages
Temporary
Placement Costs
Advertisements
Headhunter Fees
Benefits
Vacations
Payroll Taxes
FICA
Federal
Unemployment

State Unemployment
Workers'
Compensation
Pensions
Medical
Life Insurance
Continuing Education
Other
100 Contract Services
Daily Cleaning Service
Window Cleaning
Special Cleaning
Other (especially not
budgeted)
200 Supplies/Materials/
Miscellaneous
Restroom Supplies
Trash Can Liners/Floor
Cleaning Supplies
Small Tools and Equipment
Uniforms
Laundry
Repairs/Maintenance
Parts
Labor
Outside
300 Trash Removal
Routine
Other (typically not
budgeted)
400 Other

Repairs/Maintenance

41 000 Payroll, Taxes, Fringes
Salaries/Wages
Salaries
Hourly Wages
Temporary
Placement Costs
Advertisements
Headhunter Fees
Benefits
Vacations
Payroll Taxes
FICA
Federal Unemployment
State Unemployment
Workers'
Compensation
(continued)

EXHIBIT 3–1 (continued)

Pensions
Medical
Life Insurance
Continuing Education
Other
100 Elevator Contracts/Materials
Service Contracts
Small Tools and Equipment
Licenses and Inspection
Fees
200 HVAC Contracts/ Materials
Small Tools and Equipment
HVAC: Electricity Service
Contracts
HVAC: Water Service
Contracts
HVAC: Fuel Oil Service
Contracts
HVAC: Sewage Service
Contracts
HVAC: Equipment Rental
300 Electrical Contracts/Materials
Service Contracts
Small Tools and Equipment
Licenses and Inspection Fees
400 Structural/Roof Contracts/
Materials
500 Plumbing
600 Fire and Life Safety
Alarm System Purchases
Alarm System Maintenance
Fire Prevention Expenses:
Inspections, Repairs
700 Other Building
Maintenance/Supplies

Utilities

42 000 Electric
100 Gas
200 Fuel Oil
300 Purchased Steam
400 Purchased Chilled Water
500 Coal
600 Water
700 Sewer

Roads/Grounds/Security

43 000 R/G Payroll, Taxes, Fringes
Salaries/Wages
Salaries

Hourly Wages
Temporary
Placement Costs
Advertisements
Headhunter Fees
Benefits
Vacations
Payroll Taxes
FICA
Federal Unemployment
State Unemployment
Workers'
Compensation
Pensions
Medical
Life Insurance
Continuing Education
Other
100 R/G Contract Services
200 R/G Other Expenses
300 Security Payroll, Taxes,
Fringes
Salaries/Wages
Salaries
Hourly Wages
Temporary
Placement Costs
Advertisements
Headhunter Fees
Benefits
Vacations
Payroll Taxes
FICA
Federal Unemployment
State Unemployment
Workers'
Compensation
Pensions
Medical
Life Insurance
Continuing Education
Other
400 Security Contract Services
500 Security Other Expenses

Administrative

44 000 Payroll, Taxes, Fringes
Salaries/Wages
Salaries
Headhunter Fees

	Hourly Wages		Merchant Association
	Temporary		Expense
	Placement Costs		Special Events/Ceremony
	Advertisements		Political Donations
	Benefits		**Parking Operations**
	Vacations		
	Payroll Taxes	45 000	Cleaning Expense
	FICA	100	Repairs/Maintenance
	Federal	200	Utilities
	Unemployment	300	Roads/Grounds/Security
	State Unemployment	400	Administrative
	Workers'	500	Fixed Expense
	Compensation	600	Leasing Expense
	Pensions		**Leasing Expenses**
	Medical		
	Life Insurance	46 000	Advertising/Promotion
	Continuing Education	100	Commissions
	Other	200	Professional Fees
100	Management Fees	300	Tenant Alterations
	Base		(if directly
	Incentive		expensed;
	Agent Managed		otherwise, see
	Direct Management Fee		49 300)
	General Partner	400	Leasing Costs
	Management Fee		(if directly
200	Professional Fees		expensed;
	Legal Fees		otherwise, see
	Audit Fees		48 000)
	Tax Fees	500	Rent Abatements
	Other Consultants		(if directly
	Trustees Fees		expensed;
300	General Office Expense		otherwise, see
	Leasing Furniture/		48 100)
	Equipment	600	Buyouts
	Supplies/Materials Postage		(if directly
	Telephone		expensed;
	Space Rent		otherwise, see
	Repairs/Maintenance		48 200)
400	Other Administrative		
	Expense		**Fixed Expenses**
	Travel/Entertainment		
	Dues/Subscriptions/		**Fixed Expenses**
	Donations	47 000	Real Estate Taxes
	Management Accounting	100	Building Insurance
	Service		Liability
	Data Processing		General
	Errors/Omission		Boiler
	Insurance	200	Personal Property Taxes
	Car Allowance	300	Other
	Directors Fee		*(continued)*

EXHIBIT 3–1 (continued)

Amortization and Depreciation Expenses

Amortization

48 000   Amortization of Leasing Costs

100   Amortization of Rent Abatements

200   Amortization of Lease Buyouts

Depreciation

49 000   Depreciation: Building

100   Depreciation: Leasehold Improvements

200   Depreciation: Building Improvements

300   Depreciation: Tenant Improvements

400   Depreciation: Garage

500   Depreciation: Parking Lot Facilities

600   Depreciation: Operating Equipment
     Cleaning Equipment
     Repairs/Maintenance
     Roads/Grounds
     Security

700   Depreciation: Office Equipment
     Furniture
     Computers
     Copiers
     Telephone System

800   Depreciation: Artwork

900   Depreciation: Other

Financial Income and Expenses

Interest Income

50 000   Accounts as Needed

Interest Expense

51 000   Accounts as Needed

Ground Rent

52 000   Accounts as Needed

Amortization of Financing Costs

53 000   Accounts as Needed

Provision for Bad Debts

54 00   Accounts as Needed

Income Tax Expenses

55 000   Accounts as Needed
     Federal
     State
     Local
     Other

Transfer/Closing Accounts

59 000   Accounts as Needed

Reprinted with permission by Building Owners and Managers Association (BOMA) International from the *Functional Accounting Guide and Chart of Accounts*, 1988.

EXHIBIT 3–2
Chart of Consolidated Account Types

Electric
Steam
Contract cleaning
Water and sewer
Elevators
General repairs
  07 HVAC repairs
  08 HVAC contract
  09 HVAC computer
  10 Energy conservation
  12 Electrical repairs
  13 Electrical contracts
  17 Carpentry repairs
  18 Flooring
  19 Ceiling
  22 Masonry repairs
  27 Plumbing repairs
  28 Sprinkler and fire alarm
  29 Local laws
  32 Glazing repairs
  34 Roofing and
      waterproofing
  40 Skyclimber rig
  42 Janitorial contract
  44 Security repairs
  45 Telephones
  55 Air sampling
  60 Consulting fees
Supplies
  05 Oil and diesel fuel
  06 HVAC supplies
  11 Electrical supplies
  14 Electrical survey
  16 Carpentry supplies
  20 Signs
  21 Masonry repairs
  26 Plumbing supplies
  31 Glazing supplies
  33 Roof and
      waterproofing
  41 Janitorial supplies
  49 Shades and blinds
  54 Kiosk

Metal maintenance
Painting
Rubbish removal
Lobby and plaza
  maintenance
  15 Lamps for lobby
  24 Marble maintenance
  37 Window cleaning
  38 Noncontract cleaning
  41 Janitorial supplies for
      lobby
  50 Snow removal
Wages and benefits
Security
Miscellaneous operating
expenses
  02 Building office
  35 Water treatment
  39 Laundry and uniform
      cleaning
  43 Landscaping
  45 Telephone
  47 Directory service
  48 Permits and fees
  51 Office supplies
  53 Miscellaneous
  56 Building manager sundry
      expenses
Insurance
Management fee
Real estate taxes
Mortgage
Interest expense
Ground rent
Rent commissions
Rent expense
Legal and accounting
Miscellaneous administration
  expense
Capital improvements
Tenant alterations
Lease cancel
  expense

---

and prioritize it so that as he constructs next year's operational plan, he may address items of critical importance as quickly as possible. Six to eight months before producing the operational plan, the manager should solicit actual estimates for proposed work projects so that budgeted costs may be as accurate as possible. He or she should schedule projects requiring engineering, such as repairing or modifying equipment and buildings, so that accurate pricing may be established well in advance.

Although historical experience is important to both planning and strategic projections, calculations for both income and expense should be established from a zero base for greatest accuracy. That is, projections for the coming year should not simply be predicated on last year's budget, plus or minus adjustment factors, but rather based upon the review of anticipated costs for specific services and operations. The manager should calculate totals for each defined category of income and expense, and then compare these to the previous year's figures. Thus, he or she can modify the operational plan accordingly. Throughout the process of category calculation, the manager should review elements making up the individual categories in order to establish their continued need. As discussed earlier, income should be determined on a lease-by-lease basis; similarly, expenses should be computed based upon actual calculations. The following outline briefly reviews some major categories in the operating budget.

Labor

When reviewing the labor category of operating expenses, the manager must consider each staff member's job description and placement within the organization; a chart showing each individual's position can be helpful. He or she may then add to the plan of operation any jobs that were not listed and may modify the organizational structure as necessary. Although each owner's requirements for this type of chart vary, including these details in the completed operational plan is considered good practice.

Cleaning

Cleaning services may either be contracted or performed by on-staff labor. The advantages of contract cleaning include the contractor's ability to draw from his or her labor pool as required and a discounted price calculated from anticipated tenant sales. For some properties, however, it can be more advantageous for an owner to have on-staff personnel clean, particularly if spotlessness is paramount.

For these reasons, the property manager should review the present arrangement for cleaning services and determine whether to continue or to restructure it, depending upon new or modified specifications or different supervision. In establishing the budgeted amount for the next year's cleaning services, the manager should keep in mind that the labor involved reflects the largest component cost. This element is often determined through collective bargaining negotiations; a result may therefore be accurate for some years and only estimated for others.

In addition to labor costs, contracts or subcontracts for services such as window cleaning, pest extermination, rubbish removal, and sometimes security may be components of the cleaning category. Supplies, including paper products, are also frequently included.

Utilities

The components of this category vary from property to property; however, they typically include some combination of electricity, water, fuel, and steam or chilled water where central distribution of these services exists. Utility costs can be determined from a calculation of projected consumptions, using the appropriate utility rate structures. Discussions with utility companies, industry lobby groups, or both will assist in forecasting realistic rates. Actual utility history, modified by anticipated occupancy and planned changes in the building's operation provides fairly accurate utility consumption projections.

Repairs and Maintenance

The repairs and maintenance category contains the items that are the most discretionary of all those addressed in the operational plan; in the event of an economic downturn, repair and maintenance are invariably cut back first. Service contracts, which sometimes have their own category, can also be found with repairs and maintenance. The elevator maintenance contract usually presents the most significant financial commitment: however, a number of maintenance agreements, encompassing everything from maintenance of metal to flowers in the lobby, are often included. The strategies related to planning and the reasons for certain repair items in relation to rental market considerations were discussed earlier. Most repair items come from the on-site manager's wish list and are directly related to a specifically identified need. Just as he or she does for cleaning, the manager should review all service contracts to identify not only specific costs involved but also required modifications, and to examine contracts that will soon expire and will need renewal or rebidding.

Security

Property security was for many years categorized with cleaning, labor, or contract services. Recently, however, the increasing demand for first-class security services—both from security officers and from technological devices—has significantly increased the amount of money allocated thereto and placed security in a separate category. The manager should evaluate security needs and ways in which a good security system can improve the reputation of a property, to ensure that the services provided accommodate both the property's needs and the owner's cost expectations. As in other service areas, security can be obtained either in-house or on a contract basis, with the quality of personnel and system effectiveness ranging from window-dressing to omnipresent. Cost, owner preference, lease requirements, and market are the primary determinants of the type of service needed, and these, of course, will vary widely among different properties.

Management Fee

To many property managers, the most important of the budget categories is management compensation, usually structured either as a fixed fee or as a percentage of the property's income. Frequently, compensation for leasing activity is treated separately based upon an agreed commission structure. The amount received normally reflects the level of responsibility charged to the property manager; he or she functions as either a member of or the representative of ownership, and, though often under contract, the relationship between manager and owner is difficult to specifically define. The manager usually is evaluated on a performance basis—that is, his or her effectiveness in achieving the goals and expectations of the owner.

The manager should systematically apply zero-base costing to every element of the plan, asking the following questions:

- Is this required?
- What changes can make this better?

- Is the cost reasonable?
- Can the cost be verified?

The manager must consolidate these reviews to develop numbers from the operational plan that are reflected in the cost computations. To present an organized program to the owner, he or she must also review strategies for income and define an approach thereto.

The Evolution of Property Management

Twenty-five years ago, the process of budget development was all but nonexistent in the typical commercial office property. Early budgets consisted of rough pencil calculations and extremely limited supporting information. However, the process became more sophisticated over time, particularly with the movement of insurance companies and pension fund managers into the real estate arena. Only during the last decade, with the advent of the computer, have sophisticated budgets begun to emerge. Because the manager is now expected to provide greater detail in the operational plan, to modify it frequently, and often to present it in a variety of different reporting formats, an easy-to-use system of information management has become essential. Early computerized systems were inflexible and usually inaccessible to the manager actually administering the property; they were typically used only to generate monthly reports that became available for review as late as three weeks after the last records were included. Information management was therefore largely controlled by paper records permitting the on-site manager immediate knowledge of the financial condition of a property. Over time, the evolution of computerized property management afforded more flexible, though usually central, systems of reporting and recording information. These systems generally permitted only limited modification without skilled technical computer programming assistance. The mid-1980s, however, brought the personal computer to property management and provided the on-site and supervising managers with the ability to develop and modify budget forecasts easily and quickly. The variety of spreadsheet programs on the market provided an easy-to-learn, straightforward approach to budget development. Templates created by management for this purpose can greatly reduce the on-site manager's need for budget presentation formats, and they give the manager consistent results. The manager's use of a personal computer throughout the year allows him or her to track budget variance with great accuracy and provides easy preparation for the upcoming year's operational plan.

Expert Assistance

The property manager, during plan development, often requires expert assistance to help provide accurate budget forecasts. Insurance, legal, and leasing specialists are most commonly surveyed in order to develop an operating plan.

The *insurance specialist* has become increasingly helpful in recent years because the once-predictable insurance market has become quite volatile. The types and amounts of insurance are a matter of owner preference; however, changes in the insurance market can force property managers to rethink entire insurance programs from year to year. The property should be inspected every year for insurance purposes not only to aid the insurance consultant in making policy recommendations, but also to review and possibly to eliminate any hazardous activities and conditions. This review can help to reduce future claims and related premium cost. At the same time, the insurance expert should review the contractual insurance provisions to improve the owner's protection by maximizing the transfer of loss and claims risk and of premium payment from ownership to either a contractor or tenant. In addition, when the owner directly purchases labor-related insurance such as health and medical plans, workman's compensation, and so forth, input from expert council can provide useful advice about changing coverage and costs to reflect changes in market or economic pressures.

Legal assistance can be invaluable in cases of rent payment problems, and other specialized legal services are commonly required for labor problems. Perhaps the most common legal expense is that of a certiorari proceeding aimed at reducing real estate tax, which is chargeable to the tenant in escalation if the procedure is successful. Both the legal expense and the anticipated actual tax payments are significant costs that must be included in the plan.

Leasing specialists can be of great help when the manager himself does not administer the renting program for a property. These specialists can come from either outside brokerage companies or in-house leasing departments, and their information is essential not only to accurate income projection but also to unescalatable and capital expense computation. The items included in this category include such things as brokerage commissions and lease-related expenses—construction costs for new tenants, for example—and other costs related to negotiated or prospective leases. Discussions with leasing experts often help to crystallize certain types of major operation expenditures. Issues such as adding more electrical power or supplemental air conditioning, improving or modernizing elevators, and providing sprinkler systems for fire control are each closely related to the renting program, and decisions to undertake such tasks are primarily motivated by leasing needs.

THE OPERATIONAL PLAN'S EFFECT ON PROPERTY VALUE

There are three approaches utilized by the professional real estate appraiser in establishing the value of real estate:

1. The *cost* approach, wherein the appraiser determines the replacement cost of a property—that is, the cost of erecting new bricks and mortar today.
2. The *market* approach, which compares the property under consideration with recent sales of similar properties.
3. The *income* approach, which establish the value of a property by computing the anticipated future income.

Of these, the third approach is the one most frequently used for major real estate office projects and the one that the property manager can affect the most. Because the value of the project is essentially a reflection of income and expense—in other words, NOI—compounded over time, increasing the income while reducing expense for a given property can have a significant effect on value. Furthermore, the manager's ability to continually meet or exceed the projections for NOI may well make the difference in the property's ability to support financing placed on it as a result of the appraisal.

OPERATION UNDER THE PLAN

Different owners will take different positions on the function of an operational plan. To some, the plan should constantly change to adapt to unanticipated changes in the market. Other owners will treat the operational plan as an absolute guide and will expect the property manager to act accordingly. The property manager, whether for formalized reports or for internal review purposes, is best-advised to regard the operational plan as a continuous rather than static document, noting changes and adjustments in order to improve the present plan and to develop the next year's plan. Other conditions, such as economic downturns, utility cost variances, or tenant bankruptcies, may require changing the plan in the middle of an operating year. Income reductions in particular will trigger decisions to reduce expenses, and the property manager must be prepared to modify the operational plan in order to deal with these. Contingency planning in next year's strategy can greatly facilitate such mid-year modifications.

SUMMARY

The completed operational plan is a combination of income and expense projections, backup calculations, descriptive commentary on the operational cost and physical operating functions, and ownership philosophy. The document will provide the owner with a measure of the property manager's performance, and it will provide the property manager with a tool essential to fulfilling his or her fiduciary responsibility.

CHAPTER 4

DEVELOPING A LEASING PLAN

Peter G. Riguardi
Koeppel Tener Riguardi, Inc.

In the 1980s, President Ronald Reagan coined the phrase, "see-through office building." He was referring to buildings that are beautifully designed, are equipped with excellent mechanical features, and are well located, yet have few tenants. An office building is a financial failure if management is unable to attract tenants and keep them. Therefore, the developer must devise a comprehensive leasing plan before construction begins. This plan should be developed keeping in mind (1) the distinguishing features of the building, (2) what the competition is offering tenants, (3) the perception the building should create in the marketplace, and (4) the importance of strategic marketing and promotion.

Once the leasing plan is devised, a strategy to implement it must be developed. This will require the developer to hire brokers or a large sales staff with the marketing expertise necessary to successfully attract potential tenants.

DEVELOPING THE LEASING PLAN

Understanding the Features of Your Building

What features of your building will distinguish it from the other buildings in the marketplace? What advantages does your office building have in terms of location? What unique features set you above the competition? It is critical that developers consider these questions if they are to successfully attract tenants.

The developer must be familiar with the many components of the building. For example, what is the building's core configuration? Center-core buildings with windows on four sides work better for firms that need a number of perimeter offices. Side-core buildings work better for trading operations or insurance firms. What is the size and shape of the floor? For example, 10,000 square feet in the shape of a rectangle and 10,000 square feet in the shape of a square will attract different users. What are the column-spacing designs, the ceiling heights, and the power capabilities of the building? These are important features that potential tenants will consider when making a leasing decision because these features have an effect on equipment decisions. What atmosphere does the lobby convey? What is the appearance of the building from the street? What is the capacity of the air conditioning system? If it is flexible and can run long hours at low prices, it will be attractive, particularly to law firms and banking institutions.

The developer must also have an understanding of the building's limitations. How easily does the building lend itself to modifications or improvements? The developer must be honest and objective about the building. This includes having an open mind when tenants, brokers, and community groups are critical of the project.

An understanding of the importance of the building's location is also crucial in developing a successful leasing plan. Is the building close to where decision makers and CEOs from major firms live? Is it close to transportation for both suburban communities and other business? Are there restaurants and shops nearby?

Different features of a building are important and attractive to different types of tenants. A developer who first understands the building can begin to focus on the type of tenant who will be attracted by the building's unique features.

Seven World Trade Center, constructed by Larry Silverstein in the downtown area of New York, is a building that had large floor plates, a center-core configuration, and high-power capabilities; therefore, it was very attractive to the financial tenant. Seven World Trade Center was built with the idea of attracting tenants in a very fast-growing marketplace in the New York City financial district. The developers understood the building's qualities and developed a leasing plan to take advantage of its technical strengths. The plan was very successful. Initially, Drexel Burnham Lambert committed to the entire 2 million square feet; however, due to poor business, this tenant decided to back out. Nonetheless, because the Silverstein organization understood its own product and the type of tenant who required the elements of its building, it later leased space to Solomon Brothers for its world headquarters.

Identifying and Evaluating the Competition

After the developer has determined the advantages and limitations of the building and the type of tenants who will be attracted to it, the competitive buildings in the marketplace must be identified and evaluated. First, the developer should target buildings with similar features and advantages and study them. In a crowded marketplace, it is especially important that the developing firm note the unique features of its own building. Is it location? Is it style? Is it the ability to provide power to the floors? Is it the floor size? Is it a unique mechanical or architectural feature? All these issues are evaluated when tenants are comparing potential sites. The developing firm must know the features of competitive buildings as well as it knows its own. This understanding of the alternatives available to tenants is important if the developing firm is to successfully sell the strengths of its own building.

Developing a Niche in the Market

Next, the developer must decide what perception its building will create in the marketplace. Is it going to be the classy building on the block? The bargain basement? The technical building? How are the tenants, the brokers, fellow developers, and city legislators going to perceive the building? What is the reputation of the building going to be?

A few years ago, the downtown New York City marketplace was booming due to the growth of the financial community. Four buildings entered the marketplace at about the same time: Seven World Trade Center, developed by the Silverstein organization; Financial Square, developed by HRO International; 75 Wall Street, developed by Barclays Bank; and One Liberty Plaza, a retrofit by Olympia & York. All these buildings had unique features, and their developers all tried to enter the marketplace selling their strong points. Yet, depending on the tenants' needs, each building presented advantages and disadvantages.

The developers of Financial Square wanted it to be perceived as the classy, prestigious, institutional-quality building—the building beyond reproach. Only the highest-quality materials were used, and the best mechanical and ventilation systems were installed. No money was spared in marketing.

75 Wall Street, built just a few feet from Financial Square, also had a prestigious address but had limitations due to its small floor plate. Its developers used an aggressive, competitive approach. Their philosophy was "shop the neighborhood, come to us, and we'll make you a better economic deal."

Seven World Trade Center had large floor plates, strong power capabilities, and a high-quality, oversized lobby. Its developers were targeting big tenants—those who would lease 400,000 to 600,000 square feet. It was perceived as the building for big corporate users.

The developers of One Liberty Plaza pursued a different approach. Their strategy was to reposition the building, create a new lobby, and emphasize the building's prime location.

Each developer entered the marketplace and pursued a different but consistent approach. Financial Square was not a bargain basement; Seven World Trade Center was not dividing floors. Each developer had an objective and pursued a strategy to achieve it, and all had a great deal of activity within their different approaches. In any market, it is important that developers establish a niche and package their building accordingly.

Developing a Marketing Strategy

The first three steps in developing a leasing plan and attracting tenants are accomplished primarily by the developer; however, the fourth step—implementing a marketing strategy—will likely require the help of outside experts such as highly qualified public relations and advertising firms specializing in real estate marketing of buildings and developers. These firms understand the competition. They will help each developing firm to establish a building identity and fit the appropriate marketing options to that identity. Should an expensive brochure be developed? Should paperweights, baseballs, or other promotional items be given away? Should a mailing that details the project be developed? All such promotional and marketing plans can be formulated with the help of a qualified advertising or public relations firm.

Once the developing firm understands the different vehicles that can be used in a promotional and marketing campaign, a budget and schedule will be developed. When budget planning, it is important to remember that funds must be properly allocated to last throughout the leasing period. If all the money is spent on initial marketing plans, there will be none left for later marketing efforts.

One of the most organized marketing plans in New York City was pursued by the developers of 780 Third Avenue. They used a monthly mailing system to send pens, paperweights, pencil sharpeners, brochures, color pictures, and books to both the tenant and brokerage communities. This constant, unchangeable marketing campaign developed the building's identity as a sophisticated, high-quality property that would be attractive to both single-floor users and divided-floor tenants. The campaign attracted Wang Laboratories and many other fine firms.

IMPLEMENTING THE LEASING PLAN

Selecting a Staff

Each developer must decide how best to implement the leasing plan that has been developed. The first concern is whether to hire a broker or an in-house sales staff.

There are many advantages to hiring an in-house staff. They have a single-minded focus in wanting to lease the building, and they understand the building because they are there every day. Also, they are able to get very close to the various brokers who, for obvious self-serving reasons, want to get close to the developer's sales staff. The open-door policy that results between the sales staff and the brokers can be a great advantage. However, the developer must also determine whether an in-house staff is fully aware of what's going on in the marketplace and whether the staff is capable of carrying out the networking necessary to reach all the tenants.

Local brokers have such capabilities. They know the tenants; they are actively involved in canvasing them; they work on commission so there is a high incentive; and they are aware of what is going on in the marketplace. Also, a brokerage firm often has both senior and junior staff members; this offers the developer the advantages of an experienced professional and a junior person who is hungry to attract tenants and earn fees.

Developers choose different staffing options. For example, Tishman Properties, the developer of 1301 Avenue of the Americas in New York (the former JC Penney building) has a very strong and experienced sales staff in the New York marketplace. Although their staff would be more than capable of handling the marketing of this building, Cushman & Wakefield was brought in as a co-broker on the project. The tandem worked well together, attracting such tenants as Dewey Ballantine, a major New York law firm, Coopers & Lybrand, and other fine firms.

Other developing firms such as HRO International, the Silverstein organization, and Olympia & York have leased their buildings on their own, without using brokers to assist in their marketing efforts.

Whatever choice the developing firm makes, management must be cognizant of how the local brokers are involved in leasing space in the community. If the town is a brokerage town, the developer must make sure that an open dialogue and good feelings exist between the firm and the brokerage community. It can only help in leasing space.

Generating Excitement

Now the developer is ready to enter the marketplace, to let the community know what is being planned and what they should expect. At this point, it is important to create talk and excitement about the building and to orchestrate it perfectly. The perception of the building in its early stages will carry on through its entire leasing campaign and long after the building is occupied. Therefore, it is important that the community be told consistently and regularly what is being done. Positive feelings and comments about the project can be generated by ground-breaking ceremonies articles in local magazines and public relations work identifying the development team, its strengths, the quality of construction, and the advantages of the building.

Getting the Message Out

Most marketing campaigns begin at the ground-breaking ceremony. This is the developer's opportunity to tell brokers and users about the plans and goals of the property in a formalized manner. All the work the developer has done earlier, including developing presentation material, selecting promotional items, developing a schedule and budget, and selecting a brokerage and sales staff, will now be tested.

First, the developer should establish a presentation team. This team should include the finance person, the engineer, an owner's representative, and the broker. They will visit all the local brokers and space users and tell the project story in detail. This process is essential, and this group will provide users and brokers with a lasting impression of your building.

Although contacts with brokerage firms are usually done in an assembly-type presentation, contacts with space users may be done on various levels. The presentation team should visit with people who have real estate responsibilities (corporate real estate departments) or who manage real estate for their firms. At the same time, the developer and the higher-level staff should be making contacts with presidents, chairpersons, and executive vice-presidents of targeted companies to create a positive feeling throughout the community regarding the property. This one-on-one contact is more important in leasing space than any advertising or public relations.

Also, the developer must remember that the firms involved with constructing an office building should also be contacted about leasing space. Banks, accountants, lawyers, engineers, public relations firms, advertising firms, real estate firms, and others actively involved in the development of the property are potential tenants. What better way to fill your office building than to have the various people who know the building well and are actively involved in the project be your anchor tenants.

After visiting the major firms, a monthly mailing system should be developed. The mailing would be used to update all interested parties on the project's progress, and unique promotional items could accompany it (e.g., paperweights, rulers, books, etc.).

Other methods of promoting the property include speaking at various community meetings (Rotary, Lions Club, etc.), legal conferences, CFO seminars, and industry-type conference meetings (insurance, banking, accounting, shipping, advertising). These forums give the developer an opportunity to make a presentation in a more open atmosphere and to generate discussion that will lead to a positive image for the property.

As the developer's message is disseminated throughout the community, feedback from the marketplace can be expected. It is important that the developer respect the wisdom of the marketplace and respond to this feedback accurately and in a timely manner.

Today's tenant has many technical needs and has hired consultants (engineers, architects, and construction people) to handle their requirements. Therefore, technical information must be conveyed accurately, in detail, and in the language used by these consultants. The developer must remember that specialists should speak to specialists. A leasing person who knows something about engineering should not be the contact person for an engineering consultant. Instead, the developer should match the firm's engineer or in-house engineering people with the proposed tenant's engineer. Many developers today are creating easy-to-read material that can be distributed to engineers and architects and that details many of the technical features of the building. Communication of this type will do a great deal to remove potential problems.

Preparing for Tenant Visits

As the developer's message gets out, tenants will begin visiting the building. Although many developers do choose to bring tenants to the building during construction, it is difficult for the tenant to visualize the finished product. Therefore, it is very important to combine the construction site visit with a tour of a model office. Without such an opportunity, many tenants are not capable of understanding what is being built and how they might use it.

As the building nears completion, the number of visitors will increase. It is very important to have the proper staff members serve as tour guides. It is not appropriate to have a building starter or porter take potential tenants through a building. Although they understand the structure of the building, they do not know how to sell the property or convey the developer's intended image. Instead, the building agent, together with the project architect and engineer if necessary, should take the tenant through the building, explain why things were done, how things will be done, and what advantages the building has. The tenant should be treated in the same way as a visitor entering a home. An organized tour will create a positive feeling for the visitor.

It is important to build a model office in the building. This model office will serve as interim space for sales staff, locale for project meetings, and a meeting area for potential tenants and brokers. The space can be built with the materials that will be used in the standard building installation. This will give the tenants a real feel for the space that will be built.

The on-site leasing office should be staffed five days a week for nine or ten hours a day. This creates a good feeling—a feeling that the building is alive and busy. Tenants feel more positive if people are there and things are happening.

Some developers have elaborate tours. For example, at Seven World Trade Center, the tour included an audiovisual presentation of the project, expensive giveaways, and meals. The model office was a show in itself.

Monitoring Building Activity

As building activity increases, it is very important to monitor that activity. Weekly sales meetings should be held with the leasing team. Project meetings with the engineers and staff should be held. The management staff should be meeting with the sales staff. It is important that all staff members keep each other informed of their activities and keep communication open. This team approach and close monitoring of building activity is important to the property's success in the marketplace.

Negotiating Leases

As deals begin to evolve, management must make some crucial decisions. Should only large leases be considered? What about the small offer that comes in? What is the best way to handle all the activity? Obviously, large, multifloor tenants are desirable. However, they want many concessions and will have many demands. Such tenants may burden the rest of your building and discourage other medium- to large-sized tenants from leasing space in the building. Also, when a large lease expires, it will cause a major vacancy at one time. Management must be able to focus in on the large tenant and the smaller tenant at the same time. Keeping all tenants interested is essential.

It is important to have a team in place to negotiate transactions with tenants. Brokers, architects, engineers, and lawyers must work together to successfully negotiate a transaction. It is very important that the management staff be involved as well. Concessions made by the sales staff without consultation of the management staff can create problems. The management staff and sales staff must work as a team.

The perception and approach chosen by the developer before construction began must be carried out in the negotiation stage as well. If the developer has created a prestigious, first-class building, that image should be conveyed in negotiations. A consistent, thorough, and professional negotiation style is very important. If tenants and brokers enter a negotiation process and come away feeling they have not been treated professionally, this may inhibit other activity.

A fair and workable lease that can be easily used for various deals should be developed. Also, a work letter that is understandable to the tenant and the construction staff should be designed and implemented at this stage.

Continued Marketing

Developers must be careful to continue aggressive marketing after the first leases are signed. Secondary and tertiary marketing and promotional campaigns must be undertaken to attract tenants who will lease the rest of the property. If the momentum of the initial leasing successes slows, it may be difficult for the property to recover. The developer must use the initial transactions to create a new momentum and feeling about the property.

Finally, when all the space is leased, tell the community. Announcements in local newspapers and trade journals about this success create a positive feeling in the brokerage and tenant communities. It is also important to get the tenant involved in future sales pitches—there is no better salesperson for the building.

CHAPTER 5

PREPARING FOR THE MOVE

Robert De Siena
Real Estate and Facilities Consultant

Simplicity in business is a thing of the past. Technological advancements have greatly increased managers' concerns about moving as it affects employees, inventories, business deadlines, and windows of opportunity for relocating **sensitive services.** The logistics of the move, which were once handled by the corporate owner or managing partners, have become a complex planning problem. The coordinated effort required to relocate a major segment of a company now incorporates a diversified team effort coupled with a broad-based communication network. Moving a business requires matching many pieces of a puzzle together at exactly the same time in a new location without pausing. Proper planning ensures continuity of operation, transparency to customers, and a minimum of employee time lost to the organization.

As the market place expands each element of the company has developed unique operating aspects to serve the market's needs. These special operating procedures within units require development of planning subsets to handle the specific needs of each unit. This individualization precludes the owner or senior manager from implementing a singular moving plan for all departments. In today's 24-hour markets, where deadlines are critical, businesses' sensitivity to relocation has added a new dimension to moving a large segment of an operation.

This new complexity demands a strong communication channel within the organization. It is imperative that all parts thereof understand the consequences of delays in leaving the old building and in settling into the new one. Significant items of furniture or equipment missed during the move may result in deferring the move and paying rent in two locations, or may require moving furniture slated for abandonment. But without a strong communication network, deviating from the moving schedule can cause myriad problems and untold confusion for executives and employees alike.

Despite the complexity of moving a modern firm, a swift and uneventful completion is possible; the keys are planning, cooperation, and communication. Combining these elements perfectly will make heroes of the staff members.

PLANNING THE MOVE

Developing and implementing a moving plan for a large corporation requires a moving team. The role of each member must be defined, and they must establish a plan to chart the course the corporation will take during the move. The team concept evolved as the best alternative because the responsibility for coordinating a successful move affects many levels of management and multiple interfaces of organization units. Each of these units has various itineraries to follow while relocating, and if left on their own, each would focus their attention on their own specific needs, ignoring the corporate goals. The move effort requires a strict control system to prevent political jockeying.

The management team assigned to the move will cover all of the organization's assets, ensuring that essential functions are incorporated into the plan. This team generally comprises in-house personnel such as facility managers, a move coordinator, and an activity representative. Outside consultants complement the team to meet unusual workloads or to augment technical knowledge in specialized areas. A key member of management plays an important role in developing, implementing, and continually reviewing of the move's progress.

Once the team has been selected, the task that lies ahead of them is quite a formidable one. They set up the time frame for each element of the move, ranging from site selection to the actual move. The facility operation staff usually assumes the role of team leader, and they report directly to management. They will develop the plan that encompasses all aspects of a complex move. Phases of the plan include the following:

• Defining space requirements	Personnel analysis
• Acquisition of space	Comparison of space utilization

• Design & space layout	Building exterior and interior finishes
	Building systems—HVAC, plumbing, electrical
	Floor layouts
• Construction	New construction
	Corporate-owned and -developed
	Major tenancy
	Special function facilities
	Existing building corporate-owned
• Purchasing equipment and furniture	Building equipment
	Special purpose equipment— for example, UPS or security equipment
	Office equipment
	New furniture
	Refurbishing old furniture
• Telecommunication and data installation	Telephone company or private vendor
• Moving	Options for relocating operations
• Restoring of abandoned space	Restore vacated facilities

These elements should be shown on graphs for management to highlight the components that have the greatest effect on the target date. The move team should send monthly updates to the senior management, indicating any slippage and corrective actions taken to ensure timely completion of the project. This is a rather simplistic overview of the planning process; as the moving process takes specific direction, the facilities operation staff must tailor the plan to fit accordingly. The plan must also clearly define the responsibilities of each team member. The operation staff coordinates, but the team members must produce the needed results to make the relocation a success.

The Involvement of the Owner or Manager

A corporate owner or manager has considerably less involvement in moving today than he or she had in years past. Senior executives are very involved in site selection, whether the firm is moving across town or across the country. Members of corporate steering committees have significant input into these decisions, which may chart a new course for the organization. They will weigh the economic consequences of alternatives presented from political and social standpoints, but they always focus on capital and expense amounts as they affect the firm. In some instances, tax incentives offered by local municipalities enter into the calculations, as they significantly affect the bottom line. The effect of the move on employees is also of concern to this group. For example, relocating from an urban to a suburban environment may displace some staff members, resulting in a training period for new employees and a possible effect on customer service. In larger cities, the relocation may result in the same problem: losing staff. An organization must know where its employees live and how a move will influence its ability to retain valuable personnel. Managers must work closely with personnel to review their questions and concerns.

The senior staff must also help to make such strategic decisions as purchasing new furniture or equipment, refurbishing old, or moving existing furnishings. Each of these alternatives has financial consequences on the move and on cost schedules. Operating managers make recommendations that the senior officers have to evaluate. An example of the decision process is that of moving the corporate computer system. Disassembling and reassembling the system or migrating to a new system at the new facility are the two main options, and either one can be quite costly. Obviously, operating two computer centers is expensive; however, sensitivity and time constraints of the work produced may overshadow the increased cost. Furthermore, moving a sensitive area in this manner becomes evident to the customer. The move may in addition enable the organization to upgrade its equipment, thereby increasing its service capabilities. Finally, the move may be planned concurrent with the expiration of computer leases, enabling the company to make the transition at the financially optimum time. Each variable influences the organization's ability to provide service and financial results. Thus, these decisions can only be made by the top level of management.

Although it is not quite as significant a concern as computer equipment, the decision to move, refurbish, or purchase new furniture will have consequences for the cost and schedules of a move. To evaluate these options, management must be aware of the age and condition of the furniture and the cost of relocation with and without the furniture before they can render a meaningful decision. The layout in the new space will also affect this decision; for example, newer facilities with large floor plates are more easily adapted to system furniture, while older buildings with smaller core space and geometric angles may be more conducive to case goods. Another factor in the furniture equation is the company's good will toward employees. Choosing new furniture allows the employees input in the decision process. This consideration might be particularly useful when the cost difference between manufacturers is negligible and is equal to or less than the cost of moving existing furniture. The employee involvement in this decision is crucial, even though it cannot be assigned a definite dollar value.

Strategic decisions are not confined to finance. Senior managers will also become involved in planning the activities that will be performed in adjacent spaces. Management review and approval of all plans eliminates much of the political posturing that goes into all phases of planning. In the past, the entire planning process was kept within management's inner circles, but in today's major organizations, an in-house operation staff is generally responsible for all of the facility occupancy concerns. This in-house staff allows management to attend to ongoing business matters while closely controlling its operations.

Finally, the frequency of relocations in any one organization is still relatively low. It is true that churn—movement of employees or functions—is generally around 30 percent per year, but the number of employees moving at any point in time is insignificant in comparison to the total population of an organization. It is a rare occurrence when a company moves thousands of employees from one or several locations into a new facility. Thus, for this unique situation, managers take a more active role in monitoring the program's progress. They may even develop a task force to handle the planning and relocation. But at no time will they relinquish authority and control over the process. On a large scale, management will watch the progression, but when critical activities or pet operations are moved, management tends to become more involved in the planning and coordination. Management concerns center on the consequences of poorly implemented moves resulting in financial losses to the corporation; this is closely watched by stockholders, board directors, and industry analysts, none of whom senior management wishes to confront on the issue.

Human Resources Concerns

The decision to move results in a number of logistical decisions, an important one being the move's effect on the staff. Management will work closely with the human resources department to identify and overcome potential employee concerns and to plan a strategy to correct potential problems. The worst case is that in which moving to another state or region of the country is contemplated. In this situation, management might offer financial assistance to key employees to help them relocate, and may provide severance packages for those not wishing to leave the area. Despite an appearance to the contrary, this situation is not the norm. Corporate development generally highlights successful expansion into multiple locations as a trend. A major move is generally the result of consolidation with a property in the same urban or surrounding suburban areas that is owned, leased, or part of an equity partnership. Retaining employees is of great concern in the last two situations. Thus, either human resources or management must develop a program of communication. The human resources department must study employee origins and compare them to the destination to determine what results the relocation might have on the staff. In some locations, where automobiles are the usual means of transportation, moving to a suburban area may add an unacceptable amount of time to a commute. For example, in Manhattan, moving from downtown to midtown may cause the same travel problems if most of the employees live in Brooklyn or Staten Island; the opposite situation arises if the firm moves downtown and the employees live in The Bronx, Westchester, or Queens.

In an effort to remove these concerns, organizations can develop maps indicating new commuting routes and provide schedules for public transportation. The corporation may also employ commuter vans to link subcommunities and transportation depots. Management should make every effort to help employees adjust to the new location.

Many organizations attempt to counter the dissatisfaction of additional commuting by highlighting the amenities of the new location. Health and daycare facilities are two new benefits that seem to entice employees; another is a fitness center, which can reduce the tension of moving. Management can allow the employees to participate in the decision-making process—for example, on the subject of interior design. Employee participation also promotes awareness of the firm's progress in moving. Some corporations even prepare videos reviewing the reasons for relocation. These films typically include prominent features of the new building and of the area, such as shopping malls, parks, and restaurants.

Because communication is a key aspect of the relocation program, the corporation may also include the program's status in a corporate magazine or newsletter article. Rumors are the most destructive form of communication; if the company does not inform its employees about the project, they will be faced with unfounded reports and gossip. A major move is of itself very disruptive, but to keep employees guessing results in even lower productivity. Management's aim should be to eliminate this disruption during all stages of the program, especially during its planning and construction phases.

FACILITIES MANAGEMENT

About twenty years ago, large corporations began to bring in-house several disciplines associated with professional building management. Many of these activities have fit well in management structure, becoming the interface with the real estate industry and senior management of corporations. They now handle such functions as leasing, design, construction, and maintenance of owned and leased facilities, along with sundry tasks that are not usually included in the definition of corporate operations. This activity has in most instances eliminated the direct entry of outside consultants. Architects, engineers, and designers are hired by the facilities management to augment personnel in fulfilling unusual requirements. During the moving process, this organization supplements itself with consultants or develops a team of in-house personnel to meet the surge in demand. The facilities team becomes the interface with the building owners or managers. While upper management will select the geographic area for relocation, the facilities staff generally is responsible for finding the actual building and negotiating the lease. All leases must be approved by various levels of management before the facilities staff can agree to any terms.

Most leasing, design, and construction work that the facilities management performs consists of smaller moves or space needed to meet the expansion or contraction of the numerous business units within the corporation. There are projects that require relocating large numbers of staff because of market growth and the domino effect caused by the space availability within the company's portfolio. A facility staff rarely becomes involved in significant moves or other projects. Although the staff members assume the leadership role in developing and implementing an approved move plan, they must augment their staff with inside or outside assistants as required.

In the early phase of planning, the facilities management actively reviews the floor plans presented by the leasing section to determine which building has the most economical layout. With the advent of personal computer–based systems, these evaluations, which in the past might have taken months to complete, can now be reviewed in a few weeks. Software systems make it easy to take management's "what if" questions and provide feedback in a short time. Firms not capable of providing this service can obtain it from architects or from newly emerging facilities management firms. In either situation, this preliminary layout assesses the effectiveness of the space for the corporation's use. Management will then receive a recommendation for optimum utilization of the property.

Management's approval of a specific site will then set the relocation planning process in motion. The facilities managers will begin with an in-depth inventory evaluation to ensure that current records accurately detail personnel, furniture, furnishings, storage space, and the like. Using updated information, facilities management will adjust preliminary design, incorporating any major changes. For example, finding that the number of pieces of furniture to be moved exceeds the number planned for or that the number of staff members in various departments has grown without facilities management's awareness is not unusual. Local managers can acquire additional files, conference rooms, and furniture without management's knowledge. Head count increases through reorganization, temporary help, and in-house acquisitions of vacant space. Failure to incorporate all the employees and assets of each department into the plan results in underestimating the space needs of the units or forces the facilities managers to work with the department to reduce its space needs so that the space will fit the operations. Inventorying furniture and furnishings has other benefits. If management wishes to purchase new furniture and furnishings, it must sell the old assets. The inventory provides documentation to validate the location and estimate value of each unit, and it is a critical element in bid specifications for moving companies. Equipment is also becoming a more critical element in moving. Facilities management must account for all special requirements of the equipment when planning new layouts. Equipment requiring emergency or uninterrupted power systems must have space that will accommodate it.

Facilities management is responsible for developing the construction documentation, monitoring the flow of the contractor's work, and scheduling the installation of telecommunication and data networks, among other duties. Facilities managers chart all elements of the relocation project, following their progress carefully and informing management about each segment of the program. If critical deadlines either are missed or are anticipated to be, facilities managers review every available alternative to achieve the original target dates; they then present modifications to upper management before implementing changes. Alternatives are developed by consulting contractors, consultants, and users of the new building to provide the most comprehensive assessment of the situation and the best possible solution. Management appreciates neither sudden nor continuous changes to move schedules, and estimates for change must be as accurate as possible. Continually changing target dates unnerves management, causing the facilities team to lose credibility and management to expand its involvement in the move. The size of the relocation project is the main concern of management; during the past two decades, facilities management has demonstrated the ability to expertly handle smaller moves, and, because major relocations are not the norm, management views larger projects with a more critical eye.

To facilities management, a move is a multiphased project. The design phase is the first, and it requires meeting with each department that is moving, collecting current and projected personnel numbers and other data, and separating this data into different job classifications so that proper space requirements can be developed. Another factor to consider is the operation's growth potential. Departments often overestimate their needs, so facilities managers must correct discrepancies between the department's projections and management's established goals. Management's review in the final analysis will eliminate many of the remaining differences. Thus, the plan provides estimates of space requirements as well as expansion capabilities. This point is important because plans and schedules undergo considerable changes during the relocation process, especially when move projections are based on potential occupancy of a new building. The length of time between the project's inception and completion is considerable, perhaps three to five years, and the data from which the new building is designed is also that old. However, corporations are dynamic entities, introducing new products or services and eliminating obsolete ones. A common example of this problem is estimation of space requirements for a manual operation; in viewing the trend in work force size over the past few years, the number of employees multiplied by the space allotment per employee equals space requirement.

Automation of the operation during construction of the building can drastically reduce personnel and therefore space requirements. The opposite situation can occur when automation increases service capability and hence staff requirements to meet the new demands. Thus, projecting space needs remains an inexact science, but one that the facilities staff must work with during the entire project. The facilities and management staffs must freeze space requirements sometime during the project, lest construction costs get out of control.

In a contracting corporation that is forced to relocate to reduce its financial exposure caused by a merger or acquisition, staff projections and the related space requirements are considerably easier to determine. Upper management will establish target personnel levels through negotiated agreements with department managers. These levels are communicated to the facilities managers, who develop a plan based thereon. File, equipment, and conference space can become the next important planning considerations. Many corporations have in recent years established standards clearly defining the elements planned into the space as well as parameters for furniture and furnishing layouts for all levels of employees. Standards are too often interpreted by owners or agents as styles of finished spaces in an office facility. Unfortunately, this definition is very narrow when compared to its use by a major corporation. Besides the lighting, wall covering, draperies, and so forth, large corporations have standardized furniture, desk accessories, artwork, and the like. Standards are also subdivided by type of operation—senior management, customer service operations, and so on. These standard programs are both a help and a hindrance, particularly during a major relocation, because all activities scheduled for relocation inevitably do not have standard accessories. Management must then decide whether to purchase new standard furniture or move with the old. In the case of the contracting corporation, the answer is easy—existing furniture will be moved. In other situations, the value of the alternative will determine the outcome.

A different twist to this situation comes about when the company moving is a large partnership such as a law firm or an investment banking house. In-house operations staffs, if any, are small; thus, these firms rely heavily on outside consultants. In any event, the individual responsible for organizing this move will find that marching to the beats of conflicting drummers makes designing a layout more difficult. The various partners can be ranked by both their earnings and contributions, and their unique tastes can only be challenged by a partner with more seniority. The consultant and in-house staff must tread lightly when developing their plans. Operating areas are treated in much the same way as they are in major corporations, but consultants must design partners' offices on an individual basis.

The design phase involves fact-finding and layout. The next phase is that of construction documentation and bidding. This segment is critical to the final move schedule and has its own unique concerns. The selection of a qualified contractor is of considerable importance. As a general rule, most major corporations deal with a select group of contractors in their bid process. When faced with a landlord who uses a specific contractor, the corporation tries to include the landlord's contractor on the bid list or to place specific subcontractors on the approved vendor list. Internal procedure requires the corporation to obtain competitive bids to satisfy the auditors and stockholders. There are many reasons corporations and landlords prefer to work with certain contractors. The corporation, as the landlord, develops a good working relationship with a particular contractor over a period of time, and the contractors have learned and can anticipate the idiosyncrasies of the customer. The contractor provides the corporation with an extra set of eyes to review their plans, thereby reducing the need for additional (and costly) consultants. The building owner should be aware of the corporate bidding requirements. The use of construction contractors is one issue that can be resolved by discussion.

Selecting a qualified contractor is important for several other reasons, including cost control and ability to meet critical deadlines. As with all phases of a major move, corporations are concerned with construction's influence on the bottom line. Unexpectedly high construction costs may have an immediate deleterious effect on the capital segment of the balance sheet, which is sometimes funded by long-term debts or retained earnings. Construction programs associated with a major move usually significantly influence the balance sheet and therefore are closely watched by management.

However, the cost of the project to the corporation can go beyond the contractual agreements because of missed target dates. Leases in current facilities might then require extension, usually at penalty rates, and rent on the new space will commence at lease-negotiated dates, whether the space is ready for occupancy or not. Storage costs for equipment, furniture and furnishings may be incurred. Finally, opportunity costs associated with new products may be missed. These are all costs that the corporation must account for when selecting potential contractors. Thus, once a schedule is developed, the in-house staff is under considerable pressure to meet the target dates. Working with a firm that has proven itself in the past is a positive factor.

THE NEW FACILITY

Occupying a Newly Built Facility

A move becomes even more complex when construction of a new building is involved. If the corporation moving is the owner or developer, the in-house operation is responsible for adhering to the building construction schedules. This group must also coordinate special services for the corporation, such as an uninterrupted power system (UPS), emergency power distribution, emergency generators, telecommunication networks, local area networks, and security systems, as well as the overall design for the organization. The in-house personnel, though they are the general coordinators, receive help from out-of-house support staff.

When the organization moves into a developer's property, the role of the in-house staff shifts. Gone is the responsibility of controlling the contractor; this is replaced with the "concerned citizen" review. The corporation staff tries to keep the owner as close to schedule as possible. Next, the in-house staff develops schedules for installing the corporate interiors and special service requirements. The coordination becomes more complicated when different contractors are used for the base building and interior work. The staff must watch their schedules closely to ensure the contractors do not work together to hide problems in completing work. Although corporate personnel can exert less control over base building construction, they must make every effort to help contractors meet their deadlines.

Occupying an Existing Building

If a corporation chooses not to construct a new facility, it can move into an existing one. This approach requires the corporate staff to evaluate the capacity of building systems, HVAC, and electrical service to determine whether its needs can be met or whether additional systems are required. The staff will also review options for after-hours service—for example, HVAC to protect computer systems. The corporation must weigh the cost of purchasing services against the landlord's fee for providing them. It must also investigate the issues of environmentally hazardous material or possible future demolition. After these issues are settled, the corporate staff can begin to develop its moving plan. The building manager or agent is a key figure in implementing the moving program, because he or she, as the owner's representative, must review and approve the prospective tenant's plans to ensure that proposed changes will not negatively influence the owner's assets. His or her responsibilities also include making sure that any changes are in accordance with local codes and regulations. When a firm moves into an existing building, the facilities staff need no longer be concerned with the deadlines for completing a new building. Long-lead items will shift from construction to equipment and furnishings, thus reducing the complexity of the project.

Consolidating Operations

When a business moves in order to consolidate with another in an existing facility, the planning issues shift once again. A firm usually chooses this type of move to reduce its operating costs; thus, a minimal amount of capital improvement work is anticipated. It will try to utilize as much of the contracted space as possible without spending a considerable sum to move. In the best possible situation, the only expenditures will be for relocating electric and telephone service. Purchasing is kept to a minimum, and scheduling revolves around actually moving the organization.

PURCHASING

The in-house staff must sometimes incorporate another element into its planning schedule—purchasing facility and office equipment, furniture, and furnishings. The policies and procedures of purchasing vary widely among corporations; they can range from strictly centralized to local, or somewhere in between. The rationale behind organizational structure often is a mystery to the casual observer; however, making a department other than the facilities staff responsible for purchasing adds time to an already congested project schedule.

The centralized purchasing department is responsible for all purchasing in major corporations. The facilities staff develops all of the specifications for each phase of the construction work and then gives them to the purchasing staff to obtain a bid. Although many corporations believe this procedure aids control, it actually delays the completion of projects. Construction bids cause problems for the purchasing staff, because they lack the expertise to evaluate building equipment or analyze comparability unless a staff member is an engineer or architect. This process also complicates matters for the contractor because the contractor must decide whether to satisfy the facilities staff or the purchasing staff when their respective instructions conflict.

In a decentralized environment, the staff responsible for a particular job is also responsible for its purchasing. This enables the facilities staff to control the contractor and the project schedule without a third party. The process works exceptionally well during coordination of a major move.

Most large corporations take a hybrid approach to purchasing. All core business items, such as forms, supplies, and office equipment, are bought through a central unit. Unique or specialized purchases are made by the departments with the specific expertise. This procedure allows the facilities staff to control the principal purchases but requires it to use the corporate purchasing staff for additional business equipment to meet unique requirements. This dissection of responsibility makes the facility managers coordinate purchases through several organizations. Each method of purchasing—centralized, decentralized, or hybrid—requires consistency in purchasing documentation throughout the corporation. Bidding, the primary issue, is a time-consuming procedure that facilities management must include in the moving plan.

COORDINATING THE MOVE

Smaller relocations or churn projects are controlled from start to finish by the facilities staff. Small organizations do not wish to expand their size to meet one short-term demand for extra personnel during a large relocation project. Instead, they will try to utilize other personnel to supplement the facilities staff, or they will hire outside consultants to bridge the gap during critical phases. Management is keenly aware of the demands placed upon the facilities staff during major relocations; they must design space plans and monitor construction while continuing to meet the ongoing needs of the firm. These stringent demands coupled with the critical nature of a major move increase management's concern for control during this hectic time.

Management can use several organizational structures to ensure control; in all methods, the facilities staff is the focal point. Management often chooses to designate a *move coordinator*. This individual reports through the facilities operations manager with a matrix arrangement to senior management and the individual operation, and he or she typically fits into one of three categories:

1. The *High-Flier Corporate Ace*. This type of individual is highly regarded by senior managers as someone who is assured a future place at their table. Managing the move will provide him or her with a broader understanding of the organization and its specific operational needs, as well as an opportunity to demonstrate special skills. This knowledge forms a strong foundation for future assignments. Management rarely misses a chance to train an esteemed employee, and major moves are an excellent program to allow managers to learn about and to be exposed to senior management.

2. The *Self-Redeemer*. This individual was at one time considered a good management prospect, but over his last several assignments, his or her performance has been inconsistent with previous work. If senior managers still have confidence in him or her, they will provide him with opportunity to prove that recent history was a glitch in an otherwise successful career. His or her performance must withstand closer scrutiny that a more reliable employee would not be subjected to. If management loses confidence in him or her, it will act quickly to make a change or to shore up the position's support group because of the importance of the project.

3. The *Swan Song,* or "Soon-to-be-Retired Manager." This individual is a true-blue employee, usually with a long and distinguished record of successful management assignments. Now, in the twilight of his or her career, management provides him or her with one last challenge. The pride of completing a successful move for the organization he or she loves is his or her reward at the end of the stick.

The common denominator in the selection process is an individual whose skills are well-known to management—a person who they believe can complete the project with the highest quality and minimal disruption. The move coordinator will become the leader in the relocation team—the "right arm" of the facilities manager. In organizations that do not have a specific facilities operation department, the move coordinator becomes an integral member of a steering committee or assistant to a senior partner. He or she also interacts with the outside consultants.

After the move coordinator has been chosen, facilities operation staff can work more closely with design and construction aspects of the move. The move coordinator must then take responsibility for communicating with each department, informing it of the overall status of the project and the specific aspects that affect its area. He or she also coordinates the efforts of any outside consultants or in-house moving teams in gathering information about the move. Because large relocations mean interfacing with a wide variety of staff members, all of whom have their own unique requirements or idiosyncrasies, the move coordinator needs another team to help organize the moving process within and among departments. These individuals may either have the same level of authority that the move coordinator does, or they may be several levels removed. Each major department moving must appoint a facilities representative to work with the move coordinator. The representatives' work is specific to their respective areas, and they act as a conduit for information by providing the move coordinator with a skilled staff member in each department that is moving. They are thus an essential component of an effectively coordinated relocation.

The small personnel nucleus that works directly with the move coordinator, who changes from project to project, is advantageous for several reasons. They give continuity to the management process during the relocation. These representatives understand the unique aspects of their departments, which may be lost in its transition from local managers to consultants. The move coordinator, however, is ultimately in control of the overall relocation. He or she is the team's communication center. Keeping every department informed of the project's status and guiding them all through each phase of the move are the essential duties of the move coordinator. The move coordinator's responsibilities go beyond communication and include selection of and negotiation with a moving company. This responsibility is a considerable one because selecting the wrong mover adds significant cost and time to a project through delays, damages, and general disorientation.

Finding a Moving Company

In choosing a qualified moving company, the move coordinator must thoroughly investigate each candidate. He or she should know how many full time workers the mover employs; much of the preparation work is performed during the day, and without enough personnel the mover will be able to satisfy neither the move coordinator nor other customers. The move coordinator should also look at the mover's fleet size, as a small one will prolong the move and may result in hiring two or more movers. He or she should also be informed of other commitments, such as relocating another large firm, that could affect the mover's ability to adhere to tight schedules. Union affiliations should be reviewed to ensure that no conflicts exist between locals within the geographic areas of the move. The mover should point out applicable tariffs within cities and explain their effect on the corporation. References from prior moves are important to the move coordinator because a poor track record will only cause him or her unnecessary stress as the move progresses. Both the mover and the move coordinator should review procedures for handling office equipment, valuables, and pieces of art. Insurance coverage must be secured, with the certificate in hand, before the move commences. Finally, protection for the facility being vacated as well as the facility being occupied should be reviewed and specified. Many landlords require specific protection for their lobbies and corridors, and both the mover and the move coordinator must incorporate these requirements into the job specifications.

The corporation moving often deals with one or more moving companies. A typical relocation is quite small, involving comparatively few employees; thus, these relocations can be handled by most companies. A major relocation has a much larger scope. Moving 1,000 to 4,000 employees strains the capacity of a smaller moving company, and it may have to enlarge its staff from a source pool, thereby diluting the quality of service. Before the move coordinator suggests that management make a commitment, he or she should review the mover's capabilities, even if the move is scheduled in component parts of, for example, 200 to 300 employees per trip. The prolonged commitment might hinder the mover's ability to provide a consistent work force and high-quality service.

Once he or she selects several qualified moving companies, the move coordinator must prepare the bid specifications. The inventory and floor plans developed by the facilities area become the foundation for the bid. Included in the inventory is a clear definition of what is to be moved—contents of desks and files only, contents with case goods, case goods only, and furnishings. Explicit documentation brings more accurate bids. The movers should also be given specifications for freight elevators, loading docks, time requirements, and property protection, as well as basic insurance requirements. All bids should be requested in tally loads—units of measurement used by the moving industry to define the volume of items moved—to provide a common basis for evaluation. Movers should be given a brief tour of the facility to ensure that they clearly understand the bid package, and to eliminate as many of their questions and concerns as possible. To ensure comparability of quotations, any changes or modifications agreed upon with any vendor should be communicated to all bidders.

Preparing Materials and Equipment

The move coordinator must meet with each department to review file and storage space, and to develop a program of purging unnecessary files and sending vital records to storage. This process reduces the number of boxes moved and therefore the cost of the relocation. The move coordinator's primary responsibility during this stage of the move is to ensure that only *necessary* records and materials are moved. This point may require strong support from local management, but there is no reason to pay for moving unnecessary materials.

Moving sophisticated office equipment has become more commonplace; however, the more sophisticated the equipment becomes, the more temperamental it is, and the more concerned the move coordinator should be. When office equipment consisted of merely typewriters and adding machines, movers stored it in security crates to transport it between locations. No one showed much concern for damage or downtime. System downtime is now exceptionally critical, as customers must be serviced and transfer deadlines met. Today's computer systems and copy machines require greater care during move preparation to ensure full productivity. The move coordinator must often negotiate with equipment maintenance firms to disassemble equipment and prepare it for the move, and then to reassemble it after it has been placed in its new home. Reader heads or disk drums can easily be damaged in transit, and cameras and rollers on copy equipment misaligned; some equipment may require special rigging to move it from one location or to install it at another. These precautions result in fewer problems with the equipment and remove concerns of improper maintenance or noncompliance with current maintenance agreements. They also eliminate controversy with the movers over who will repair equipment and how long it will be out of service. In some instances, if the mover moves equipment without aid of the maintenance company, existing maintenance agreements may be void. The move coordinator is responsible for making all necessary arrangements. Proper care and handling of the company's equipment will eliminate many potential concerns of management.

Freight Service

Among his or her many tasks, the move coordinator finds the responsibility of coordinating freight car utilization. This may sound simple enough, but this one element can become the tightest bottleneck in the move project. Most buildings have inadequate freight service, and competition for it is fierce. The freight car's daytime hours may be short because of a scanty labor force or other tenants vying for the same time slots to maintain their ongoing operations. Competition during the evening centers on using the freight cars to remove the daily trash. Most freight system owners do not allow the use of passenger cars for transporting furniture or equipment because of weight restrictions or possible damage to the cab's interior. This seemingly simple task thus becomes quite complex. The move coordinator must work closely with the building managers of both the premises to be vacated and occupied when scheduling freight cars to ensure that all parties are properly coordinated with their metaphorical watches synchronized. Delays on either end can cause a quick escalation in cost and long hours of waiting.

The move coordinator must also investigate the capacity and size of the freight elevators. Larger pieces of equipment may require special consideration when being moved between buildings. What is moved out of one building may not fit into another. Some items must be placed on top of the elevator cabs, and others might require other special arrangements. Being unaware of these problems tends to irritate management. The move coordinator must be familiar with this aspect of the move assignment.

Final Clean-Up

Sometimes the easiest part of a move is the move itself. Returning to the scene after a move vividly demonstrates how well the file-purging programs work, which furniture or equipment was deemed expendable by the departments, and what artwork was overlooked. The move co-ordinator must evaluate the remains of corporate property to make sure that no critical or valuable material was left behind. Touring the va-cated premises with a departmental representative will provide neces-sary guidance to complete the task. If furniture was left behind, the move coordinator must arrange for all desks and file cabinets to be emptied, ensuring against the loss of valuables. He or she must then make arrangements to sell the furniture or to donate it to a charity. Al-though used furniture does not return a high percentage of the original value, it does provide some money while reducing the cost of clean-up. For example, if wood desks are sold at $40 per desk, a corporation moving 500 employees would receive $20,000, and it would no longer need to move the furniture.

Most leases call for the premises to be vacated in at least broom-swept condition. Thus, the move coordinator must negotiate with the building maintenance organization to remove all loose trash before re-turning the space to the landlord. However, there are some leases that require the tenant to return the facility in its original state. This is most often the case when private stairwells, lawyers' libraries, or special equipment was installed. The cost of these repairs can be settled through negotiation or through actual repair of the facility, but facilities man-agement, not the move coordinator, must fulfill these responsibilities.

Newly Occupied Areas

The move coordinator's responsibility does not end the night of the move. Relocated departments usually require assistance in settling into their new homes. When possible, the move coordinator should use the team to satisfy a department's needs. If the problem involves construc-tion, the move coordinator and the facilities staff should act together to correct the problem as quickly as possible. However, when questions arise about clean-up or keys for desks and files, the move coordina-tor should respond. During these final hours, the move coordinator is monitor of the front line.

The remainder of the move team concentrates on the next target date. The move coordinator can then work on satisfying the needs of the moved departments. Management's assessment of the relocation's success includes not only transporting an operation from one facility to another, but also the level of departmental disruption and the amount of downtime.

THE MOVERS

The movers' work usually begins early in the week before the move. Working from the floor plans for both the space to be vacated and occupied, they must, with the aid of the move coordinator, correlate data to devise a plan ensuring that the contents of one individual's space move swiftly and efficiently to their new location. Of course, the smaller the move, the less intricate the planning; but when the program calls for hundreds of people coming from several locations, the plan quickly becomes very complex.

A typical moving plan develops in the following manner:

1. The mover assigns departments to be moved an alphanumeric code, which is placed on the tags of all its items.
2. The mover then color-codes the tags for the new space; this will aid in delivering the items.
3. The mover places the color-coordinated alphanumeric tags in the new facility for distributing materials.

This system is also included in the floor plans to aid the movers on the night of the move, and it acts as an audit to ensure that all items have been moved and accounted for.

The mover provides local managers with all the preparation assistance they need. Although the assistance may be necessary, it might be outside the contractual agreement, resulting in additional charges to the corporation. The move coordinator should therefore process any requests for additional services.

The mover's duties are usually clear enough: A team of movers will go to the sending point on the night of the move, follow procedures for protecting corridors and passageways as defined in the contract, and load the dollies with boxes or furniture. This process is followed by positioning move teams in the departing floors, in freight or lobby entrances, and on the trucks. The movers on the floors bring the items to the elevator and fill it. The ground-level mover transports the items to the truck. The last group packs the truck. This process is reversed on the receiving side, except that items are directed to their locations by the color and alphanumeric code on their tags. Using this coordinating system allows smooth flow of materials with little downtime caused by indecision. The efficiency of this system enables the mover to complete the task in a minimal amount of time.

In any move, there are items that require special handling. For example, office equipment and pieces of art are rarely boxed for shipping. The mover has special bins for transporting security items. The department moving should prepare an inventory of the equipment to be moved, noting age and condition in case some mishap occurs in transit. Art may require special packaging that depends on its value. The movers should prepackage the artwork and preload as much nonessential material on dollies as possible to avoid delays on the night of the move. They must work with the move coordinator to ensure that all file cabinets and typewriters are unbolted for ease of relocation. Although the unit moving may find these procedures disruptive, they help make the move smoother.

Before the movers are finished, the move coordinator or departmental representative and the mover should inspect the area to ensure that everything has been moved. A rule of thumb is, "If it looks important, take it." It is less costly to move an item while the movers are on the premises, and, if the item is not taken, it will be discarded in the final clean-up and lost forever. The department can make a more rational judgment about the necessity of the item in the calmer period after the move.

The mover's responsibilities are not completed when the furniture, equipment, and files are in the new headquarters. The departments that moved need some initial help in adjusting to the new environment. After all, the best-laid plans of mice and men often go awry. The building's configuration is inevitably inconsistent with the floor plans. Thus, files protrude in aisles, desks abut objects not shown in drawings, and electric and phone outlets do not align with furniture. All of these complications require minor adjustments on the receiving side, which the movers can easily perform with guidance from the unit. The movers must unload and bring in the business equipment and remove the empty storage boxes. The faster the staff becomes acclimated to its new home, the more productive the organization will become. Therefore, removing small obstacles early will enable the company to move forward at a faster pace.

CORPORATE ACTIVITY

Moving is very disruptive to an operation, which includes customers' wants and managers' needs. Thus, the more planning that goes into the move, the more successful it will be. The cooperation and participation of departments or units to be moved are as essential to a successful move as the facilities staff and the move coordinator are. Each element of an organization has its own unique aspects or requirements that must be communicated to the facilities staff while designing the program. The departmental representative must review all plans developed for his or her activity to determine whether they meet the needs of the area. He or she should find out whether there are sufficient positions to cover current staff or possible future growth, whether the layout is conducive to the work flow of the operation, and, if required, whether emergency power or supplementary air conditioning is provided. To units being moved, the placement of support equipment is as important as the furniture layout. The facilities staff may understand the organization's mission, but they rarely obtain the ongoing intimacy necessary to understanding operational needs; area managers or designated representatives must ensure that these needs are met. The unit moving should feel comfortable with facilities management's final plan and sign it off. However, the department's responsibility does not end with the sign-off. As the move date draws closer, assigning employees to their position becomes critical. This office map determines the placement of telecommunications and data equipment. Selecting instruments and special features will closely follow. Although not given the high priority on management's list of concerns, the cost of sophisticated features on a telephone system adds considerable expense to the bottom line. Departmental managers should judiciously incorporate this equipment into their operations budget if no corporate standards exist.

Moving as efficiently as possible is the responsibility of local managers. Together with the move coordinator, they should review their department's filing needs, purging the unnecessary, transferring to storage vital records, and in general making sure that only essential material is moved. The manager should also inventory storage areas, eliminating obsolete equipment that is gathering dust or reducing supply purchases to marginal levels. The fewer items to be moved, the lower the cost of the move. The local managers should also assess the quality of their equipment or equipment leases. If possible, they should arrange for new equipment to be delivered to the new location rather than transport the old. This procedure may require higher levels of authorization, but the area manager must present this option to management. Furthermore, if new equipment is installed at the new location, facilities management must be notified of any special requirements. Because local managers may not understand power requirements, the facilities staff should review with them any changes in equipment to ensure that manufacturers' specifications for power and environment are met.

Finally, the local manager is responsible for boxing all materials and working with the movers and the move coordinator to ensure that all boxes, furniture, and equipment are properly tagged. On the evening of the move, the local manager should have sufficient staff on hand to help identify the status of items missed through oversight or specifically not included in the move. Moving items left through oversight at a later date is costly, and managers on the receiving side of the move can make decisions as questions arise. Form often does not follow function, and drawings do not match space layouts.

The Cost of Downtime

The move team must reduce the downtime or non-productive time of employees during a move as much as possible. However, as the moving time grows closer, employees depart from their normal work routines to some form of move preparation. During the weeks immediately before and after the move, the company will experience its greatest negative influences. Research shows that employees are affected significantly more on the day of and the day after the move. Boxing, purging, and storing files must be completed, along with the labeling and tagging of items to be moved, while the period after the move is lost to refiling and locating material to perform daily routines. These studies indicate a loss of productivity or downtime of approximately 38 percent during the week before and the week after the move.

From the results of this study, the downtime cost per employee would be approximately $639.42, based on an average salary of $35,000 plus a 25 percent benefits cost. When this figure is multiplied by 1,000 to 3,000 employees moving, the one-time cost in lost productivity would range from $639,420 to $1,918,260. These statistics may be conservative, considering the blend of employees and managers, but it represents a real dollar loss to the corporation. To reduce downtime, some firms require departments to come in over the weekend to unpack and set up their operations. This adds a slight cost greater than that stated above, since weekend work is paid for in premium wages. However, customer services are then minimally interrupted by the relocation.

SUMMARY

Major moves bring into focus many different elements of the corporation of the organization. Communication among these elements is essential to the move's success. Management's concerns center on cost, lost opportunities, and downtime, while personnel managers are concerned with its effect on employees, whether the firm is moving across town or across the country. The facilities staff is the overall coordinator of the program, with special emphasis on the design and construction phase of the project; the staff also oversees the actual move. The move coordinator, a one-time specialist, handles the logistics of the move and interfaces with the in-house operations and the movers. Each department must take the necessary steps to effectively prepare for its move. Moving is a team effort, and if the team does not function smoothly, delays will beleaguer the entire staff, resulting in higher costs and management complaints.

A major move is not a common occurrence for large corporations. Successful completion can be achieved with proper planning and responsiveness to the changing environment. Through cooperation and teamwork, the move can be completed on time and within the budget, thereby meeting everyone's satisfaction.

CHAPTER 6

UTILITY REDISTRIBUTION

Jay A. Raphaelson
Utility Programs & Metering Inc.

INCOME AND EXPENSE

Much of the real estate community believes that utility redistribution is purely a technical function, generally delegated to either the engineering or the construction department. However, many organizations do not consider the fact that the effect of utility redistribution is companywide. Once the building owner secures power from the local utility, he or she must act in place of the utility company. Not only must the owner make sure that he receives the best value from the local utility, but he must also wisely allocate this power throughout the building, ensuring that he does not exhaust his distribution capabilities and that he is properly compensated for distributing resources.

The redistribution of power affects virtually every division within the real estate organization. Once a building is on the drawing board, the owner and his or her staff must make decisions about the amount of power that will be brought into the building. They must also make related decisions concerning HVAC systems, water distribution, metering systems, and so forth. Because this task generally falls to both the architects and the engineers, they must incorporate these decisions into the building design. When the property design is completed, management must consider certain leasing decisions including the following:

- The amount of power allotted to each tenant.
- The method of charging tenants for power.

- The amount of air conditioning to be provided.
- Whether the air conditioning should be metered.
- The method of serving overtime air conditioning.
- Whether to charge for condenser water or chilled water.
- What would happen if the tenant required additional power.
- The method of compensating the landlord for base building expenses.

Once these leasing decisions have been made and building construction has begun, the construction division must meet all its structural requirements. When the tenant takes occupancy, the operations department is responsible for ensuring that the tenant receives the amounts and types of utilities to which he or she is entitled, according to the terms of the lease. The accounting department monitors the building's income versus the services provided therein. The asset manager must be able to differentiate between income, expense, and profit, if the owner chooses utility redistribution as a profit tool for the building.

The management of utility redistribution is actually a minibusiness within the property. The building management acts as a utility company, and it may be governed by the rules and regulations set forth by the local regulatory commission. This chapter discusses utility redistribution within properties and the allocation of the costs thereof.

ALLOCATING POWER TO THE TENANTS

After arranging for power service with the local utility, the building owner must decide how to allocate this power among the new tenants. There are three generally accepted ways of redistributing this power: direct utility metering, sub- or checkmetering, and rent inclusion. Each method has distinct advantages and disadvantages. The building owner must check with the local utility and regulatory authority to determine whether any restrictions are placed on submetering or rent inclusion programs.

Direct Metering

Direct metering virtually removes responsibility from both the landlord and the tenant for utility redistribution. The landlord must provide the appropriate service taps and dedicated power for the tenant; once power is connected, the tenant is directly responsible to the public utility. Any further utility issues are resolved between the tenant and the utility. If the tenant fails to pay its bill, the utility can terminate service. The tenant usually believes that there are certain advantages in dealing directly with the public utility. The first of these is integrity; it is dealing directly with a third-party contractor with published rate schedules that are routinely controlled by a regulatory authority. Another advantage is that the tenant has control over its own usage. If it wishes to receive the advantage of utility rebates, energy conservation measures, or any type of electricity control, it has direct responsibility and will receive the benefits of these cost-saving measures. The tenant must also maintain its own checks and balances to ensure that it is receiving the best utility value for his money. It must ensure that it is on the most advantageous rate schedule, that its meters are read correctly, that it maintains an effective power factor, and that service is sufficient for its needs. A major disadvantage is that in cases where a tenant requires more power for its space, it may be extremely costly to receive additional service because the landlord might not have the additional risers, transformers, or other necessary equipment to furnish extra power within the property. This means that the tenant must procure the needed power directly from the utility, and it may be an expensive proposition.

The landlord receives some of the same benefits that the tenant receives. There is no responsibility to the local utility once power has been delivered to the space. Any problems with electric service are strictly between the tenant and the utility. However, the landlord must consider two disadvantages. The first is the case where multiple risers service each tenant space; if each tenant has a separate dedicated riser rather than a common buss, these lines take up substantial space within the building. More tenants mean more space taken up by this electrical equipment. The landlord must make a cost analysis to determine whether more revenue can be generated from renting additional space than from filling it with electrical equipment.

Another consideration for the landlord is the effect of tenant relocation on the power. Each utility meter services a specific area, and there is no guarantee that each subsequent lease will cover the same space configuration as that of the original lease. A meter obviously cannot recognize a demising wall dividing a space that was initially for one tenant and is now subdivided for two. The meter will continue to register consumption from the electrical panel for both spaces. Workers must take steps during construction to ensure that each space is properly metered. This may involve splitting electrical service, installing additional panels and meters, and tracing the electrical lines to make sure that all parties are billed correctly. It is a fairly common occurrence to have power terminated from one space while it continues in another. In some areas, the utility may be responsible for tracing each service to guarantee each tenant proper billing as each new service is applied for. In many cases, however, unless a utility is specifically told that a space has undergone construction, it will reassign a meter in name only, regardless of how much power is actually served to a given space.

An extremely important consideration for the landlord—and the main disadvantage of direct utility metering—is the potential loss of usable power. During lease negotiation, the landlord and tenant discuss the amount of electric service available; the tenant must predict what his or her power requirements will be and negotiate accordingly. This is not an easy task because office equipment has changed dramatically within the last five years and continues to evolve quickly. Tenants therefore tend to overestimate their power needs for the term of the lease. The landlord must compare the amount of power available to the property and the amount of power it is prepared to allocate for dedicated use by each tenant. Once this power is assigned to a prospective tenant, recovering it for use elsewhere in the building is extremely difficult, if not impossible. Consider the following situation, for example. During the course of lease negotiations, a landlord commits eight watts per square foot to a tenant for its electrical requirements. Over the next several years, it is determined that it is using only four watts per square foot, and its power needs are not likely to increase in the foreseeable future. The landlord cannot recover the four watts per square foot of idle capacity assigned to the tenant. This additional power could become critical near the end of a building's leasing program. The landlord must ensure that enough power is available for the last tenant to sign a lease, so that this tenant does not require additional—and expensive—power capacity that may already be available to the property.

Many owners have started to include a "use or lose" provision in their leases. They state that a specific amount of power will be available for a tenant's use. If the tenant does not use this allocated power within a specified time period, the owner retains the right to recover it at no additional cost.

Submetering

Submetering, or checkmetering, offers many of the advantages of direct utility metering. The landlord must check the rules and regulations governing submetering in his or her particular area. Many states prohibit checkmetering entirely; other states leave it to the discretion of the local utility; and still others place no restrictions on this type of metering. Some areas regulate submetering because the landlord has the potential to overcharge the tenants with this type of metering system. The utility has no control over an agreement between the two parties, and in states that do not have any legislation which establishes limits on charges, a landlord can charge a tenant whatever the market will bear even with a meter. The meter continues to register actual consumption, but the landlord, who assumes the responsibility as a utility, may establish its own rate schedule. However, if a submetering system is properly administered, both the landlord and the tenant can enjoy a beneficial relationship. The tenant still has control over the amount of power used in its space. If the tenant wishes to take steps toward conservation, which may lower its energy cost, it may do so within the guidelines of the lease. Each tenant can generally rest assured that the landlord has installed meters that meet or exceed government standards for revenue metering.

The landlord enjoys certain advantages with a checkmetering system. It enables him to control the power allocation during a tenant's lease if the tenant's electrical needs change. An electric meter that records usage allows the landlord to monitor variations thereof. He therefore may take advantage of the flexibility of this system. Although he still must ensure that each space is properly metered, he may link multiple meters through a computerized metering system that will save a significant sum that would otherwise go toward additional wiring as tenants' spaces are re-leased. In areas where it is permissible, the landlord may negotiate with the utility to make a profit through a submetering system. This profit may be written directly into the lease, or it may be accomplished by supplying the tenant with electric service at a price equal to that which it would pay directly to the utility. The landlord may then be eligible for a lower rate from the utility based upon total volume.

In a commercial application, installing the correct type of electric meter in each tenant space is important. Most commercial buildings have a rate schedule predicated on demand, which is generally defined as the highest surge of electricity within a specific time period—usually fifteen minutes or a half hour—within the monthly billing period. The tenant should have the same type of meter as the building. The tenants' bills can then be rendered in the same format as that of either the building or of directly billed customers. Many building owners install kilowatt-hour (kwh) meters only. They then determine the average cost per kilowatt-hour from the monthly bill and apply this rate to the tenants' registered consumption. This type of billing method does not fairly allocate the tenants' costs, as it is predicated on only one component of the electric bill. For example, a firm that utilizes a lot of computer equipment and supplemental air conditioning is demand-intensive when compared to a sales or accounting firm that does not have such heavy electrical requirements. In this particular case, the accounting firm would be subsidizing the computer firm's greater demand for electricity. The additional cost of meters which register actual demand and consumption is insignificant when compared with the revenue that a tenant with smaller demand requirements could lose.

Rent Inclusion

The third method for utility redistribution is rent inclusion. Rent inclusion is the practice of assigning a consistent monthly value for electricity and including it in the rent. This billing method is either accomplished by a cost-per-square-foot allocation or by an electrical survey. A rent inclusion value can range from 50 cents per square foot to 3 dollars per square foot, depending upon the owner's actual cost of electricity, market value in a particular area, or both. In many depressed areas of the country, this value is understated; a market value that has no relevance to the cost of the service supplied may have been determined. However, if one owner charges 50 cents per foot for electricity and another charges 75 cents per foot, the tenant perceives this difference as a savings in base rent, regardless of the fact that a survey to determine the proper value may be conducted later. Another misconception is that the 50 or 75 cents per foot is entirely for electricity used in that tenant's space. Instead of performing a survey, some owners compare their income from tenants to their total utility expense and place the difference in rent escalation at the end of the year. This method makes the building whole, but the landlord risks the tenants' discovery that they may be subsidizing other tenants' utilities through rent escalations. When a rent inclusion value for electricity is negotiated by the cost-per-square-foot method, it is not usually based on prevailing rates or on the tenant's usage. The lease serves as a contract for the landlord to provide a given amount of power during specific times for "normal" equipment for a negotiated sum. This sum may not, however, have any relation to the actual cost of utility service. Furthermore, many landlords determine this value and then fail to provide a method for increasing or decreasing it as utility rates change. The owner has negotiated a specific profit margin, and he should maintain it throughout the term of the lease. Therefore he should include provisions to adjust this value whenever necessary. Rates should be revised on a regular basis so the tenant knows that the landlord is aware of and maintaining its lease obligation.

Before a survey is conducted, the landlord's surveyor prepares an inventory of all the electrical equipment in the tenant space. Each piece of equipment has an electrical rating that either is listed on the unit itself or is available from the manufacturer. The surveyor must ascertain how each piece of equipment is being used, so he conducts interviews with both tenants and building personnel to assess the operation of the equipment. A thorough survey can fulfill dual purposes: not only will it provide an estimate of what the tenants' charges should be, but the survey can be compared with the building's electric bills and hence used as a tool for energy conservation. Many tenants, in fact, use the evaluation to reduce their monthly bills through energy conservation. A survey determines things that a meter cannot; for instance, sign-in and sign-out sheets can help determine occupancy hours and when basic lighting is turned on or off.

A significant amount of electricity is wasted in daily office procedures. For example, cleaning personnel generally turn off light switches on the wall but rarely turn off cubicle lighting. The ever-present personal computer or video display terminal left on twenty-four hours a day, seven days a week, not only wastes electricity but also creates additional heat that is much harder to compensate for by air conditioning on hot summer Monday mornings. Copying machines that have on and off switches on the inside completely shut themselves off, while those with switches outside the unit are similar to instant-on television sets; the basic components are turned off, but the heating element stays on to eliminate an extended warm-up period.

A survey is a snapshot of a specific area taken at a specific point in time. The landlord must take care to periodically reinspect the tenant's premises to ensure that it does not significantly increase the amount and use of its equipment without the landlord's approval. This survey, which also determines demand, allows the owner to find the wattage per square foot utilized in the space and to compare it with the lease provision.

Even though it is an extremely useful tool, the survey can potentially create serious landlord-tenant disputes during the term of the lease. It tends to be one of the least-discussed items in the lease because both landlord and tenant consider the provision to be electricity-rather than cost-oriented. If the landlord raises the utility charge after the tenant moves in, the tenant usually refers to the initial rent inclusion value and claims that the landlord has misrepresented the issue. On the other hand, tenants that recognize the importance of this issue have a distinct advantage when negotiating this part of the lease; they are often able to negotiate caps in the lease for both cost figures and power requirements. They may be more familiar with rate schedules and could end up purchasing power from the landlord at a lower price than the landlord can obtain from the utility.

Everyone involved in purchasing and redistributing power must realize that it is a dollars-and-cents issue. The owner must decide both how to distribute power and whether the cost thereof must be negotiated separately and considered an asset. There is potential in this area for either significant loss or gain. As utility rates escalate, many institutional owners and lenders evaluate utilities and their relation to a building's potential income, expenses, and overall value.

KNOWING THE LOCAL UTILITY

The landlord must ask itself two basic questions:

- Is enough power available?
- How much will it cost?

Determining the amount of power required for a particular property requires evaluations by consulting engineers. Making a wise decision about the issue of cost requires both expertise and common sense. Many organizations believe that utilities are infallible; they are in the business of selling electricity. If a potential customer initiates rate negotiations during a building's planning, rather than after such issues have been decided, it has a definite advantage. It should keep the following question in mind: "How can I get the electric service I require while paying the smallest possible amount for it?"

The potential customer needs some basic information before establishing a utility rate. It should obtain a tariff from either the utility or the regulatory commission, which contains most of the approved rate schedules. It also includes a list of rules and regulations for securing electric service. Using the tariff, the potential customer can find the best rate schedule for its needs. After reviewing the schedule, however, it should obtain a copy of any "off-tariff" rates that are in effect for other customers in the area. These rates might not be in the published tariff: they are the result of negotiations with another customer. If the customer in question meets the same criteria that another customer has negotiated, the utility must provide it with an exact or similar rate schedule. If it has a unique requirement, a separate rate may be negotiated specifically for its property. Many utilities have negotiated rates in order to prevent loss of revenue; because electricity is the only product that it sells, the electric company, when faced with the possibility of a potential customer using an alternative energy source or receiving power from another utility company, is more likely to negotiate.

Utilities have multiple rate schedules, and the cost of supplying each customer sector varies; so, during rate negotiations, the customer should find out whether its rate is based on the actual cost of supplying service to the property. In most cases, the commercial and industrial sectors subsidize the utility's total revenue base. The ratio of revenue created by the commercial and industrial base to the utility's total revenue can be helpful information when negotiating a rate. After all, the issue at hand is the percentage of its profit that the utility can make from a single customer.

Before beginning negotiations, it is helpful if the potential customer investigates incentives available within or outside of the utility. Many utilities sponsor rebate programs based on the installation of energy efficient equipment and lighting in the property.

Some utilities offer incentives for buildings in areas that have excess power, especially those that are undergoing revitalization. Old industrial sectors are being converted to commercial office complexes, and many large organizations are moving their back offices to these areas to take advantage of lower rent and utility rates.

Many utility services compete against themselves through different divisions. For example, a single utility company may sell electricity, gas, and steam, all of which can fuel a building's base HVAC system. Each division within the utility is responsible for generating sales, and when one competes with other divisions, the customer usually has an advantage. Finding lower cost alternatives does not stop with the utility company; there are often local and state incentives, too. In some states, utilities used in the manufacture of a resaleable product, which would normally be taxable, are tax exempt. A customer may also purchase power that the local utility will redistribute through an alternative grid. State and municipal programs have established criteria for eligibility, but they certainly merit investigation.

Obtaining power from the local utility for a new building can create a difficult situation. The problem typically develops in the following way. The building requests a certain amount of power from the utility. The utility usually wants some proof that the power will be used, as it wishes to avoid the expense of bringing more power than necessary to the building and installing additional equipment. However, an accurate estimate of power needs is often difficult to obtain when the building is not pre-leased. On the other hand, a tenant wants assurance that his power needs will be met; if he will require an unusually large amount of power, a building owner may be unable to guarantee this for the tenant. There *is* a solution, however. The utility can make arrangements to supply power in stages; the owner can thus negotiate a lease based on the utility's agreement to provide power when and if need is demonstrated. The tenant will know that power will be available, but that the landlord will recover and redistribute unused power. The utility can keep this power in its bank and utilize it elsewhere until the developer requires it.

The key to dealing with any utility is asking questions. Utilities are regulated monopolies that have a certain amount of competition and are governed by a regulatory authority. If the building owner purchases electricity (or any utility) just like it would any other product, it greatly increases the likelihood of obtaining the best rate for the service provided.

OVERTIME SERVICES

Most building owners define base operating hours in their leases. The hours are typically 8:00 A.M. to 6:00 P.M., Monday through Friday, and 8:00 A.M. to 1:00 P.M. on Saturday. When a tenant uses the building outside of the standard times, the landlord must decide whether to bill the tenant for overtime services. In most cases, standard lighting and equipment are included in either the survey or in the direct or submetering. A significant concern, however, is overtime air conditioning.

In some cases, maintaining the air conditioning unit is the tenant's responsibility, but the landlord supplies condenser water or chilled water for its operation. The production of this water is recorded on the landlord's electric meter, and the tenant should bear responsibility for the cost of overtime cooling. Many building owners charge market value for overtime air conditioning without having supporting evidence. This figure is often challenged during a lease negotiation or an operating escalation review. An owner who can support its fees is better-equipped to handle any negotiations with or challenges from its tenants about overtime charges. A typical condenser water cost analysis includes components such as fans, pumps, pneumatics, chemicals, repairs, supplies, preventive maintenance, service life, and water consumption and lighting for mechanical engine rooms where equipment is monitored. Exhibit 6–1 is a typical condenser water cost analysis.

A more complex problem arises when the owner prepares an overtime allocation for a central plant. It must consider the cost of equipment that operate for the entire building, as well as the equipment operating for specific zones.

An appropriate overtime air conditioning charge excludes the utility demand component—the building's peak demand, usually incurred during normal business hours. Because overtime air conditioning is generally provided during off-peak periods, the building's demand will be much lower than it is during the daytime. Exhibit 6–2 is an example of an overtime HVAC evaluation. The owner should evaluate such reports annually and upgrade them according to changes in utility costs, material costs, and equipment.

EXHIBIT 6–1
Condenser Water Cost Analysis for 1988–1989

SUMMER SEASON
$97.36/mo./ton @ 4 mos.   = $389.44

WINTER SEASON
$114.92/mo./ton @ 8 mos.   = $919.36

                            TOTAL P.A. = $1,308.80/yr/ton

                            TOTAL P.M. = $109.07/mo/ton

I. *SUMMER OPERATION*

A. *FANS*
1. Cooling Tower CT-1   =   30.08 Kw
2. Cooling Tower CT-1A   =   30.08
3. Cooling Tower CT-2   =   30.08
4. Cooling Tower CT-2A   =   30.08

                  TOTAL   =   120.32 Kw

120.32 Kw @ $.103434/KwHr @ 58%   = $ 7.22

B. *PUMPS*
1. Condenser Water Pump #1   =   70.16 Kw
2. Condenser Water Pump #2   =   70.16
3. Domestic Water Pump #1   =   28.30

                  TOTAL   =   168.62 Kw

168.62 Kw @ $.103434/KwHr @ 58%   = $10.12

C. *PNEUMATICS*
1. Air Compressor   =   3.57 Kw
2. Drier   =   .71

                  TOTAL   =   4.28 Kw

4.28 Kw @ $.103434/KwHr @ 58%   = $ .26

D. *CHEMICALS*
$8,100.00 P.A. @ 58% @ 8,766 Hrs P.A.   = $ .54

E. *WATER CONSUMPTION*
209.05 Tons @ .3209 @ $1.42/100 cu.ft   = $ .95

F. *LIGHTING*
1. 35th Floor MER   =   1.43 Kw
2. Sub-cellar MER   =   4.89

                  TOTAL   =   6.32 Kw

6.32 Kw @ $.103434/KwHr @ 58%   = $ .38

EXHIBIT 6–1 (continued)

G. *REPAIRS, SUPPLIES & PREVENTIVE MAINTENANCE*
  1. Repairs & Supplies   = $2.27/Hr
  2. Preventive Maintenance
     and labor $186,338.50
     P.A. @ 20% @ 8,766 Hrs/
     P.A.   = $4.32/Hr   = $6.59

H. *SERVICE LIFE*
  $15,952.92 P.A. @ 8,766 Hrs P.A.   = $ 1.82

                  TOTAL   = $27.88/Hr

               TOTAL P.M.   = $20,352.40/Mo

          TOTAL/MO/TON
  @ 209.05 Connected Tons   = $97.36/Mo/Ton

II. *WINTER OPERATION*

  A. *FANS*
    1. Cooling Tower CT-1   =   30.08 Kw
    2. Cooling Tower CT-1A   =   30.08

                  TOTAL   =   60.16 Kw

  120.32 Kw @ $.103762/KwHr @ 58%   = $ 6.24

  B. *PUMPS*
    1. Condenser Water Pump #1   =   70.16 Kw
    2. Condenser Water Pump #2   =   70.16
    3. Domestic Water Pump #1   =   28.30

                  TOTAL   =   168.62 Kw

  168.62 Kw @ $.103762/KwHr @ 58%   = $15.75

  C. *PNEUMATICS*
    1. Air Compressor   =   3.57 Kw
    2. Drier   =   .71

                  TOTAL   =   4.28 Kw

  4.28 Kw @ $.103762/KwHr @ 58%   = $ .26

  D. *CHEMICALS*
    $8100.00 P.A. @ 8766 Hrs P.A.   = $ .92

  E. *WATER CONSUMPTION*
    209.05 Tons @ .3209 @ $1.42/100 cu.ft   = $ .95

F. *LIGHTING*
    1. 35th Floor MER   = 1.43 Kw
    2. Sub-cellar MER   = <u>4.89</u>

                  TOTAL = 6.32 Kw

  6.32 Kw @ $.103762/KwHr @ 58%   = $ .38

G. *REPAIRS, SUPPLIES & PREVENTIVE MAINTENANCE*
    1. Repairs & Supplies   = $2.27/Hr
    2. Preventive Maintenance
       and labor $186,338.50
       P.A. @ 20% @ 8,766 Hrs/
       P.A.   = <u>$4.32/Hr</u> = $6.59

H. *SERVICE LIFE*
    $15,952.92 P.A. @ 8,766 Hrs P.A. = <u>$ 1.82</u>

                  TOTAL = $32.91/Hr

           TOTAL P.M. = $24,024.30/Mo

          TOTAL/MO/TON
  @ 209.05 Connected Tons = <u>$114.92/Mo/Ton</u>

EXHIBIT 6–2
Sample Overtime HVAC Evaluation

I. *COOLING—TOTAL HOUSE*
  A. *Turbine/Compressor Sets*
    1. Steam
      a. Turbine
        1,320 Tons @ 16 Lbs/Ton @ $14.04/1000 Lbs @ .81   = $240.19
    2. Electric
      a. Compressor Heaters
        9.84 Kwhr/Hr @ $.159544/Kwhr = $ 1.57
      b. Condenser Vacuum Pump
        7.72 Kw @ $.159544/Kwhr = $ 1.23   = $ 2.80

  B. *Fans*

1. HVAC Fans Top & Bottom 2nd to 16th Floors	=	98.66 Kw	
2. Spill & Return Fans 2nd to 16th Floors	=	39.47	
3. HVAC Fans 17th to 29th Floors	=	26.48	
4. Spill & Return Fans 17th to 29th Floors	=	9.10	
5. Exhaust Fans 2nd to 29th Floors	=	.25	
6. Supply Fan Elev MR 16th Floor	=	1.07	
7. Supply Fan Elev MR 16th Floor	=	.03	
8. Toilet Exhaust	=	5.82	
9. HVAC—Lobby	=	2.40	
10. HVAC—Locker Rooms	=	.97	
11. Exhaust Fan—Elev Pit	=	.67	
12. Supply Fan—Refrigeration Room	=	10.11	
13. Peripheral Fans	=	112.51	
14. Cooling Tower #1	=	16.06	
15. Cooling Tower #2	=	16.06	
16. Cooling Tower #3	=	16.06	
		355.72 Kw	
355.72 Kw @ $.159544/Kwhr		=	$ 56.75

EXHIBIT 6–2 (*continued*)
Sample Overtime HVAC Evaluation

C. *Pumps*
  1. Condenser Water Pump #1   =   57.42 Kw
  2. Condenser Water Pump #2   =   57.42
  3. Chill Water Pump #1   =   35.14
  4. Chill Water Pump #2   =   35.14
  5. Peripheral Pump South Zone   =   12.63
  6. Peripheral Pump West Zone #1   =   9.78
  7. Peripheral Pump West Zone #2   =   9.78
  8. Peripheral Pump North Zone   =   9.78
  9. Peripheral Pump East Zone   =   9.78
  10. House Pump 32.39 Kw @ 15%   =   4.86
  11. Hot Well Pump #1A   =   1.02
  11. Hot Well Pump #2A   =   1.02
  13. Vacuum Pump   =   3.33
  14. Condensate Pump   =   3.33
  15. Condensate Pump—Converter
      1.99 Kw @ 65%   =   1.29
                             251.72 Kw

    251.72 Kw @ $.159544/Kwhr   = $ 40.16

D. *Pneumatic System*
  1. Air Compressor 3.40 Kw @ 35%   =   1.19 Kw
  2. Air Drier   .70 Kw @ 75%   =   .53
                             1.72 Kw

    1.72 Kw @ $.159544/Kwhr   = $ .27

E. *Chemicals & Analysis Service*
  $4,000.00 PA @ 2,520 Optg Hrs PA   = $ 1.59

F. *Labor*
  1. One Engineer @ $16.35 Per Hr + 30% FB   = $21.26
  2. One Helper   @ $12.95 Per Hr + 30% FB   = $16.84   = $ 38.10

G. *Filters*
  $5,000.00 PA @ 2,520 Optg Hrs PA   = $ 1.98

H. *Water Consumption*
  1320 Tons @ .3209 @ $.70/100 Ft^3 @ .81   = $ 2.40

I. *Preventative Maintenance & Repairs*
  1. Scheduled Maintenance & Repairs
    a. Amortized Maintenance   = $9.69
    b. Tools, Oil & Grease, Seals,
       Belts, Traps   =   2.78
    c. Plumbing   =   .80
    d. Thermographs   =   .40
    e. Paint   =   .40
    f. Refrigerant   =   .79

  2. *Labor*
    $14,212.08 PA @ 2,520 Optg Hrs PA   =   5.64   = $ 20.50

                                 TOTAL: $404.74

SUMMARY

A reasonable charge for a tenant's utility bill is approximately 10 percent of his rent, which varies with the size and complexity of each tenant's installation. Utilities represent a significant portion of any business's budget, and unless a building owner keeps pace with the utility-related changes that affect his or her property, he or she will surely fall short in utility revenues. More and more organizations are making a business of utility management, including designing efficient properties, specializing in rates and billing, and even representing tenants against owners on a contingency basis.

Utility management in properties used to be as simple as income versus expense. Today, many professional organizations work with utilities, governmental agencies, and multibillion-dollar corporations to properly allocate utility cost. These costs must be managed efficiently and professionally in today's everchanging marketplace. Managing income and expense effectively greatly enhances the value of the owner's portfolio through the tenant's improved perception of his or her ability and through the efficiency and awareness created within the organization.

PART 2

DEVELOPING NEW CONSTRUCTION

CHAPTER 7

FINANCING THE PROJECT

Bertram Lewis
Sybedon Equities Corp.
Dale Goncher
Columbia University

INTRODUCTION

An understanding of commercial real estate financing requires a familiarity with three distinct areas: (1) the capital markets and those who participate in them as providers of funds for real estate; (2) the processes of valuation and assessment of risk; and (3) the techniques of creating secured and other participating interests in real property.

The objectives and constraints of the participants in the capital markets must be understood since the method in which each participant accesses funds affects the type of lending, loan term, and pricing it will engage in. Valuation and risk assessment processes also must be understood; the emphasis of each process may vary depending on the type of lending or participation involved. In addition, the techniques, ranging from interest rate swaps to wraparounds and from participating mortgages to subordinated ground leases, must be understood; one or more of the available techniques may be involved in any single financing transaction.

Each of these three topics is complex and ever changing. Increased globalization of capital markets, new regulations, tax law changes the underlying economics of real property in local markets, and varying perceptions about inflation may cause changes to take place in lending patterns. In this chapter, we will focus on commercial income-producing real estate and the process of arranging debt, not equity, financing.[1]

REAL ESTATE CAPITAL MARKETS

The overall availability of capital and terms upon which it is loaned for real estate projects are determined by the total supply of capital in the capital markets—both domestically and offshore. The past decade has been a period of enormous growth and increased sophistication in the capital markets.

The providers of real estate capital are intermediaries who must access capital and turn it into real estate project financing. Real estate intermediaries must compete with the other users of capital, such as consumers, governments, and industrial corporations (and their intermediaries); therefore, the price of real estate capital is always related to overall market supply/demand conditions. Furthermore, the increased volatility of interest rates and focus on shorter maturities in the marketplace increases the difficulty of obtaining financing for the relatively long-term investments needed in real estate.

Traditionally, there has been a greater flow of lendable funds into real estate during periods of low interest rates and, conversely, of equity funds during periods of high interest rates, reflecting high inflationary expectations. Available lendable funds tend to flow out of real estate when the competition for such funds causes yields to rise dramatically or when real estate values are perceived to be declining. In the 1980s funds were readily available and supported by tax subsidies, and there was a climate of deregulation. However, as the 1990s begin, the climate has changed. There is now a "credit crunch," due to excessive inventories, tax reform, and a renewed emphasis on regulation. Until the supply and demand for real estate products again become more balanced, with the prior excess production absorbed into the market, property values will likely decline and funding will be more difficult to obtain.

Expanded sophistication in the capital markets and competition for the available capital has had a dramatic effect on the tradition-

---

[1]Changes in federal and local tax codes can affect the financing process dramatically. However, this subject is so complex and changeable that it cannot be adequately covered in this chapter.

ally diverse real estate industry. There has been a movement toward larger development firms and institutions that can achieve economies of scale, diversify operations in several markets, and meet tightened credit requirements. The small- and medium-sized investor-developer is increasingly at a disadvantage because of the heightened creditworthiness necessary to obtain funding, particularly for a new venture.

Today, the primary players in the real estate debt marketplace are the life insurance companies, pension funds, and commercial banks. Occupying a somewhat smaller role are the commercial finance companies, thrifts, special purpose partnerships, and real estate investment trusts (REITs). An increased number of foreign banks and insurance companies entered the domestic market in the 1980s, but their activities were largely equity related or, on the debt side, limited to participating in loans originated by domestic banks or making loans to firms with whom they had already established banking relationships. As these offshore investors gain experience, it is likely that their activities will broaden.

A knowledge of how various lenders operate leads to an understanding of why some lenders will offer liberal prepayment privileges while others will not, why some lenders will fix interest rates while others prefer to "float," and why some lenders generally offer nonrecourse loans while others rarely do. Borrowers must match their needs with those of the different types of lenders.

Life Insurance Companies

The life insurance companies are the most diversified sources of real estate capital, investing both in debt and equity. Their direct investment in commercial real estate loans represents approximately 25 percent of the total amount of such debt outstanding from 1987 to 1990. They have three principal sources of funds: (1) annuity and life insurance premiums, (2) direct borrowing (typically through the sale of guaranteed investment contracts, or GICs), and (3) the sponsorship of joint and separate accounts primarily for pension funds. The providers of funds (through premium payments or direct lending) look to the creditworthiness of the life insurance company to achieve their goals of return and repayment. Accordingly, they are not involved directly in the outcome of specific investments of the company. (So-called universal life policies do permit policyholders to specify how cash values are to be invested. To that extent, the policyholder's yield could be more directly related to the outcome of a particular class of investments.)

However, in the case of joint and separate accounts sponsored by the insurance company, the pension fund's investment outcome is directly related to the performance of the account in which it invested. Life insurance companies frequently offer a variety of joint accounts with differing investment objectives that generally have one of two basic structures: (1) open-end funds, which have an infinite life and generally permit periodic redemption and sale of new participations, and (2) closed-end funds, which have a limited life. Open-end funds are primarily invested in real estate equities. The separate account is usually established to meet the specific investment needs of the beneficiary, who often retains the right to approve specific investments recommended by the life insurance company.

Insurance commissioners in each state regulate the life insurance companies. New York State generally has the most stringent requirements and tends to set the regulatory standard for the industry. A.M. Best, the most well-known rating agency for life insurance companies, rates these companies and their investment products.[2] Obviously, those with the highest ratings pay the least to attract capital.

The life insurance companies lend on either a direct or correspondent basis, depending on the particular institution. Correspondent lending relies on intermediaries to analyze, recommend, originate, and sometimes service the loan. Generally, life insurance companies are intermediate- and long-term lenders, avoiding construction loans. Their loans are often made without recourse, which means that in the event of default the lender's recourse is limited to the pledged interest in the real estate. They tend to lend at a fixed rate of interest and attempt to match the term and rate of their loans to their liabilities (this is called matched funding). This often makes it difficult, or expensive, for a borrower to obtain an advance lending commitment at a predetermined fixed rate more than a few months in advance of funding or to obtain a liberal right of prepayment. Because of the focus of some of their joint accounts, insurance companies seek a higher yield and hence "participate" in the income of projects they finance.

Pension Funds

Potentially, the pension funds have the largest domestic pool of long-term capital available for real estate, but only small amounts have

---

[2]Recently, Standard & Poor's also began rating life insurance companies.

found their way into direct real estate loans. Pension funds hold assets for the payout of various public and private pensions. The passage of the Employment Retirement Income Security Act (ERISA) in 1974 brought about the "prudent investor test." This "test" affirmed the desirability of investment diversification. This, in conjunction with high inflation in the late 1970s and early 1980s, caused substantial pension fund money to flow into real estate investments, primarily equity.

With few exceptions, pension funds are not direct lenders in real estate, lacking both the staff and expertise. Pension funds are the principal purchasers of GICs offered by life insurance companies and participants in joint and separate accounts sponsored by those companies. They also provide real estate funds through other intermediaries such as commercial banks, independent advisors, REITs, and special partnerships. Pension funds are more of an indirect influence on available real estate capital. Pension fund assets consisted of 5 percent in real estate equities in 1989, representing $94 billion. This is exclusive of approximately 1 percent of assets in mortgages and their additional investments in GICs, bank certificates of deposit (CDs), and other forms of debt, of which a significant amount is employed in financing real estate.

Pension fund investments in real estate tend to be in long-term loans at fixed interest rates or in equity ownership. Fund managers generally attempt to match to their investment yields and maturities to pension fund liabilities. They are conservative investors and generally avoid development risk situations. Accordingly, they tend to lend on properties that are already income producing and do not usually seek recourse against that borrower.

Pension funds are not formally regulated except by the common law applicable to the term *prudent* and the desire of corporate treasurers to achieve a respectable level of earnings in the pension fund, consistent with safety. Pensions are funded by a combination of principal payments from the corporation and earnings. To the extent that earnings can be prudently increased, the funding obligation of the corporation may decrease. On the other hand, low earnings increase the funding obligation of the corporation.

Commercial Banks

The primary sources of funds for commercial banks are deposits and other types of borrowings. At the retail level, these are checking accounts, passbook savings, CDs, and money market accounts; at the wholesale level, these includes jumbo CDs, commercial paper, and securitized note issues. Commercial banks also have access to long-term funds in their trust departments and as intermediaries and advisors to pension funds. Commercial banks are also the most active players in the interest rate swap market, where floating rates can be swapped for fixed rates and vice versa.

Both federal and state governments regulate commercial banks, mandating that all loans be backed by a minimum amount of capital. Loans that are classified as substandard by bank examiners require the establishment of a reserve against capital, thus constraining overall loan growth. Ceilings on the maximum loan to appraised value and on loans to one borrower are commonly required. Generally, commercial banks lend at floating rates, in the form of construction and intermediate-term loans. These loans tend to be prepayable on a relatively liberal basis and often require personal guarantees and/or additional collateral.

To the extent that most commercial banks offer federally insured deposits (up to $100,000), it might be assumed that all have a similar cost of such funds. In reality, the cost may vary as a result of the degree of aggressiveness of different banks for such funds and the overhead associated with attracting such funds. As with other lenders, commercial banks also seek to match maturities and interest rates on both sides of the ledger (i.e., assets and liabilities). From 1987 to 1990, commercial banks held approximately 45 percent of the total commercial mortgage debt in the United States, which accounted for approximately 35 percent of commercial bank assets. This level of concentration is historically quite high and likely to be reduced as a result of regulatory pressure and revised bank policies.

Thrifts

Savings and loans and savings banks have short-term deposit sources of funds similar to commercial banks but are not usually sellers of commercial paper or very large CDs. Thrifts also can borrow for varying terms from the Federal Home Loan Bank at rates that are published regularly for their district. Well-managed thrifts usually operate on a matched funding basis. (A failure to do so was an important element in the insolvencies in this industry in the late 1980s and thereafter.) Because of the problems in this industry, the thrifts are subject to increasing regulation, including ceilings on loan-to-value ratios, risk-based capital requirements, and lowered limits on loans to any individual borrower. Thrifts have traditionally provided construction loans and permanent mortgages in the residential market and for commercial properties in their geographic area. During the 1980s, many thrifts broadened their products and their geographic scope, with less than satisfactory results. From 1987 to 1990, thrifts held approximately 20 percent of the total commercial mortgage debt, a percentage that is likely to diminish.

Other Markets

Commercial finance companies issue short-term floating rate commercial paper, placed domestically or offshore, and often have intermediate- and long-term debt as well, usually at a fixed rate. The commercial paper market is "regulated" by the rating given the company by the credit rating agencies (Standard & Poor's, Moody's, etc.) Companies without a high credit rating may need a third-party guarantor in order to participate in this market. Most of the major credit companies are subsidiaries of major industrial corporations or bank holding companies. Generally, they provide short- and intermediate-term financing at floating rates geared to the prime rate, the London Interbank Offered Rate (LIBOR), cost of funds, or other indices.

A real estate investment trust (REIT) is a trust with pass-through tax treatment that must conform to specific requirements of the Internal Revenue Service (IRS) and is often subject to Securities and Exchange Commission (SEC) disclosure rules as well. REITs are primarily equity investors (REITs that invest in mortgages will likely require participation). Some REITs were created with an indefinite life, while others are intended to liquidate at a certain point. All REITs are required to pay out substantially all of their earnings, thus depriving them of retained earnings as a future source of capital. They raise capital through new share offerings and by borrowing, usually from commercial banks.

Various limited partnerships have been created to respond to specific types of financing, such as second mortgages and shared appreciation mortgages. These entities usually are intended to have a finite life and do not typically seek new funds beyond what is available at the inception of the partnership.

Such non-bank and non–insurance company lending for commercial real estate purposes represented approximately 10 percent of total lending from 1987 to 1990.

VALUATION

To obtain financing, a borrower must find a lender who considers the project acceptable in terms of anticipated yield and the perceived level of risk. The lender will examine the borrower's creditworthiness and detailed information on virtually every aspect of the project, ranging from design to management to market considerations.

Physical Aspects

Traditionally, the *three* most important factors in real estate were "location, location, location." Today, financing and market timing would also be added to this list; however, location would still be considered the most important factor.

For an office building, the prestige and convenience of a location determine its marketability and ultimate success. Such factors as accessibility (for both occupants and their visitors), availability of services (e.g., restaurants and hotels), and the nature of the neighborhood (i.e., whether it is established or developing) can have a dramatic effect on the assessment of location — an admittedly subjective process.

The location, however, must be considered relative to the perceived market demand. Does the location fit the project design and market segment being sought at a cost that makes the project feasible?

The physical structure must also be examined. Quality of materials, suitability of design, and the existence of amenities relative to the target market and the competition are all considerations. Well-planned floor layouts and core components, an appropriate type of construction and materials, and a high efficiency ratio (the relationship of usable area to gross area) are features that add to a building's marketability. Amenities such as an advanced telecommunications system may be attractive but their feasibility must be demonstrated (i.e., will tenants pay for it?). Parking and transportation needs must also be adequately understood and addressed. The physical characteristics of the building must be related to the needs of those who will occupy the space, and the needs must be met at a price the tenant is willing to pay. Lenders consider these physical aspects when making real estate financing decisions.

Economic Aspects

The economic analysis of a project—that is, the valuation process—is another important aspect of real estate financing decisions; however, it is but one of the many considerations that go into lending decisions.

For income-producing real estate, the first step in the valuation process is to evaluate the existing and projected cash flow in order to determine the net operating income (NOI) for the projection period. The gross rental income (GRI), the starting point in the analysis, is usually estimated from the rents being generated in the market for similar buildings and adjusted for anticipated changes in market conditions. The term "rent" includes base rents, lease-specified tenant reimbursements, and ancillary income such as parking. Tenant concessions are often considered to distinguish effective rents from stated rent (including free rent periods, signing bonuses, high allowances for tenant improvements, and so forth). From this GRI projection, a vacancy factor is customarily subtracted to reflect anticipated vacancies, turnover losses, and credit-related losses. This produces a level of income referred to as the effective gross income (EGI).

Next, an analysis and projection of operating costs is made, separately identifying those costs that tend to vary with occupancy and those that are relatively fixed. The lender will refer to its data bank and other sources for historic figures on the cost of operations as a guide to reviewing the borrower's estimates. Once established, the operating expenses will be subtracted from the EGI to determine the projected NOI. This data produces a series of cash flows over the projection period.

The next step is to determine the disposition or residual value of the property. The cash flows and disposition value (which are analogous to bond interest and principal redemption) provide a framework for valuation. Disposition value is usually established by a simple capitalization approach. The projected NOI at an assumed point of disposition is divided by the assumed rate of return required by buyers at the disposition date. For example, if the projected cash flow in year 10 is $800,000 and it is assumed that buyers will demand an 8 percent capitalization rate, the assumed disposition value is $10 million. (This process of simple capitalization applied to a current year's NOI is another approach to valuation.)

The final step in this discounted cash flow approach is to select a discount rate and apply it to each year's cash flow and the disposition value. The result is the present value of the perceived future benefits that will accrue to the owner of the property.

This is a very subjective process. Rents are *projected,* expenses are *projected,* a disposition value is *assumed,* and a rate of capitalization is *selected* to apply to the *estimated* cash flows. In truth, value is in the eye of the beholder. For the would-be borrower, the task is to find a lender whose "eye" for value approximates his or her own.

This discounted cash flow approach is widely used. There are many refinements and variations to it that deal with sensitivity analysis, internal rate of return, net present value calculations, and methods for selecting discount and capitalization rates; however, the subjectivity of the process remains. Not only is determining value a subjective judgment, but that value may only be valid at a particular time. For example, in an auction market, market value might be established at the lowest price a motivated seller was willing to accept, which matched the highest price a motivated buyer was willing to pay, at that time. Even then, other buyers and sellers may not agree that the price established represented true value. In real estate, the lender seeks to establish its estimate of value, which is likely to be at variance with the estimates made by others. In an ideal setting, the lender with the highest valuation estimate would probably be the one to provide financing.

Customarily, the lender will apply two tests to the cash flow and valuation analysis. First, the loan-to-value ratio will be determined—with the loan not to exceed 75 to 80 percent of the estimated (or appraised) value of the property. Second, a debt service coverage analysis will be made to establish how much cushion the lender will have between the projected NOI and the debt service (interest and amortization) on the proposed loan. This is usually done by dividing the NOI by the debt service payment to produce a debt service coverage ratio. A required ratio of 1.15 to 1.2 would not be unusual.

Risk Assessment by the Lender

Lending involves risk taking. The lender who denies making risky loans is really saying that the risk is worth undertaking for the potential return.

Risk comes in two forms—risk that is intrinsic to the transaction and risk that is extrinsic. Extrinsic risk includes risks associated with government or political action, market supply and demand factor, uninsurable casualty losses, and declining value of the currency (inflation). A lender is aware of these risks and must determine whether such perceived risks are within a tolerable range. The same can be said of the borrower.

There are also many intrinsic risks in real estate transactions. How lenders and borrowers perceive these risks and work to eliminate them is crucial to the success of the project.

Evaluation of Borrower

Real estate lending invariably involves a security interest in the fee ownership or other interest in the property (e.g., a leasehold). Because it is secured lending, the creditworthiness of the borrower may not be as important a consideration as it is other lending situations. In fact, it is not uncommon for real estate loans to be non-recourse—that is to specifically provide that the lender's recourse in the event of default is limited to the pledged interest in the real estate. With such a loan, the borrower is exempt from personal liability.

While it is unlikely that nonrecourse lending will disappear, the problems in the real estate industry that surfaced in the late 1980s and early 1990s have caused many lenders to reexamine their policies on this subject. Even in instances of nonrecourse lending, lenders want to know more about the financial capacity of the borrowing parties than ever before. Furthermore, it is reasonable to anticipate some level of personal guaranty on most types of construction loans, land loans, bridge loans, and junior mortgages. As underwriting standards have strengthened, the borrower's ability to invest cash equity has also become a more important factor. In the 1980s highly leveraged, nonrecourse (or limited recourse) loans were commonplace; in the 1990s low-leverage, high cash equity and personal guaranties will be more the norm.

Along with the financial analysis of the borrower, an evaluation of his or her background and experience will be made. Does the borrower have the prerequisite experience in all aspects of development and property management? What is the borrower's standing and reputation in the community? Has the borrower been successful before in completing a project on time and on budget and in keeping the project fully rented? There is little doubt that the lending excesses of the 1980s will remain an enduring reminder that the capacity of a borrower is as important as the economics of the project.

Security

Personal guaranties are often a reality of commercial real estate lending, particularly in development stage ventures or highly leveraged transactions. In construction projects, two distinct types of guaranties may be sought. The first is a *guaranty of repayment,* which obligates the guarantor to perform the obligations of the borrower, including the payment of interest and principal. The second is a *guaranty of completion,* which obligates the guarantor to complete the project without liens for the sums available and by a predetermined date. This guaranty is similar to a performance bond but somewhat broader in scope because it includes both hard and soft costs of the project. The latter type of guaranty may be the only guaranty in a construction loan situation where the interim lender has a take-out or permanent loan commitment from another lender that is dependent only on the timely completion of the project, and will be funded at that time.

In some states, lien laws may enable suppliers and vendors to achieve a priority claim against the property ahead of a first mortgagee. Personal guaranties (to either the lender, the title insurer, or both) are more commonplace in such states.

In addition to, or instead of, guaranties, a lender may require other collateral or a letter of credit as further security. (A *letter of credit* is an agreement in writing that obligates another bank, the issuer of the letter of credit, to make available a certain sum for the account of the customer to a named beneficiary, upon the conditions for funding stipulated in the letter.) A fee is usually paid to the issuer that relates to the time that the letter of credit is in place; the issuer may require collateral from the customer, which could include specifically identified stocks, bonds, or interests in other properties. Generally, loans made as a result of drafts against letters of credit are due on demand and are guaranteed by the borrower.

Project Quality Risks

Projected rents for an unleased office building are obviously less predictable than rents projected for a substantially leased building. The rent projected to be paid by a creditworthy tenant is more secure than that of a nonrated tenant. A lease that provides for net rents, where the tenant pays the operating costs, is more predictable than a gross lease, where the landlord pays the operating costs. A project with an agreement to fix real estate taxes for a period of time (often called an agreement for payments in lieu of taxes, or PILOT) is more secure than a project without such an agreement.

These illustrations indicate that inputs into a projection have different degrees of predictability. Those with lesser certainty are riskier. The qualitative differences must themselves be evaluated (which is why some lenders, for example, will not make construction loans). Generally, the discount and capitalization rates selected in the valuation process will reflect the riskiness of the inputs, as will the loan-to-value ratio, debt service coverage, and interest rate (and perhaps initial discount) on the loan. Lenders do not knowingly make "risky" loans, but they do understand the relationship between risk (to their level of tolerance) and return.

All real estate loans involve a risk to the lender of higher than anticipated inflation (producing a repayment of the loan in cheaper currency than was initially advanced). Loans that do not self-liquidate involve risk that higher interest rates prevailing in the market at the time for refinancing may not permit refinancing to take place at a reasonable cost. Construction loans generally involve these risks along with two others: (1) the risk associated with the construction process itself and (2) the risk of marketing the space (assuming little or no preleasing) once construction is complete. The lender's underwriter is responsible for eliminating these risks wherever possible and for pricing the transaction to account for the risk.

RISK ASSESSMENT AND MANAGEMENT BY THE BORROWER

In an ideal borrowing situation, the borrower might seek to be exempted from personal liability and to avoid making any equity investment in the property. Under the right circumstances (usually involving an existing rental property for which the lender is willing to accept greater-than-usual risk in exchange for equity participation), these goals can be achieved. Competition among lenders can also make them less risk-adverse (as occurred in the 1980s) and can create limited or nonrecourse opportunities for borrowers on highly leveraged financings. Obviously, low-leverage financing may make a lender more comfortable and less concerned about recourse to the borrower.

Hedging

Risks that are extrinsic to the specific transaction (e.g., fluctuations in interest rates, changing character of a neighborhood, etc.) are also of concern to the borrower but are not easily managed. However, interest rate risk can sometimes be managed by hedging the transaction and/or locking in long-term, fixed rates. Sometimes, the ability to prepay and take advantage of future refinancing opportunities can be negotiated.

One method of hedging the transaction is through an interest rate swap, typically with a commercial bank as the counterparty. An interest rate swap is an exchange of a series of cash flows (e.g., those at a floating rate for those at a fixed rate). The swap agreement specifies that in exchange for paying the counterparty a series of fixed rate payments, it will pay out a series of floating rate payments (or vice versa). The counterparty matches its portfolio with offsetting transactions to make a profit on the spread. The interest rate swap is not an exchange of principal and does not release the borrower from liability on the underlying loan or the lender from credit risk of the loan. If a highly rated commercial bank is the counterparty, the credit risk of that counterparty defaulting on the payments is usually minimal.

Matching Loans to Liabilities

Just as lenders attempt to match their loans and liabilities to reduce risk, borrowers who wish to reduce risk must do the same. For example, an office building investor must try to match lease terms and financing terms. It would be very risky to finance a property with long-term, fixed-rate leases with floating rate debt; the low-risk choice is to match the predictability and volatility of the income stream with the financing terms.

Repayment and Limiting Liability

A borrower is expected to assume the burden of repaying a loan. The borrower's insolvency would ordinarily constitute the only circumstance in which repayment might be compromised, but, even then, the lender would look to the asset itself as a source of repayment. This is often the case in real estate financing, particularly regarding development stage transactions. The availability of limited or nonrecourse financing will shift some or all of the burden of an unsuccessful project to the lender. In such circumstances, the lender's focus shifts from the borrower's credit to the value of the asset being pledged as security and (hopefully) built-in safety mechanisms, such as an acceptable loan-to-value ratio and the ability of the lender to approve new leases.

Although borrowing establishes a debtor-creditor relationship, the borrower may not have to repay the debt except out of the proceeds of the project being financed. This ability to limit liability, when combined with so-called equity kickers (that is, additional interest based on project revenues) for the lender may create a type of security that may be subject to judicial interpretation: at what point does the loan cease to be a loan and become equity?

Options to Reduce Risk

Suppose that you, as the borrower, are convinced of the feasibility of developing a new office building and that conditions in the mortgage market are reasonable. What are the likely approaches to financing your project? If the construction lender agrees with your assessment of the market, you have a good track record, there is equity in the project, and you are willing to guaranty both completion and repayment (and you are creditworthy), a mortgage will likely be available. If you are uncomfortable with the risk of this approach, there are several options: prelease a significant block of space (which could involve equity participation by your major tenant), invest significantly more equity, negotiate a loan "floor and ceiling" (with the latter loan level being subject to leasing requirements), offer the lender a kicker (e.g., participation in the project) in exchange for limited liability, or defer the project to a time when lending standards might become more liberal.

No two projects are alike; consequently the financing must be tailored to each specific situation. The areas of variability and negotiability include: loan amount, cost (including interest and fees), rate, prepayment privileges and penalties, equity investment, lender participation, maturity, extension options, degree of personal liability, and repayment schedules.

FINANCING STRUCTURE

Obtaining the most favorable financing is often difficult. An experienced intermediary, such as a mortgage broker, can help by finding the institution most likely to approve the loan and by facilitating the negotiating process.

Loan Cost

Interest rates are often quoted in basis point spreads over indexes (1 basis point = 1/100 of 1 percent). For example, a fixed rate may be set at a spread against Treasury securities of comparable maturity. A floating rate may be spread against the prime rate or LIBOR (a rate at which banks lend dollars to one another for various terms in the London market). Other price considerations are points (1 point = 1 percent of the total loan amount) charged up front, which may be refundable or nonrefundable. Refundable points represent a good faith deposit that is returned to the borrower at closing or retained by the lender if the loan does not close through no fault of the lender. Nonrefundable points represent fee income to the lender and often include at least partial recovery of the lender's costs of originating and underwriting the loan. A par lender does not charge a nonrefundable fee. This may be the case with an insurance company that utilizes the services of a correspondent (who will usually charge a fee). Each lender has varying requirements for good faith deposits and origination fees, which may change as competitive conditions change. (There was a time in the late 1950s when some lenders were paying origination fees to mortgage brokers.)

Construction Financing

Construction loans provide all or part of the funds required to cover the costs of production, from development planning through initial leasing. These are high-risk loans for relatively short time periods. Funds are usually disbursed in stages corresponding to the level of completion of construction to assure the lender that the funds are properly employed in the project. Payment and performance bonds at the general contractor and subcontractor level may be required to help defray some of construction risk. This growing principal loan usually involves a capitalization of the required interest. The lien laws of various states will further specify the mechanics of funding, since the lender will always want to preserve its lien position (construction loans are almost always first mortgages). There are two categories of construction loans:

1. A construction loan with take-out is a construction loan made with some sort of financing in place to repay, or take out, the loan at the end of the construction period. This can be in

the form of a standby, interim, or permanent loan from the same or a different lender. If a different lender is involved, there will often be an agreement (buy-sell or triparty) in which the construction lender agrees to deliver the loan to the next lender who agrees to accept it.

2. An open-end construction loan is the type of construction financing used when no take-out is in place. It is assumed that new financing will arranged in the future to repay the construction loan.

Interim Financing

Interim financing is used as bridge financing by those borrowers who are unwilling or unable to obtain long-term permanent financing. It may be used in new projects to take out the construction lender. It may also be used when it is perceived that there are temporary unfavorable conditions, such as low loan-to-value ratios or premium interest rates on permanent financing. This financing is a temporary measure preceding a more permanent financing stage. Loan terms are usually no longer than five years.

Standby Loans

Standby loans provide credit support for construction or other interim loans and may resemble take-outs in most respects. A standby loan is distinguished from other take-outs by the intent of the parties. The standby lender commits to a loan for a fee but has little interest in actually consummating the loan; it is hoped that by the time funding is required, another lender will be available. In order to provide the borrower with an incentive not to close the standby, the loan terms are often less favorable than what other lenders will require.

While most standbys involve first mortgages, they can also be employed as second or other junior mortgages. For example, a second mortgage standby may cover a gap between a conventional lender's floor and ceiling loan amount. This standby loan may permit a construction lender to increase its funding level from the floor amount of the take-out to the ceiling amount, on the theory that the construction loan will be fully retired by the funding from both take-out sources if the conditions for the ceiling loan funding are not achieved.

Permanent Financing

Once the development and leasing stages of a project have been completed, permanent financing should be arranged. This is generally a longer-term loan that is more likely to be non-recourse, that will probably involve the payment of amortization as well as interest, and that may be at a fixed interest rate. A list of common permanent mortgages follows.

1. A self-liquidating mortgage is a fully amortizing loan that calls for level payments of principal and interest in the periodic (usually monthly) payment. The balance of principal gradually declines to zero over the life of the mortgage, which is normally 20 years or more. Prepayment is usually available near the midpoint of the loan term, albeit at some penalty.

2. A bullet mortgage is an interest-only loan that usually requires no principal repayment until maturity. Typically, no prepayment is allowed except on a cost-of-funds or yield-maintenance basis. (These loans are usually matched against GICs.) The loan term is typically 5 to 10 years.

3. A balloon mortgage is a partially amortizing loan in which the amortization period is longer than the loan term. This leaves a balance or balloon due at maturity. Loan terms of 5 to 20 years are typical.

4. A variable rate amortizing mortgage is an amorizing loan (of the self-liquidating or balloon variety) with an interest rate that is tied to a predetermined index and is reset periodically. This loan is often used with a ceiling (cap) that limits the maximum rise in the rate and sometimes with a floor (collar) that additionally sets a minimum rate, regardless of the index.

5. A fixed rate accrual mortgage is an interest-only loan in which the periodic payment is at a fixed payment rate (pay rate) and the difference between that and the contract rate (or accrual rate) is deferred for some period of time. This feature can be useful if a property's NOI is expected to increase in the near future, and the increased cash flow will then be available to pay the deferred interest. (If the contract rate is a variable rate, this loan is called a floating rate accrual mortgage.)

6. A participating mortgage is a loan in which the lender has a right to participate in future revenues (usually a percentage of

gross income above a predetermined level) including, in some cases, refinancing or sale proceeds above a certain threshold. Depending on the nature of the participation, the lender can become an equity partner. The lender's participation in revenues is sometimes referred to as a *kicker*.

7. A convertible mortgage is any mortgage loan that gives the lender the option to convert some or all of its mortgage into a full partial equity ownership at a future date.

8. A participating-convertible mortgage is a loan in which the lender receives the periodic payments, part of the revenues, and has the option to convert into equity. This vehicle has been used to effect a practical transfer of an interest in equity while endeavoring to defer the sale for tax purposes.

There is an inherent danger associated with participating and perhaps convertible mortgages—the potential loss of lien security. The theory is that with regard to third-party creditors, one cannot be both a lender in a project and hold an equity position. Legally, it is uncertain when the character of a participating mortgage changes the lender's role from a provider of debt to a provider of equity. This has added significance if the lender has regulatory constraints on its ability to own equity. Nonetheless, as the needs of the marketplace dictate, participating mortgages will continue to be used.

Loan Covenants

Loan covenants are used by the lender to control certain rights or privileges otherwise exercised by the borrower. However, if the lender reserves too many borrower rights for itself, it may lose its legal identity as a lender.

The lender may require the establishment of one or more specialized accounts for designated purposes. One of the most common is the real estate tax account, into which monthly deposits are usually made so that when taxes are due, sufficient funds are on hand. Another is a reserve for replacements account, which may permit accumulated funds to be used for tenant or building improvements.

A restriction on the ability to have additional debt (even though subordinated) is often encountered but is by no means universal. Lenders who favor this restriction wish to limit the demands on the properties' cash flow and also to avoid complexity if their loan is to be reworked. (In the latter case, a junior lender would have to consent to a modification in the senior debt.) Lenders who are less concerned believe that a responsible borrower and junior lender would not permit excessive strain on the cash flow and that the participation of a substantial junior lender indirectly adds credit support to the transaction.

The lender may also invoke covenants that influence the borrower's ability to execute new and renewal leases. The rent structure of a property is critical in determining NOI and value; therefore, a series of ill-conceived leases (even though they are usually subordinated to the mortgage) could affect the value of the mortgage as well as the property. As a result, office building mortgages frequently provide for lender approval of new, modified, or renewal leases. There may be certain standards set forth and approval required if there are adverse deviations from the standard.

Another restrictive provision is the due-on-sale clause, which states that a sale of the property causes immediate acceleration of the due date of the loan. A similar clause permits a sale subject to the lender's approval of the purchaser. Some have questioned whether such provisions are intended to give the lender comfort in knowing who the borrower is or are intended to give the lender another look at the loan and how it relates to current interest rates. Some courts have ruled that lenders must act "reasonably" in approving a new owner and may not use this provision to generate early prepayment when it may suit them.

There are many other restrictive covenants, such as the use of casualty insurance awards (to reduce the loan or rebuild the property), changing the use of the property, accepting prepaid rent from tenants, and so forth. A real estate mortgage involves more than the negotiation of the amount, interest rate, and term. The negotiation of such restrictive covenants must also be undertaken.

Leases

Leases for office buildings are usually gross leases with escalation clauses. The landlord is typically responsible for paying all operating costs in the initial year of the lease, with any subsequent increases in such costs passed through to the tenant as additional rent. There may also be other additional rent provisions such as increases related to the Consumer Price Index (CPI), porter wage adjustments, or payments that effectively amortize certain leasehold improvement costs. From a loan underwriting point of view, the pass through of increased operating costs (including real estate taxes) often makes the loan more secure.

Leases are liens in real estate. It is necessary to establish lien priority by agreement to avoid establishing liens by date. All leases should have a standard subordination clause, making the lease junior to any and all mortgages placed on the property. Most tenants will understand the need for this and accept such a provision even though technically they could be removed from the building in a foreclosure action brought by a lender (since they have a junior claim to that of the lender). In practice, lenders want to retain tenants and will usually forego this right. However, in a situation with a long-term, below-market lease, the lender might determine that termination of the lease was in its best interest.

To accommodate the concerns of some tenants on this subject (usually the larger lessees), the lender might consent to a nondisturbance provision, which states that as long as the tenant performs its obligation under the lease it will not be disturbed even under foreclosure. The circumstances for granting nondisturbance should be agreed upon when the loan is being negotiated.

Lending Syndicates

The increased size and risks of projects and regulatory requirements regarding loans to one borrower has led many lenders to organize lending syndicates in which several lenders participate in a particular loan. This enables diversification and gives lenders with limited origination capacity an opportunity they might not otherwise have. From the borrower's perspective, loan syndication should be avoided for two reasons. First, the loan must be "sold" several times instead of once. This lengthens the period of negotiation and raises the likelihood of having to make further modifications after the deal has been "fully negotiated" with the lead lender. (This would not be the case if the lead lender made an unconditional commitment and accepted the burden of being able to "lay off" participation "as is.") Second, the loan may later have to be renegotiated because of unanticipated adverse circumstances. Recasting a syndicated loan can be very complex because multiple principals will have different ideas on how to solve the problem.

LAYERED FINANCING

The basic legal interest in real estate is the fee. The process of leasing and financing real estate involves partitioning the fee into different interests, generally known as liens against the fee estate. The documents that establish these lien interests also establish the relative security claims of the parties. For example, a first mortgage or a typical lease creates a security interest in the property that is senior to the interest of the fee owner. Modern financing transactions utilize various fee-splitting techniques to create separate claims against the fee interest, which can be separately pledged and financed.

Leasehold interests can be created for a portion of a property (e.g., a typical office lease) or for the entire property. In the latter case, the leasehold interest may merely indicate that a single tenant will use and occupy all the property, or it may create a financing vehicle in which the tenant has no interest in physically occupying the space. Given an adequate term and cash flow, the created leasehold and the remaining fee interest could be financed separately. By agreement, the fee owner and the lessee would have established relative priority positions; therefore, the leasehold mortgage might be subordinated to the fee position or might be senior to it.

It is also possible to segregate the land and building and create a leasehold estate for the building alone. Under this situation, the lessee would pay the owner of the land a rent that reflected the value of that land. The interest of either party could be financed.

Exhibit 7–1 shows a project with multiple interests. As the rent paid by the tenants in the building flows down, each participant siphons off its share. If the participants with the higher lien priorities (at the bottom of the diagram) do not get the money they are entitled to, those participants above them will be forced out (foreclosure). Such complex structures are often devised to accommodate varying business and/or tax strategies of the parties, historic circumstances, or a desire to achieve greater financing leverage than otherwise possible.

Wraparound Mortgage

Suppose you own a property that has an existing mortgage of $1 million at 9 percent interest, with 10 years remaining until maturity. Suppose further that the property has a value of $2 million and a new lender is willing to make a first mortgage loan of $1.6 million (80

EXHIBIT 7–1
Multiple Interest Positions in a Project

1 Building Tenants	Makes payments to "owner" (#2). Leases usually subordinated to all interests other than "owner."
2 Operating Leasehold	Operates property and pays rent to its landlord (#3). Position could be financed (not shown).
3 Passive Leasehold	Holds long-term lease. Receives sufficient payments (rent) from its tenant (#2) to meet obligations to those below.
4 Mortgage on Passive Leasehold	Holds security interest in leasehold. Receives payments from mortgagor (#3). Security interest is ahead of those above but junior to those below.
5 Fee Owner	Owns land (or land and building) that it has leased in exchange for agreed rent payments. Has not subordinated to leasehold mortgage.
6 Fee Mortgage	Has highest priority claim. Relies on receiving a portion of fee owner's (#5) rent receipts to pay interest and amortization.

percent of value) at 10.5 percent interest. The conventional approach would be to retire the existing $1 million out of the proceeds of the new financing. However, the interest on $1.6 million at 10.5 percent is $168,000, while the present loan costs $90,000 (9 percent of $1 million). Hence, the "new" money ($600,000) has an effective cost of $78,000 ($168,000 less $90,000), or 13 percent.

A wraparound mortgage would be a better choice in this case. The new lender would advance the $600,000 to you and would assume the payment obligation of the existing debt. Instead of paying off the original mortgage now, it will be paid over time by the new lender at the 9 percent interest rate. In effect, the new lender is borrowing that money for the transaction from the old lender instead of using internally generated funds such as deposits. The level of risk to the new lender is unchanged.

If the wraparound loan in this case was written at 10 percent interest, the borrower would save $8,000 a year, reducing the cost of the new $600,000 from 13 percent to 11.7 percent. The yield to the new lender would be the same, 11.7 percent:

Received from borrower ($1.6 million at 10%)	$160,000
Paid out to original mortgagee ($1 million at 9%)	$ 90,000
Retained	$ 70,000
Return on $600,000 invested	11.67%

In practice, wraparounds are more complex, particularly when different amortization assumptions are introduced. Since they are a form of secondary financing, the consent of the first mortgagee may be needed. In the example provided, the present mortgagee might well object if its consent was required. Why should it get stuck with a 9 percent loan for another 10 years when current rates are obviously higher?

SUMMARY

To be effective, borrowers and their agents must understand the lenders. They must be sensitive to lender's policy and regulatory constraints, conversant with valuation and risk assessment approaches taken, and aware of the interrelationship of the lending process with the capital markets and the overall process of developing and managing real estate. They also must realize that the process is always in flux as a result of competitive forces, economic conditions, and other externalities. Regardless of the complexity, deals will be made as long as there are users for real estate who are willing to pay for that use.

CHAPTER 8

SELECTING THE CONTRACTOR AND NEGOTIATING A FAVORABLE CONTRACT

Robert F. Cushman
Pepper, Hamilton & Sheetz

Alfred P. McNulty
Applied Project Management Group

EARLY DESIGN CONCERNS

Formal Estimates

As the design stage nears completion, owners should obtain an updated estimate of the construction costs. This estimate can be in the form of a single general contract bid, or, if the drawings are not complete enough to develop a bid, it can be in the form of a construction manager's estimate, which is usually based on compiling the proposals of the specialty trades.

A general contractor begins this estimating function by identifying each cost item. For most of the work, a general contractor engages specialty trade subcontractors and depends on their bids for 85 to 100 percent of the direct work items in making cost tabulation. The general contractor first prepares a detailed estimate of the work that will be performed by his or her own forces. Historically, this has been the concrete, masonry, and carpentry work; however, this work is increasingly being performed by the speciality trades as well. A general contractor may perform part of the work in order to cut expenses or to allow for better control of the pace of the project.

A construction manager also depends on the specialty trades for the direct work item costs and seldom performs any work with his or her own forces.

The total estimate must also include the costs of on-site and off-site management, insurance, permits, and temporary facilities (often constructed by a general contractor's forces as they are difficult to identify, but might include temporary barriers and clearing and rubbish removal). Additionally, when a guaranty is required, the estimate will include an intangible item—the cost of the risk. The amount will be based on the contractor's sense of security with the guaranty. Often the competitiveness of a situation dictates how much risk the contractor will take and how much risk he or she will leave the owner.

Subcontracting

The construction manager or general contractor must assemble a team of specialty contractors that will work well together and must determine each subcontractor's ability to perform a quality job expeditiously. The work of each subcontractor affects the work of the others; the real price of a project is influenced by the quality and timeliness of each subcontractor's work.

Quality work cannot be accomplished without fairness in negotiation. Many contract negotiations are concerned with identifying who has assumed what risks. In the traditional bidding system, the architect's documents are the major determinant of the scope of the work. Each subcontractor must bid competitively based on complete documents. If the trade subcontractor feels the desired detail or quality expectations are not precisely set forth in these documents, he or she will often demand more money to provide for the risk involved. The general contractor will work in much the same way. Managers and designers must discuss and resolve any uncertainties in the drawings or concerns over field procedures before contracting. They must also clarify their interpretations.

Off-Site Management

Off-site management duties include the coordination of shop drawings. During the construction process, shop drawings are required to be prepared by the subcontractors to define certain work (e.g., the prefabrication of structural steel, cabinet work, light fixtures, and piping assemblages). These drawings are a refinement of the architect's design, and, after they have been prepared by a specialty contractor; they are reviewed by the architect. Expeditious delivery and approval of shop drawings are very important. When material is fabricated and delivered it must fit into the space provided and connect to adjacent work neatly.

Off-site management also includes the distribution of information to individuals performing the field work. Shop drawings should be distributed to all subcontractors for their review. The subcontractors should be encouraged to ask for clarification of details rather than to follow their standard practice.

Adjustments in the design must also be conveyed to the subcontractors by off-site management. As the architect or engineers continue their analysis of the design, even after the completion of their documents, new concerns may be found that can lead to adjustments. Or the owner may learn of new developments or opportunities that will be beneficial. These revisions must be distributed quickly to the subcontractors and must be incorporated into the planning of the work; contracts must also be adjusted fairly.

Scheduling of the field work generally determines the off-site activities. Off-site management must anticipate the time necessary for shop drawing review and the time necessary for fabrication, and must provide for the delivery of the fabricated material for field installation in sequence. Flexible and imaginative solutions often are necessary to circumvent unanticipated obstacles. Occasionally adjustments in the details of a design are necessary in order to find a substitute material when the desired material cannot be available on time.

On-Site Management

The contractor's most significant role is providing on-site management. The on-site manager is responsible for coordinating the work environment (providing for scaffolding, proper all-weather access, storage space, planned aisles, etc.). The on-site manager must also provide support for all construction activities, such as temporary water, power, and light; protection from the weather for the individuals doing the work; and protection for the work that has been installed. Moreover, the workers need dressing rooms, lunch areas, drinking water, toilets, and telephones, which the contractor or construction manager must provide.

The on-site manager also must interpret the design documents for the journeymen. For this reason, the contractor's superintendent must have knowledge of the whole project (each specialty trade foreman generally sees only his or her portion of the work). Much of the superintendent's time is spent explaining the design documents to individual journeymen and in refining the design for the details that are required.

The contractor's superintendent often determines the basic layout of the site, providing column lines and elevations from which the specialty trades can work. But each day minor adjustments must be made in the dimensions to accommodate for the tolerances needed for connecting devices, elbows, traps, radius restrictions, access requirements, and the like, which were not shown on the design documents and frequently were not on the shop drawings. These job site realities can often result in conflicts between subcontractors. The superintendent must be vigilant in adjusting these dimensions in order to prevent such conflicts.

When material is late or when a pending design change causes an interuption in the work, the superintendent must be creative. Unforeseen field conditions (e.g., a storm that damages equipment or material, a flood, accidents, etc.) must also be overcome. It is important that the on-site manager is flexible enough to work under such circumstances.

Quality Control

All workers have a responsibility to perform quality work. Each individual journeyman must perform his or her work properly, and the contractor for whom he or she works must provide supervision to ensure that he or she does so. Superintendents must watch for faulty work and see that it is corrected immediately, before it is repeated or enclosed by work that follows.

Specific responsibility for quality control is most often delegated to the architect, the consulting engineers, and to special testing or inspection agencies. The thoroughness of the inspection depends on the priorities of the owner and on the requirements of the regulating bodies. Inspection costs will affect the bids; some architects and owners have reputations for demanding unusually high quality levels that add to the cost of the specialty trades. For example, a specialty trade contractor would run the risk of removing and redoing a portion of work if unusual tolerances for concrete or masonry uniformity are required. This risk would be reflected in the bid. However, this extra cost may be consistent with the owner's priorities.

Time Control

Before the work begins, the contractor or construction manager will prepare a schedule of the major construction activities. Depending on the sophistication of the contractor and/or the complexity of the project, this may be a bar chart or a detailed network schedule; in any case, it will deal only with the significant tasks. The contractor will assume that related secondary tasks will be performed within the time sequence of the primary tasks identified. Each task depends on those before and restrains those following.

The field managers must establish a pace for the work and a crew size that can remain constant. Frequently, work begins with a small crew, builds to an optimum crew (which is constant), and then is reduced to a small crew for the final tasks and adjustments to the work. If one specialty trade contractor falls behind schedule, the following subcontractors must reduce their crews to meet that pace, and the entire project will be delayed. Similarly, if a strategic material is late or is delivered in a form that is unusable, the dependent activities will stop, the crews will be reduced quickly, and the rhythm of the project will be disrupted. The major goal of both off-site management and on-site supervision is to maintain the schedule. Once it is disrupted it is very hard to reestablish; the manager should be prepared to spend money to overcome delays.

Money Administration

The proper administration of money involves monitoring and supervising an orderly cash flow from the owner to the individual journeyman to the material suppliers. The architect and construction manager or general contractor determine the value of the portion of the work installed during each month by each specialty trade (usually on a prearranged schedule of the value of each portion of the specialty contractor's work); a certain amount is withheld to ensure completion of the remainder of the work; and payment is made on a monthly basis. Since the journeymen must be paid weekly, the specialty trade contractors need this money to support their operations. Most material supplies require prompt payment as well.

A vital element in cash advances is a statement by the architect that the work has been performed to the quality level required by the contract. If the quality level is not met and corrections are required, funds must be withheld to ensure compliance. The owner and bank rely on these value and quality reports when making payment.

Adaptability

Unexpected field conditions, unanticipated regulatory requirements, owner adjustments resulting from new developments or concerns, or design adjustments made by the architect or engineers result in changes to the project's schedule and cost. For example, changes may require prefabrication of some item and may delay or change work that is nearly completed.

The failure to administer these changes effectively and quickly can have a serious negative impact on the success of a project. Such adjustments and changes must be made with minimum disruption of the initial schedule. This requires that designers and contractors work quickly to determine design and cost adjustments. The construction manager or general contractor must establish an effective system to process approved changes quickly into change orders with appropriate cost and time adjustments.

THE RISKS

Since profit is often tied to risk, the fee charged for construction services will run from a minimum amount, (based on the cost of management) to a substantially higher amount (the cost of the management plus the cost of the risks, when assumed by the contractor). The cost of management includes direct wages, supporting facilities, and the dollars needed to entice the contractor to assign his managers to this project as opposed to another (the opportunity cost). The cost of management also includes the use of money utilized by the manager to service the project. The cost of the risk will be discounted if the contractor feels he can pass some of the risks back to the owner.

Construction risk to the owner falls into one of four categories: (1) the bid that is higher than available funds, (2) the difficulty of optimizing contractor performance and time within the contract, (3) change order exposure, and (4) difficulty in coordinating existing owner operations with new construction.

A High Bid

The greatest risk to the owner and to the designer is an unexpected high bid, one that is higher than available funds. Traditionally, the architect's estimate at the conceptual stage, which sets the budget for the project, is based on a per-square-foot basis. A good estimate will allocate different prices for each type of use. These allocations are based on past experience adjusted for the particulars of the planned project.

Unfortunately, many factors can negatively influence the estimate between the time of this conceptual budget and the receipt of the actual bid based on completed documents. For example, the time span can change significantly, or the program can develop special features that are foreign to historical experience. Frequently, the final area dimensions are 5 or 10 percent greater than those used in the initial budget estimate. Furthermore, construction costs change due to the cycles of competitive activity in the local area. Even with careful cost review at the design and drawing stages, the bids may be surprising. This may require some redesigning or additional funds to increase the budget.

The construction management system reduces the likelihood of a high bid because the costs are professionally monitored as the design develops. Moreover, the construction manager provides input during the design stage to improve the value effectiveness while the documents are being prepared. The construction manager also markets to the bidders more effectively.

Contractor and Subcontractor Performance

The preparation of a general contractor's bid requires three to four weeks. During that time the general contractor prepares a detailed estimate of the work that it will perform with its own forces and of the temporary facilities and management that are its responsibility to supply. The general contractor will also invite specialty trade contractors to provide bids for the direct work. Approximately 90 to 100 percent of this direct work will be purchased by the general contractor either from material suppliers or specialty trade subcontractors. In a competitive bid situation, the general contractor wil be seeking the lowest bids from suppliers and subcontractors. Those providing the lowest bids may be subcontractors who the general contractor prefers not to employ. Nevertheless, this subcontractor's low bid must be used by the general contractor without review in order for him to be competitive. Assembling a team by low bid only can be risky for the owner because it may not provide the best project team.

Competitive bidding can also be risky for the general contractor. Often it is difficult for designers to be specific in the contract documents. Sometimes misinterpretations of the documents can lead to increased problems and costs. Also, after a general contract has been awarded and the subcontracts are entered into, the subcontractor who helped win the bid may find that the initial figures were too low. Knowing this, the general contractor often includes the cost of anticipated risk in his bid. The general contractor may have to assume the costs of these misunderstandings.

The competitive bid process, with no negotiation or selection criteria other than the price, places the contractor in an adversarial position with the owner and the designers. The contractor's interest is often best served by providing the minimum amount of work value required by the contract documents at a minimum cost. On the other hand, the intent of the designer and the owner is to achieve the maximum quality that can be interpreted from the documents without regard to the contractor's costs. In the competitive bid environment, there are pressures on the general contractor to provide management at the lowest cost possible. For smaller projects this may mean a carpenter foreman is assigned as the superintendent. Most likely, this superintendent will focus more on the carpentry work than on the general management of the project. Thus the general contractor acts as little more than another trade subcontractor. General management of the project is compromised.

The trade contractors influence the cost of a project as well. They want to select the optimum crew size to perform the work—starting with a small crew, building to a maximum, and maintaining that maximum until the crew can be reduced in an orderly fashion. This may be contrary to the schedule of the general contractor.

Trade union rules also may influence performance and cost. For example, under union regulations if four workers are assigned to a project the foreman also may work with his tools. However, with the addition of one or two more workers, the foreman may be required to manage full time and perform no work whatsoever.

Material delivery also affects contract performance and cost. Contractors may wish to deliver all their materials at one time and may require storage space at the site and early progress payment, or they may choose to deliver intermittently, which can add to their cost and risk of delivery. Either way, there are costs to the project.

Change Orders

Contract adjustments and change orders will modify a small facility contract by 3 to 5 percent. Contracts for larger and more complex projects will generally be modified by higher percentages. These change orders must be fed into the system smoothly if work is in progress, but very often they are not. To protect themselves, trade contractors may reduce crews or may withdraw from the work area until a contract adjustment request has been analyzed and a change order issued.

Negotiation of these changes can be complicated when they are filtered through the "neutral" general contractor to the owner and design professionals, who may have limited knowledge of the actual costs and field problems. Because of time delays and work slowdowns, the cost and risk of these changes may be far greater to the owner than the dollar increase paid to the trade contractor. With a professional construction manager, the owner has an ally in negotiations.

Coordinating Existing Owner Operations and New Construction

Since much construction consists of additions or renovations to existing buildings, the contract often provides for the isolation of the construction activity from the operating areas of the existing structures. In practice, however, operations and construction often fall all over each other. If, in a competitive bid agreement, the obligation of the contractor not to interfere with the operation of the facility is developed and if stringent rules in this regard are defined, the contractor must address this risk by adding a high coordination cost in the bid. However, a sense of cooperation between the administrator and the contractor's superintendent or project manager is more effective than a stringent contract.

THE TRADE-OFFS

The choice of the construction process will depend on the owner's evaluation of the trade-offs between the risks assumed by the contractor or construction manager and the risks that the owner is willing to bear. These trade-offs are difficult to quantify.

A Guaranteed Price versus the Time Required to Establish It

An early start of a project may guarantee a lower financing rate. However, there are risks associated with this fast-track approach. Whether the risk involved is worth the financing benefits must be determined.

The traditional design process permits the establishment of column lines and the floor loading requirements fairly early so that the structural designer may proceed with working drawings. Similarly, working drawings for the envelope of the building (the windows, facade, and roof) can also proceed while the design of the specialized spaces such as interior areas are still in design development. Consequently, there is opportunity for construction to start on the structure and envelope before the interior design is final and available. This work can be performed during the first six to eight months of construction on a normal project, and interior trade contracts can be added when their design is complete and prior work is ready for trade field sequence. There are risks in adopting this procedure because a major change in the interior program can require a change in the facade or the structure.

While the basic concepts of the mechanical and electrical design (which may be 40 percent of the total project cost) can be developed and put in place early, the later portions of the mechanical and electrical design (e.g., the communications systems, ventilation control, coordination of ductwork, and placement of conduit to the architectural features) cannot. However, there is a danger in proceeding with the structure and envelope without knowing the mechanical and electrical contract costs. These are the trades that most frequently give rise to the major cost surprises. If construction of the structure is underway, the options for adjusting the total project cost are significantly reduced by a high mechanical or electrical bid.

The trade-off of fast-tracking is the additional risk resulting from reduced flexibility in dealing with higher prices downstream. The least risk is undertaken when the planning for the structural and envelope work construction has proceeded substantially, perhaps almost to completion, but is still subject to cancellation when the mechanical and electrical prices are received if they are out of line.

A Guaranteed Price versus a Reduced Level of Management

The competitive bid process forces the general contractor to cut costs, which means only minimum management will be provided. However, it is in the owner's interest to have the best management available to control costs, time, and quality. The solution may be to hire a separate construction management organization that has developed the best techniques for effective management and allows the best talent within their organization to focus on the major problems (routine matters can be handled by lesser professionals within the organization). The construction manager's sophisticated systems can provide techniques for estimating costs during the early stages and can be a most welcome aid to the designers. They can provide a logical time schedule and a monitoring system for early warnings if trouble is anticipated. They also can effectively distribute information to involved participants, particularly to the decision makers of the organizations involved.

The trade-off is that such skilled management has a high cost the owner. Hopefully, the marketing techniques employed by the professional construction manager for obtaining specialty trade bids will more than offset this cost.

Value Engineering

Value engineering is a special technique that isolates secondary or even tertiary option portions of the design by cost to determine if the value exceeds the cost. The results can lead to an alternate design or approach that can produce nearly the same results at reduced costs. Today, value engineering is employed by most design professionals and consultants. However, sophisticated construction managers (and specialty trade contractors who have the best understanding of costs within their specialties) can present the most meaningful options and accurate cost estimates available to an owner so that the value trade-off decision can be made.

Assignment of Risk to Reduce Costs

There is a trade-off between assigning risks to others (and the cost to the owner of that assignment) and assuming the risk yourself. Risk can frequently be best assigned to the person who can best handle it.

For instance, if the owner can best control the schedule in terms of the regulatory approval process, he or she should assume that risk. Likewise, the owner may assume the risk for subsoil conditions or can assign this risk to the excavation and foundation contractor at a price.

Magnitude of the Owner's Role

The construction management approach requires more active participation by the owner than the general contractor bid approach. It provides tools so the owner can effectively participate. It allows the owner periodic insights and time to monitor the budget, construction timing, and value input. Also, the construction manager is aware of the owner's secondary and tertiary desires. As the project advances there may be opportunities to fulfill these desires at little extra cost. One technique is to develop a formal list of items that have been cut for initial budget reasons but which are still desired. There may be opportunities to purchase these items at a minimal cost or as a trade-off for another feature.

Using a general contractor, the owner delegates participation and in the process reduces his or her control.

THE CONSTRUCTION APPROACH OPTIONS

The following construction approaches are available: (1) a single bid by a general contractor, (2) four or five prime bids by which the mechanical, electrical, plumbing, and sitework may be separated from the general trades, (3) the construction management approach, with the manager acting either as a prime contractor or as an agent through whom an owner awards 20 or 30 direct contracts, (4) a negotiated, maximum fixed-price contract with a general contractor, and (5) a design/build arrangement with a guaranteed price.

General Principles

When chosing a construction approach, owners must be aware of their priorities. Quality is important, of course, but there is a level of quality that should be acceptable within the budget allocations; improvements in that quality can add substantially to construction costs. Time is also important, but the time elements of the total project may involve some precalculated risk.

Fast-tracking (beginning the structural work before hiring all the subcontractors) is available with all five options. Under the single bid, an early purchase can be made of the structural elements and key mechanical equipment; the foundations may even be started. These purchase orders can be assigned to the low bidder. Under the multiple prime approach, the same advance purchases can be made and then assigned to the appropriate prime, or they may be kept in place as additional primes. Under the construction manager approach, the construction manager can award the contracts sequentially rather than at one time. After a substantial number of contracts are finalized, the construction manager can be in a position to give a guaranty of cost.

The owner must determine how involved in the construction process he or she wants to be. The single bid requires the least participation; the others require more but, in turn, give the owner more control.

The owner also must evaluate whether his or her staff is able to assume the responsibilities that each of these options requires. If not, the owner should reinforce the staff as needed.

The Single Bid

In the single bid approach, the design documents are completed and offered to a select group of general contractors. Or, if legally required, the bid requirements are advertised in newspapers or magazines so that contractors capable of posting appropriate bonds can bid the project. The single bid method makes the contractor responsible for managing the field activities and completing the work in accordance with the plans and specifications. The administration follows a formal routine as is set forth in the contract package. The single bid approach not only provides a guaranteed price before work starts, but it is the most politically acceptable method of having the work performed. The construction agreement usually provides penalties if the work is not completed by a given date, although this is seldom enforced.

Prime Bids

This approach is used when the owner desires to separate the mechanical, electrical, plumbing, and sitework from the general contract.

This separate prime method, in which the major trades bid publicly, is required by statute in some states. The general management of the project is usually assigned to the general contractor, although the legality of assigning the owner's management responsibility has been challenged. The owner has a direct contract relationship with the major subcontractors, and, generally, the engineers and architects (as the owner's representatives) can deal with the subcontractors effectively on a direct basis.

This method also ensures that *each* low bid is available to the owner. In the single bid approach, the lowest electrical and lowest mechanical bid may not have been given to the low general contractor. Moreover, the low general contractor may not have chosen the lowest prime bidder for the team.

The disadvantage of the multiple prime approach is that the coordination of five independent organizations whose success is dependent on each other is often casually performed and indeed is sometimes unenforceable. Variations on this option give the general contractor additional power—for example, the right to withhold payments to the contractors if they are not performing in accordance with the project schedule. In another variation, the owner provides a project coordinator in the field whose tasks resemble those of the construction manager.

A Construction Manager

A construction manager will provide advice and guidance during the design development stage, and when the documents are ready, he or she will call for and evaluate competitive bids of the specialty trade contractors and present the evaluated bids to the owner for selection. These trade contracts can then be entered into directly with the construction manager, who acts as a general contractor, or the construction manager can act as the owner's agent, with the contracts being written directly between the trade contractor and the owner. The construction manager, working from incomplete plans, must judge what is intended. For this reason, the construction manager is often better organized to provide the specialized management services desired. The bidding general contractor is accustomed to measuring and counting that which is on the documents as a "given," with little interpretation. Other tasks undertaken by the construction manager include accounting for monthly payments, filling in design detail for pricing purposes, and advising designers of options.

Moreover, the construction manager is positioned (because a fee is received for this service) to serve the owner and is the owner's advocate in relationships with the trade contractors. The construction manager has no obligation to them because his or her future growth will come from future work from the owner and not through the help of the trade subcontractors in competitive bidding situations.

A Negotiated General Contract

In a negotiated general contract situation, the general contractor receives his or her agreement after negotiation with the owner, rather than by competitive bidding. The price may be fixed or it may be established at cost (with a contingency), plus a fee with a guaranteed maximum. The advantages of this are similar to those of the single bid approach.

The Design/Build Method with a Guaranteed Price

This method is practical for preengineered buildings or standard industrial enclosures but is not really suitable for a more complex project. For example, in a complex medical building there must be interplay between the operating staff and the designers. A guaranteed price could be a serious restraint to developing an effective design. On the other hand, the administrator may feel more comfortable when he or she is assured that the key requirements will be met with the available funds before he or she is committed to a sizable design fee. The administrator may need a specialist to assure the staff that requirements will be fully satisfied by the design before approving it.

THE SELECTION PROCESS

Legal regulations often dictate which construction options are available. For example, a financing agreement may require that a single guaranteed price be available before the work commences (or before the first monies are committed). This can eliminate or substantially restrain the fast-track option. There also may be a regulation requiring competitive bids or multiple primes. Even if applicable law requires advertised competitive bids available to all who can produce a bond, a method can be developed that will not leave everything to chance. For instance, a construction manager can be retained as a coordinator of the separate prime contracts, or the owner can expand the process by requiring as many as 15 prime bid packages.

The first step, after determining which of the construction options are legal, desirable, and economically feasible is to identify the best candidates either for competitive bidding or to serve as a construction manager. The architect, engineer, and members of the owner's board of directors can help the owner determine the candidates. The owner or his or her project manager or construction consultant then should speak to these candidates. This dialogue should give the owner greater insight into the values of each option and an opinion as to how well the individuals will act under each contractual arrangement. The objective of the selection process is to identify the best candidate and then to guide that candidate into a position where he or she is most likely to be the successful candidate. If competitive bidding is required, then it is important that the three or four best contractors in an area be encouraged to bid. These contractors cannot legally be given any special favored position, but they can be encouraged to take advantage of the opportunities to question the architect and to understand the building requirements completely. If a negotiated arrangement with a construction manager or general contractor is possible, then the objective must be to develop a process to discover which of the candidates is the best qualified.

The administrator and his or her board must assemble a team of capable, compatible, and creative specialists who must render assistance during design and procurement stages as well as off-site management and on-site supervision. Because each technical skill is indeed related to an individual, care should be taken that the appropriate individual is available. The team must include specialists in areas such as structure, foundation, mechanical and electrical work, and estimating and scheduling. Routing systems and procedures and past results must be evaluated by managers with ingenuity.

Before interviewing the candidates, the evaluating team should prepare a thought-provoking checklist of issues and problems to enhance the dialogue. A specific value should be placed on each player on the team so that when the competing candidates are evaluated (say, on a 1 to 10 basis) and a weighing factor (which might be 1, 2, or 3) is multiplied, the total will help distinguish the candidates.

Each individual whom a company intends to assign to the project should be evaluated. In large companies, the variation of performance ability and historical achievement of particular employees can be significant. Since the project manager or field superintendent will be responsible for much of the decision making, these people should definitely be interviewed as part of the candidate evaluation process. It should be required in the construction and design agreements that the organization assign these specific individuals to the project if they are found to be acceptable. The interview process will be enhanced by detailing for these individuals what the project should entail, what services the owner seeks, and the exact role they are expected to play.

The interview panel should include as many decision makers as possible. The project manager or construction consultant and the building committee of the board of directors should be included. If there is a critical financial source, consideration should be given to including that organization or individual as part of the selection process, perhaps by placing a representative on the interviewing panel.

Immediately after each interview, the panel should evaluate the candidate. The members of the panel should share judgments with each other. Often the panel members have different backgrounds and skills (indeed, they should be chosen with this aim in view). Because they will observe different characteristics in the candidates, open dialogue will provide combined insights far greater than any one member could develop.

Presumably, all candidates chosen to be interviewed were selected because they possessed the skills necessary to perform the required tasks. The candidate who is ultimately selected should be the one who is perceived as the most able to observe the priorities of the required facility. In addition, that candidate should be perceived as the most compatible with the selection committee—the one who makes the committee feel the most comfortable in delegating to him or her the responsibility of carrying out their objectives.

THE APPROPRIATE COMPENSATION

The selection committee must develop a specific agreement on the services to be performed and agree upon appropriate compensation for these services. Presumably, the invitation to the interview has included a list of the services required, and the candidates have included in their presentation a statement of the compensation they would seek. Usually, the selection committee delegates one of their members to negotiate appropriate refinements to the arrangement. The committee will have learned from their collective interviews what services should be removed from or added to the agreement.

The appropriate fee results from the balancing of the desire for the best services from the contractor or construction manager and the cost of these services. The base costs include salaries, related indirect expenses, and the cost of the support features to the individuals who will be assigned to the project. Usually, the salaries and related expenses of individuals who are clearly assigned to a project will be included as a cost of the project and not as part of the fee. For example, the superintendent, the engineer, or craftsmen performing direct work and assigned to the field office, as well as the management of that field office, are part of the cost of the work. It is more difficult to slot the project manager and the cost of off-site people in the home office who may be assigned to the project on a frequent but part-time basis. Such cost often is determined on a time-card basis with an agreed hourly rate that incorporates the direct salary and fringe benefits plus an allowance for support costs (e.g., lighting, rent, office equipment, telephone, etc.). Secretarial and clerical workers are hard to identify as they are generally assigned on a part-time basis and do not normally keep time cards. The most satisfactory resolution here is to estimate the cost of these off-site services and establish them as an element within the fee.

One intangible element in determining the fee is opportunity cost—that is, the cost of assigning an organization's time and energy to a project. Factors of opportunity cost include the cost of building and maintaining an organization between projects, the sales cost (preparing for the interview), and the cost of general management.

Another factor that influences the fee is the sum of money that the provider of construction services must advance. This amount can be substantial if the general contractor or construction manager is required to pay for labor and/or materials and then wait four to six weeks for payment. It can be minimized by an arrangement in which the owner pays the trade contractors directly.

Yet another element in the fee is risk. This risk, factors of which have been addressed throughout this chapter, can be minimized by a well-financed project. However, there is always risk: risk related to nonpayment; risk related to liability for error that may occur; potential risk in the time and cost required to manage the correction of faulty work; risk in performing changes that may arise and may not be compensated for; and risk in the noncompensated delays resulting from changes and adjustment. If the project takes longer than anticipated, nonreimbursable costs expand. There is also the ever-present organizational risk that work will not be continuous or that the project will be delayed or canceled, which generally means the contractor must absorb the cost of employees between assignments or while an assignment is being reorganized. These risks are compensated with the contractor's money that otherwise would be the contractor's profit.

Consequently, compensation negotiation must include identification of the items that are to be reimbursed at cost and those less tangible items that will be identified, quantified, and gathered into an amount called a fee. This fee can be paid by agreement on a monthly basis or it can be based on the time frame in which the costs will be incurred. For example, the procurement and planning process requires a large amount of off-site management time that should be paid for at an early stage. Similarly, insurance and other organizational costs may be incurred at the beginning. The trade-off is the desire of the owner to ensure the enthusiastic service by the contractor to the very end of the project and a desire to have a slower payment schedule that lasts beyond field construction. Very often a fee is divided into a percentage of construction costs and paid on a monthly basis proportionate to progress.

In these negotiating and contracting stages, the owner should obtain assistance from an experienced project manager or construction consultant and, certainly, from an experienced construction lawyer and accountant. A good contract, a fair contract, but a contract tailored to the owner's needs and risk assumptions can save thousands of dollars. Good professional advice at this stage of a project's development is a necessity.

THE FORM OF THE AGREEMENT

The Cost Plus Agreement

The cost plus contract form is recommended in the following instances: if changes are expected during construction; if it is impractical to prepare complete drawings and specifications prior to construction; or if the owner desires construction to commence prior to the completion of the construction documents or in the case of emergency work. Under this agreement, the contractor, usually awarded the contract as a result of negotiations, is reimbursed the cost of performing the work and paid a fee. The American Institute of Architects (AIA) Document A111 (1978 edition) is the standard form of agreement between the owner and contractor where the basis of payment is the cost of the work plus a fee.

The Construction Management Form

A construction management arrangement will fit into one of these three categories: (1) the architect is the construction manager, (2) a consultant becomes the construction manager, or (3) a general contractor becomes the construction manager. AIA Document B-801 and Associated General Contractors of America (AGC) Document No. 8 are the standard forms that may be adapted for use in any of these construction management situations.

Protecting the Owner

When a contractor encounters difficulty during construction or has underbid or underestimated the project, the owner can expect a claim for additional compensations based on a claim of differing site conditions, changes to the work, construction changes (e.g., errors, omissions, or ambiguities in the specifications), delay, disruption (e.g., owner-supplied material is unavailable or the owner is slow in approving drawings), or forced acceleration as a result of a refusal to grant appropriate extension.

Good planning and project scheduling, careful recordkeeping, aggressive contract administration, and proper project management can help minimize contractor claims; however, the best protection is an owner-oriented construction document that requires the contractor

1. To include in the bid a contingency deemed sufficient to cover unanticipated site conditions.
2. To disclaim any owner representations pertaining to the site or any reliance thereon.
3. To remain liable for any loss or damage that arises from the work (and not be limited by the terms of a warranty).
4. To maintain job progress and proceed with extra work that may be disputed, regardless of a subsequent resolution of the compensation issue.
5. To waive certain types of claims for delay damage, accepting an extension of time to complete as the sole remedy.

The owner should take a hard line in contract negotiations as a defensive measure (although all contracts require trade-offs, of course).

The use of experienced construction counsel makes it more likely that the project will be completed on budget, on time, and without a multitude of contract claims.

Just as the owner has expectations of the contractor so too are there expectations of the architect. The owner must require more from the architect than a design and a downstream certification that the project was built by the contractor in accordance with the plans and specifications. For example, the owner should require the architect

1. To design a project free of defects, to meet industry standards, to be in compliance with applicable codes and restrictions, and to warrant design adequacy (a warranty owners seldom receive).
2. To be the interpreter of the design generated, the judge of the quality of the construction work performed, and the initial arbitrator of job disputes.
3. To be the owner's representative and protect the owner through construction—to make sure that the owner obtains a defect-free building. This includes inspections before the end of warranty periods.
4. To design to a fixed limit of construction cost—or redesign without cost.

The services agreement with the architect must also be tailored to fit the delivery system contemplated and the needs of the project. The owner must remember that it is his or her project; the owner must be satisfied with the agreement even if it means using an architect who is less prestigious but more accommodating.

These assignments of risk will have a cost to the contractor and the architect. The related increase in fees will usually be worth the insurance of the owner's risks.

The Lump Sum Fee

In reality, concept and design represent 15 percent of the fee; the other 85 percent is the cost of technical skill. When evaluating a fee, the owner must be assured that the architect or contractor is correct as to costs, is capable of delivering with the quality factor anticipated, is able to deliver on time, and is skillful. The owner must be sure that the mechanical, electrical, foundation, food, equipment, and landscape consultants employed are of the highest caliber and that the architect or contractor has quality people for the project. For this reason, we believe that the best way to develop a coincidence of interest and not a conflict of interest is the traditional lump sum fee method of delivering service (both architectural and construction) rather than a percentage basis fee. Although not appropriate in all situations, it is our opinion that this approach brings a dedication to the right answers, the right design, and the right research the first time.

CHAPTER 9

SELECTING THE ARCHITECT/ENGINEER

Joseph C. Canizaro
Joseph C. Canizaro Interests

A very important step in the development process is the selection of the architect/engineer. This selection helps determine how successfully the owner's program and vision are executed.

THE PROCESS

Prior to selecting the architect/engineer, it is important that the owner evaluate his or her objectives, program, budget, site, and approach toward executing a project. The owner then should compile a list of criteria that he or she feels is critical to the selection of the architect/engineer. This list should be matched against a list of architects/engineers who by reputation, recommendation, or actual experience match the list of criteria.

Expressions of interest and qualification statements should be solicited from the firms on the list. An evaluation of the responses should enable the owner to develop a short list of firms to be invited to participate in the formal proposal and interview process.

The participating firms should submit detailed proposals in response to the owner's program for the project. (The proposals should address personnel, schedule, compensation, and so on.) As part of the interview process, the owner should visit the firms' offices to determine the personality and method of doing business and to meet and evaluate proposed personnel. The owner should evaluate the results of the interview and the contents of the detailed proposals against the list of criteria established earlier in the process. This evaluation should result in selection of an architect/engineer who will give the owner the product he or she expects.

Once the selection of a firm is made, the negotiation and finalization of the architect's/engineer's contract completes the selection process.

Establishing Objectives

The selection of the architect/engineer must fit the owner's plan for executing the project. If the owner has a large, experienced in-house staff, then it is not critical that the architect/engineer have a great deal of specific project experience and a large, experienced staff to handle project management duties. If, on the other hand, the owner has a small in-house staff that lacks specific project experience, then the architect/engineer would need to have extensive project experience and a project staff capable of guiding the owner through the project development process.

The owner also must determine the architect's/engineer's role in the project. Is the owner looking for a full-service firm that can offer a full range of architectural and engineering services? Does the owner intend to select an architect and then select individual engineering disciplines? This decision probably is determined by the size and experience of the owner's in-house staff. Obviously, it takes more time and experience to select and manage a group of firms than to manage one firm that provides all the required services.

Determining Services

The owner must also decide the exact services that will be provided. This is especially true for the architect's services. Is one architect going to provide design, production, and construction administrative services, or, as is becoming more common for the larger, high-profile projects, is one firm going to provide design services while another firm provides production and construction administration services? Often high-profile, national design firms are teamed with a local firm that provides the production and construction administration services. This gives the owner the advantages of the reputation and prestige of a national design firm and the representation and knowledge of a local firm. The disadvantage to this structure is that the owner must play a very active role in the coordination of the design and production firms.

Other specialized services an architect can provide include facilities planning, preparation of financing packages, and zoning application services. The need for these specialized services should be determined by the owner as part of the planning process.

The owner must weigh similar decisions regarding the services of the engineer. There are full-service firms that offer a range of engineering disciplines: structural, mechanical, plumbing, and electrical. More commonly there are firms that offer structural engineering and firms that offer mechanical, plumbing, and electrical engineering services. In some cases, firms specialize in just one of the mechanical, plumbing, or electrical areas. The owner must decide which type of firm will best serve the project and whether the owner or the architect will contract directly for engineering services. If the owner chooses to contract directly for engineering services, it is important that he or she seek the advice of the architect.

Developing a Program

Before the owner solicits proposals from the architect/engineer, he must have a finalized program for the particular project. The process of developing a program defines the objectives and parameters for the project and helps to avoid costly and time-consuming misunderstandings during the course of the development of the project. The more detailed the written program for the project, the better and more detailed the proposals from the architect/engineer.

The program should describe the site, address the physical requirements for the project, and address the schedule for the project. It also should describe the owner's approach toward handling a project and should describe the in-house project team. The program should outline the economics of the project and explain the budget within which the architect/engineer will be expected to execute the project. Other miscellaneous information that communicates the scope, image, and feel of the project should also be included.

Many owners are resistant to developing a written program so early in the life of a project. However, this program should be seen as a document in progress that will be revised during the life of the project. It will serve as a benchmark, as a measuring device, for the entire project team as a project moves forward in the development process. Once the architect/engineer has been selected, the program should be reviewed and revised. It should serve as a measure of the success of the architect/engineer throughout the course of the project.

If the owner is unable to develop a definite program for the project, it is often because various issues are unresolved or seem to conflict. One solution may be to hire an architect and, if necessary, engineers to participate in a predesign or conceptual review of the project. This process forces the owner, with the help of the architect/engineer, to clearly identify the various issues influencing the proposed project. Once the issues are identified, various solutions can be reviewed and refined. The refinement process should allow the owner to more easily develop a detailed program for the project.

Establishing Criteria

Once a written program has been developed and decisions about the structure of the architect/engineer team have been made, the criteria for the selection of the architect/engineer will become much clearer. The criteria should be developed in a formal document and should be reviewed against a preliminary list of architectural/engineering firms. In developing this preliminary list, the owner should draw on past experiences with architects/engineers, solicit suggestions from contractors, contact other owners who have developed similar projects, identify architects/engineers responsible for similar projects that the owner is working on, and obtain input from professional organizations such as the American Institute of Architects.

Contacting the Firms

Once a preliminary list of firms fitting the selection criteria has been developed, these firms should be contacted to determine interest in and qualifications for the project. The firms should be provided with an abbreviated project program—just enough to describe the scope of the project and provide information necessary for generating a specific response. The architect's/engineer's response should include a qualification statement addressing the history of the firm, giving financial information, and providing a list of projects the individual firm has executed that are similar to the project being contemplated.

The response from the invited firms should be evaluated against the list of selection criteria, and a short list of firms that will be invited to make formal proposals should be developed. This short list should be limited to three or four firms. The formal proposals should address fee, project personnel, schedule, scope of services, and initial design approach to the project.

In inviting a formal response from a short list of firms, the owner should include information on his or her own organization. This information should explain the history of the company, the key players in the company, and the past projects developed by the company. This information will be useful to the architect/engineer in tailoring a formal proposal to the owner's experience.

Design Competition
Depending on the size or type of project, the owner might choose to have firms on the short list compete for the project through a design competition. For the most part this involves only the architect. The design competition usually involves paying the competing firms a small design fee and giving them the time necessary to develop their design solutions. The owner often can use the competition to market or gain public support for his project. Design competitions give the owner a clear look at each firm's design solution prior to a final selection of the architect. Design competitions are usually pursued only for large commercial or public projects.

Evaluating Proposals

The evaluation of the formal proposal should focus on how each proposal meets the owner's list of criteria. It is often helpful to develop a matrix based on the list of criteria to graphically compare each firm's response. The matrix should help rank the proposals received from the individual firms. It may identify a firm that clearly does not measure up or a firm that obviously has not properly addressed the project program. However, in most cases, the formal responses will not clearly identify the best choice for the owner.

Participating in the Formal Presentation

Visiting the Firm
The owner must visit each architect's/engineer's office to listen to a formal presentation. The owner should evaluate the impression he or she gets from these office visits. Does the firm project the type of image with which the owner wants to be associated? Does the firm have dedicated and enthusiastic employees? Is the firm organized with clear direction and leadership? The impression that

is developed during this visit is a very important component of the selection process. A long, intense, intimate relationship is about to be formed. The chemistry that is developed between the owner and the architect/engineer will determine to a large extent the final success of the relationship.

Meeting Personnel

During the architect's/engineer's formal presentation, the actual personnel who will be assigned to the project should be introduced. The architect/engineer should give a detailed review of the professional and educational backgrounds of the proposed personnel. These staff members should give a brief oral presentation on past project experience that is relative to the owner's proposed project. This gives the owner some insight into the personality and the communication skills of the proposed project personnel, both of which are critical to the success of the relationship between the owner and the architect/engineer.

Determining the Firm's Strengths

The architect/engineer should supply a written list of past projects complete with client names and telephone numbers. The owner should contact these clients for recommendations and comments and might even visit some of the projects executed by the architect/engineer. At such a visit, the owner should be aware of the initial impression of the project, its overall quality level, the success of the construction detailing, the way in which the project has aged, and the apparent success or lack of success of the project. Contractors who worked with the architect/engineer on past projects can also provide insight into a firm's performance.

The owner also should question the architect/engineer about the design and construction budgets for past projects and should question the past clients about the architect's/engineer's success in meeting those budgets. This is an important selection criterion.

If a national firm is being considered, the owner should request information on other out-of-town projects and on the architect's/engineer's knowledge of the specific location of the proposed project. Lack of knowledge of local building codes and construction practices can be a costly problem for the owner to overcome.

The formal presentation process also should include a discussion by the architect/engineer about ideas or visions for addressing the owner's program for the proposed project. The owner should listen carefully and critically to this discussion to see how closely the architect/engineer comes to ideas that the owner already has developed about solutions to the program. The owner should judge the creativity of the architect's/engineer's response as it will indicate the level of creativity within the firm.

The process for obtaining owner input and approval during the design and documentation process also should be reviewed during the presentation. The architect/engineer should detail his or her method of developing a project and the decision-making process that is integrated into the development process. The owner should be satisfied that the architect's/engineer's decision process will work with his or her own decision process. If there are conflicts, they should be discussed.

During the final presentation, the architect/engineer should give the owner the opportunity to ask questions; the owner should give the architect/engineer the same opportunity. If all questions are answered, there should be no misunderstanding about the architect's/engineer's proposal.

The owner should investigate the financial strength of the architect/engineer as well. The size and work load of the firm influences the financial stability. The owner should be satisfied that the financial condition of the architect/engineer is sound.

Discussing the Schedule and the Fee

During the formal presentation, the architect/engineer should provide a detailed schedule for executing the project. If this schedule does not meet the owner's project schedule, this conflict should be discussed and resolved. If necessary, the architect's/engineer's fee proposal also may need to be revised to account for schedule revisions. The architect/engineer should discuss the firm's existing and anticipated work load and the work loads of the proposed project personnel so that the owner is aware of potential conflicts.

Discussion of the architect's/engineer's proposed fee structure is appropriate as well. The method for calculating the proposed base fee and for calculating additional service fees should be clearly understood.

Making the Selection

Following the office visits and formal presentations, the owner should review the selection criteria matrix and make any necessary revisions. At this stage, one of the firms should begin to emerge as the best firm in terms of meeting the owner's selection criteria and establishing a positive relationship. If the owner cannot identify a single, clear choice in the process but narrows the choice to two firms, it may be necessary to revisit the remaining two firms. It is important that the owner take whatever time is necessary to choose a firm that he or she feels comfortable with and feels can successfully execute the project. Confidence is important to the success of the relationship and to the success of the project.

Negotiating a Contract

Once the owner has made a decision on which firm will be selected, the other firms should be notified of this decision. The contract negotiation process with the chosen firm will need to address several issues: the method of compensation, the exact scope of services to be included and those services that will be considered extra services, the form of the contract, and insurance requirements. The owner should have addressed these issues in the project program that was provided to the architect/engineer prior to the selection process, as that is the best time to identify differences in such philosophies.

Compensation for architects is determined by two methods: (1) percentage of the final contractor's construction cost or (2) a square-foot fee. The square-foot fee seems to be the most popular because it fixes the fee at the beginning of the project and removes the perception that the architect benefits from increased construction cost. For commercial building projects, engineers generally quote fees on a square-foot fee basis, and both architects and engineers generally quote reimbursable expenses (travel, phones, reproduction costs, etc.) as an extra to the base fee. In most cases, reimbursables are handled on a pass-through of actual cost; however, in some cases a markup of reimbursable costs is negotiated to cover administrative expenses.

Fees are generally paid to the architect/engineer based on the completion of specific phases of work during the design and documentation process. These phases are generally the schematic design phase, the design development phase, the working drawing phase, and the construction administration phase. It is important for the owner to remember that once the approval is given for the architect/engineer to proceed from one phase to the next, revising decisions made in the preceding phase will result in additional fees from the architect/engineer.

The scope of services that the architect provides may include the various engineering disciplines that the project requires plus the various consulting services (e.g., elevator, acoustical, parking, and so on) that might be required. The owner must decide whether to contract directly for these services or to have the architect contract for them. If the owner chooses to contract for the engineer and consultants, the architect will still have to coordinate their work, a responsibility that should be addressed as part of the fee and scope of work discussions. In either case, the architect should submit to the owner a list of the engineers and consultants required to execute the project and specific recommendations as to firms. This list should be discussed and agreed upon regardless of who will be contracting for the services.

Another important negotiating issue is the role of and the service provided by the architect/engineer during the construction process. Most architects/engineers provide limited services during the construction phase of a project as part of their basic services. These limited services include periodic visits to review the progress on the construction, drawing review, and attendance at regularly scheduled project meetings. If the owner requires on-site, day-to-day representation by the architect/engineer, this extra service must be added to the contract. The size, experience, and sophistication of the owner and his or her staff will help determine what services will be required of the architect/engineer during the construction of a project. It is important that the owner has adequate representation, supervision, and quality control; this may be provided by either his or her own staff or personnel of the architect/engineer. This issue should have been addressed in the written program for the project, and the architect's/engineer's response would be an important selection criterion.

Most architects/engineers prefer to use the standard contract forms provided by the American Institute of Architects (AIA). However, most owners find them to be biased on the side of the architect/engineer. As a result, many owners use custom-drafted contracts that are based on the AIA contract but that been edited and revised to address the particular needs and concerns of the owner and of the specific project. If this issue is not identified and discussed during the selection process, it can be highly sensitive and can add considerable time and expense to the contract negotiation process. If the owner intends to use a custom-drafted contract, he or she should include that intent in the project program or should explain it during the interview process. If the owner has a standard contract form he or she uses on a regular basis, it should be made available to the short list of firms being interviewed. During the selection process, the owner should ask the architectural/engineering firms for their comments on the custom contract form and should let their responses be an important part of the selection criteria.

Evaluating Insurance Coverage

Liability is an important issue to both the architect/engineer and the owner. Unfortunately, due to the soaring cost of professional liability insurance, most architect/engineers carry professional liability policies with very small limits of coverage. Usually, these policies are blanket policies. Firms that are very busy with many projects with a high dollar value are very vulnerable under such coverage, and owners looking to the architect's/engineer's professional liability policy for protection are also in a very weak position.

There is a growing trend among owners to secure project professional liability insurance for the architect/engineer. Although this insurance is expensive, its cost must be weighed against potential exposure presented by a particular project (for very complex projects, such coverage can make good economic sense).

The owner also should be satisfied that the architect/engineer carries adequate limits for personal liability insurance and that the insurance adequately covers the architect's/engineer's personnel at and on their way to and from the project's construction site. The owner should be named as an additional insured party on the architect's/engineer's personal liability policies and should obtain certificates of insurance.

SUMMARY

The selection process involves not only the careful interviewing of architectural/engineering firms but also careful consideration of the proposed project's program and objectives of the owner. The selection of the architect/engineer is also more than just a quantifiable process based on cost; it is the start of a long, intense, creative relationship involving individuals with strong personalities. The success of that relationship depends on subjective and emotional intangibles. Therefore, the owner must take the time to make a solid and informed decision when choosing his or her architect/engineer.

CHAPTER 10

THE EFFECTIVE USE OF THE INTERIOR ARCHITECT

Margo Grant
and Yee Leung
Gensler and Associates/Architects

The role of the interior architect in the effective management of your real estate investment is to assist and advise in developing strategies that add dollar value to your property. His or her goal is to support marketing plans for leasing space as early as possible and for as long as possible, thus maximizing the worth of the investment.

Interior architects offer a broad range of services, including design and space planning, from which building owners and tenants can derive long-term benefits. The services provided by an interior architect are especially useful to three primary segments of the real estate market:

- *Owners or developers of existing buildings or of speculative buildings under construction.* An interior architect can help design public spaces, provide tenant finishes and planning services, and generally improve the efficiency and marketability of the building.
- *Major tenants of those buildings.* An interior architect can assist a tenant in the planning, design, and move-in process. While representing the tenant's interests, the interior architect will also assist in negotiations between tenant and owner to achieve the most satisfactory resolution of planning and design objectives.
- *Owners, such as corporations or other business entities, who will also occupy the new facility.* When the building owner will

also be the building occupant, the interior architect's participation during the initial programming phase can result in data that assist the base building architect in planning spatial and functional amenities for the facility. As a result, the building, designed from the inside out, satisfies the user's current and future needs.

Acting as a consultant to either the owner or the major tenant, or moderating between both parties, the interior architect can make recommendations for core development, planning efficiencies and footprint parameters, and modifications. The interior architect can help the base building architect to develop improvements in the building's efficiency and marketability by using strategies that focus on planning depths, optimum modules, column spacing, and building systems coordination.

CREATING A QUALITY ENVIRONMENT

The events of the past decade show that superior buildings remain viable in soft market economies. The increasing quality levels of both new and rehabilitated structures in large cities has raised tenant expectations by elevating comparison standards. The interior architect is fully qualified in terms of professional expertise, knowledge of current market conditions, and prior experience, to advise owners on the most beneficial short-term and long-term means of attracting and securing tenants in the competitive 1990s market. As an owner, you should be aware of some criteria that your building should meet, including what you see (visible features) *and* what you don't see (invisible building elements and systems).

What You See

Enhanced and upgraded building standards in public spaces include such features as the following (see Exhibit 10–1):

- Lobbies.
- Typical floor corridors.
- Elevator cabs.
- Lighting.
- Finishes, materials, and colors.
- Public area furniture such as seating, concierge consoles, and guard or security stations.

EXHIBIT 10-1

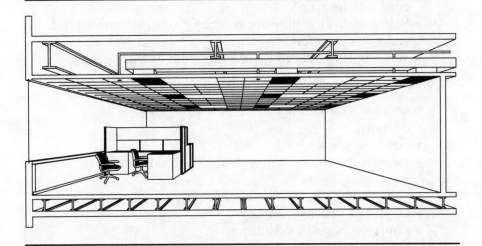

Building standards should remain high in tenant spaces so that only minimal above-standard modifications that raise the aesthetic and functional quality of the space will be necessary to expedite occupancy.

Owners should encourage prospective tenants to work with an interior architect to ensure that the levels of aesthetics and function of tenant spaces are maintained throughout the interior. The interior architect should become involved in the process as early as possible, preferably in the pre-lease phase, so that requirements of scale, planning, and function can be integrated into the project without interrupting the schedule.

What You Don't See

Enhanced and upgraded building systems ameliorate operational costs for both owners and tenants. Communications, lighting, and electrical and mechanical systems account for more than 35 percent of the total cost of constructing a contemporary building. These infrastructural systems are concealed, but they have great effect on the bottom line. Today's advanced building technology addresses issues that owners should consider as requisite marketing tools in the electronic office environment. This contemporary technology includes innovative techniques for distributing electrical, telephone, data, and communications wiring and energy conservation measures such as the following:

- Optimum control systems for heating, ventilation, and air conditioning (HVAC).
- Selective light control for reduced electrical consumption and visual comfort.
- Window treatment to reduce heat gain or loss and glare.

Additional concerns include these items, among others:

- Life safety and support.
- Security.
- Handicapped access.
- Internal transportation, such as elevators, escalators, stairways.
- Federal and local code compliance.
- Upgraded structural capacity.
- Improved acoustical isolation.
- Efficiency ratios.

OWNER-ORIENTED INTERIOR ARCHITECTURAL SERVICES

Benefits

The interior architect offers an array of comprehensive professional services in related disciplines that separately address individual components of a building project, and that together provide an integrated solution to concerns of building owners and investors. These services are most appropriately begun in the pre-design or pre-construction phases of a project and contribute significantly to the overall success of the marketing process. When the owner is also to be the occupant, a wider range of services is provided.

The services most relevant to the building owner or investor include the following:

- Renovation of existing buildings.
- Adaptive reuse of buildings.
- New buildings designed from the inside out on a speculative basis for generic tenants or for an owner or occupant.

The end-use of these buildings include any or all of the following:

- Corporate headquarters.
- "Back office" operations.

- Professional occupancy, such as a law firm; a financial, banking, or investment institution; or a health care facility.
- Retail.
- Hospitality.

Studying a building for modifications early in the process results in an economically sound project with benefits for the owner or developer through high-grade, tenant-attractive buildings. The emphasis should be on tailoring a speculative building—whether the project is pre-existing, in the design phase, or under construction—to the specific requirements of the targeted users. The owner or developer can receive any of the following benefits through using the services of an interior architect:

- A planning module that meets anticipated tenant needs.
- A building configuration that optimizes space utilization.
- Flexible systems that avoid expensive future alterations.
- Maximum energy conservation and management techniques.
- Calculations of usable and rentable areas to determine accurate tenant charges.
- Basic marketing data for the leasing agent's use.
- Project controls that expedite planning and design implementation and move-in.

Examples of Services Provided to Owners or Developers

The application of building design consultation and analysis services to owners and developers is illustrated in the following examples of real work situations:

- *Core Rotation.* In a building to be occupied by an oil conglomerate, the interior architect's investigation demonstrated that rotating the core of a high-rise structure by 90 degrees and making other minor adjustments eliminated wasted space and permitted a coordination of structural systems.
- *Core Reconfiguration.* For a building in the design stage, the interior architect reviewed base building drawings and recommended a reconfigured core in order to provide a dedicated ground-floor elevator lobby for the primary tenant. The interior architect also evaluated the elevator situation, and, by adjusting both crossover floors and floor service between low-, mid-, and high-rise levels, enabled the developer to attract

a major tenant by accommodating specific initial occupancy needs and future growth plans.

- *Building Footprint Modification*. After reviewing base building drawings for a financial institution, the interior architect concluded that slightly modifying the radius of a curvilinear building footprint increased efficiency and flexibility.
- *Wire Management Efficiency*. In a building designed for an owner-occupier, the interior architect found that four strategic points for the risers and vertically stacked communications and electrical closets would simplify future changes in wire management.
- *Building Services Coordination*. By modifying the configuration of the freight elevator and conveyor shaft in a building to be occupied by a leading financial institution, the interior architect ensured that building services, such as mail circulation and garbage removal, were discharged to a dedicated service lobby, thus separating these activities from the typical work environment.

In all five situations, the base building modifications in the design stage resulted in a more efficient, functional, and marketable project.

TENANT-ORIENTED INTERIOR ARCHITECTURAL SERVICES

For a major tenant, the interior architect's contribution to the evaluation and design of the work environment is an important factor in establishing and maintaining high functional and aesthetic standards. The interior architect can coordinate all building elements so that both the owner and user receive long- and short-terms benefits, thus adding value to both their interests. Detailed scope of services can encompass prelease, basic, and supplementary services. Those listed below are usually tenant-oriented, unless the owner is also the user.

Prelease Services

Facility Master Planning
1. Global programming for space requirements.
2. Workplace standards development.

3. Building analysis.
4. Test space layout.

Programming
1. Confirmation of project goals and objectives.
2. Detailed survey of each department or operation unit.
3. Interviews of selected personnel to confirm space requirements.
4. Preliminary workplace space standards.
5. Qualitative requirements of the space.
6. Outline of requirements for special engineering systems.
7. Summary and detailed reports of all findings, including preliminary budget of furnishings and construction costs.

Prelease services can include floor plan review (core, stairs, and planning qualities), building systems review (engineering and structure), and lease workletter analysis.

A study by the Buffalo Organization for Social and Technological Innovation (BOSTI) showed that a positive work environment significantly affects job performance and satisfaction. BOSTI found that the value on job performance of a good office design can be calculated at approximately $2,000 per year per employee. This finding supports the argument for professional interior architectural services as an integral part of an intelligent business plan related to the concerns of both owners and tenants.

The following are some of the concepts involved in facilities master planning.

- *Global Programming for Space Requirements*. The purpose of global programming it to establish future growth projections. The interior architect meets with client representatives to become generally familiar with overall functional requirements. These are translated into square-footage needs and significant qualitative requirements that project the parameters within which planning is based within a predictable range in yearly increments, and they lead to the development of optimum space-leasing strategies. Experienced interior architects can use their knowledge of trends of various industries to assist in the process.
- *Workplace Standards Development*. Standards are developed according to the user's functional and status requirements for

either private offices or open workstations in different sizes and configurations.

- *Building Analysis*. The ability of the interior architect to advise clients on building selection and lease suitability is based on thorough knowledge of market conditions and space planning requirements. The services included in this project phase can be organized into two categories: initial building analysis and detailed building analysis.
  - *Initial Building Analysis*. Feasibility studies lead to long-term space planning strategies and include (1) calculating loss factor by comparing rentable to usable square footage, and (2) evaluating plan efficiency by examining floor and module size, perimeter area available for exterior office, depth of core to window, circulation patterns, and vertical transportation.
  - *Detailed Building Analysis*. When the client's requirements are compatible with the building footprint, a detailed building analysis is generally appropriate. This process comprises the following steps.

    1. Preparation of more detailed plan studies that specifically locate program requirements such as individual offices, workstations, conference areas, and specific support areas.
    2. Review of the planning-level operational characteristics of the HVAC system, electrical distribution, fire protection, security, elevators, and structural capacity for floor loading and modification, as well as the ceiling and lighting systems.
    3. Workletter analysis and negotiation, which can encompass any of the following:
       - Review and evaluation of building standard systems, including power and air conditioning criteria.
       - Comparison of alternate landlord proposals.
       - Development of negotiating posture for raw space with a cash allowance or building standard quantity allowance.
    4. Preparation and review of schedules and budgets to ensure maximum value to the client. Soft costs associated with a major relocation can be identified at this point.

- *Space Layout*. Test layouts are prepared to determine compatibility with the global space program. These are diagrammatic space studies determining general location of important areas such as circulation, offices, and support stations.

Basic Services

Schematic Design
1. Identification of areas that require base building revisions.
2. Vertical stacking and horizontal block diagrams.
3. Planning and design concepts for all areas.
4. Workstation concept based on functional requirements.
5. Furnishing standards, color palettes, and finish materials.
6. Formal presentation for client review, including budget update.

Design Development
1. Detailed plan drawings of each area.
2. Integration of engineering designs for various building systems.
3. Detailed studies of special finishes, ceiling conditions, millwork, and other special features by use of renderings, models, mockups, and other three-dimensional studies.
4. Detailed development of furniture systems.
5. Formal presentation for review, including budget update.

Construction and Furniture Documents
1. Detailed plans and elevations for construction drawings, including ceilings, power, telephone, millwork, finishes, and furniture.
2. Large-scale detailed plans, elevations, and sections.
3. Specifications establishing quality of all materials and installations.
4. Coordination of all engineering and other special consultant work.
5. Preparation of all required bidding or contract documents.

Construction Observation
1. Review of all shop drawings and samples for conformance to design intent.
2. Periodic visits to the project site to monitor progress and quality of work.
3. Review of contractors' applications for payments.
4. Coordinating and scheduling of the move.
5. Responding to general contractor questions.

Supplementary Services

Supplementary services are additional tasks that the client may request from a professional design firm and include, but are not limited to, these examples:

1. Services in connection with areas or work outside the project area and scope of basic services, such as redesign of base building elements (restrooms, core facilities, and so forth).
2. Consultants' preparation of rendered views, models, or mock-ups of specific areas for explanatory purposes.
3. Graphics programs.
4. Artwork, interior planting, oriental rug selection, antiques programs.
5. Custom furniture design.
6. Preparation of record drawings.
7. Preparation of facilities management standards manual.

DETAILED CASE STUDIES

The following case studies illustrate interaction among owners, developers, tenants, and the interior architect, emphasizing how various elements of the scope of services can coalesce into a completed project. The issue of relocation versus renovation or retrofit of existing space is common in the contemporary marketplace. Each case represents a different set of options and a different range of building types.

Tenant Relocation to a Landmark Status Building

To support its image as a leader in its industry, a professional service firm decided to relocate to a more prestigious address. Through effective use of an interior architect, the firm leased and renovated two contiguous rectangular floors in a 1930s landmark building that met the following programmatic criteria.

- A flexible design that allowed four small operating units unified by some physical identity within the two floors.
- Accommodation of as many people as possible, with comfort and efficiency, in the smallest possible space— this was especially critical, considering the ever increasing cost of space.

- Availability of large amounts of natural light, with a preference for operable windows.
- Availability of heat and air conditioning for after-hours operations and special electronic equipment.

Several properties were rated against these criteria and on the basis of ratio of rentable square feet to staff relative to total rent. Although the rent on the landmark property was slightly higher than others considered, the client felt that the benefits, including the high proportion of perimeter space with access to natural light, justified the additional cost. The total area of 35,000 square feet was allocated in the following way: 50 percent to open space, 20 percent to private offices, and the balance to support facilities. Two hundred twenty square feet was the average amount of space allotted to each of the 158 staff members.

The entire space was gutted and reconfigured for improved efficiency and productivity. The problem of low floor-to-ceiling height (11 feet) was solved by close coordination of structural members and services. Building standard finishes in the elevator lobbies were replaced with wood floors and wood paneling that continued in the main reception area. A stair was cut to link the two floors. Adjacencies were reconfigured and communications systems were brought up to state-of-the-art levels. As a consequence of the planning efficiencies, the firm's ability to service a growing number of clients substantially increased, and staff morale and productivity measurably improved.

Tenant Renovation of Existing Space During Occupancy

A major publishing company occupied approximately 250,000 square feet in a 1920s building. As the organization grew, staff was housed in non-contiguous floors as leases became available. Lighting was poor, and writing, editing, and typesetting operations needed to be computerized, requiring significant reorganization of in-house activities. Responding to the challenge of advising the client, the interior architect focused on strategic planning. The ultimate question was whether to relocate or to undertake a major renovation of the existing facility.

The interior architect, through interviews with key members of the organization, determined the ideal workstation size and consolidated previously dispersed departments by restacking the floors. With a clear idea of the desired outcome, alternative options were tested, utilizing the programmatic data developed by the interior architect. The client decided to remain at the current address.

However, during the renovation, only about 5 percent of the 250,000 square feet could be used for "swing" space to station temporarily dislocated staff, and construction had to progress on a complex level so that the budget would not be eaten up by overtime. Moreover, personnel had to be moved as little as possible, and critical functions moved only once.

The interior architect, therefore, not only created a distinctive and coherent design, but also prepared a phasing chart, orchestrating construction and the final move. In total, 120 separate moves involving 50 departments were scheduled within a time frame of 40 months. This schedule was detailed in roughly 25 stacking and phasing operations that showed in intricate detail the renovations of half-floors at a time, with dates, times, and activities for both the publishing house and other building tenants, all of whom were affected.

Acting on behalf of the major tenant, the interior architect also negotiated with the building owner, who collaborated with them to cause as little disruption as possible to the construction schedule. Although the interior architect failed to convince the building owner to undertake a major rehabilitation of the elevator services, they reached a compromise. The owner agreed to provide staffing, at no cost to the tenant, for after-hours elevator and janitorial services for garbage and debris removal, with access to truck-loading docks. The tenant's long-range passenger elevator problem was solved by a new interior stair between contiguous floors.

Tenant Relocation to New Space in a Speculative Building

With its lease due to run out, a professional partnership needed to relocate to a large block of space within a limited time frame. The interior architect established a program of requirements that compared the current space with six other buildings. For each building, the interior architect provided a "snapshot" analysis, calculating efficiency and identifying negative factors such as small core-to-window wall depth, or a small floorplate, that would necessitate distributing office functions over too many floors. A new building compatible with the programmatic requirements was found, and the project was designed and built on a fast-track schedule.

Additional usable square footage was discovered when structural columns, encased in a material that matched the exterior finish of the building, were found to be considerably smaller than their enclosures. A significant amount of floor space was gained by reducing the column enclosures on the twelve floors. Sound baffles were installed to reduce sound leakage from one floor to another at these junctures.

The interior architect designed special floor loading to handle extensive movable file systems. An entire floor was dedicated to computers, management information systems staff, word processing, and production. An internal stair was cut to connect all 12 floors.

Although the building lobby was still incomplete, special requirements for security, signage, and aesthetics were in place. The interior architect worked with the base building architect and building owner to accommodate the client's needs. This activity included redesigning the reception desk and cutting through the building core to install a vertical conveyor for delivering packages on all floors, thus obviating the need for messengers to enter the office space.

The interior architect studied the options of reusing existing furniture and of purchasing new. The recommendation was to reuse only items that would save money because of appropriateness or ease of moving. The entire project was completed on a fast-track 15-month schedule from programming to move-in and punchlist follow-up.

New Building Designed from the Inside Out for an Owner-Tenant

A pharmaceutical firm, planning a 250,000-square-foot administrative office building on a suburban campus, engaged an interior architect at the beginning of the project to provide the building architect with the programmatic data that resulted in a building designed from the inside out.

In addition to offices and general work spaces accommodating support functions, the program called for special areas such as an auditorium, conference center, library, a cafeteria with private dining capability, credit union, ATMs, a retail store, health unit, and cardiovascular fitness center. The interior architect incorporated both objective and subjective considerations into the design criteria. These considerations include future growth, ratios of enclosed offices, and support space to open work areas, versus the desire for maximum perimeter area. From this analysis came the program that detailed space projections and specified appropriate floorplate sizes.

Budget limitations assumed that reusing furniture would be cost-effective. The interior architect's solution was to raise the value of the existing furniture by creating an environment in which it would fit nicely. A color palette was developed both to enhance the beige and dark oak finishes of the furniture and to act as a neutral backdrop for seasonal changes in the countryside visible from the interior.

The interior architect's determination of programmatic requirements in the early stages of the project ensured that the building met the tenant's needs. Identification of a minimal core-to-perimeter floorplate and establishment of the most efficient planning module for the client's use had significant influence on the base building design. The finished product includes efficient, flexible workspaces in identifiable groupings linked by coherent circulation.

FLOORPLATE ISSUES AFFECTING OWNER AND TENANT

Building owners and tenants are often unaware that the floor area that determines the rent is not wholly usable space. Floorplate efficiency can vary considerably from building to building. The most efficient configuration represents the highest occupancy rate of usable space in the rented area.

Floorplates of approximately the same area can yield vastly different amounts of actual usable and rentable space. Factors affecting the usable space include the efficiency of the building's core design and location, circulation patterns, and window-to-wall configuration, among others.

Usable versus Rentable Areas

Figures for calculating rentable versus usable areas vary, but some general definitions apply:

- *Net gross area.* All the space on the floor plate within the inside face of the exterior wall.
- *Nonrentable area.* Typically includes all shafts, base building stairs, elevators, and other floor penetrations.
- *Building common areas.* Typically are prorated to each floor as part of the rentable area. Included may be elevator lobbies, space housing mechanical equipment, janitor closets, electrical and communications rooms, washrooms, and so forth.

- *Rentable area*. Calculated floor by floor by deducting the non-rentable area from the gross floor area, then adding the prorated building common areas.
- *Single tenant usable area*. The per-floor rentable area, minus the floor common areas.
- *Multi-tenant usable area*. The single tenant usable area minus prorated multi-tenant corridor and floor common areas.
- *Efficiency ratio or loss factor*. The ratio of usable to rentable space.

Floorplate Configuration

The shapes of contemporary buildings now appearing on our city skylines fall into four basic categories:

- *The square box*. Generally considered to offer excellent planning opportunities for a company requiring a balance of enclosed private offices of uniform size and open-plan interior spaces (see Exhibit 10–2).
- *The long rectangular slab*. Generates space-planning options for companies requiring a large number of private offices, such as law firms and professional service organizations (see Exhibit 10–3).
- *The atrium building*. Increasingly popular for establishing a special corporate environment. This configuration (shown in Exhibit 10–4) effectively permits more windows and brings more natural light to the interior. The disadvantage is that interior utility space for storage or support services is sacrificed.
- *The new multisided and curvilinear shapes*. These offer the possibility of planning unique, high-visibility spaces (Exhibit 10–5). Sawtoothed configurations and other unusual shapes and sizes of bays may increase the number of private offices.

Multisided geometric forms vary widely in efficiency, and several considerations should be reviewed when evaluating an unusual floorplate shape. The key to any such evaluation is to determine whether the novel geometry is an advantage or a hindrance to one's business needs.

The ideal floorplate shape varies from client to client, since the company's operations and culture ultimately dictate the most appropriate plan. To arrive at the most suitable floorplate, the interior architect must analyze the client's office size and shape standards, workflow

EXHIBIT 10–2
Square Box

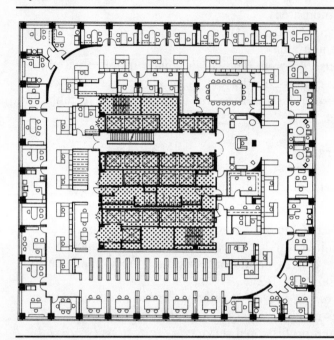

EXHIBIT 10–3
Rectangular Slab

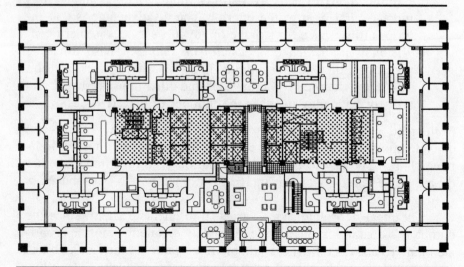

EXHIBIT 10–4
Atrium

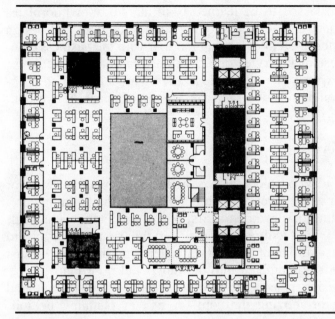

EXHIBIT 10–5
Curvilinear Shape

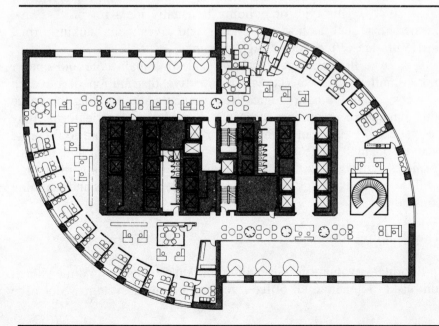

patterns, optimum departmental adjacencies, privacy and status considerations, and space and furniture standards.

The ultimate lesson to be learned from the study of floorplates is that every project can be improved by sound planning and design strategies. The interior architect, being familiar with the business community and professional service organizations, can bring a wealth of experience and expertise to the problem solving associated with obsolescence versus modernization, and the leasing of space in overbuilt markets.

The Building Core

The interior architect considers three basic factors in planning interior space: the columns, the exterior wall modules, and the building core. The core, consisting of elevators, stairs, rest rooms, and mechanical, electrical, and service facilities, orients everything on a floor toward itself and generates all major circulation patterns on the floor. It must therefore be properly integrated into the functional floor plan.

In the predesign phase, the interior architect may recommend either modifying or moving the core for greater planning flexibility. For example, if the core is located to one side of the building, the remaining unbroken area can efficiently accommodate open office space. A centralized core with a consistent distance from the core wall to the perimeter facilitates flexible space planning for private or open offices. This type of building is usually ideal for professional partnerships, such as law, accounting, and investment banking firms, where private offices are in high demand.

A large floorplate can accommodate one main core and one or more smaller "satellite" cores for effective distribution of building services, thereby meeting egress requirements and dividing the space into manageable planning segments. Unusual geometric forms may be made more efficient by rotating or realigning the core to increase usable square footage and improve circulation. A qualified interior planner or designer can help an owner avoid a building plan that, while visually exciting, might create difficult dimensions and planning constraints.

The Building Module

In floorplate evaluation, the building module is the basic dimensional unit used to generate all office sizes and planning systems. Since the cost of nonstandard, nonmodular interior construction can be significant, identifying an appropriate building module is critical.

The module, often developed together with window mullion spacing, dictates office widths. For example, a 4-foot building module establishes perimeter offices of 8, 12, or 16 feet; a 5-foot module allows 10-, 15-, or 20-foot offices. The client should be aware of how much the module will affect interior planning, based on corporate standards and objectives. A building owner should be concerned with providing the most efficient office space for potential tenants, giving them adequate flexibility to downscale office sizes.

The most frequently used modules are those of four and five feet. A great advantage of the 4-foot module is that many building systems such as lighting, ceiling, HVAC, raised computer floor panel systems, and other building materials are manufactured in compatible increments—for example, 2- by 4-foot ceiling tiles and 1- by 4-foot lighting fixtures.

However, this module has limitations for office sizes; 8 feet by 12 feet is too small, while 12 feet by 12 feet is not conducive to efficient furniture placement. The popular 5-foot module results in a 10- by 15-foot office, which has almost the same square footage as the 12- by 12-foot one and generates a more suitable office arrangement. Manufacturers of building components such as lighting and ceiling and floor tiles are in the process of developing a 5-foot module for their products, which will increase the practicality of this dimension.

The interior architect can make a valuable contribution to analyzing alternative floorplates and other base building design considerations. Not only does the building configuration strongly influence space planning; it also becomes an extension of the client's image. The client can be assisted in reaching a decision by comparing planning solutions based on alternative building configurations and established corporate requirements. By reviewing its options through drawings, floor plans and renderings, management can select the building configuration best-suited to its needs.

SELECTING AN INTERIOR ARCHITECT

The profession of interior architecture is a relatively recent extension of traditional building architectural services. Base building architects are usually more concerned with the exterior configuration and the structural and mechanical components of a project, while the interior architect's attention is focused on the interests of the owners and users of the interior environment. The interior architect's expertise extends to strategies that increase the marketability of the buildings by improving the qualitative, quantitative, functional, and aesthetic aspects of the interior spaces.

An interior architect employs a multidisciplined staff of architects, interior designers, space planners, programmers, project managers, and technical specialists. Other professional firms offer more specialized services in the fields of interior design, interior decoration, and space planning. In all cases, these professionals offer partial services that must be supplemented by other consultants.

For the above reasons, building owners and their tenants should retain the services of an interior architect for long-term strategizing and maximum return on investment. The interior architect's interdisciplinary organization offers access to the many specialties that encompass the complexities of projects of any size. These services bring bottom-line benefits to both owner and tenant.

Tangible and Intangible Criteria

Interior architecture is a highly specialized profession involving mastery of diverse yet related skills and based on understanding the relationships among functional, technical, and aesthetic components of buildings. Through education and experience, the interior architect is equipped to work with the base building architect, consultants, and owner and user representatives to develop a mutually acceptable design.

For the owner or developer, the interior architect emphasizes a highly efficient space—it should be flexible enough to meet a variety of tenant needs, as well as competitive and leasable in the marketplace. For the tenant or user, the objective is to tailor an otherwise speculative office building to meet his or her particular requirements. Selecting the most suitable interior architect requires careful investigation of both objective and subjective criteria. Objective criteria include the following:

- The firm should be experienced enough to plan, visualize, schedule, and manage the entire process from beginning to end.
- The firm should possess the depth of staff required to address multidisciplined issues such as programming, design,

- project coordination and management, construction administration, move-in, and, where applicable, post-occupancy evaluation.
- Project execution can extend over a number of years; therefore the firm should have the financial and staff stability to go the full course.
- The firm should be committed to using computer-aided drafting and design (CADD) as creative planning and design tool. Interactive systems that react to changing information and its assimilation should be available to maintain a database that addresses information about facility management, strategic planning, design development, construction documentation, building evaluation, site analysis, and rentable area measurement.

Although tangible assets of experience, efficient management systems, and appropriate tools are quite significant, of equal importance are the intangibles of chemistry, attitude, and sensitivity to specific needs. The interior architect with a history of long-term client commitment will serve the project well as it goes through many complicated and sometimes frustrating stages before completion.

The Selection Process

Your interior architect will have a long-term effect on your investment, the ultimate success of your marketing, and user satisfaction. There are numerous sources of information for selecting a design firm:

- Personal recommendations from friends, colleagues, and professional contacts who have recently relocated, renovated, retrofitted or built from the ground up.
- Local chapters of the American Institute of Architects (AIA), the American Society of Interior Designers (ASID), and the Interior Business Designers (IBD), which provide lists of member firms.
- Design magazines present projects that can give you an idea of current trends in building, interior, and systems design, and can lead you to the firm that expresses your image and expectations.
- Referrals from real estate consultants, furniture dealers, moving consultants, and members of other related industries knowledgeable about the design profession.

- Some professional magazines publish annual lists of "giants" in interior architecture, showing status by revenues, locations, business volume, number of employees in various categories, and major recent installations.

Once you have compiled a list of prospective design firms, the next step is to visit completed projects to compare your conceptual project with the finished products. You will become aware of often dramatic distinctions in style and tone that result from differences in planning, lighting, and the use of color, wall, and floor finishes.

You should develop a list of several firms from which to make your choice. Carefully check the references and credentials of each to answer these questions:

- Did the firm work well with the client?
- Was it attentive to the project during all phases?
- Were budgets, schedules, and deadlines respected?
- What was the greatest problem in the relationship?
- What was the greatest benefit?
- Does its experience and expertise meet the requirements of your project?

When you are assured that the firms in question are qualified and well-recommended, a meeting should be arranged to test the chemistry between their team and yours. Most reputable firms will be happy to schedule a formal presentation, which will include examples of their work and a proposal of the services they could offer you. A written request for proposal (RFP) is a sound method of defining the work anticipated in your project and eliciting the approach, process, budgeting, and scheduling methods of each candidate.

Other criteria include (1) physical proximity of the interior architect to the project is important; that is, if the firm is not in the area, is it willing to deal with the distance factor in a way that is satisfactory to you? (2) Are your design objectives in agreement? For example, are you looking for a high design image that perhaps expresses the signature of the interior architect more visibly than yours? Or do you prefer a firm that will translate your objectives into a set of solutions that expresses your corporate culture and helps you to implement your business plans?

The ability of your interior architect to consider the practical implications of design decisions is a critical criterion of professional competence. Naturally, materials should be selected for their aesthetic qualities, but long-term maintenance should also be kept in mind. Your interior architect should offer practical solutions that meet the project's aesthetic goals while creating cost-effective solutions that will keep expenses down over the long-term occupancy of the space.

Finally, the intangible issue of chemistry cannot be overemphasized. Do you like these people? Can you be assured of working with them compatibly for the duration of the project? Do you trust their professional advice? Whether you are an owner or a tenant, the management of your investment represents a large dollar value. You must feel secure that your interior architect appreciates the risk factors involved and the degree of responsibility to your interests.

WORKING WITH YOUR INTERIOR ARCHITECT

Communication is one of the most critical factors in your relationship with your interior architect. Therefore, once you have made your selection, you must designate teams representing owner and interior architect. Lines of reporting should be defined so that decisions can be made as expeditiously as possible.

Effective management procedures should monitor project progress and satisfy schedule, budget, and quality parameters. Your interior architect will request that you take the following steps to aid this process:

- Designate a representative to provide day-to-day working decisions and serve as liaison with the project team.
- Make prompt decisions about the project schedule. Delay in the decision-making process may affect the fee and overall project costs.
- Provide drawings and specifications clearly showing the base building work and its structural, electrical, mechanical, fire protection, and plumbing systems.
- Provide specifications and environmental requirements for equipment.
- Provide a detailed inventory of all furnishing to be reused (the interior architect can provide this).
- Establish roles and responsibilities.
- Determine project goals and objectives.
- Establish a program of regular meetings

At project start-up, the interior architect assigns a team to your project who will remain dedicated to it throughout. A project schedule and a series of regular review meetings must be set. The schedule shows dates for completion of work phases, important presentations or meetings, decisions, and target occupancy; progress reports will be issued. Budget preparation is a priority at project initiation. Continuous updating is the key to successful budget control.

THE INTERIOR ARCHITECT'S TEAM

The larger interior architectural firms are usually organized on a matrix principle, divided into separate studios led by senior members of the firm. Studios are then divided into teams employing a variety of disciplines. On a typical project, the team consists of the following members:

- The *project principal* (1) ensures that all work is performed to the satisfaction of the client, and (2) reviews the project approach, participates in selected meetings, and reviews all work.
- The *project designer* (1) sets the design concepts and direction for the project, (2) works closely with the client to establish the aesthetic and functional guidelines for the project, and (3) participates in all major presentations and in other aspects of the project as needed.
- The *project manager* (1) administrates the project from day to day, (2) establishes budget and schedules, (3) monitors progress against targeted objectives, and (4) coordinates all team members and consultants to meet the established project schedule.

Other team members supporting these principal players include some or all of the following:

CADD operators.
Furniture and finishes specialists.
Interior designers.
Project architect.
Space planners.
Technical director.

Depending on the scope of services and the complexity of the project, either the interior architect or the owner or client may retain the services of these or other outside consultants:

Acoustics.

Audio/visual.

Cost estimating.

Electrical engineering.

Fire safety.

Food services.

Lighting design.

Mechanical engineering.

Security.

Structural engineering.

Telecommunications.

Vertical transportation and material handling.

FEE STRUCTURE AND COMPONENTS

Fee Components

Of major concern is the issue of professional fees. In the overall picture of project costs, fees for professional design services represent a relatively small portion of total expenditure. A typical budget breakdown for a large project (50,000 square feet and over) yields the following figures (see Exhibit 10–6).

The cost of fees should be balanced against the long- and short-term savings gained from professional advice. Base building modifications recommended by the interior architect can effect significant economies, and building core rearrangement at the predesign stage can increase space efficiency, which, over a potential 20-year time span, can yield impressive profits. An increase of 5,000 square feet of rentable space, representing 1 percent of a 500,000-square-foot project, at $15 per square foot, yields an additional income to the building owner of $1.5 million over the 20-year span.

Fee Computation

Typically, fees for basic professional services are calculated on an hourly basis at standard billing rates for the staff assigned to your

EXHIBIT 10–6
Typical Budget Breakdown for a Large Project

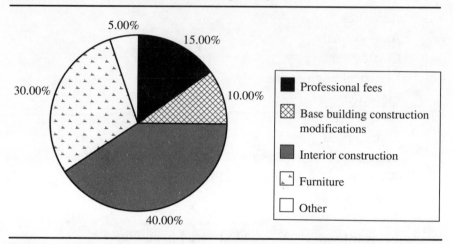

project within a "not-to-exceed" lump sum fee—for example, $3.50 per rentable square foot. Alternate fees, billed at hourly rates, can be charged by prior agreement for full-time "on-site" construction observation or for special private office design, including material and furniture selection, custom millwork, and custom furniture.

Exhibit 10–7 shows the percentage of fee allocation to each of the six phases of a typical project.

EXHIBIT 10–7
Fee Allocation of a Typical Project

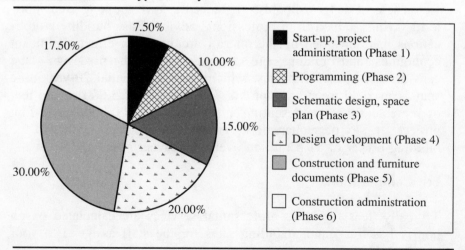

Fees for prelease services are also charged on an hourly basis to a predetermined maximum. These fees are greatly dependent on the complexity of the project, the number and complexity of buildings to be evaluated, and the number of presentations required to communicate the interior architect's findings.

Phases 3 through 6 usually comprise basic services. Programming, though defined as a prelease service, is often included in basic services, and the labor hours required are added to the maximum fee. Supplemental services are also billed on predetermined hourly rates, to a maximum fee established upon determination of the scope of work. In addition, such reimbursable expenses as the following will be billed:

CADD and computer equipment usage.

Data communications.

Delivery and messenger services.

Facsimiles.

Long-distance telephone calls.

Models.

Out-of-town living expenses.

Permit fees.

Photography.

Printing.

Renderings.

Reproducibles.

Reproductions.

Sales taxes.

Shipping.

Telecommunications.

Travel.

SUMMARY

The interior architect is in the unique situation of representing the interests of building owners—and ultimately their tenants—on many issues that, when resolved, positively affect the long-term profitability of the investment. The interior architect brings to these issues a global overview based on experience and an appreciation of the changes occurring in the contemporary business climate. The related and comprehensive services that the interor architect offers can result in a flexible environment with the built-in capacity to respond to change and growth, within a spatial envelope that accommodates the aesthetic and technical components of a marketable property.

CHAPTER 11

SUPERVISING CONSTRUCTION AND AUDITING COST

Joseph C. Peters
Cushman & Wakefield

THE GENERAL CONTRACTOR

A dictionary would define *contractor* as one who agrees to furnish materials or perform services at a specified price.

A general contractor was at one time a firm that had all of the equipment and trades within its own organization to construct a building without depending on other organizations for help. In today's world of specialization, the general contractor calls on a host of subcontractors to furnish the materials and labor for actual construction.

The complexity of the modern office building, with its multitude of materials and systems, has virtually made it economically impossible for one firm to do all the work. Therefore, in the office building market there are essentially two kinds of general contractors: a base building contractor and a tenant contractor. The base building contractor is a core and shell contractor, essentially starting with excavation and finishing the building to its rough state on the interior of future tenant floors. However, practically all base building contractors will perform tenant work.

On the other hand, the tenant contractor is a general contractor who specializes in tenant construction work and does little or no base building work. This type of contractor is prominent in larger cities. Tenant work begins on floors after the core and shell are completed, or in tenant space in existing buildings; all work within the tenant space and in other areas required for tenant occupancy is included.

Both the base building and tenant contractors are set up to work in basically the same fashion, as agents to the owner or tenant. They work with various subcontractors to orchestrate and execute the owner's or tenant's plan.

The general contractor is reimbursed by charging a fee that is typically an agreed-upon percentage of the total cost of the subcontracted work. The GC also receives reimbursement for out-of-pocket field costs, called *general conditions*. General conditions are defined as the general contractor's cost to manage and supervise the trades and to provide necessary services to the project such as protection, labor for clean-up, temporary electric and water, hoisting, and so forth. General conditions costs are limited to costs associated with field work (work performed at the job site) or field overhead and are not associated with home office costs. Some base building contractors, particularly larger firms, perform some of the trade work such as excavation, concrete, and carpentry work; however, this has become less common in the industry.

In the last 25 to 30 years, a new term has been associated with the general contractor — *construction manager* — which means anything the contractor and the owner want it to. The American Institute of Architects (AIA) and the Associated General Contractors (AGC) have guidelines that specifically outline the various services that a construction manager provides. A general contractor and a construction manager are essentially the same for preconstruction services. Both can help select consultants, comment on constructability of design, and provide budget and scheduling information. The main difference between a construction manager and a general contractor is that a construction manager does not enter into contract with a subcontractor in his or her company's name but as an agent for the owner. This process obviously has certain legal disadvantages for the owner and is the main reason why knowledgeable owners avoid using construction managers.

AGREEMENTS

In the construction industry there are three basic types of owner-contractor agreements:

- Stipulated sum (fixed price).
- Cost plus a fee.
- Guaranteed maximum price.

In 1915, the American Institute of Architects established standard owner-contractor documents of the kinds mentioned above, and have continued to modify and improve them over the years. The AIA format is the industry standard and is the basis of most agreements between the two parties.

Stipulated Sum (Fixed Price)

The stipulated sum agreement is that in which both the owner and the general contractor agree on a price either by competition or negotiation. This agreement is combined with other documents such as drawings, specifications, and general and supplementary conditions. Because the price is fixed on a set of drawings and specifications, it is only appropriate to use this agreement when the drawings and specifications are complete and when the owner and design team do not anticipate any changes.

The American Institute of Architects' Document A201 contains the definition of general conditions. This document is the "boiler plate," or standard contract language used with stipulated sum, cost plus a fee, or guaranteed maximum price agreements. General conditions are the clauses that address the relationships between the owner and contractor, contractor and subcontractor, and contractor and architect. This agreement also discusses all of the components and issues of a construction project, such as payments, changes to the work, duration of work, disputes, corrective work, termination, and similar issues. Supplementary conditions are additional clauses typically prepared by the architect, which address any special conditions related to the project that are of a more technical nature, or special procedures required of the contractor.

Cost Plus a Fee

Most projects today are done on the cost plus a fee basis; some of these are later converted to a guaranteed maximum price. A cost plus a fee contract is one that includes the cost of the work plus a fixed or percentage fee, and it is used when the owner wants to shorten the overall project schedule. In this approach, the contractor starts construction before the drawings and specifications are completed; this procedure is called the "fast-track" approach. The combination of a fast-track approach and a cost plus a fee construction agreement is used more often than any other method in the building of major base building and tenant projects.

The cost plus a fee contract has several advantages. First, under this agreement, the general contractor is enlisted as a team member early in the project and therefore contributes to discussions during the design phase. The GC's timely input on schedule, cost, construction techniques, and value engineering options is beneficial to the project at this stage. Second, the contractor follows a bidding and selection process for each of the various subcontractors. As each subcontract is awarded, the owner has increasing verification of the eventual price. In addition, the owner has control over decisions on modifications should a particular trade come in over the budget. This sometimes happens because of market forces, unforeseen circumstances, or owner-generated changes. But, unlike a lump sum contract, in which timely changes are difficult to make, the cost plus a fee contract allows the owner to directly participate in reviewing subcontractors' bids, which often lessens the time and cost involved. Another significant feature of this process is that all accounting is open, and all bills are subject to a complete audit throughout the project.

The disadvantages to this method primarily affect the contractor. The cost plus a fee contract entails a lot of work and can appear to take more time. In addition, open accounting requires extensive bookkeeping and closes many avenues for hidden or inexplicable charges. The participation of the owner's consultants can eliminate short-cuts, favoritism, and other special treatment traditional in the business.

Guaranteed Maximum Price

A guaranteed maximum price (GMP) is the same type of contract as a cost plus a fee contract, except that the costs are fixed, or guaranteed not to exceed a set limit. If the cost exceeds the GMP, the contractor is responsible for the overage. If the cost is less than the GMP, the savings will be given to the owner or split by a negotiated amount between the owner and contractor. By agreeing to give the contractor a portion of the savings, the owner provides an incentive to negotiate and "buy" the subcontractors' work aggressively and to control cost overruns.

The disadvantage to this type of agreement occurs when the contractor is requested to guarantee his price before the documents are at least 75 percent complete. Motivated by the desire to meet the GMP, the contractor will actually control the design. If the design team does not agree with the GC's intent and insists on the design shown on the completed documents, the general contractor usually requests an increase in the GMP with change orders, and change order costs can add up quickly.

There are several ways to get around this problem so that the GMP becomes less of a risk to the general contractor.

1. Do not request a GMP early in the documentation phase. Wait until the documents are at least 85 percent complete, thus reducing the possibility of many change orders.
2. Request that the general contractor purchase at least 75 percent of the trades before committing to a GMP. By doing so, the contractor will substantially reduce his or her risk, and, therefore, the GMP will have less uncertainty for both owner and contractor.
3. Establish a list of allowances with the general contractor and design team representing the completion or further development of the documents and include these allowances as part of the GMP.
4. Understand and list all exceptions and qualifications to the GMP and determine whether they will influence the final cost by adding change orders.
5. Establish a contingency fund that you as an owner can control if changes are required.

Even though a GMP is more complex than a cost plus a fee, it emphasizes the fact that costs are fixed and changes are more costly to make, thereby instilling discipline. Because of this psychological edge, meeting the budget could be easier with a GMP than a cost plus a fee agreement.

WHAT A GENERAL CONTRACTOR CAN CONTRIBUTE

Preconstruction

As mentioned earlier, a construction manager and a general contractor provide the same preconstruction services.

Preconstruction services are those provided by a GC when he or she joins the project team in the early stages of design—generally when the project is of a fast-track nature. The GC typically attends all of the project design meetings and actively participates with the architect, consultants, and the owner, discussing the following issues:

- Budget.
- Schedule.
- Constructability.
- Staging.
- Materials.
- Labor availability.
- Value engineering.

One of the great advantages of the fast-track process is the fact that the general contractor is selected in the preliminary stages of design, and therefore becomes a valuable team member providing input on these important issues.

A general contractor should not be selected until the Design Team has established the requirements and design objectives of the project, as the creative design must initially develop without building constraints. The best time to select a general contractor to participate in the preconstruction services is at the end of the schematic phase. This gives the owner and design team an opportunity to use the schematics as an important part of the RFP (request for proposal) to the contractor. Questioning invited contractors for their ideas and input on construction cost, constructability, and schedule will provide valuable information to the design team and will be beneficial to selecting the correct general contractor. The architect should approve of the general contractor, since many of the services that the contractor performs, particularly giving insight on constructability and value engineering, affect the architect's design.

Project Cost

The difficulty of maintaining the budget causes the greatest stress for project owners. Unfortunately, most owners learn their true project cost after most of their design options have been forfeited. The best way to control cost is to select a project team that considers meeting the budget as important as meeting the design and construction requirements. In this way, cost control will be implemented at the start of a project. An owner must quickly become familiar with the relationship between the opportunity to control cost and the accuracy for estimating cost—the key to staying on budget.

At the end of the schematic phase, the design documents define all of the quantitative and qualitative aspects of the project. This means that the project team will understand the base building project, including foundation, structural systems, exterior skin, HVAC, electrical, plumbing, and vertical transportation (elevators and escalators). The same principle applies to interior renovation projects. The owner should know what he or she is buying.

All of the systems defined at this stage represent more than 80 percent of the total building cost. Although the systems are well defined, the estimated costs are not. The project team needs a combination of historical data and quotations from general contractors in the marketplace to establish a reasonable estimate.

If the project team selects a general contractor early (at end of schematic phase), the GC's primary activity is to establish an estimate based on the schematic documents. If this estimate exceeds the owner's budget, or if the project is economically unfeasible, the project team still has a 50 percent chance of making changes in the design without impairing the schedule (see Exhibit 11–1). Such revisions might include a less expensive facade, elimination of a basement level, shortening the building, selecting an alternate structural system or a less expensive mechanical system, or revising the elevator system, among many possibilities. The general contractor contributes substantially to value engineering by drawing on his or her past experience with the cost and schedule implications of these potential changes.

During design development, the second large block of time on the chart, the project team studies and refines the design and prepares specifications for major building materials and systems. With the general contractor as part of the project team, the team can obtain pricing from subcontractors, thereby increasing the accuracy of cost estimates to 90 percent by the end of design development. However, the opportunity to make design changes to meet the budget without significant schedule changes or delays decreases to 20 percent. Late changes tend not to involve major building components and instead concern the selection of alternate materials, such as using precast concrete in lieu of granite on a facade, reducing the quality of interior finishes, or simplifying a landscape design. Once the project reaches the construction document phase (see Exhibit 11–1), the opportunity to meet cost requirements decreases to a level where the team cannot easily prevent cost overruns. A project team that considers the

EXHIBIT 11–1
Project Flow from Schematics to Procurement

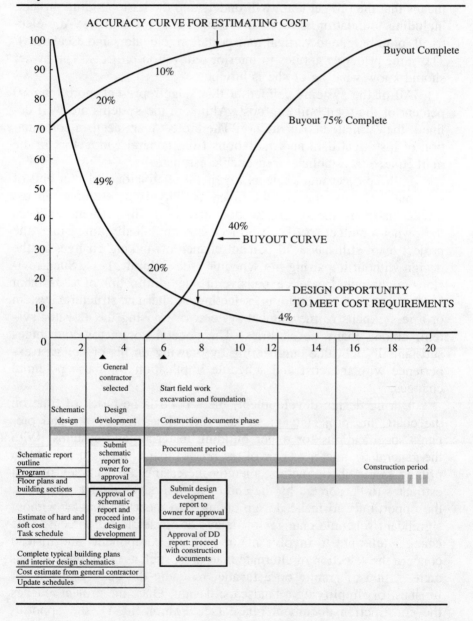

importance of cost is critical, so that they will respect the budget during the early stages of design and present the owner with the opportunity to make major project decisions that will control expenditures.

Schedule

When thinking about the complexity of developing a major highrise office building or even moving into tenant space as small as 10,000 square feet, one cannot help but contemplate the time required to successfully complete the task. One must consider the following points:

- The hundreds of people that will be involved.
- The fact that the success of completing an item of work is dependent upon the successful completion of prior items of work.
- The fragility of scheduling a project from its inception to the point two or three years later when it will be complete.

An industry adage used (sometimes too often) to explain the success of a project is, "On time and in budget." It sounds quite simple to the listener, but genuine success of a project requires dedicated teamwork and cooperation from everyone.

When developing a schedule for a project, no matter what its size, one must remember to keep it simple. The term *simple schedule* does not mean that it is insufficient, but rather that it represents those items of work for which specific project team members are responsible. A well-run project may have several schedules that further deal with the various facets of the project:

- *Project Schedule*—the overall concept of a project depicting the general items of work for predevelopment, design, construction, lease-up, or move-in. This schedule is used primarily by the owner, project manager, architect, and contractor.
- *Design Schedule*—a representation of the various design document phases and approvals required at the end of each phase. This schedule is used by the owner, architect, design consultants, and project manager.
- *Construction Schedule*—a detailed representation of the construction tasks required by the various trades. This schedule is used by the owner, project manager, architect, general contractor, and subcontractors.

- *Tenant Schedule*—the depiction of the work for a tenant, including design construction and move-in. It is used by the tenant, owner, project manager, interior architect and tenant contractor.
- *Cash Flow Schedule*—a representation of the funds required over the construction period to pay the monthly cost of the project. This is used by the owner, funding institution, and project manager.
- *Subcontractor Schedule*—a sequential outline of the work of a particular subcontractor in detail. It is used by the general contractor and the subcontractors.

The statement that a schedule must be simple may seem inappropriate for a complex project. However, in order for a schedule to be effective, it must capture the attention of those who are responsible for the work. Intricate computerized schedules such as CPMs (critical path management) depict the complexity of a project but do not focus the attention of the project team on the immediate issues. The schedule should represent the critical items of work that are dependent on the completion of the previous item of work. Many of these dependent items of work become linked and comprise a path through the schedule, called the *critical path*.

The critical path, which unfortunately is understood by only a few on a project, needs to be established early and updated periodically throughout a project, because it may change, depending on project requirements and developments. It should be understood and followed by all team members and discussed at project meetings. Some general contractors emphasize this path on the schedule and make it a special item for the project meetings.

Just as all must help maintain the budget, everyone (owner, architect, consultants, project manager, contractors, and so forth) must be responsible for his or her part of the schedule. Keeping the schedule simple will guarantee the concentration necessary to maintain this focus. From this responsibility, the team members will develop a commitment to provide the special efforts and find creative solutions when schedule problems occur. If there is one guarantee in this business, it is that you will have problems—probably lots of them—that will affect your schedule. Therefore, the schedule needs to be discussed at every project meeting in part and in whole. Even in the beginning of a project when the architect and his or her consultants want to focus only on design, they should be aware of how the design will affect their ability to develop the necessary documentation within the project schedule restraints. Design documentation is often not sufficiently detailed to obtain proper and accurate bids on a fast-track project. Because no one prepared thorough documents, the project later usually acquires significant change order costs, and these always exceed the cost for the labor to better develop the design documents in the first place. For better control of your project, you have to concentrate on scheduling and give it the same careful review and analysis at each meeting that you would to the design.

Constructability

Constructability is an area that demonstrates the creativity of the general contractor. It deals with many issues such as methods, staging, and manpower requirements. The experience of the general contractor and, specifically, the experience of the individuals assigned to your project, strongly influences the benefits of working with a particular contractor. Selecting a GC who has a great deal of experience with the kind of project you are contemplating is therefore of great importance. The contractor's creativity is, of course, valuable throughout the project, but even more so in the beginning during the design phase.

The following two examples demonstrate how clients have benefited from a contractor's experience in construction.

1. A general contractor was asked to review the schematic design documents of a garage structure in a large city. After a few minutes of glancing through the documents, the contractor noted a precast spandrel beam that in his judgment was too long and would be impossible to truck to the site. After working with the architect, the beam was redesigned into two separate members that could be delivered to the site without logistical problems.
2. In a large interior project for a major law firm, the tenant general contractor realized that the amount of architectural woodwork specified was greater than any of the local woodworking shops could fabricate within the given time period. The aggressive construction schedule that the contractor established could have been jeopardized because of the amount of woodwork required, so he requested that the interior architect divide the woodwork into two or possibly three separate bid

packages. Each of the qualifying woodworking subcontractors then bid each package as if they were separate projects. The law firm was therefore able to select the best price from each package, ending up with three different woodworking subcontractors capable of meeting the schedule for their portion of the work. The client also benefited from the additional competition created by bidding three separate packages and thus obtained a lower total price for all of the required architectural woodwork.

Value Engineering

Value engineering is the analysis of all the components that make up a system and the process of substituting less expensive components without changing the purpose or function of that system. All projects go through some sort of value engineering program. A contractor of any size will always have ideas on how to build something more economically. The key to good value engineering is to avoid cheapening the systems to a point where the initial project is substantially changed.

Another advantage to the fast-track approach is that the contractor is part of the project team in the early stages of design and understands the project requirements. The GC's value engineering respects the design intent and therefore produces results that are acceptable to the owner and the design team. A word of caution: If a project has serious budget overruns in the design phase, value engineering is not the answer. The only solution is to redesign to the budget or increase the funds necessary to build the project as designed.

BIDDING AND SELECTING SUBCONTRACTORS

The general contractor hires a variety of subcontractors to actually furnish the labor and materials for the construction project. If the general contractor has been selected on a lump sum basis, the selecting and bidding procedures for subcontractors will be done solely by the general contractor as part of establishing the lump sum. Therefore, there will be either limited or no approval of the subcontractors. However, if the owner has selected a general contractor on a cost plus or GMP basis, the general contractor follows a bidding procedure that may involve the entire project team. To secure the best price from the most appropriate firms, the general contractor solicits written bids from the firms qualified by the project team.

Using the entire project team to develop the bidders' lists is important for several reasons. First, the subcontracting firms under consideration should be financially stable and established in their field. Second, the architect or designer must be sure that the firms are capable of executing the design requirements of the project. The subcontractors should also have proven track records for projects of similar magnitude. Most importantly, the general contractor and subcontractors must be compatible so that they can work together toward a common goal.

As the bidders lists are established for each of the trades, the following procedure takes place. The architect submits the design documents and preliminary budget to the general contractor for review. The general contractor in turn bids the project by trade, issuing to the bidders the architect's drawings and pertinent specifications. The bidders are given a period of time to study the documents and are often asked to visit the job site to become familiar with the field conditions. Then they will be invited to attend a meeting conducted by the general contractor to answer questions. Obviously, the advantage to having all the bidders present is to ensure that all are receiving the same information and to discourage favoritism. The subcontractors are required to submit written quotations for their work to the general contractor. These bids will be opened publicly with the entire project team present, to prevent further behind-the-scenes negotiating.

After bidding is opened, the written quotations are analyzed by the general contractor, who compiles a spreadsheet noting the major concerns. The spreadsheet compares the budget to the submitted bids, subcontractor qualifications, and the bids to the general contractor's time schedule, as well as states the general contractor's recommendation (see Exhibit 11–2). The project team reviews the spreadsheet and either approves it or requests further modifications or information of the bid analysis. The general contractor cannot move ahead until the owner signs off the approved subcontractor. Once all agree on a bidder, the general contractor prepares the contract documentation and awards it to the approved subcontractor.

This may seem a lengthy process, considering the many trades that can be involved in any given project. However, it is to the owner's advantage to seek the experience of the project team, the architect, the engineer, and the general contractor to choose the best team of subcontractors.

EXHIBIT 11–2
Subcontractor Proposal Analysis for Superstructure Concrete Work

John T. Client
Vice President
QRS Corporation
Corporateville, USA

Project: QRS Headquarters Building

Date: April 10, 1990

Dear Mr. Client:

We hereby submit three copies of our tabulation of the sub-bids we received for the Superstructure Concrete work in connection with the QRS Headquarters Building at 123 Main Street. Our recommendation regarding the award of this subcontract is stated at the end of the analysis. We ask that you kindly authorize the award of this subcontract by approving where indicated on the spreadsheet (page 2). Please return two signed copies of the spreadsheet and all sub-bids, if any, submitted herewith, to our office at your earliest convenience.

Budget: $1,050,000.00

LIST OF DRAWINGS & SPECIFICATIONS, INCLUDING REVISIONS & DATES:

DRAWINGS:
From I.R. Design, Architects:

A1.1, A2.1 through A2.8, A3.1 through A3.8, A4.1 through A4.5, A5.1 through A5.5 dated November 1, 1989.

From M. Technical, Structural
Engineers:

S.1 through S.12, dated December 1, 1989.

SPECIFICATIONS:
From I.R. Design, Architects:

Sections 03310, 03320, 03410 & 03412, dated October 1, 1989

EXCEPTIONS:
Dewatering.
Slab on grade at garage.
Winter protection/heat.
Foundation concrete.
West retaining wall.
Standby light & power.

Grouting for curtainwall.
Exposed concrete walks.
Grading for slabs on grade
  and walkways.
Sales tax.

(1)

204

Concrete Bid Categories	Poor & Inc.	Phil	Ace S&M	Concrete	Salamander
BASE BID:	$971,185	$1,027,043	$1,498,376	$986,000	NO BID
Equipment pads	$5,000	INCL	INCL	$5,000*	
Slabs on grade	INCL	INCL	INCL	INCL	
Sump pits	INCL	INCL	INCL	$5,000*	
Slabs on metal deck	INCL	INCL	INCL	INCL	
Stair pans/landings	INCL	INCL	INCL	INCL	
Garage curbs/ walks	$54,650	INCL	$56,500	$55,000*	
S.O.G. garage equip. rooms	INCL	INCL	INCL	$10,000	
South entry plaza	INCL	INCL	$55,800	$56,000	
Encase electric conduit	$16,750	$14,900	$21,200	$15,000	
P & P bond	INCL	INCL	INCL	INCL	
Insurance	INCL	INCL	INCL	INCL	
TOTAL	$1,047,585	$1,041,943	$1,631,876	$1,132,000	
Final negotiated price	$1,000,000	$975,000	$1,631,876	$1,132,000	
UNIT PRICES:					
Slabs on grade/SF	+2.50/ −2.00/	+2.50/ −2.00/	NO BID	+3.75/ −3.00/	
Slabs on metal deck/SF	+2.50/ −2.00/	+2.50/ −2.00/	NO BID	+3.50/ −3.00/	
ALTERNATES:					
1. Sales tax	$19,500	$15,830	$28,500	$22,350	
2. Storage building w/o associated sitework	$27,175	$24,739	$32,610	$40,927	
3. Fountain	$10,340	$4,975	$9,700	$8,265	

*Indicates XYZ Construction estimate of work omitted by bidder.

RECOMMENDATIONS:
Award a lump sum contract to Poor & Phil Construction Corporation $975,000.00 based on price, excluding sales tax.

APPROVED:

QRS Corporation   XYZ Corporation

_____   _____
(Client Firm Name)   (Contractor)

_____   _____
(Client Contract Name)   (Contractor Contract Name)

_____   _____
(Title)   Title

_____   _____
(Date)   (Date)

(2)

CONSTRUCTION

No matter how many years of experience you have in the business of development, design or construction, the beginning of construction is always exciting to anyone who is actively involved with a project. Focus is on the general contractor at the beginning of a project, but after a year, team members may not be as willing to listen to the GC's daily reports. The contractor must therefore precisely lay out communication procedures with the project team. The GC must devise a format to convey construction problems and job status, as well as frequency of reports, whether weekly or monthly. A discussion of the various types of meetings and required paper flow that a contractor may use follows.

Project Meetings

The traditional way in which the contractor interfaces with the project team is through weekly or monthly project meetings run by the project manager or the general contractor and attended by members of the project team representing the owner and the design side. These meetings are extremely important because they serve as the main conduit for resolving issues, finding solutions to field problems, and reporting on the project's cost and schedule status. The contractor who has the talent to run these meetings efficiently and without an adversarial style will be successful in obtaining the necessary assistance from the other team members to help complete the project. The general contractor's project manager normally takes detailed minutes of the meeting and then distributes them among those attending. The minutes of the previous meeting are used as part of the agenda and are reviewed as old business or open items. New business issues make up the other part of the agenda and, of course, become old business on the next set of minutes.

For a productive meeting to take place, the project manager must be able to run the meeting with a sense of urgency and also understand how to motivate the other team members to respond to requests with the same urgency. He must also have total control of the meeting and the full attention of its participants. This attention and sense of urgency are together one of the keys to a successful project. Many projects have suffered serious delays, cost additions, and construction problems because meetings were not controlled and well-run. Many construction problems will also be discussed at these meetings, and tempers can be lost among those attending. Despite these drawbacks, the project manager must remain calm, be a strong leader, and control the meeting so that all issues are resolved.

A seasoned project manager loathes surprises. Therefore, he must be a good communicator and find the time to speak on a daily basis with all members of the team, keeping them informed of their areas of concern. This intense communication helps ensure the project's success. It enables the project manager to be aware of critical issues and start the process of resolving problems with the rest of the team. It also helps him motivate the team during the actual construction of the project because he can adjust priorities to properly focus the work effort.

RFI Meetings

As part of the project meeting many General Contractors include on the agenda a section called "request for information" (RFI). During a typical RFI meeting, the contractor distributes a list of items shown in order of priority, for which he needs either information or resolution from the project team.

Just as the project manager hates surprises, so do his fellow team members. As a good communicator, the manager should inform the appropriate people before the meeting that he will be requesting help or information in solving a problem. For the owner or tenant, these times exemplify the importance of the team approach. The compatibility of the design team and the contractor are indeed tested at RFI meetings, and their ability to work together in solving problems will become evident.

Change Order Review and Approval

Change orders are a part of every project. They are the byproduct of the complex nature of building a project. Once the construction document phase, or construction phase, is reached, there is little you or the project team can do to prevent cost overruns. However, much can be done in reviewing change orders and granting approval to changes that are justifiable.

Change orders generally fall into four categories:

- *Scope changes*. These are changes in the documents either to add or delete specific work requested by the owner or design team.

- *Document changes*. Because design documents are never complete and often contain errors or omissions (even with CADD systems), they require changes for either correction or completion and adherence to design goals or programs.
- *Field changes*. During construction, there are often unknowns that are not revealed during the early phases of field inspection, soil borings, or site analysis. Therefore, these problems must be resolved during construction.
- *Contractor claims*. This is a change to which the contractor or subcontractor feels he or she is entitled because of either delay or an addition or deletion to the work as stated in the construction agreement.

Regardless of the kind of change, each must be reviewed by the architect and other design consultants. The architect must prepare a written statement to the owner describing the change, the reason for the change, his or her estimate of the cost, and whether the change should be approved or rejected.

Change orders take up a large part of the project meeting and must be discussed in detail. If all team members share a good relationship, their individual viewpoints on each change will be respected. Their opinions on whether a change should be rejected or approved should not slow down the progress of the work. In many projects, disputed change orders are settled after the project's completion. However, few are resolved this way when a project team has mutual respect and understanding for various points of view.

Schedule Review and Update

During the early phases of design, the construction schedule is established and its critical path predicted based on the GC's past experience. However, during actual construction reality takes over, and the critical path as well as the total construction schedule may seem as if meant for a completely different project. The importance of the contractor's discipline in updating the schedule weekly cannot be stressed enough. All too often the schedule is forgotten, and weeks go by before the project team can measure the construction's progress.

The general contractor and the field staff have a tendency to build the project day by day. However, this is the best way to lose control of the subcontractors and the project team, as their production and cooperation will decline if the GC neglects frequent updates and schedule reviews. For example, when the general contractor enters into an agreement with a subcontractor, they agree to three basic elements: scope, cost, and time. Within the subcontractor's agreement is a schedule of his or her particular trade work to fit into the overall schedule. If a sub falls behind, the contractor must do more than give warning. The GC must demonstrate through the subcontractor's schedule and the main project schedule that the sub's progress is not in accordance with his contract. The subcontractor must then make up the lost time at his or her own cost and do so in a way that does not adversely affect the project schedule.

By telling the project team of the weekly progress, the contractor can direct everyone's focus on the problem delaying the work. This is extremely important when the design team takes more time than necessary to prepare or review shop drawings, subcontractor awards, change orders, and other necessary contractual documents that are required to keep the project on track.

Cost Reporting

With the aid of computers, contractors have become expert at reporting cost. For many years, the general contractor's cost report looked like the diagram in Exhibit 11–3. This report is updated monthly and reflects the approval awards and extras, pending awards and extras, and the status of each trade, whether under or over budget. It is extremely important for the owner or tenant to control the funds being disbursed to the various trades. This report form lacks anticipated total cost, which does not appear as one of the column heads because *real anticipated costs*—the contractor's "gut feeling" of the project's destination—cannot be obtained by adding or subtracting any of the columns in the chart. A good contractor accounts for things that have not reached the paper stage, considering such items as pending delays in material shipment, discussion between an owner and architect for additional design changes, or possible delays caused by weather conditions.

A contractor will not often stick his or her proverbial neck out and try to predict project cost. However, by predicting the cost this way, the GC helps the rest of the project team to focus on possible cost overruns early enough to prevent them.

EXHIBIT 11–3
Sample General Contractor's Cost Report

Trade item	Budget	Subcontractor Award Extras	Cost to date	Remaining to complete	Under run	Over run

AUDITING CONTRACTOR COST

One important safeguard in the control over construction cost that owners often overlook is an audit of the general contractor. Perhaps the most common reason for the lack of auditing by owners is inexperience. Quite simply, most owners or tenants have never been involved with a construction project and are unaware that they *can* audit the contractor. One may rest assured that no contractor will volunteer or suggest this idea to the client. However, by auditing the contractor's monthly requisitions and accounting records, the owner or tenant will gain assurance that construction costs are appropriate, accurate, and reasonable.

Construction Audit Defined

In broad terms, auditing can be defined as any function that involves the review of another's representations to determine their validity. Construction auditing is more narrowly described as a systematic examination of a contractor's requisitions, records, and related operations to determine mathematical accuracy and adherence to the owner-contractor agreement.

Establishing the Audit

Like most individuals, contractors are never very receptive to an audit of their accounting records. It is therefore prudent to establish the owner's or tenant's "right" to audit the contractor. This is accomplished by specifically stating in the owner-contractor agreement that the contractor shall make all accounting records and supporting documentation related to the project accessible to the owner for his or her review and audit. Should any of the American Institute of Architect (AIA) standard owner-contractor agreements be used, specific articles deal with the contractor's responsibilities for maintaining complete accounting records so as to provide for proper financial management of the project. The articles also contain the necessary clause that grants the owner or his or her representative access to all the contractor's accounting records related to the contract.

Once the owner or tenant has established the right to audit the GC's contract, the decision as to when to begin auditing the contractor may be made at any time. You should note, however, that the earlier the auditing begins, the more effective a control it becomes. By deciding to audit before the contractor is selected, the auditor can help establish auditing and accounting procedures for the project, assist in interviewing potential contractors, and participate in negotiating certain sections of the contract.

In addition, by conducting the audit during construction as opposed to after it, certain other advantages may be gained. Specifically, a more thorough review of costs is possible when conducted on the supporting documentation each month rather than on the entire cost documentation after the project is completed. Continual periodic review also affords the owner or tenant greater control over any disputed costs. If questionable cost items arise during the audit of an ongoing project, contractors are more agreeable to a quick resolution when they know that the owner or tenant still has the power of the checkbook.

The Contractor Requisition

The main document that will be audited for the construction project will be the contractor's application for payment, or, as it is more commonly called, the *contractor's requisition*. The requisition is essentially an invoice from the general contractor for reimbursement of cost incurred on the project. The cost can be broken down into four main categories: subcontractor costs, general conditions, change orders, and fee. All costs and the form and frequency of requisitions are specifically detailed in the owner-contractor agreement.

Subcontractor costs are those not originating from the general contractor. A subcontractor is an entity who has a direct contractual obligation with the general contractor to perform a service, supply material for the project, or both. Examples of subcontract costs include electrical, HVAC, plumbing, fire protection, demolition, dry wall, and masonry, among others. The actual cost of a particular trade or subcontract is based upon a set of bidding documents for the work to be performed. The subcontractor reviews the documents for the proposed project and determines a price for performing the work. The subcontract should be awarded based upon a competitive bidding process and should be attended by the owner and other team members. At least three bids for each trade should be included to obtain the best price; the lowest bid price is usually selected. After a subcontractor is awarded the contract for a particular trade, the general contractor requires a complete breakdown of the subcontractor's total cost. This breakdown of costs for materials and labor constitutes the subcontractor's schedule of values and is used to determine percentage complete for the requisition.

General conditions costs are direct costs of the general contractor incurred in performing his or her duties. These costs are controllable by the general contractor and, accordingly, represent an area of primary audit significance. The general condition costs to be reimbursed (Exhibit 11–4) and those not to be reimbursed (Exhibit 11–5) should therefore be specifically defined in the owner-contractor agreement. Keep in mind that the purpose of defining these costs in the owner-contractor agreement is to limit the general contractor to only those costs that are both reasonable and necessary for performing duties. Special efforts should be made to ensure that the general contractor does not overstaff the job and that no home office salary or overhead costs are reimbursable.

Change orders are written orders to the contractor signed by the owner and architect authorizing a change in the work to be performed or an adjustment to either the contract price or project schedule. The formal written change order indicates the total cost of the change and includes all the subcontractor costs and the contractor's additional general conditions and fee. The contractor's portion of the change order cost is usually defined in the owner-contractor agreement.

Fee is what the owner agrees to pay the contractor as compensation for his services in performing the owner-contractor agreement. Essentially, the fee represents the contractor's profit and is usually calculated as a fixed percentage of the construction cost. The construction cost is therefore defined within the owner-contractor agreement. For purposes of calculating fee, the general contractor's general conditions are included in the construction cost.

Once all the subcontracts have been awarded and the contractor has determined general condition costs and total fee, the contractor should put together a listing of scheduled values to be billed to the owner. This list should be of sufficient detail to enable the project architect and owner to determine the percentage complete for each item. The form of the requisition itself typically follows that established by the AIA. Specifically, the contractor should submit the requisition using the AIA "Continuation Sheet" (G703) shown in Exhibit 11–6 and the AIA "Application and Certificate for Payment" (G702) shown in Exhibit 11–7. The G703 contains several columns with specific headings to help standardize the requisition; note that column C should contain the individual scheduled values that were previously agreed to by the owner. This column, when multiplied by the percentage

EXHIBIT 11-4
General Conditions—Examples of Costs to Be Reimbursed

- Field office labor wages and benefits
  Management
  Accounting/clerical
  Secretarial
- Field labor wages and benefits
  Foreman
  Carpenters
  General laborers
  Teamster
  Operating engineer
- Field office rental
- Field office equipment and supplies
  Furniture rental/purchase
  PC rental/purchase
  Fax machine rental/purchase
  Copy machine rental
  Miscellaneous office supplies and paper
- Jobsite communication
  Portable radios
  Telephone equipment rental and monthly expense
  Mobile phone
- Blueprinting and reproduction
- Postage and express delivery
- Jobsite safety
- Rubbish removal
- Site surveying
- Job progress photos
- Temporary services
  Electric
  Heat
  Sanitary
- Jobsite security
- Licenses and fees
- Expediting travel expenses
- Temporary equipment rental
  Scaffolding
  Personnel hoist
  Material hoist
  Power tools
- Sales and use taxes
- Structural testing and inspection

EXHIBIT 11–5
General Conditions—Examples of Costs Not to Be Reimbursed

- Home office wages and benefits
  Management
  Technical
  EDP
  Accounting
  Secretarial
- Home office overhead
  Allocated G&A expenses
  Rent
- Contractor's capital expenses
- Contractor's negligence costs
- Fines and penalties
- Legal costs
- Lost or stolen equipment
- Bonuses or gifts
- Contractor's normal commuting expenses
- Moving expenses
- Meals and refreshments

complete agreed to by the architect, will determine the total completed and stored to date amount (that is, column G). The G702 is actually a summary document used to show the current payment due. It is also the form that the architect signs in order to certify the current percentage complete. Most of the information contained on the G702 comes from the G703 and any prior G702 forms.

The Audit Procedure

The owner-contractor agreement stipulates how often the contractor may bill the owner for construction costs incurred. Typically, requisitions are submitted monthly and payment is due within the previously determined period of time.

The first step in auditing the requisition actually begins before its submission. As part of the audit process, the auditor must work with the project team, in particular the general contractor, and establish a meeting to review a draft of the requisition. The draft is more commonly known as the "pencil copy" and is the contractor's interpretation of the sum currently due, based upon a review of the subcontractors' requests for payment and current general conditions. The contractor must establish a cutoff date with the subcontractors for submission of their invoices for work to be completed by the

EXHIBIT 11–6
Sample G703 Form
CONTINUATION SHEET

AIA Document G702, APPLICATION AND CERTIFICATE FOR PAYMENT, containing
Contractor's signed Certification is attached.
In tabulations below, amounts are stated to the nearest dollar.
Use Column I on Contracts where variable retainage for line items may apply.

AIA DOCUMENT G703   (Instructions on reverse side)   PAGE   OF   PAGES

APPLICATION NUMBER:
APPLICATION DATE:
PERIOD TO:
ARCHITECT'S PROJECT NO:

A	B	C	D	E	F	G		H	I
			WORK COMPLETED						
ITEM NO.	DESCRIPTION OF WORK	SCHEDULED VALUE	FROM PREVIOUS APPLICATION (D + E)	THIS PERIOD	MATERIALS PRESENTLY STORED (NOT IN D OR E)	TOTAL COMPLETED AND STORED TO DATE (D + E + F)	% (G ÷ C)	BALANCE TO FINISH (C – G)	RETAINAGE

SAMPLE

SAMPLE

1. AIA copyrighted material has been reproduced with the permission of the American Institute of Architects under license number 91066. Permission expires June 1, 1992. FURTHER REPRODUCTION IS PROHIBITED.

2. Because AIA Documents are revised from time to time, users should ascertain from the AIA the current edition of this document.

3. Copies of the current edition of this AIA document may be purchased from The American Institute of Architects or its local distributors.

4. This document is intended for use as a "continuation" (consultants are further defined by Senate Report 94-473 on the Copyright Act of 1976). This document is not intended to be used as a "model language" (language/provision from which to be used to be modified by inserting specific amendment sheets and/or by appending separate amendment sheets and/or fill in provided blank spaces.

AIA DOCUMENT G703 • APPLICATION AND CERTIFICATE FOR PAYMENT • MAY 1983 EDITION • AIA® • © 1983
THE AMERICAN INSTITUTE OF ARCHITECTS, 1735 NEW YORK AVENUE, N.W., WASHINGTON, D.C. 20006

G703–1983

EXHIBIT 11-7
Sample G702 Form

1. AIA copyrighted material has been reproduced with the permission of the American Institute of Architects under license number #96046. Further reproduction is prohibited.

2. Because AIA Documents are revised from time to time, users should ascertain from the current edition of this document.

3. Copies of the current edition or this AIA document may be purchased from The American Institute of Architects or its local distributors.

APPLICATION AND CERTIFICATE FOR PAYMENT   AIA DOCUMENT G702   (Instructions on reverse side)

4. This document is intended for use as a "consumable" (consumable is further defined by Senate Report 94-473 on the Copyright Act of 1976.) This document is not intended to be used as "model language" (language taken from an existing document and incorporated, without attribution, into a newly created document.) Rather, it is a standard form which is intended to be modified by appending separate amendment sheets and/or filling in provided blank spaces.

TO (OWNER):

FROM (CONTRACTOR):

PROJECT:

VIA (ARCHITECT):

CONTRACT FOR:

APPLICATION NO:

PERIOD TO:

ARCHITECT'S
PROJECT NO:

CONTRACT DATE:

PAGE ONE OF   PAGES

Distribution to:
☐ OWNER
☐ ARCHITECT
☐ CONTRACTOR
☐
☐

CONTRACTOR'S APPLICATION FOR PAYMENT

Application is made for Payment, as shown below, in connection with the Contract. Continuation Sheet, AIA Document G703, is attached.

CHANGE ORDER SUMMARY	ADDITIONS	DEDUCTIONS
Change orders approved in previous months by Owner TOTAL		
Approved this Month		
Number	Date Approved	
	TOTALS	

Net change by Change Orders

1. ORIGINAL CONTRACT SUM .... $
2. Net change by Change Orders .... $
3. CONTRACT SUM TO DATE (Line 1 ± 2) .... $
4. TOTAL COMPLETED & STORED TO DATE .... $
   (Column G on G703)
5. RETAINAGE:
   a. ____ % of Completed Work $
      (Column D + E on G703)
   b. ____ % of Stored Material $
      (Column F on G703)
   Total Retainage (Line 5a + 5b or
   Total in Column I of G703) .... $
6. TOTAL EARNED LESS RETAINAGE .... $
   (Line 4 less Line 5 Total)
7. LESS PREVIOUS CERTIFICATES FOR
   PAYMENT (Line 6 from prior Certificate) .... $
8. CURRENT PAYMENT DUE .... $
9. BALANCE TO FINISH, PLUS RETAINAGE .... $
   (Line 3 less Line 6)

The undersigned Contractor certifies that to the best of the Contractor's knowledge, information and belief the Work covered by this Application for Payment has been completed in accordance with the Contract Documents, that all amounts have been paid by the Contractor for Work for which previous Certificates for Payment were issued and payments received from the Owner, and that current payment shown herein is now due.

CONTRACTOR:

By: Date:

State of: County of:
Subscribed and sworn to before me this   day of   , 19
Notary Public:
My Commission expires:

ARCHITECT'S CERTIFICATE FOR PAYMENT

AMOUNT CERTIFIED .... $
(Attach explanation if amount certified differs from the amount applied for.)
ARCHITECT:

In accordance with the Contract Documents, based on on-site observations and the data comprising this application, the Architect certifies to the Owner that to the best of the Architect's knowledge, information and belief the Work has progressed as indicated, the quality of the Work is in accordance with the Contract Documents, and the Contractor is entitled to payment of the AMOUNT CERTIFIED.

By: Date:
This Certificate is not negotiable. The AMOUNT CERTIFIED is payable only to the Contractor named herein. Issuance, payment and acceptance of payment are without prejudice to any rights of the Owner or Contractor under this Contract.

AIA DOCUMENT G702 • APPLICATION AND CERTIFICATE FOR PAYMENT • MAY 1983 EDITION • AIA® • © 1983
THE AMERICAN INSTITUTE OF ARCHITECTS, 1735 NEW YORK AVENUE, N.W. WASHINGTON, D.C. 20006.

G702-1983

last day of the period that the requisition will cover. Although the contractor's accounting staff needs time to prepare the pencil copy, the subcontractors' cutoff date should be as close as possible to the pencil copy meeting date to minimize the degree of estimated costs by the subcontractors.

Once the pencil copy is prepared, the project team meets to review the requisition and determine the current percentage complete for each subcontractor. Those present should include at least the general contractor's project manager and accountant, the architect, the owner, and the owner's auditor. Depending on which subcontractors are currently being billed, certain owner's consultants, if hired, should also be present to evaluate their particular areas of expertise. Examples would include an MEP (mechanical, electrical, and plumbing) specialist to review electrical, HVAC, and fire protection systems, and a structural engineer to review any concrete or steel work.

To determine percentage complete, the owner, architect, and owner's consultants must review the individual subcontractors' total completed and stored to date amount and percentage by scheduled value line item as presented by the general contractor. Presumably the general contractor will have reviewed the subcontractors' invoices prior to the pencil copy meeting and adjusted any line items as appropriate. The general contractor should never raise a subcontractor's total requested amount; the owner should not pay more than a subcontractor bills. The owner's, architect's, and consultants' evaluation of percentage complete should be based on their walkthrough of the site prior to the pencil copy meeting. Any deletions or decreases made by the owner or architect are in most cases challenged by the general contractor. In any event, all final adjustments should be mutually agreed upon and documented by the contractor's accountant and owner's auditor.

After all the subcontractors' percentage complete amounts have been agreed upon, the current period general conditions are reviewed for reasonableness and compliance with the owner-contractor agreement. This typically involves making sure that all current items agree with appropriate supporting documentation such as vendor invoices, receipts, payroll records, employee expense reports, and, if necessary, cancelled checks. In addition, the auditor should check for proper approvals by the contractor's project manager and correct job coding by the contractor's accountants. Specifically, certain general conditions costs will be paid from the contractor's home office and charged to the project. The auditor should be certain that such coding is valid. Any adjustments to the current general conditions by the owner or an accountant should be mutually agreed upon and documented by the contractor's accountant and the owner's auditor.

After the project team has agreed upon all the subcontractor percentages and general conditions amounts on the pencil copy for the current period, the contractor's accountant prepares the requisition. The completed requisition and all supporting information are then sent to the owner's auditor for final review. The auditor's final review at a minimum consists of the following:

1. Verification that all prior requisition totals by line item have been properly carried forward to the current requisition. If the AIA G703 form is used for the requisition, the auditor's review ascertains that amounts appearing in column D, "Previous Applications," agree to column G, "Total Completed and Stored to Date," of the prior requisition.
2. Verification that all completed and stored-to-date totals by the subcontractor are in agreement with the pencil copy totals. The auditor should also check the mathematical accuracy of the totals.
3. Review of each subcontractor's current invoices to verify that all completed and stored-to-date totals per the requisition are less than or equal to total amounts billed by the subcontractor.
4. Review of each subcontractor's retentions to ensure mathematical accuracy and compliance with terms of the owner-contractor agreement.
5. For reductions in retention previously held on a subcontractor, the auditor should verify that a fully executed and notarized partial waiver of lien has been submitted. The partial waiver of lien should indicate the total of all payments made to the subcontractor through the prior requisition.
6. For any materials stored off-site, verification that all amounts per the requisition agree to the applicable subcontractor's bill of sale and certificate of insurance. In addition, an affidavit from either the general contractor or the owner's representative evidencing inspection of the material stored and proper segregation of the owner's material from that of others at the warehouse should be included.

7. Verification that all general conditions costs included in the requisition are in agreement with the pencil copy totals.
8. Verification that all change orders billed have been fully approved by both owner and architect and that the costs agree to the executed change orders.
9. Review of the general contractor's fee calculation for mathematical accuracy and compliance with terms of the owner-contractor agreement. If fee retention is applicable, its calculation and compliance with terms of the owner-contractor agreement should also be reviewed.
10. Verification that all amounts on the AIA G702 agree with the supporting G703 amounts and amounts from any prior G702.
11. Verification that the G702 has been signed by the contractor and notarized.

Should any of the above procedures detect an error, the auditor should contact the general contractor to discuss the error. Depending on the dollar amount of the error and the amount of time necessary to correct the requisition, the auditor either sends the requisition back to the contractor for resubmission or makes the correction himself.

After the requisition has been reviewed and adjusted if necessary, it is sent to the architect for his review and signature on the AIA G702. The architect is then responsible for sending the certified requisition to the owner for payment. In addition to the audit procedures outlined, the construction auditor should from time to time, depending on the duration of the project, perform additional audit tests to ensure that costs are in compliance with the contract terms. These additional tests include the following:

1. Detailed review of the contractor's payroll system to determine that wages and benefits included in general conditions are actual costs paid to employees and outside agencies.
2. Payroll payout of the contractor's field labor to determine that laborers billed for in general conditions are actually working at the job site.
3. Detailed review of contractor's actual insurance costs for the project to determine accuracy of amounts billed in general conditions.
4. Agreement of all subcontractor's scheduled value amounts to the actual executed contract between the general contractor and the subcontractor.

Final Requisition

In form, the final requisition presented to close out the construction cost for the project is similar to all previous requisitions presented. The obvious difference is that the final requisition is the contractor's last invoice and, as such, details all costs as complete. All audit procedures previously described should be performed on the final requisition as well. One notable difference is that the general contractor must provide final lien waivers from all subcontractors for the project. The amount indicated as total payment to be received for the project must agree with the subcontractor's original contract value plus or minus the value of all change orders applicable to that subcontractor. In addition, the general contractor must provide the final lien waiver by evidencing all payments received from the owner. The purpose of the final lien waiver is to protect the owner from future claims by any contractor or subcontractor.

PROJECT CLOSE-OUT

In the final stages of a project, the primary objective is to ensure that all work is complete and that all final documentation is signed off and given to the owner. The three elements needed to substantiate completion are the architect's final inspection, any required inspections by government agencies, and the certificate of substantial completion signed by the owner and the general contractor.

Punch List

The end of the job can be the most difficult part. Emotions run high just before the owner's move-in deadline. Afterward, the contractor and crews can lose momentum, with diminished interest in the small details left to be done. This is the time when a thorough but reasonable punch list is needed as a guide to complete the work. The *punch list* is a compilation of items that are missing or require adjustment, touch-up, or some other such action. The list is prepared by the architect from his physical inspection of the project site. It often includes input from the engineers and other consultants on the project. The general contractor is responsible for distributing the architect's punch list to the various subcontractors and making sure that the work is completed in a timely fashion.

The punch list should be a master list of all the required work. Issuing multiple lists can create redundancy and blur the focus of the subcontractors. Punch list items should be reasonable; if the content is too nitpicky, it will not be taken seriously, and the more critical items could be overlooked. It should also stick to the original scope and specifications. The owner or a member of the project team may be tempted to modify a condition when it can actually be seen in the field, but in the interest of completing the project as originally contracted, these changes should be held aside for future, if any, consideration.

Final Documentation

When the punch list work has been completed, the general contractor submits to the architect the final application for payment. Before the architect approves final payment, the following documents must be completed and received by the owner:

1. Certificate of occupancy. The architect or code consultant can help obtain this for the owner.
2. Certificates of inspection for the following items:

   - Elevators
   - Fire protection
   - Mechanical
   - Electrical
   - Kitchen equipment
   - Public assembly

   The general contractor is responsible for coordinating this effort to its completion.
3. Sign-off of all punch list items by the architect and engineers.
4. Guarantees and warranties.
5. Certificates of insurance where required for products and completed operations.
6. Operating and maintenance manuals.
7. Spare parts and maintenance materials.
8. Keys and keying schedule.
9. Orientation of owner's personnel.
10. All documents of record on the project (shop drawings, equipment cut sheets, and so forth).
11. Record drawings ("as-builts") from appropriate subcontractors.

12. Evidence of compliance with all federal work programs, if applicable.
13. Evidence of payment and release of liens.

Before the owner can make a final payment to the general contractor, all outstanding liens must be released. The general contractor must receive the final release of lien from each of the subcontractors on the final contract amount, including all change orders and other revisions. After this, the general contractor submits the release of lien to the owner for all amounts paid by the owner, including general conditions and the general contractor's fees and insurance. The final application for payment can then be issued. The general contractor prepares and signs this standard document and submits it to the architect for signature. The fully executed document is sent to the owner, and, provided all final releases of lien are in order and other pertinent documents have been received, the owner can pay the final bill of the general contractor. The project is complete and, hopefully, a success.

PART 3

ACQUIRING EXISTING PROPERTIES

CHAPTER 12

EVALUATING THE INVESTMENT POTENTIAL OF OFFICE BUILDINGS

Stephen B. Siegel
Chubb Realty, Inc.

When evaluating the investment potential of an office building, the most common mistake is assuming that its current and future performance can be analyzed without regard to its environment. The financial viability of any office building is as dependent on national, regional, and local economic trends as it is on the size of its floor-plates, creditworthiness of its tenants, strength of its rent roll, or the amenities in the immediate area.

Therefore, when seeking new investment opportunities, the identification process begins with a broad-based, macro-trend analysis and continually narrows the field of prospective investments until a specific building is selected. Through a series of comparative analyses, it becomes a process of elimination ending with the most appropriate building for the chosen investment criteria.

It should be emphasized, however, that the investment criteria strongly influence the final set of office buildings selected and provide the focus of the analytical process. When choosing the criteria, the elements to consider fall into four major categories:

1. Economic environment.
2. Real estate market conditions.
3. Property characteristics.
4. Expected financial return and investment structure.

Regardless of the degree of formal analysis, the process of identifying potential acquisition targets requires considering these seven questions:

1. What are the long-term national economic trends?
2. How will different regional or metropolitan markets respond to these trends?
3. Which metropolitan areas offer the most opportunity to meet desired investment goals?
4. What are the current and expected future real estate environments for target metropolitan areas and their submarkets?
5. Which submarkets offer the best opportunity?
6. Which buildings within the target submarkets provide the greatest present and future potential?
7. What price should be paid?

INVESTMENT CRITERIA

Investment objectives play a pivotal role in determining the criteria for purchasing a property. The dollar amount, degree of risk, and desired rate of return provide the parameters of selection. The determining factors for an investment strategy can be divided into the following categories, which define the type and location of properties.

- *Expected return and investment structure.* Aside from the most obvious consideration—the amount one wishes to spend—the expectations of the investor regarding the type, timing, and rate of return per dollar invested, as well as the amount of risk and leverage that are acceptable, set criteria for the property selection process.

    Consideration should be given to the importance of receiving current income, appreciation potential, or a combination of both. Decisions need to be made about the level of risk that is acceptable and the corresponding rate of return. Similarly, the investment structure, or combination of debt and equity, also influences the investment decision. Equally important is the way in which the investor participates in a real estate investment—as a single owner, joint-venture partner, syndication, limited partnership, financing source, or some other form of involvement.

- *Property Characteristics.* Deciding to invest in an office building opens a whole set of questions regarding the characteristics that a potential investment should possess. For example, basic considerations include the size of the building, its physical condition, age or stage of development, desired occupancy, and preferred location (that is, central business district or suburban).

Other less obvious, but no less important, questions include the following:

1. Should the building make an architectural statement, or have a landmark status?
2. Is a single-occupancy building preferred?
3. What type of tenants are desired?
4. What are the preferred lease terms?
5. What other special attributes might be especially important to the property investment decision?

• *Real estate market.* The desired size, composition, and conditions of a real estate market should be part of the real estate investment decision. For example, if an investor has a particular knowledge of a given set or type of market, he would probably do best "sticking with what he knows." The type of property desired also affects the selection of market type or location, as does the expected rate of return.

• *Economic Environment.* The size of the metropolitan area, stability of the economic environment, and the rate of expected growth are each important to the investment decision. These can frequently be influenced by the type of property sought. The degree of market risk acceptable to the investor further limits the selection.

Putting all these components together results in a set of well-thought-out investment criteria against which various office buildings can then be measured.

LONG-TERM ECONOMIC TRENDS

Although national economic trends affect the performance of any real estate property, office buildings are especially sensitive to general business conditions. Job creation rates are a key determinant of demand for office space. The growth potential of a particular industry could affect a building's—or an entire market's—occupancy level. The expected rate of inflation is a factor in rental rates and appreciation. Interest rates, which greatly influence the amount of capital available to finance acquisitions, dictate the level of debt service, and thus potential current income from a property. Last but not least, commercial real estate has been, and will continue to be, a business-cycle-sensitive investment. These indicators provide points of reference for comparing the performance of buildings.

Careful consideration should be given to a wide variety of factors that influence the national economy:

- *Employment growth*. Will the economy create jobs at a faster or slower pace than in the past?
- *Industry trends*. Which industry groups will be expanding or contracting, and at what rate?
- *Population growth and migration patterns*. Will the nation's population grow more rapidly or at a slower pace in the future? How will this affect the working-age population?
- *Household formation*. Will the number and size of households increase or decrease, and at what rate?
- *Income and housing trends*. Will personal income growth outpace inflation? Will disposable income rise? Will the housing market enjoy strong growth or face weakening demand?
- *Interest rate movements*. What is the outlook for interest rates? Will they rise or fall? How far? How fast?
- *Rate of inflation*. Will inflation remain at current levels? What factors can change the rate and direction of inflation? Will the stagflation (high inflation coupled with declining economic growth) of the 1970s recur?

When constructing the most likely scenario for future economic conditions, current values of these variables should be compared to their past values to estimate the current stage of the business cycle and the direction and magnitude of changes to expect in the future. This process helps to determine if, and to what extent, changes in any of these variables affect the future strength of metropolitan or local markets—and individual buildings—in terms of prices, rents, supply, demand, profits, and rates of appreciation.

Furthermore, the expectations for the future economic climate in the nation affect the level of interest in real estate as an asset class, as opposed to other forms of investment. When the economic future appears bright, demand for real estate properties rises, causing competition and prices to increase. In contrast, if economic conditions seem to weaken, interest in real estate investment wanes, competition drops off, and prices stagnate or decline.

Opportunities abound in either scenario. However, as the 1980s amply demonstrated, success is easier to achieve in a period of rapid economic growth than during a period of slow economic growth. The 1990s are not expected to experience the economic boom of the 1980s. Therefore, the degree of success will be even more closely related to the investor's aptitude in identifying unique opportunities created by changing national economic trends and their influence on various markets throughout the country.

REGIONAL AND METROPOLITAN MARKETS' RESPONSES TO TRENDS

Regardless of whether all markets or specific ones are to be analyzed for potential investment opportunities, a comprehensive review of past, present, and future economic conditions is an integral part of determining investment potential. Comparing a particular market's historic and anticipated growth trends with those of the nation as a whole is an important step in analyzing a metropolitan market. A given market's expected reaction to projected national trends sets the tone for its future economic activity as well as for its attractiveness as an investment. This, in turn, provides the foundation for screening markets for economic conditions that match preselected investment criteria, and ultimately for developing an investment strategy in a particular market or markets.

The specific behavior of a given metropolitan area in relation to the nation provides insight into the probable future growth pattern for the market. Some metropolitan areas' economies tend to follow the nation's cycles, while others move in the opposite direction. For markets tracking national trends, the degree of volatility and timing of cyclical highs and lows may be equal to, less than, or greater than those of the nation. Understanding these similarities and differences helps to gauge the pattern and probable strength of future economic trends for a particular market.

In more specific terms, each metropolitan area's economy should be reviewed against its own and the nation's historic and projected economic patterns for a specific set of variables. The same basic elements that were reviewed for the national economy can form the basis for the metropolitan level analysis:

- *Population size and growth*. How large is the population base? How rapidly is it growing on a percentage and an absolute basis? How does its rate of growth compare to the national population growth rate? To its own historical rate of growth? What is the age distribution of the population? How is it changing?
- *Employment size and growth*. What is the size and rate of growth of the area's employment base? Is employment growing at a faster pace than that for the nation? Is the rate of employment growth increasing or decreasing compared with historic trends? How diversified is the employment base?
- *Industry trends*. What are the major industry groups? Which ones are growing or shrinking? Who are the major employers, what industry are they in, and how well are they doing? Do they dominate the employment market, or is there an even distribution of industry types and establishment sizes? What ancillary companies or industries service the major employers? How substantial are these? Are many industries expected to be strong performers in the future, or does the area contain numerous industries facing difficult or uncertain futures?
- *Household formation*. Is the rate of household formation greater than or less than in the past? How does this compare with the national trend?
- *Income trends*. Is personal income growth increasing? Is the area's median income above the national median? At what rate is it growing? Is disposable income—purchasing power—high or growing quickly?
- *Housing trends*. What are the type and quality of housing? What is its relative affordability? How is it changing? At what rate is the stock increasing?

FACTORS LEADING TO ACCURATE CATEGORIZATION OF METROPOLITAN AREAS

Analysis of economic characteristics, such as population size, employment and industry composition, and growth potential, allows grouping of metropolitan areas with common traits. Further analysis can then be limited only to those metropolitan areas meeting specific, predetermined investment criteria. Investors can thus begin to narrow the selection.

Numerous grouping schemes can be employed to complete this task. Perhaps the most straightforward is a broad-based, five-category process that places metropolitan areas into the following categories based on their current stage in the economic life cycle. Whether reviewing single or multiple metropolitan regions one should place them into one of these categories. Doing so facilitates comparison with other markets with similar behavior patterns and at comparable stages of the economic lifecycle.

• *High-growth emerging markets.* This group usually includes metropolitan areas that generally are either small to medium in size, such as Charlotte, North Carolina, or Louisville, Kentucky, or those that are relatively new as active office employment markets, such as Las Vegas, Nevada, or Riverside, California. Frequently, growth in the latter has been a relatively recent phenomenon related to a change in the local economy, such as becoming the recipient of "spill-over" growth from a nearby major metropolitan market (such as the way in which northern New Jersey benefits from a close association with New York City). These markets are prone to boom-bust cycles, especially if growth is from a single source, such as a rapidly growing industry. If such an industry should suddenly lose its momentum due to obsolescence, increased foreign competition, or other factors, the effects on the local economy could be devastating.

As a result, this group of markets can be high-risk, ventures as growth is often erratic and not always sustainable. High-growth areas are often sensitive to changing economic conditions, such as the fortunes of specific industries, population migration patterns, or growth management policies. What factors can change or impede growth in the future?

• *Strong, steady growth market.* Generally, markets offering strong, steady growth are medium to large and continue to diversify their economies. The population growth for these areas tends to be at or above the national growth rate and employment growth usually is supplied by several unrelated industry groups. Frequently, metropolitan areas that are evolving into, or have already become, regional business hubs fit into this category. Examples include Washington, D.C., Columbus, Ohio, and Atlanta, Georgia.

This type of market is generally less volatile because it is more insulated from the national business cycle. The diverse nature of its industry composition and sources of economic activity make it less sensitive to changes in a single industry. Although this type of market does not typically achieve rapid growth rates, it often produces a sustainable level of continued economic growth over relatively long time periods.

• *Slow, stable growth market.* Many of the nation's larger metropolitan areas fall into this category. Having already established a well-diversified economic base, these markets generally have distinct multiple sources of continuing economic development. Examples could include Chicago and San Francisco. Although their growth rates may be slower than the nation's, the absolute increase from an already large base provides a stable, albeit unspectacular, rise in economic activity.

• *Declining or stagnant market.* Metropolitan areas that face the problems of declining population and stagnant or eroding employment typically are those areas that became victims of changing times. Several of the nation's older industrial-based metropolitan areas have gone through long periods of decline for many reasons, as the national economy has increasingly focused on service industries.

It should be noted that some so-called Rust Belt markets, such as Cleveland, Ohio, have displayed remarkable economic resiliency, while others have been less successful in diversifying and rejuvenating their economies.

• *Re-emerging or turnaround markets.* Metropolitan markets regaining lost momentum can be classified as re-emerging or turnaround markets. Prime examples are many of the metropolitan areas located in the Midwest or in the Oil Patch, including Cincinnati, Dallas, and Houston.

These markets once had economies that grew quickly before falling into a period of decline as their respective major industries lost their competitiveness. When economic trends change or an area replaces stagnating industries with new ones, the market begins to reverse its declining trend.

The above method also can be implemented in the dissection and review of each distinct market contained in a given metropolitan area. This process offers a blueprint for the basic analysis of the economic viability of a market and its components regardless of the geographic level of aggregation.

MARKET AREAS OFFERING THE BEST OPPORTUNITY TO MEET DESIRED INVESTMENT GOALS

One of the most important elements in matching properties with pre-determined investment criteria is knowing where to look for them. The size and quality of property sought often dictates the type of markets to examine. For example, if an investment goal includes purchasing a 1 million-square-foot "trophy" building, the type of market to be analyzed would not include smaller cities in the high-growth emerging market category, or even the suburban markets of many of the larger metropolitan areas. Neither the level of business activity nor the rents in these markets is sufficient to support this size of project. In contrast, if the investment objective is to purchase a high-quality building one-tenth as large, New York would be an unlikely target, as such properties are mostly peripheral to the central business areas and appeal almost exclusively to small, price-driven tenants.

Therefore, understanding the characteristics of a particular market or group of markets is vital to determining whether there is a match to the investment criteria. For each of the five market categories, the appropriate investment strategies differ, as specific investment opportunities are more readily available in one market group than in another.

For example, emerging markets may provide opportunities for purchasing an office building at an attractive price (before the investing herd has discovered the market) and offer rapid appreciation potential. On the other hand, such a market can pose an unacceptably high degree of investment risk for certain types of investors. Because this category of market usually does not have a long-term track record and because rapid economic growth is not sustainable indefinitely, the risk of investing is generally much higher than in more established markets. Furthermore, because the range of product type—size, quality, and type of tenancy—may be somewhat limited as well, the available properties in such a market may not meet the criteria of more conservative investors.

A market offering strong, steady growth poses less risk to an investor. Its future economic performance and resultant demand for office space can usually be estimated with greater certainty, but, in return, the potential for appreciation will probably be constricted, reflecting this lower level of risk. Furthermore, demand for properties of this type is generally greater than in more risky emerging markets.

This will certainly affect the availability and the prices of properties located there. However, the generally wide range of property types available offer the opportunity to satisfy several different investment strategies.

Slow, stable, growth-oriented markets provide a safe haven for an investor. However, the goal of such an investment is generally not as much a high rate of return as it is preservation of capital with some current income. Similar to a market growing at a steady pace, the future economic performance can be estimated with greater probability than for a smaller, emerging market. It is important to distinguish between two possible future scenarios for these markets: they can continue to grow at a stable rate, or they might slowly slip into decline or stagnation. Market trends must be examined carefully to ensure that a consistent level of growth will be maintained. Properties in stable markets generally attract investors interested in moderate appreciation potential and a steady stream of income at rates competitive with alternative fixed-income investments.

Markets that are in a period of decline or have stagnant economies offer special challenges. These markets are probably best left to sophisticated investors who are willing to accept the higher degree of risk inherent therein. Even in this type of market, investment potential does exist. For example, properties located here frequently wind up in the "distressed" real estate category, requiring specific expertise in rehabilitation or "work-outs." These present opportunities to improve a property's performance through physical changes, debt restructuring, rent roll increases, or other measures, which could result in a significant profit. On the other hand, this type of investment requires knowledge, experience, and usually hands-on management. Therefore, investing in declining or stagnant markets is not for everyone.

Re-emerging or turnaround markets also offer unique opportunities. Investment in this type of market requires careful monitoring and understanding of the economic environment and a good sense of timing. Even though properties can be bought for what may seem like a bargain price compared to replacement cost, investing in this type of market also carries risks, which are high, especially if the economic recovery is short-lived. Financing may be difficult—or at least more expensive—to find, and the rewards are usually not immediate. An investment in turnaround markets requires patience, creativity, and some luck.

Each market type offers different degrees of risk and reward and is therefore attractive to different groups of investors. Regardless of which market type meets the chosen investment criteria, a complete understanding of the economic environment and the future direction of the specific market are requisite for selecting an office building.

CURRENT AND EXPECTED REAL ESTATE ENVIRONMENTS FOR TARGET METROPOLITAN AREAS AND THEIR SUBMARKETS

Each metropolitan area possesses unique real estate characteristics, and local market conditions are most strongly affected by area-specific events. However, certain measures of activity and elements of composition are nearly universal. These commonalities provide a way to identify the underlying determinants of supply and demand. Furthermore, they can be used either to assess the current and probable future health of a given metropolitan area's submarkets, or to compare real estate conditions of multiple markets.

The method of analyzing a real estate market begins with a review of the entire metropolitan area, which is then replicated through successive levels of disaggregation, from the submarket to a specific building. The composition of a real estate market and the level of activity that is generated usually can be measured by analyzing local trends with the following criteria:

- Inventory.
- Vacancy rates.
- Absorption.
- Leasing activity.
- Rental rates.
- Construction activity.
- External factors.

Through the review of this set of variables for each market and submarket, a detailed history documents the direction, rate, and orderliness of real estate development over time and across geography.

Although history can be an important guide in any investment endeavor, it does not always provide a complete picture because individual markets and submarkets are constantly evolving. An understanding of the changing variables that create, alter, or limit the supply and demand for office space is therefore essential. Both the general market conditions and the interaction of the submarkets in the metropolitan area should be reconnoitered. This narrows the selection to specific submarkets offering the buildings most likely to meet the predetermined investment criteria. These questions should be answered for each metropolitan area under review:

• *What are the size, composition, and geographic distribution of the office building inventory?* Real estate market analysis begins with a description and quantification of the inventory, or total stock of office buildings, of a market. Though it is important to know the square footage and number of office buildings in the total market, equally important is classifying the amount of office space by age, class of building, and geographic dispersion. The number and average size of buildings provide further understanding of the character and demand for different product types within each submarket.

This information is useful in eliminating markets that do not meet investment criteria. For instance, some markets have too small an inventory base or average building size. Similarly, if a central business district is the desired location, this analysis could eliminate markets that do not have one. It could also help identify markets with an aging building stock, which could indicate opportunities for replacement construction or renovation projects.

• *What has the trend been for vacancy rates?* Data should be gathered for each submarket by class of building for both sublease space and space being marketed directly by a landlord. The level, behavior, and interaction of vacancy rates can explain a great deal about the overall health of a market, as well as the changing geographic and building quality preferences of its tenants. Through the careful analysis of vacancy rate trends, current or potential excesses or shortages can be identified. For example, if vacancy rates are rising, one must determine the cause of the increase. Perhaps construction activity has temporarily outpaced a still healthy demand for space, which could be a positive sign. However, tenants could be consolidating or relocating to other markets which is usually negative. Worse yet, construction activity may be increasing at the same time that demand is declining. If so, this is a market to avoid!

Similarly, reviewing sublease vacancy rates could show that subleasing might negatively influence a market's rental rates or slow leasing of buildings under construction or recently completed, by providing competitive space at more attractive rates. Such an exercise could also show that much more space is available in the market than a vacancy rate that measures direct availabilities (as many publicly available reports do), otherwise indicates. Market intelligence could thus prevent the serious mistake of constructing an unneeded office building or purchasing a property for more than its real value.

A comparison of vacancy rates in class A properties (highest quality, well-located properties) and in class B properties (older buildings or those in less desirable locations) could reveal much about a market. Class A vacancy rates could be dropping at the expense of class B space, as has recently been common. The fall in class A vacancies could result from tenants upgrading their space at attractive prices, or it could be evidence of permanently changing space needs of the tenant base. It does not, however, indicate that the occupancy level is growing at a healthy rate for the market. On the contrary, it is a sign of imbalance, usually created by an oversupply of class A space, which causes rents to stagnate or decline, and landlord concessions (for example, monetary contributions toward capital improvements to tenant spaces or waiver of rental payments for specified periods of time) to become generous, encouraging class B tenants to occupy class A space at bargain prices. As a result, projects experience diminishing economic vitality—and value.

By identifying these trends, significant opportunities could be uncovered. For example, perhaps the tenant base is shifting to higher quality space. If this is the case, as the class A vacancy rate drops, activity could move to other markets where higher quality space is more readily available or could be more easily or economically constructed, especially if site availability or strict growth control policies limit continued development. An alternative is additional construction of high-quality space. The market could also be a candidate for renovation projects, which not only are cost-effective, but necessary to remain competitive and retain market value. Furthermore, if site availability or growth control were factors limiting new construction, total rehabilitation (upgrading of systems) or partial renovation of existing properties becomes even more appealing, especially in a market retaining its popularity as a business location. Or, if renovation is not a feasible alternative, class B buildings could become prime targets for sales, alternative uses, or replacement construction.

Another consideration for space availability is the number of properties that can accomodate a range of tenant space requirements, or that possess unique features, such as large, unobstructed floor space. A market could have a rising vacancy rate, but relatively few large blocks of available space, or an insufficient amount of a particular type of space. Therefore, almost regardless of vacancy rate trends, this situation could indicate a new construction opportunity or a reason to purchase a building that could satisfy this rising demand.

• *How strong has leasing activity been, and what portion has resulted in absorption?* First, a word of caution: Do not confuse leasing activity with absorption. Leasing activity is defined as the total square footage of new leasing transactions completed in the market, while absorption is the net increase or decrease in the amount of occupied space. Leasing activity reflects tenant movement among buildings in a market, and absorption measures the growth or contraction in realized demand for office space.

Leasing activity provides a measure of market velocity—that is, the rate at which tenants move among buildings. Analysis of leasing activity provides insight into the size and type of tenant active in the market, as well as an estimate of the number of transactions that can be expected during a given time period. This information is extremely useful for estimating the length of a lease-up program, the probable size distribution of tenants, and which industry groups are likely to be active in the market. Reviewing this information over time provides an indication of what changes are occurring in the market in terms of tenants' size, preferences, rate of activity, and willingness to relocate to another building or another submarket. This information is vital in evaluating the potential of a particular building to attract the type of tenants currently active in the market as well as for estimating a leasing schedule.

Absorption measures the change in office space occupied. Review of absorption trends should include a comparative analysis across submarkets and by class of building. Absorption also should be reviewed in relation to the price and availability of supply. This will highlight tenants' locational preferences as well as possible imbalances among cost, supply, and demand for office space.

One should identify which submarkets are experiencing a steady or rising level of absorption and which submarkets have stagnant or declining occupancy levels, as well as look for submarkets showing signs of recovery—for example, slowing rates of negative absorption, or slightly positive absorption following a long period of negative absorption. One should also investigate the reasons for these trends and answer several questions: For submarkets with rising occupancy, is the tenant base expanding? Are new businesses locating there? Why? Will it continue? In relation to other submarkets, is the space more suitable to the tenants, is it more cost-effective, is it in a better location, or is it simply more readily available than in other areas?

If the strong absorption is merely a spillover from a neighboring submarket that is temporarily experiencing tight supply conditions, then it is unlikely that the trend will continue. However, the neighboring submarket may have depleted its buildable space, experienced a sharp rise in the cost of land acquisition or building construction, lost its appeal as an office center, or be facing other growth-limiting factors. If so, this spillover trend will probably continue. In this case, the market should be reviewed for opportunities to purchase an existing office building or to construct a new one.

For markets with stagnant or declining occupancies, is business contracting; are businesses moving out by choice or by necessity? Is the supply of space no longer suitable for the tenant base? Has the rent become too expensive, the building stock aged, or the submarket lost its economic viability? Or is there just not enough space to meet current demand? If the last choice is the reason, then this may be an ideal time to buy or construct a building. On the other hand, if any of the earlier factors are the reason for declining or stagnant absorption, one might find opportunities for niche purchases or renovations.

A similar analysis should be conducted by class of space. For example, class A space may show strong absorption at the expense of class B space either because tenant preferences are changing or because class A space is offered at rents not significantly greater than class B rents. This again could be the result of either the oversupply or the aging of class A space. In contrast, class B space could show strong absorption, while class A space is stagnating. In this case, there could be a scarcity of class A space but a strong need to be in that submarket, or the tenant base may not need class A space and be unwilling to pay for it. The economic strength of the tenants who tend to occupy one particular class of space also affects the rate of absorption by altering the demand for additional office space, or even the need for the amount already occupied. Careful monitoring would be advised before deciding to buy or build here.

• *How have rental rates performed?* The level of rental rates in a market contribute significantly to the value of its properties. Therefore, the potential investor should carefully review the range of rates, the spread between class A and class B rents, geographic differences, and the direction of change in rental rates. Equally important are trends in concession packages.

Although the range of rents available closely correlates with the array of office space available, the spread between class A rents and class B rents provides an indication of the degree of competition in a market. The absence of a significant difference between the two rental ranges usually means that either no substantial difference exists between properties classified as class A and class B, that supply is exceeding demand for class A space, or, though less likely, a tight market exists for class B space, causing rents to drop in an effort to stimulate occupancy.

Comparing rents for similar property types in different submarkets is also useful, as it identifies current and future competition for any submarket under review. Although rents generally reflect differences in acquisition and construction costs between markets, this analysis will also quantify the premium that tenants are willing to pay for similar space in an area that is either better-located or more prestigious.

The most important consideration in evaluating rental rates is the difference between actual *contract* rents and proforma, or *asking,* rents. This difference could make or break the economic feasibility of a project. Concession packages also have significant influence on the effective rent received for office space. Depending on how generous these are, the economic feasibility of a purchase or the construction of a new project could be seriously impaired. A thorough knowledge and understanding of these factors is essential in evaluating the potential income that can be generated in a specific market.

The growth in rental rates over time provides a good indication of the profitability and value increase of properties. An investor must consider whether rents have been increasing, decreasing, or stagnating; their rates relative to the rate of inflation; and their likely direction. Because projecting future rental streams is essential to placing a value on a property, realistic estimates are needed for the direction and rate of change of a market's rents.

• *What are the trends in office building construction activity?* The amount of annual addition to the stock of office buildings is an important indicator of the growth of a market. The geographic dispersion of construction activity provides insight into the direction of economic growth, and the quality of new buildings can frequently indicate the preferences of the tenant base. An indication of the current and future strength of a market and its submarkets can be derived from reviewing the location, type, size, quality, rent structure, and leasing activity for buildings under construction or recently completed. The potential investor needs answers to the following questions:

1. Where has most of the construction activity occurred? Why?
2. Has the activity remained in well-established business centers, or are new submarkets emerging that will compete for tenants?
3. If so, what advantages does the emerging market offer to make it attractive?
4. Similarly, what are the size, quality, and amenities of projects under construction?
5. How do these compare to the characteristics of existing buildings?
6. If the new construction is different from existing buildings (for example, with higher quality, larger size, or more amenities), is the market in transition to a higher profile market, or is there only limited demand for these new projects?
7. Are tenants willing to pay for the new construction, or are these projects leased at discount rates?
8. How quickly have these projects been leased?
9. How have the projects affected the market?
10. Are they simply taking tenants from other buildings, or are they accommodating actual needs of an expanding business base?
11. Finally, how much new construction is expected to be completed annually over the next several years, and how will it affect market vacancies and rental rates?

Compare the expected annual addition in supply to estimates of future demand (based upon projections of employment growth) to gauge the direction of future market conditions. The amount of expected new construction may be more than the market really needs. If so, market conditions can be expected to become more competitive, and rents will probably be adversely affected. If not, market conditions could tighten, placing upward pressure on rental rates.

These situations point to several opportunities. First, if new construction is not sufficient to meet future demand, obviously there exists an opportunity to construct a new building. On the other hand, the higher rents of new construction could create the opportunity to purchase and upgrade an older existing building, especially in traditional high-demand markets. The results would be comparable space at a lower rent in a desirable location.

• *What external factors will influence the future growth and development of submarkets in the metropolitan area?* This is a very important consideration when evaluating the future potential of various submarkets in a particular area. For example, is residential development moving away from the traditional nodes of business activity and creating the need for new employment centers? Are growth management policies redirecting future commercial activity back to (or away from) the CBDs, or limiting the type or supply of space in a particular area? Will impact fees (that is, charges levied on developers by local governments to finance community enhancements in return for permission to construct new projects) significantly raise the cost of new construction? Have new infrastructure plans opened the development potential of new geographic areas?

All these, as well as numerous other external factors, have a significant effect on the future development pattern of a market area. For example, many believe that recent trends in limiting the amount of new construction allowed in a market will increase the attractiveness of renovating existing buildings in many markets, as well as encourage a more stable balance between supply and demand. This, in turn, should have a positive effect on rents and values.

Once the answers to these questions are known, an analysis can be conducted to determine whether the existing and anticipated supply of office space will meet the needs of the business community. This analysis should compare the future demand, derived by analyzing the area's economic and business trends, to the current and future composition and conditions in the real estate market. Through this process, opportunities to fill gaps—unmet or insufficiently met space requirements—can be identified.

When assessing the future space needs in any market, it becomes important to look at the type of tenants, how their needs are changing, and how this will affect the current or future supply of space. In other words, has the market recognized the gap? If not, which type of office space will encounter the greatest imbalance between supply and demand? Where within the metropolitan area will this gap be widest?

Identifying and capitalizing on these unmet office space needs in a market creates the basis for a successful—and profitable—real estate investment. The analysis of a market does not only explain the relative balance between supply and demand in a given market. Through careful evaluation, key gaps, or mismatches between supply and demand, can be identified. Buildings that can fill these voids are the ones that will be successful.

SUBMARKETS WITH THE BEST OPPORTUNITIES

Market characteristics, composition, and prevailing conditions, combined with expectations for the future economic environment, create specific submarket opportunities. As already illustrated, not every submarket is suitable for every type of office building. Similarly, a single submarket has needs for different types of office buildings at different stages of its lifecycle. For example, a market that has traditionally housed back-office centers may, in its next stage of growth, be primed for a first-class front-office building. Alternatively, a large high-profile office center may have reached its buildable limits, and renovation of existing buildings can become a profitable venture. Evidence of these emerging needs is generally supported by the changes in the local market characteristics and statistics.

Therefore, based upon the analysis of various submarkets in a metropolitan area, the task of the investor is to match the appropriate type of office building to the needs of different submarkets, or, conversely, to identify the submarket or submarkets that present the best opportunity for a particular type of office building investment. The matrix in Exhibit 12–1 presents several scenarios of market characteristics and changing conditions along with the type of office building investment opportunities that may be indicated.

BUILDINGS IN THE TARGET SUBMARKETS PROVIDING THE GREATEST POTENTIAL

Once the submarket and office building type have been determined, a list of comparable buildings can be developed. This process hones the analysis to the micro-level, focusing on a selected group of buildings

EXHIBIT 12–1

Comparison of Various Investment Opportunities Based on Market Conditions

	Renovate	*Existing class A building*
Inventory	Any size base; high percentage of class B or older class A buildings	Medium to large base; at least 50% class A
Vacancy	Rising class B; steady or declining class A	Low to moderate level; steady or declining class A
Lease activity	High percentage of small- to medium-sized transactions	Wide range of size for non-high-profile tenants
Absorption	Steady or rising class A; declining class B	High level of class A absorption
Rental rates	Wide spread between class A and class B	Rising class A rentals
Construction activity	Low to moderate level	Low level
External factors	Growth control; few buildable sites	Few buildable sites; expanding economy

in the market. Within this peer group, intensive analysis of individual properties' performance will identify the building or buildings that present the most potential as investment vehicles.

Comparisons of the buildings' competitive and operational factors should be made. Consideration should be given to such factors as location, physical condition, the building's stature in the marketplace, occupancy level, types of tenants, history of turnover, rent levels, and management efficiency, in order to estimate the market viability and the financial health of each building. Through this analysis, their strengths and weaknesses can be identified. This process leads to the selection of the single building that either is in the best competitive condition or can benefit the most from the investor's particular real estate expertise (for example, turning around distressed properties, upgrading and releasing existing buildings, conversion to alternate uses, and so forth).

EXHIBIT 12–1 (continued)

Investment-grade bldg.	New construction
Medium to large base; high percentage of class A	Any size base; no class preference
Low to moderate level for class A; steady or declining class A	Low or declining level of class A
High percentage of high-profile tenants and large space needs	Active; major users; strong activity
Steady or rising level of class A	Steady or rising level of class A
Strong class A rentals on upward trend	Strong class A rentals on upward trend
Low to moderate level	Low level
Growth control; increase in high-profile firms	Expanding economy; increase in high-profile firms

To determine which buildings have the greatest comparative advantage, an audit of several factors should be conducted. For example, one of the first points to consider is the building's relative location within the marketplace. Which buildings offer the easiest access to transportation, or to the center of business activity? Another important consideration is how the occupancy level compares to other buildings. Which buildings have a history of high tenant turnover? Why? What type of tenants occupy the buildings? How is this changing? Is the architectural style appealing? Is the building design functional for the type of tenants in the market? What is the physical condition of the various buildings; have they been kept in good repair? How efficient is the management of the building? How do rental rates compare to those for other similar buildings? The answers to these questions depend largely on the desired investment type. For example, a decision to purchase an existing class A building would result in different choices depending on whether an investor was looking for a distressed property or a well-managed building with a stable long-term occupancy.

The characteristics of a desirable distressed property might include a good location, strong architectural appeal, and basic design functionality, but below-market occupancy and rents. This type of building may have become a victim of high turnover or might have lost market competitiveness—thus commanding lower rentals—because of lax or inexperienced management. And with lower income, capital improvements and repairs probably have been neglected. This may create an opportunity to purchase a building that offers good to excellent growth potential at an attractive price. In contrast, if a well-maintained building with a stable long-term occupancy was the investment goal, then different considerations would be important.

Whether the economic viability of the building can be improved by the investor is the point to consider about a distressed building. This requires analysis of the type, extent, and cost of a modernization program, which could include new electrical, mechanical, and life safety systems; asbestos removal; window replacement; renovation of public areas; new elevators; and a host of other improvements. How much would this improve the value of the building? Could this lead to an upgrading of the type of tenant, an increase in the occupancy level, or both—perhaps through an aggressive marketing program? Would these changes increase rental income enough to justify the expense of the modernization program?

Regardless of the type of building sought by an investor, the goal is still to identify those that will benefit from changing economic and real estate conditions as well as from the unique set of talents that the investor brings to a project. This combination should further enhance the value—and the profitability—beyond the price.

PRICE

Once a specific property in a particular submarket has been matched to the investment criteria, the investor must consider what a reasonable price for the property would be. The first task is to determine the price at which the projected rate of return is adequate for the level of risk involved.

Several methods can be used to estimate a fair price for an office building. One of the most common methods of measuring value is the capitalization rate, or *cap rate,* which is an indication of the current yield. The cap rate is calculated by dividing net operating income by the purchase price. The resulting percentage is a tool for comparing similar investments on a full equity basis (prior to considering debt service).

Turning the cap rate formula around, an investor who has established a target cap rate (or desired current yield) can readily divide the net operating income by the cap rate to determine the price that should be paid for a property.

Another approach involves comparing recent sales of similar buildings. When using this method, buildings should be compared on the basis of location, size, age, style, amenities, physical condition, and tenancy. After adjusting for differences in these variables and for differences in financing, a comparison of purchase price should be conducted on a per-square-foot basis.

The replacement cost method also provides a relatively easy way to calculate a point of comparison when evaluating the price for an existing building. This method entails comparing the purchase price (per square foot) to acquire a building to what it would cost to acquire the site and build it from scratch. In general, the price that an investor is willing to pay for an existing property should not exceed 75 percent of new construction prices. However, certain exceptions apply. For example, high occupancy by quality tenants, location, rents at or above market levels for long-term leases, or favorable financing terms could justify paying more for a building because of the lower level of risk involved.

A rate of return can be calculated by assessing the debt structure, potential growth in earnings, and estimated future sale price at the end of the holding period. This method allows the investor to consider planned capital improvements, higher occupancy, creative financing structures, and better lease rates, among other factors. It also allows for the estimation of performance under different market and economic scenarios and therefore various levels of risk. This provides a more complete picture of the investment potential of a building with one caveat: The calculations are only as good as the projections.

Each method of calculating a purchase price should be evaluated in relation to the amount of leverage or debt to be used to finance the acquisition. A highly leveraged property provides the greatest potential for capital appreciation, and therefore a higher expected return. However, this high-growth strategy also provides the highest risk and the least amount of current income. Conversely, the most conservative investor would reduce the risk by applying no leverage at all. With an all-equity purchase, the current income will be greater, but the potential for capital appreciation is curtailed.

In the end, evaluating the investment potential of an office building entails multiple levels of micro- and macro-analysis, which incorporates review of general economic conditions as well as financial returns and investment structure. Certainly, investors have been able to profit from investments in office buildings without such thorough and detailed analysis; such an investor usually benefits from a healthy dose of good fortune and a broadly rising market. Prudent investors, however, do not rely solely on luck and timing for their success; The risk is too great if the market sours unexpectedly.

Through painstaking research and financial evaluation, compelling investment opportunities in office buildings can be realized almost regardless of the stage in a market's economic cycle. For investors who perform such analysis the financial rewards can indeed be great.

CHAPTER 13

FINANCING THE ACQUISITION

Kevin F. Haggarty
Cushman & Wakefield, Inc.
Scott C. Liebman
Cushman & Wakefield, Inc.

Real estate, because of the sheer magnitude of a typical investment, is perhaps more than any other investment dependent upon financing. Historically, the availability of leverage allowed real estate investors to optimally deploy their available equity capital to acquire multiple properties. Obviously, a key part of the decision in purchasing a real estate investment is how to finance the acquisition. In this chapter we will focus on financing the acquisition of real estate and, in doing so, expand the definition of financing to incorporate equity, since in today's markets, capital has taken on a variety of different meanings. Depending upon the investor and the risk/reward criteria, the financing possibilities range from all equity to as much debt as can be obtained.

We will focus first on the ramifications of using debt to provide leverage, and then cover alternate financing structures, underwriting issues, capital sources, and the financing process. We intend to provide an overview of the implications of financing a real estate acquisition with various types of capital. The capital markets are always evolving and the specific structures discussed here may become dated or obsolete. However, the underlying principles apply to whatever financing structure is employed.

An abbreviated glossary is provided at the conclusion of this chapter for terms that may not be familiar to the reader.

The concept behind debt financing is to maximize the deployment of capital for both the equity investor and the lenders. Depending upon the characteristics of a particular transaction, different capital structures of debt and equity should be utilized to maximize the owners' leverage and minimize their risk. One key to creating the optimal capital structure is to understand the ramifications of leverage. Essentially, leverage is the effect on financial cash flows provided by debt; typically the greater the amount of debt, the higher the equity investor's returns. This is true whenever the leverage is positive — that is, the rate of return on the debt is lower than the overall rate of return on the total investment. In these situations, the equity receives a higher return, since it is taking a greater share of the overall return because the lender is receiving less. For example, consider a transaction with an all-cash return of 14 percent. If financing can be structured at a 10 percent interest rate for 75 percent of the value of the transaction, the remaining 25 percent of the equity investment will benefit from and achieve a higher level of return because of the positive spread between the financing return and the overall return. However, when the debt costs more than the equity, it is known as negative leverage, since the use of debt actually lowers the equity investors' return.

Before one can understand the concept of leverage and how it should be properly utilized, it is necessary to review the risk/reward spectrum. The classic risk/reward spectrum is simply as follows: the higher the risk, the higher the potential reward. Exhibit 13–1 provides an example of a risk/reward spectrum using real estate as the prime example. Leverage actually alters the risk/reward spectrum by lowering the equity investors' risk profile. Although this seems counterintuitive at first, since highly leveraged transactions are typically the most risky investments, leverage reduces the amount of equity invested and, therefore, maximizes the return on equity. In reality,

EXHIBIT 13–1
Sample Risk/Reward Spectrum

Low risk/ low return	Low-medium-risk/return	Medium risk/ return	Medium-high-risk/return	High risk/ high return
Treasury bonds	Net leased property (high-credit tenant)	All-cash investment	Leveraged renovation of real estate	Real estate development

what leverage does is shift the risk from the equity to the debt, since the lenders are making a proportionally larger investment in the transaction. Leverage provides the equity investor with the mechanism for reducing capital investment and thereby lowers risk level.

The key to determining the proper amount of leverage is to understand the investors' criteria. Some large institutional investors prefer all-equity investments that are, in theory, the least risky form of investment, because, as long as the property's value does not completely collapse, the investors will not lose their investment. Investors who leverage their investments do so in order to increase their returns and to maximize the deployment of their equity capital. Unfortunately, in the event of a problem with the property's cash flow, the leveraged investor could be forced to give a property back to the lender if unable to meet the debt service. This is the double-edged sword of leverage. Properly utilized, it can be extraordinarily successful, but if too much leverage is used and the property's cash flow is insufficient to support the debt service, the equity investor could wind up losing all of its investment.

Properly structuring the financing of a real estate acquisition requires that the investor assess all of the key factors, including (1) the investors' risk/reward profile; (2) the investors' investment strategy; (3) the properties' cash flow characteristics; and (4) the capital markets. Each of these factors must be included into the capital equation in order to structure a financing that achieves the investors' goals.

The process outlined above—detailing the factors that must be incorporated into a financing transaction—can be partially defined by using the term *underwriting*. Underwriting is a term that is used in many different contexts, but, in this chapter, it will cover the analysis of financing a transaction from both the borrowers' and lenders' points of view. Prominent parts of underwriting a transaction include the financial analysis of the property, developing an understanding of the specific and national real estate markets and economy, and defining the borrowers' profile.

Once a borrower has completed his underwriting analysis, a lender must then be found who is willing to finance the property. The capital markets are truly global in today's environment, so a wide variety of lenders must be explored. Potential lenders include insurance companies, commercial banks, pension funds, savings and loan associations, foreign investors, and other capital sources. Obviously, the lenders contacted for a particular financing will vary, depending upon the transaction type, size, location, and borrower. Later in this chapter, when specific transaction structures are discussed, the lender profiles will be outlined in more detail.

The marketing of a financing is a process with many moving parts. Once the first section—underwriting—has been completed, the actual marketing of the financing takes place with either the borrower or its agent contacting the appropriate lending institutions. During this process, a lender will be selected who will have offered the most attractive terms, and the borrower and lender will commence negotiations. The documentation required varies in type and complexity and is dependent upon a number of factors, ranging from the financing structure sought to local requirements or to lenders' particular standards.

EQUITY VERSUS DEBT

How much equity? How much debt? Those questions are difficult to answer, and the answers reflect myriad factors. Leaving an investor's risk/reward profile out of the equation for the moment—since each investor is different—brings the question down to the particular property. Is it fully leased? Does it require significant capital improvements? Are leases turning over in the near future? What is the condition of the local market? Does the property have a weak or strong major tenant? These are among the many issues that must be incorporated into the debt/equity equation. The dilemma facing an investor is what level of equity they should commit to the property. Ideally, the amount of equity is the minimum amount necessary to safely support the financing while satisfying the investor's risk/reward requirements. Any equity above that level merely lessens the investor's overall return and increases his level of risk. Depending upon the investor and market conditions, the debt/equity mix could range from all equity to almost all debt.

The proper debt-to-equity ratio cannot be defined here; it varies in every instance and with every investor. However, as a basic rule, the greater the downside risk, the more equity required to support the debt. For example, compare two buildings—one fully leased to credit tenants with little lease turnover during the next 10 years, and a second property that is 50 percent leased and requires significant capital improvements over a several-year period, in addition to lease-up costs. In the first instance, an investor will only need enough equity to provide a cushion for the debt. However, in the second building, the investor must contribute sufficient equity to support the cost of bringing the building to a fully leased and renovated state. Whether this equity is contributed at the time of purchase and debt is used to fund the lease-up, or if the equity contributions are split between the initial acquisition and during lease-up, it is clear that a greater amount of equity is required than in a fully leased, stable property.

For the sake of simplicity, going forward we will assume that the investor will try to maximize its leverage and minimize its equity contribution. Although this ignores some basic risk/reward parameters, it provides a framework for discussing the debt financing techniques available to finance the acquisition of a property.

FINANCING METHODS

Fixed- versus Floating-Rate Financing

The growth in size and sophistication of the capital markets has provided real estate owners with a wider variety of debt-financing structures. Probably the most significant change has been the opportunity to use floating-rate financing for more than just construction loans. Historically, real estate owners financed their acquisitions with fixed-rate financing, often with amortization provisions. Now, however, owners can take advantage of the capital markets and utilize floating-rate financings, which fluctuate at a pre-defined spread over a base index during the permanent loan term as well as the construction loan term. Floating-rate financing allows the investor to take advantage of a declining interest rate environment while obtaining immediate financing. Conversely, real estate owners are subject to the risk of higher interest rates if rates move upward. Fortunately, interest rate swings can be mitigated through the use of hedging products such as interest rate swaps, caps, and collars, all of which will be discussed later in more detail.

What is important to recognize is that owners are no longer locked into one or two types of financing. They are now able to utilize capital market financing techniques, much as a multinational corporation does.

Bridge Financing

Bridge financing, also known as acquisition financing, is temporary financing utilized either to acquire a property before the placement of permanent financing or to cover the period when substantial improvements will be made to the property and its cash flow. Typically, bridge financings are utilized as stopgaps until the property's cash flow has been stabilized and the property can be refinanced with a permanent loan.

Bridge financing is similar to construction financing (not discussed here, since the purpose of this chapter is to cover acquisitions) in that it is usually priced with floating rates and is typically recourse (at least to some extent) to the borrower. Floating rates were discussed earlier and defined as interest rates that "float" over a base index. In today's market, lenders are increasingly pricing their loans at a spread over LIBOR (London InterBank Offered Rate), but using the prime rate or some other rate as a base is not unusual. The spread over the base index is variable, depending upon the strength of the borrower and the attractiveness of the real estate asset, because the loans are typically guaranteed to some extent by the borrower. As a result, to the extent that a borrower has strong credit, he or she will be able to borrow "bridge" funds at a more attractive rate than a weaker-credit investor.

Bridge lenders are generally commercial banks or credit companies because they procure their primary capital sources at a floating rate. Savings and loans were once active bridge lenders, but the current state of the industry has, for the most part, eliminated them from any type of real estate lending.

Key factors that bridge lenders consider are the quality of the real estate, realism of the projections, ability of the borrower to deliver the performance promised in the projections, and the financial strength of the borrower. Good-quality real estate always goes a long way in making lenders more comfortable with a loan, but they must also be convinced of the reasonableness of the projections and accept the downside risk. Furthermore, the borrower's ability to complete a renovation, lease a property, and create the projected cash flow is a critical factor in the equation. Finally, as downside protection, the lenders look to the borrower's financial strength to ensure that if something goes wrong they can get their loan principal back from the property and other assets of the borrower.

Some bridge lenders seek to participate in the potential returns of the transaction to compensate for the higher level of risk entailed in the financing. For example, the lender may agree to fund the transaction in return for a percentage of the profits resulting from the spread between the ultimate permanent refinancing or sale proceeds and the

EXHIBIT 13–2
Sample Property Acquisition Figures

Purchase price	$50,000,000
Equity	10,000,000
Acquisition bridge financing	$40,000,000
Renovation and	
lease-up costs	7,500,000
Interest carry	2,500,000
Total bridge financing	$50,000,000

initial bridge financing. In effect, the lender becomes an equity partner in return for funding the transaction.

The debt service on bridge financings can be structured in a variety of different ways, depending upon the property's cash flow. Unlike a construction loan, in which cash flow is low until lease-up, a property acquired with a bridge loan may generate significant amounts of cash. As a result, bridge loans are often structured with a pay-and-accrue formula, in which the lender takes available cash flow as partial payment of interest, accrues the shortfall, and adds that amount onto the money funded.

Funding for bridge loans can also take a variety of structures, depending upon the transaction. Typically, the bridge lender funds a significant portion of the initial acquisition with the balance of the acquisition price covered by equity, and then provides the necessary money required to stabilize the building's cash flow. As an example, consider the property acquisition scenario in Exhibit 13–2. Referring to the example, after the acquisition, renovation, and re-lease of the building, the cash flow increases from $2.5 million to $7.2 million. As a result, the investor can place permanent financing on the property for a total of $60 million (assuming a 10 percent interest rate and 1.20 debt coverage ratio), and can thus repay both the bridge financing and the entire equity investment. In other words, the real estate investor has created a situation in which he will have unlimited returns, because he no longer has any equity dollars invested in the transaction.

Permanent (Long-Term) Financing

Permanent, or long-term, financing can take many forms, including five general types: (1) bullet loans; (2) participating debt; (3) convertible mortgages; (4) zero coupon financings; and (5) equity. Unlike bridge financing, most long-term financing is non-recourse to the borrower and relies entirely on the real estate as collateral. Bullet loans are by far the most prevalent type of long-term financing, while the other types are available for more specialized situations.

Bullet Loans

The primary criteria for evaluating the amount of a bullet loan are interest rate, debt service coverage, and loan-to-value ratio. Insurance companies and commercial banks, the principal bullet loan lenders, set criteria for these loans and the majority thereof reflect those un-derwriting terms. The generic bullet loan is priced at a fixed spread over treasuries, at a 70 to 75 percent loan-to-value ratio and a 1.05 to 1.25 debt service coverage ratio. Although this is the standard, every transaction varies. As an example of a bullet loan, consider the stabilized property outlined in Exhibit 13–2. With cash flow of $7.2 million, a bullet lender might loan $60 million based on a 10 percent interest rate and a 1.20 debt coverage ratio. This would provide the lender with a cushion of $1.2 million before the property could not service the debt out of cash flow.

Bullet loans can often be structured with earn-outs, which can increase the level of financing as the property's cash flow increases. For example, if an owner expects cash flow to increase significantly in the second year of the loan because of lease rollover, the financing could be structured to provide for additional funding based on prede-termined formulas as the cash flow level increases. Alternatively, the owner could guarantee a portion of the loan with letters of credit or alternative means in order to convince the lender to provide additional funding.

Bullet loan terms vary—a typical one ranges from three to ten years. The loan term is dependent on the borrower's needs, the property's cash flow, and, ultimately, the lenders' capital sources. On longer-term loans, lenders frequently require amortization of a portion of the loan. Amortization, however, is usually not a large amount, since the amortization term is an extended one, such as 25 to 30 years.

The interest rates on bullet loans are usually fixed at a spread over treasuries for the entire loan term. Alternatively, commercial banks might price the loan at a spread over LIBOR, plus its swap costs (to fix the rate), plus a credit spread. Although the rate is usually set at commitment, many lenders are willing to provide floating-rate options that may be locked in a fixed rate within a specified time. This type of structure is becoming increasingly popular as lenders and owners seek to develop creative and flexible solutions to financing problems.

The advantage of a bullet loan to real estate owners is that they are not giving up any of their equity and hopefully, over time, will completely finance their equity. In other words, the level of the debt financing will reach a level where the owner no longer has any money invested in the transaction. Another advantage of bullet loans is that the interest rate is fixed and owners know the full extent of their exposure. Furthermore, the sources of bullet loans are typically very active, and real estate owners can depend on debt financing to be available. Disadvantages to bullet loans include moderate loan-to-value ratios and debt service coverage requirements, which prevent owners from fully financing their investments. Bullet loan lenders are also rather inflexible in the terms and conditions of their loan documents, which sometimes creates problems.

From a lender's perspective, bullet loans are steady sources of income from conservative investments that balance out investment portfolios. Lenders also prefer bullet loans, since they match well with funding sources that often require fixed rates of return.

Many insurance company bullet loan lenders require prepayment penalties if a borrower prepays a loan. The rationale behind this is that a significant portion of an insurance company's investable funds come from guaranteed investment contracts (GICs) that provide the investor with a guaranteed yield for a specified period of time. As a result, the insurance companies impose prepayment penalties to ensure that they can provide their GIC investors with the guaranteed returns. In most cases the prepayment penalty is in the form of *yield maintenance,* which means that the borrower is required to pay a penalty equal to the amount a lender would need to receive to invest the balance of the funds at a lower interest rate with an equivalent overall yield. For example, a 10-year, $50-million loan was made at 9.5 percent, interest only, and the loan was prepaid in the beginning of the seventh year when the interest rate on a comparable new loan would only be 8.5 percent. The prepayment penalty would be calculated so that the lender's overall return is 9.5 percent over the 10-year term of the initial loan, assuming that the funds were reloaned at 8.5 percent for

EXHIBIT 13–3
Sample Prepayment Penalty Calculation

Current debt service ($50 million × 9.5%)	= $4,750,000
New debt service ($50 million × 8.5%)	= $4,250,000
Years remaining on the loan	= 4 years
Annual shortfall	= $ 500,000
Prepayment penalty	
Net present value @ 9.5%	= $1,602,241

the final four years of the initial loan term. Although the actual formulas are more complicated, the basic calculation is shown in Exhibit 13–3.

Convertible and Participating Mortgages

Because of what had been rising property values and low initial rates of return on acquisitions of top quality buildings throughout most of the 1980s, property owners had not been able to generate the maximum amount of financing proceeds from traditional lending sources without resorting to more expensive second-mortgage financings. As an alternative, hybrid financings like convertible and participating mortgages were developed to provide a means to finance those low–initial cash flow but high-quality properties.

Convertible Mortgages   Convertible mortgages can be, in many instances, a proxy for equity because the lender has the option to eventually become an equity partner in the transaction. The fact that convertible mortgages can become equity raises some questions about the cost of the transaction versus conventional debt, since equity, owing to its higher risk profile, generally carries a higher return. Obviously, the ability to generate a higher loan-to-value ratio combined with attractive coupon rates makes convertible mortgages desirable to many owners. What makes convertible mortgages attractive to a lender or investor is that overall return approximates equity yields, but, during the loan period, he has a secured investment with limited downside risk because of the coupon payments. As a result, the loan has the potential to become very much like an equity investment with a guaranteed return. The option to convert into an equity position in a joint venture with a quality partner at the end of the loan term is the attractive feature of convertible debt. Simply put, the lender or investor has the best of both worlds—the security of debt and the yields of equity. Furthermore, coupon rates, though typically below bullet loan rates, are above what the riskier, pure equity yields would be.

From a borrower's perspective, convertible mortgages offer several advantages. The primary advantage is that the borrower can maximize financing proceeds, owing to the lower coupon of the convertible mortgage. In addition, many convertible mortgage lenders are less sensitive to debt coverage ratios. During the loan term, however, while the borrower is minimizing debt service with lower coupons, lender participation in cash flows can substantially increase the total debt service. The borrower also has the advantage of minimizing the tax impact due to the deferral of capital gains taxes until the actual conversion date. Perhaps most importantly, the borrower is able to maintain control of the property throughout both the loan period and the joint venture after conversion.

Structuring the economics of convertible mortgages is in many respects a circular calculation. The key variables include the loan amount, coupon, participation, loan term, option price, and any post-conversion preferences. The goal in structuring a convertible mortgage is twofold: (1) arriving at a transaction where the lender or investor achieves an overall internal rate of return (IRR) approximating what an equity investment in the property would yield; and (2) providing the borrower with the maximum financing proceeds at the lowest possible initial yield and overall cost.

Several years ago the principal goal in structuring a convertible mortgage was to achieve a 100 percent loan-to-value ratio. However, because of some repayment issues to be discussed later, this is changing. Nevertheless, most borrowers appear to be driven by the highest possible convertible loan amount, and, as a result, the key variables in structuring the transaction become coupon, participation, loan term, and residual interest. Coupon rates are traditionally set at below-market rates; the actual amount below market is dependent upon both the yield curve and which coupon is required to achieve the desired yield. Recent trends indicate that coupons are being stepped up at different points during the term of the loan rather than being fixed at one point for the entire loan term. In addition, participation in cash flow is becoming increasingly prevalent in convertible mortgages. The actual term of a convertible mortgage varies and can be adjusted to satisfy the needs of both the borrower and the lender or investor. The level of residual interest, or the conversion amount, is also a significant variable from a yield perspective. Perhaps more important is what it means from control perspective. Yields can also be increased for the lender or investor through a preference return after conversion or through a preferred capital account.

Major issues in structuring a convertible mortgage are what the conversion option price will be and whether any debt will be repaid upon conversion. There are two general ways to structure the repayment issue upon conversion: (1) the lender can convert the entire loan into an equity position; or (2) the lender can convert a portion of the loan into equity and be repaid the remainder of the loan. In the first case, the repayment of the convertible loan is not an issue, since there is no loan being repaid by the borrower. However, this structure will lead to a lower overall loan amount, because in a typical transaction, the lender or investor is converting into a 50 percent interest in the property, and projected future values for the time of conversion often do not allow for a high initial loan amount, such as 100 percent of cost, converting into only a 50-percent ownership interest several years later.

The second case, where only a portion of the loan converts into an equity position and the remainder of the loan is repaid, contains several important issues. The primary concern is where the borrower will get the funds to repay the nonconverted portion of the loan. The obvious option of placing a non-recourse mortgage on the property is not always a viable one, because the entire property will then be encumbered by the mortgage, even if the loan amount relates to only the borrower's 50 percent interest. As a result, the lender or investor could lose his entire equity position in the event that the borrower or partner defaults. This whole issue can be avoided if the convertible mortgage lender or investor agrees to encumber his interest as well as the owner's with non-recourse financing upon conversion.

The borrower could alternatively arrange recourse financing to pay off the non-converted portion of the loan, but his credit then becomes a major issue, and he must have enough credit for institutional lenders to be comfortable with this solution. As a result, more and more convertible mortgages are being structured with a total conversion of the loan into equity.

By going this route, however, the original purpose of convertible mortgages—placing higher loan-to-value financing—is necessarily altered. To get around this lower loan-to-value problem, more convertible loans are being structured with yield-enhancing methods such as cash flow participation during the loan term and post-conversion preferences for the lender or investor to allow the higher initial financing and therefore higher loan-to-value figure.

In all cases, one must remember that a convertible mortgage is, in essence, a joint venture. Once the lender converts into equity he is a full partner of the borrower. This means that at the time of the convertible loan funding, lender and borrower must together negotiate a full joint-venture agreement and agree upon all the key clauses such as those about buying or selling and significant property decision mechanisms.

The following hypothetical example of a property illustrates different convertible mortgage structures. The property in question is a class A, high-quality, multi-tenant office building with a value of approximately $234 million. The three convertible mortgage structures all have 10-year terms and a target IRR of 10.25 percent over a 15-year holding period. The actual IRR for each of the three structures is within four basis points of the target; however, as you will see, the loan size and structure is different in each case. Exhibit 13–4 highlights the three structures, as well as a conventional bullet loan, which can be used as a benchmark.

EXHIBIT 13–4
Bullet Loan versus Convertible Loan Structures

	Bullet loan	Structure I	Structure II	Structure III
Loan amount	$136 million	$170 million	$200 million	$210 mill.
Loan-to-value	58%	73%	85%	90%
Debt coverage ratio	1.10	—	—	—
Average coupon (or coupons)	9.25%	8.13%	7.5%	7.5%
Cash flow participation	—	50%	50%	50%
Principal amount converted	—	100%	50%	50%
Lender ownership after conversion	—	50%	50%	50%
Preference	—	10%	—	8%
10-year cash-on-cash return	9.25%	9.08%	8.04%	7.88%

As Exhibit 13–4 illustrates, a borrower who would only be able to raise $136 million through conventional financing might be able to raise up to $210 million using a convertible mortgage structure. This dramatic increase in financing may more than compensate for the fact that the borrower is giving up 50 percent of the equity upon conversion and paying a higher overall rate (IRR), 10.25 percent, as compared to 9.25 percent. The difference between structure I and structures II and III is that in structure I: the lender converts the entire loan into equity with nothing being repaid. Structures II and III can only be done if the lender or investor feels comfortable with the credit of the borrower and his ability to raise recourse financing to pay 50 percent of the loan upon conversion or is willing to encumber his partnership interest in the property only and not encumber the property itself. Structure III is different from structure II only in that the lender or investor will receive a preference return after conversion, which lifts the yield enough to allow for the additional $10 million loan amount.

All three convertible mortgage structures work (from an economic point of view), which shows the diversity of structures available in a transaction. However, from a business perspective, the lender or investor must get comfortable with the borrower to the extent that he will eventually become his joint-venture partner.

Unfortunately, because of their structural parameters and complexity, convertible mortgages clearly cannot be the solution to every real estate owner's problem. However, they can be a useful financing mechanism for owners with a large portfolio of properties who are seeking long-term financing partners, and, as a result, should consider it an innovative mechanism for unlocking the greatest amount of equity value in a property.

Participating Mortgages. Participating mortgages, like convertible debt, are a hybrid between debt and equity. Participating loans are closer than convertible mortgages to true debt because, although he participates in the property's cash flow and appreciation, the lender does not have the option to convert into an equity interest. In other words, the participating lender benefits from the equity appreciation, but only during the loan term and at maturity of the loan.

Participating loans are structured with a base coupon rate and a percentage share of available cash flow above that level in the same manner for convertible mortgages. Participating mortgages are increasingly being structured with stepped coupon rates as the cash flow increases, in order to maximize both the loan amount and the lender's yield. Occasionally, the loans are structured with an accrual feature to raise the loan-to-value ratio, although this negates a portion of the participation since any accrued shortfalls are paid first. In effect, accrual features make the loan less risky from a lender's point of view, as a greater portion of the debt service is guaranteed. Participating lenders also share in any appreciation in value of the property by taking a percentage of the spread between the value at the end of the loan term and the original financing amount.

Overall, a participating lender seeks to generate a total return at least equivalent to an equity investment, but with the bulk of that return coming from annual cash flow, rather than from residual participation. Additional upside potential is generally regarded as "nice but not necessary" to meet his investment parameters. Interestingly, the IRR on the typical participating loan is often higher than what the yield would be for an equity purchaser. This is a curious paradox, because the risk of the participating lender is less than that of an equity buyer. Furthermore, the participating lender has the benefit of the loan coupon, while an equity investor does not. Perhaps the answer to this question is that a participating lender is only going to benefit once, while the equity investor theoretically can benefit as long as he chooses to own the property.

Like convertible mortgages, participating loans can lead to higher loan-to-value ratios through the use of lower coupon rates, which results in better debt service coverage. However, some participating lenders are more sensitive to debt coverage than convertible lenders, and loan-to-values therefore cannot be "pushed" as far as convertible loans. This is changing, as the traditional participating lenders are beginning to make convertible mortgages as well. Conversely, without the need to finance the repayment of a nonconverted portion of a loan, participating loans do not have the problem of structuring this portion of transaction, and can thus allow for a higher loan amount.

As additional protection, some participating lenders structure their loans with a "look-back" feature that ensures a minimum yield to the lender. It basically provides for a higher participation in residual proceeds to counteract lower-than-expected participation in cash flow. From an analytical point of view, the look-back is the equivalent of a minimum IRR that must be achieved. To calculate the look-back, the appropriate residual participation is increased at the end of the loan term until the IRR goal is reached. The look-back rate is usually lower than the projected overall yield to allow for a margin of error in the projections.

Participating lenders are typically credit companies and pension funds, both of which have different yield criteria, owing to their different sources of funds. Yield criteria aside, both lender types structure their loans in a similar manner, although the product type may vary. For instance, a credit company may be a more viable candidate for a high-risk property because of its higher cost of funds, and a pension fund a more likely lender for a class A, central business district building. Credit companies are more likely to structure the loan with an accrual feature, since their loans are typically higher risk deals. Credit company loans are often priced using the prime rate as the base index, whereas pension funds are more flexible in their coupon rates and usually relate the coupon or coupons to treasury bonds. In both cases, one should recognize that the pay rate is usually below the base index.

Interestingly, even though participating loans are structurally different from convertible mortgages, they are virtually identical from an analytical perspective. In most instances, the coupon and cash flow participation structure is very similar for the two types of loans. Analytically, the calculation of the appreciation benefits is identical, because when analyzing a convertible mortgage, one typically assumes a sale of the end of the loan term, just as for a participating loan. Structurally, of course, the two loans are different in that the participating lender's involvement with property ends with the loan term, while a convertible mortgage lender becomes an equity investor.

Zero Coupon Financing

Zero coupon financings are not widely available and are only applicable in a limited number of circumstances. However, it is important to understand how they work and in what situations they are effective. Zero coupon financings, as their name implies, are loans with no current payment of interest; the interest accrues and is repaid when the loan is due. The advantage of zero coupons is obvious—no payment of debt service out of cash flow—but the disadvantages are less noticeable. Unlike most conventional financings, whose balances either stay flat or amortize, zero coupon mortgages constantly increase. This can cause a problem when the property's value does not inflate rapidly enough to allow repayment of the loan. Remembering that zero coupon financings are constantly ticking time bombs is the key to effectively utilizing this financing source.

The zero coupon market is relatively small, and lenders are not easy to find, with the majority of the financings being provided by the public market. Other major lenders include pension funds, insurance companies, and smaller niche lenders who may not require current cash flow and can afford to wait for the interest to be paid at a later date. However, because no current debt service is paid, zero coupon loans carry a higher rate than conventional financing.

Another factor to consider is that the loan-to-value ratio of zero coupon loans is vastly different from that of conventional financing. Although a typical conventional bullet loan is given at a 75 percent loan-to-value, many zero coupons are made at much lower levels, and even the accreted value is often below that loan-to-value level. This means that the transaction must be capitalized with other sources of funds—usually with equity, but occasionally with other types of financing. Placing zero coupon financing in a secondary position to pay current debt carries risks, but, in the past, when capital was plentiful, it provided borrowers a way to generate maximum financing on a property.

Of course, placing the zero coupon financing in a second mortgage position increases the interest rate, but it also limits the loan amount to levels that fit within the parameters established by many lenders. Consider the following example with a property that, owing to its quality and location, has a value of $100 million with only $5 million of current cash flow. In this case, an owner may only be able to achieve a first mortgage bullet loan of $45 million (10 percent interest rate and 1.10 debt coverage ratio), which represents a 45 percent loan-to-value. The owner must then fund the balance of acquisition with equity. However, the projections indicate that the property's cash flow in 10 years would be $14 million, allowing for, under identical circumstances, a bullet loan financing of $127 million. Since the owner would only need $45 million to repay the first bullet loan, $82 million would be available to repay a zero coupon financing. In this example, a lender might be persuaded to make a second mortgage zero coupon financing of, for example, $15 million at 11 percent (allowing for a premium for the second position), which would grow to approximately $45 million in 10 years. This type of financing would provide the lender with a conservative loan-to-value ratio on the projected value of the property—$280 million at the same 5 percent going-in capitalization rate. Furthermore, and perhaps more importantly, the total repayment of $90 million for both the first mortgage bullet loan and the zero coupon second mortgage debt at the end of the loan term or terms is less than the value of the property today.

One must understand that zero coupons are not right for every situation and that the lending market is very limited. Furthermore, remembering that the loans often accrete at a rate that is faster than the rate at which a property appreciates is imperative. As a result, sufficient room must be left in case property values do not inflate as rapidly as the financing.

Equity

Early in this chapter, we defined the concept of financing to include both equity and debt. Equity can, in many instances, be the appropriate capital source for a transaction. Equity investors typically seek a preferred return, possibly with accruals, and a percentage of the total equity in the transaction. In addition, they often look for a return of their invested capital before allowing distributions to the other equity sources. This type of equity is not true equity in that it has a preferred position in the capital structure, but it carries a higher level of risk than secured debt.

Instances where equity is the appropriate capital source vary and depend upon the transaction. One possible scenario is an investment in a property that needs substantial renovation. A purchaser of such a property has two basic options: bridge financing or an equity partner. One advantage of using equity is that the current coupon to be paid on the preferred return is usually lower than that of a bridge financing. However, instead of merely participating, the equity investor requires an actual ownership position. Simply put, the trade-off is a lower coupon or preferred return for a more substantial portion of the profits. The key to developing the best capital structure is maximizing everyone's returns; equity can be an effective capital source. As the 1990s unfold, capital—especially debt capital—is becoming scarce, so equity capital has assumed an even greater role in real estate finance.

Securitized Offerings and Structured Financing

As real estate has evolved into a global investment class, so have its financing structures. In addition, the size of some transactions has increased to a point where such transactions are not viable for a single lender, and tapping the public markets for additional or alternative sources of funds has become necessary. Theoretically, any real estate financing can be securitized and financed in the public market. However, owing to the cost of securitizing a financing, it is usually not practical for amounts smaller than $50 million.

A separate but related issue (since a private offering can also be rated) is obtaining a rating from a significant agency such as Moody's or Standard & Poor's. Such a rating is important because it demonstrates the solidity of the financing to the ultimate financing source, but it is not necessary for all transactions. Each financing must be analyzed to find out whether the benefits of a rating provide significant enough savings to make the process worthwhile.

Examples of securitized offerings include conventional interest-only loans, participating loans, and convertible mortgages. Structurally, they are virtually identical to non-securitized offerings, with the exception of the protection necessary to satisfy the requirements of the bond trustee. Theoretically, securitized offerings should offer lower interest rates to the borrower, since the transaction would ideally be structured or tiered to attract various investor classes along the yield curve. Counteracting this savings, however, are the higher costs of structuring the transaction and the limited amounts of flexibility for the borrower as he is dealing with an array of investors who work through a trustee with limited latitude.

Another method of securitizing a financing, whether it is publicly or privately placed, is to structure the financing with multiple tranches of debt and equity. Doing so allows for optimization of the yield curve because various parts of the financing can be placed with different classes of investors who require different levels of returns. A simple example of what could be termed a structured financing, although it is a typical real estate structure, is a transaction financed with three classes: (1) a bullet loan (senior debt); (2) a second mortgage (subordinated debt); and (3) equity. In the truest sense of the term, however, structured financings involve several tiers of subordinated debt. For example, consider the $500 million dollar financing of a property with $40 million in cash flow shown in Exhibit 13–5.

Each tranche would be placed with different investors and the returns matched to their requirements. In this example, the senior subordinated lender would receive a projected 14 percent IRR, the junior subordinated lender a 20 percent IRR, and the equity an IRR

EXHIBIT 13–5
Sample Structured Financing

Cash flow	$45 million
Senior debt ($400 million @ 9%)	36 million
Available cash flow	9 million
Senior subordinated debt	
($50 million @ 10%)	5 million

The senior subordinated debt also receives 25 percent of available cash flow and residual or refinancing proceeds.

Available cash flow	$4 million
Junior subordinated debt	
($30 million @ 12%)	3.7 million
	(including participation in cash flow)

The junior subordinated debt receives, in addition, 25 percent of available cash flow and residual or refinancing proceeds.

Available cash flow	$0.3 million
Equity ($20 million)	0.3 million

The equity investor receives the balance of available cash flow and residual and refinancing proceeds.

of 30 percent. The increasing returns reflect where the return comes from, shifting from cash flow to residual as the available cash flow diminishes.

FLOATING RATES AND INTEREST RATE HEDGES

Many financings are based on a floating rate and vary according to the base index. The lender will price the transaction at a spread over the index, typically LIBOR, the prime rate, or treasuries, and the interest rate will float with the index. Which index is utilized is dependent upon a number of factors, including the lender and the project type.

The advantage of floating rate financing is that it gives the borrower tremendous flexibility in playing interest rate cycles. For example, if an owner believes that interest rates are heading down, a floating rate financing allows him to take advantage of the lower rates by refinancing to a fixed rate loan at the bottom of the trough.

Alternatively, when interest rates rise, an owner does not have to tolerate a high rate for a long term, and he can wait until rates are lower before converting to a fixed rate. An additional benefit is that floating-rate debt carries no prepayment penalties designed to protect a lender's yield. However, using interest rate swaps, caps, or collars could cause an incremental cost of unwinding the transaction. This is, however, a trade-off for hedging the risk of floating-rate debt.

One advantage of the global capital market is that there are lenders who are always looking to place fixed-rate debt. As a result, floating-rate borrowers have the opportunity to hedge their positions by utilizing swaps, caps, collars, options, and so forth to minimize the risk of floating-rate debt. In other instances, where only a floating-rate financing is possible, a lender may require a hedging program in order to minimize risk if interest rates rise. Examples include requiring a borrower to purchase a cap on a floating financing in order to protect against the possibility of cash flow insufficient to cover the interest payments, and the situation in which the lender has the option to convert the loan to a fixed rate through interest rate swaps.

The costs of hedging floating risk debt vary and are dependent upon the type of hedge, the term of financing, the rate being hedged, and the borrower's credit. Ultimately, the cost of the hedging program must be factored into a floating rate financing in order to accurately determine its entire cost. Using an interest rate swap as an example, consider the following situation: A $50 million loan is priced at 75 basis points over LIBOR, which, for the sake of this example, is assumed to be 8.75 percent. Therefore, the initial floating interest rate is 9.5 percent. Creating a swap whereby the borrower trades that floating rate obligation for a fixed rate of 9.5 percent might cost 40 basis points per year of the loan. The total cost of the financing is therefore 9.9 percent.

The key factor in floating rate financings is the base index. LIBOR and treasuries fluctuate much more rapidly than does the prime rate. This is an important consideration in a volatile interest rate environment; the prime rate generally lags behind market movement by a significant period, whereas LIBOR or treasury bill interest rates gyrate tremendously. The hedging technique utilized is unimportant. However, the owner or borrower *can* have unlimited flexibility in structuring a floating rate loan that has fixed-rate advantages.

GUARANTEES

Lenders are always looking at how they will be repaid and whether there will be adequate value, cash flow, or both to ensure repayment of the loan. This is most important with non-recourse loans, which are only secured by the real estate asset. Lenders thereof are generally more conservative in their underwriting standards than in instances where they have access to other collateral in the event of trouble. A mechanism utilized to make lenders more comfortable with higher loan-to-value ratios and lower debt coverage levels is the partial guarantee put up by the borrower. These guarantees can range from an escrow account to a letter of credit to a negative pledge of other assets, all of which provide the lender with additional security for the loan.

Recourse loans are simpler because the borrower *must* pledge assets—letters of credit, marketable securities, partnership, interests, or other nonfinanced real estate assets—as collateral for the loan. As a result, the lender is secure; in the event of default, the lender would receive the assets secured by the loan and the other collateral. Clearly, with non-recourse loans, the interest rate is heavily dependent upon the credit strength of the borrower and the quality of the collateral.

UNDERWRITING

The key to obtaining financing is the ability to convince the lender that the transaction makes sense from both economic and safety perspectives. We have defined this task as underwriting. The crux of underwriting from a financial perspective is the valuation of the property and the development of cash flow projections. Market issues must also be covered thoroughly, concentrating particularly on the property's competitiveness with other buildings in the market. Engineering, environmental, and title reviews, as well as other legal studies, must also be performed. We, however, will concentrate mainly on the financial aspects and only briefly discuss the market issues in this chapter.

Valuations and cash flow projections are dependent upon the information utilized to create them. Therefore, the initial operating expenses, rent roll, and capital expenditures must be understood and checked for accuracy before beginning work. Mistakes in these items will undermine the entire project. Once this information has been verified, assumptions must be developed in order to create the projections. One must first realize that predicting the future with absolute accuracy is impossible. Therefore, one should concentrate on coming up with assumptions that are *realistic* indicators. For example, it is nearly impossible to estimate that market rents will grow at 2 percent per annum for the next two years, 8 percent for the next three years, and 5 percent thereafter, A better approach is to use a steady growth factor, perhaps 5 percent, which will give the same results at the end of the projection period. In this way, one does not attempt to make year-by-year predictions, merely the end result. Another important consideration to remember is that very few projections will be accurate; the goal therefore is to create a realistic platform which can be utilized to analyze and reanalyze the property.

Assumptions cover more than growth rates. Other important considerations include market rents, lease-up periods, leasing concessions, and projected capital expenditures. These are crucial market issues that require a great deal of homework for full understanding. Assembling the assumptions and developing cash flow projections and a valuation is only the beginning. Once completed and checked for accuracy, the projections should be tested to reflect alternate scenarios. The importance of this step is sometimes overestimated, since the base situation should be reasonable. However, testing gives an indication of what can happen if problems develop or if the market changes. One must keep in mind that financial projections should be used only as an analytical tool and not as an absolute prediction of the future. Projections are merely a useful tool for analyzing a real estate investment opportunity and comparing it with other investments so an educated investment decision can be made.

Reasonable projections are also important because they show lenders that the borrower has done his homework and understands the market and the property. Unreasonable projections tend to turn off lenders, who will choose to spend their limited time on other projects that do not require as much diligence.

LENDERS

In today's complex financial markets, an investor can find myriad ways to finance an acquisition. We will discuss here the six most common types of lending institutions.

1. *Commercial banks*. Throughout the 1980s, commercial banks were the largest real estate lenders in the United States, supplying almost any type of financing, ranging from construction loans to long-term mortgages (bullet loans). The majority of commercial bank loans have floating rates, but hedges allow a lender to fix the rate for the borrower. Commercial banks' credit review background makes them likely lenders for recourse loans, such as bridge and construction loans, in which the borrower's credit takes on increased importance. Furthermore, the tremendous market share of commercial banks make them the likely choice for financing projects throughout the United States.

As the economies of the world increasingly mix together, the distinctions between domestic and foreign banks lessen. Differences still remain, particularly among types of real estate security, but many distinctions are blurred. For example, as foreign banks increasingly fund their lending activities from the same sources as domestic banks, the spreads over which loans are priced become virtually identical and are more dependent upon a particular bank's appetite for the deal than upon nationality of the bank.

2. *Savings and loan associations*. The excesses of the 1980s and the uncertainties of the consequences of the Financial Institutions Reform, Recovery, and Enforcement Act (FIRREA) on S&Ls make discussing their capabilities difficult. Savings and loans will obviously have a much smaller role in the real estate lending market than previously. However, the traditional niche of the S&L in commercial real estate lending has been in floating rate loans, often on development or redevelopment transactions. Whether this will continue is uncertain and will not be clear until the effect of FIRREA is fully felt. At this time, it appears that S&Ls will be much more conservative in their lending practices and have stronger underwriting criteria; they probably will revert to their origins, namely, residential mortgages.

3. *Credit companies*. The major credit companies have expanded into real estate lending and typically offer high-rate but high-risk loans. Bridge loans and participating second mortgages are not unusual for credit companies. They should be looked upon as a source of high-risk capital in situations that require a sophisticated lender.

4. *Life insurance companies*. With the exception of commercial banks, life insurance companies are probably the largest real estate lender in the country. The majority of their loans are fixed-rate medium- to long-term loans, as well as equity investments. However,

life insurance companies will also make construction loans, usually in conjunction with a take-out, and fund joint ventures. Since they are also the largest equity buyer of commercial real estate, usually on behalf of pension fund investors, they supply forward commitment purchase contracts of projects to be built.

As the capital markets have evolved, many life insurance companies have become more flexible in terms of structuring financing to meet the needs of borrowers. For example, they structure loans with a floating rate over the short term, giving the borrower the option to fix the rate for the remainder of the term whenever desired.

Foreign life insurance companies have become active equity investors in domestic real estate as well as occasional convertible mortgage lenders. However, most do not provide straight financing, and, in the case of Japanese life companies, are prohibited by law from doing so.

5. *Pension fund investors.* These investors could theoretically become one of the largest real estate investors, if they commit the percentage of their capital that has been publicized. However, the reality is that the pension funds will probably not be able to locate the quantity of institutional property that they wish to invest in, so this increased funding would be meaningless without expanding their investment horizons. To date, most of the pension fund money has gone into participating and convertible loans and equity investments.

Since the late-1960s, most pension fund investment in real estate has been done with commingled funds and separate accounts handled primarily by the major life companies and some selected independent advisors. Toward the end of the 1980s, more of the experienced pension fund investors, both private and public, were making investment decisions through their own staffs or through specialized advisors or partners, including a few developers and real estate services companies. It is too early to detect a pattern, but this movement seems driven as much by the need to diversify as by dissatisfaction with some of the returns generated by traditional advisors during the last decade. Foreign pension funds are active equity and convertible loan sources for real estate in the United States. They typically utilize many of the same criteria as do domestic pension funds.

6. *Public markets.* The public markets have not been utilized to a great extent because of the complexity and cost of issuing public debt. Although securitizing real estate was the "thing to do" in the 1980s, most real estate could not practically be securitized. This market historically remained relatively quiet, except for very large and specialized financings as well as the residential market.

The difficulty that the real estate industry is now experiencing in raising capital, however, could lead to a resurgence of securitized and credit-enhanced borrowings as a creative way to tap alternative sources of capital. In times of scarce capital or higher interest rates, securitized financings become more viable, but they will now be seen as one of many financing options as opposed to the panacea for all financing needs that many touted them to be in the early 1980s.

THE PROCESS

Understanding the mechanics of financing the acquisition of real estate is, unfortunately, only the beginning of the process. The actual process of securing financing is a long and difficult one that reflects the imperfect nature of the underlying asset and the inefficiency of the real estate capital markets.

We have already discussed underwriting and the various components that make up the valuation of a real estate asset. Another part of the process is assembling a detailed memorandum describing the property, the market, the borrower, and, perhaps most importantly, the terms and conditions of the desired financing. There is no one correct format for preparing a financing memorandum; however, a good memorandum will thoroughly describe all important aspects of the transaction in a forthright manner. When preparing a memorandum, one should place oneself in the lender's position and critically review the information. One must also remember that capital sources see a tremendous number of investment opportunities; they can only examine a few and close on fewer still. Therefore, the more accurate, complete, and reasonable one's material is, the more receptive a capital source will be to the opportunity presented.

Completing the underwriting is only the beginning. Simultaneously, a marketing strategy needs to be assembled that addresses, among other things, transaction structure, capital sources, timing, and use of an advisor. An advisor can be a helpful part of a transaction because he or she brings a third-party viewpoint and numerous contacts and relationships with capital sources. As negotiations progress, it is often useful to have an objective person in the middle to mediate disputes. A time schedule can be helpful, but one should not count on its accuracy. The capital-raising process is quite involved, and the documentation itself requires long periods of time. As environmental concerns have increased, the due-diligence period has lengthened correspondingly.

Transaction structure and size determine the capital sources, so the transaction structure drives the process. Figuring out the proper structure requires defining objectives and tailoring the structure to meet them. A variety of structures were discussed earlier, and, although these are certainly not all of the variations, they give a broad outline about structuring deals.

Marketing a transaction is a time-intensive process that requires extensive contacts. Closed transactions result from strong relationships and inherently good deals, not just "dialing for dollars." Therefore, a well-thought-out marketing strategy identifying likely players and a comprehensive offering memorandum are crucial. This is not to say that a capital source could not appear out of nowhere, merely that someone who knows the market has a better idea of who might want to finance a certain transaction. Depending upon the size of the transaction and the location of the key players, face-to-face meetings to present the financing are usually best. Although these are not always possible, preliminary phone conversations to screen investors are important so that only those truly interested receive materials for review. The screening process has a second positive consequence — capital sources are more receptive to subsequent financing requests if their time was not wasted on earlier deals.

The actual process of documenting a financing varies with transaction structure and capital source. Bullet loan lenders typically have applications that must be negotiated prior to issuing commitments. Other lenders negotiate a letter of intent. Regardless of the document, the process takes time and effort. Other issues that must be covered in documenting a financing include title searches, title insurance, and environmental audits, which are becoming increasingly important in identifying potential liabilities. Environmental issues that frequently appear are asbestos, ground water contamination, and toxic waste. Determining the nature, extent, and cost to fix environmental problems is of paramount importance to capital sources who are concerned with limiting their exposure. Lenders also seek indemnities to protect themselves from environmental liabilities. This part of the process is taking on increased importance, and the requirements to satisfy lenders will probably expand as every one involved learns all of the issues and develops solutions to the problems.

Closing the transaction requires constant attention by all parties to ensure that all of the legal and documentation issues are satisfied. Problems can develop at any time, and they must be quickly solved in order to keep the deal on track. An industry adage is, "Each deal dies at least once before it closes."

SUMMARY

Financing the acquisition of real estate is difficult, but once completed allows the effective financial management of a property. The proper capital structure is crucial in achieving the balance necessary to manage a real estate asset effectively and achieve the maximum return with the lowest level of risk. Only a few of the details of the financing process have been discussed here, but we hope that this chapter has highlighted the key points and dealt with the relevant issues.

GLOSSARY

amortization The principal repayment of a loan during the term of the loan. Typically, on loans with an amortization feature, the debt service is a combination of interest and principal based on a calculated schedule.

application Documentation submitted by borrowers outlining the financing desired.

balloon payment The payment made by a borrower at the end of a loan term to retire the remaining principal of the loan.

basis point One hundredth of a percent. 100 basis points equals 1 percent.

bridge financing The temporary financing provided to a borrower that enables him or his to acquire a property. In many cases the bridge financing provides for increased funding as the property cash flow increases.

bullet loan A conventional fixed-rate loan usually provided by insurance companies. Bullet loans often have amortization features. The term *bullet* refers to the principal amount due at the end of the loan term.

cap A capital markets technique that allows a borrower to set a limit for how high a floating rate loan can float.

capital markets The generic term for the international pool of money available for financings.

collar A capital markets technique that enables a lender to set a floor for how low a loan can float. Typically used in conjunction with caps.

commitment Documentation provided by a lender committing him or her to fund a loan based upon the terms specified in the application agreement.

construction financing Financing provided to developers enabling them to build a property. Funds are provided, up to a predetermined ceiling, based upon a construction draw schedule. Interest payments typically accrue or are funded as part of the construction draw schedule.

convertible mortgage   A loan that has the option to convert into equity in the property at a specified time.

debt coverage ratio   A ratio used by lenders to assess a property's ability to service a loan. The standard ratio is net operating income divided by debt service, although lenders may also look at a ratio with cash flow as the numerator.

fixed-rate loan   Loan in which the interest rate is fixed at a predetermined level (or levels) at funding.

floating-rate loan   Financing in which the interest rate is determined by a spread over a predetermined index such as LIBOR, prime rate, or treasuries. When the underlying indices change, so does the interest rate on the loan.

hedge   Capital markets technique that allows borrowers to minimize the risk of arranging floating-rate financings.

interest only   A loan in which only the interest is paid during the loan term and the entire principal is paid at the time the loan is due.

LIBOR   The London Interbank Offered Rate.

loan-to-value ratio   The ratio between the loan amount and the value of the property.

maturity   The date when the balance of the loan is due.

mortgage   A generic term often used as a substitute for financing. Property used, the term refers to the lien that a borrower gives a lender on the property.

non-recourse financing   A loan in which the lender's sole security is the property.

participating financing   Financing in which the lender participates in the cash flow of a property after debt service. In addition, the lender may also participate in the residual or refinancing proceeds at the end of the participating loan term.

prime rate   Interest rate set by U.S. commercial banks.

recourse financing   A loan in which the lender has security in addition to the property.

residual   The value of the property in excess of the loan amount due at the maturity of the loan.

stabilization   The point at which a property's cash flow is considered to have leveled off and is stable prior to lease turnovers, rent steps, and so forth.

swap   A capital market technique utilized to convert a floating-rate financing to a fixed-rate, or vice-versa.

tranche   A term that defines a particular part of the capital structure. For example, the debt might be called the *debt tranche* and the equity, the *equity tranche*. It also applies to the various funding amounts when the loan is advanced in more than one stage.

yield curve   The line that connects the interest rates of varying term securities. Typically used in reference to treasury bonds.

CHAPTER 14

ASBESTOS MANAGEMENT

Carl Borsari
Schulweis Realty, Inc.

HISTORY OF ASBESTOS IN THE UNITED STATES

Asbestos is probably the most environmentally debated building material to be used in the last 100 years. Asbestos was originally developed and used as an insulating material, a fire-proofing material, and for a variety of other commercial and industrial applications, owing to its resistance to heat and chemicals. It came to be used on a large scale initially as pipe and boiler insulating material; starting in the 1950s, it was used extensively as a fire-proofing material in steel construction for both steel columns and beams, as well as metal decking. It was literally a miracle material, one that received preferential treatment as an insulating material, until the danger of asbestos was finally realized. Unfortunately, however, large-scale use of asbestos in the United States did not start to decline until 1973.

The general public is unaware of the nature and source of asbestos. The Occupational Safety and Health Act (OSHA) describes asbestos as "the naturally occurring minerals chrysotile, amosite, crocidolite, tremolite, anthophyllite, and actinolite, provided that the fibers have a length greater than 5 microns, with a diameter less than 3 microns and at least three times longer than it is wide." In layman's terms, asbestos is a natural mineral rock mined from the earth, just like other minerals, such as iron and copper. The difference, however, is that asbestos, when crushed or pulverized, divides in fibers rather than dust particles (which is the case with other minerals). These fibers are the inherent danger of asbestos.

282

In commercial office buildings, the two most common types of asbestos present are chrysotile and amosite. Chrysotile (white asbestos) is characterized by long fibers, which enables it to be woven into cloth and mixed into heat-resistant products. Chrysotile accounts for over 90 percent of the asbestos present in the United States. Amosite (brown asbestos) is a trade name derived from the asbestos mines of South Africa. Amosite is characterized by short fibers. It is chemical resistant and was used for pipe insulation and in cement products.

Studies Uncover the Dangers of Asbestos

Various studies of people involved in the manufacture or installation of asbestos—such as that performed at naval shipyards and for manufacturing companies like the Johns Manville Company—uncovered the fact that people with occupational exposures to asbestos, who worked with it on a day-to-day basis, had an increased potential to develop cancer as a result of fibers getting into their lungs. When these fibers became airborne, workers subsequently inhaled them, causing serious health problems—namely, asbestosis, mesothelioma, and lung cancer. Each of these diseases is the result of the inability of the body's natural defenses either to expel or otherwise eliminate the fibers.

Diseases Associated with Asbestos

Asbestosis is a disease characterized by fibrotic scarring of the lung. It is prevalent among workers who have been exposed to large doses of asbestos fibers over a long period of time; there is a clear relationship between exposure and development of this disease. The latency period for asbestosis is 15 to 30 years. Most scientists agree, however, that asbestosis is not a concern for building occupants or maintenance workers.

Mesothelioma is the disease of greatest concern among asbestos removal workers, but it is also the rarest. Unlike asbestosis, this disease, a cancer of either the chest or abdominal cavity, is not linked with dosage. In fact, there have been incidents in which people have contracted mesothelioma with extremely limited exposure. As with asbestosis, there is a latency period of 30 to 40 years from exposure to onset.

Lung cancer is caused by many different elements, of which only one is asbestos. Employees exposed to industrial concentrations of asbestos are at risk of contracting lung cancer. A cigarette smoker who also works with asbestos is more than 50 times more likely to contract lung cancer than a nonsmoking non-asbestos worker. Like asbestosis and mesothelioma, there is a long latency period between initial exposure and the occurrence of the disease—20 to 30 years. There appears to be some relationship between exposure and development of the disease, but these levels have not yet been quantified.

One should note that these diseases are related to industrial occupational exposures—manufacture and processing—of asbestos and asbestos products, where workers wore little or no protective equipment. There is almost no incidence of office occupants contracting these diseases as a direct result of their limited exposure to asbestos in the typical office setting. Nonetheless, legal action has resulted in claims relating to all levels of asbestos exposure.

EPA Ban of Asbestos

In response to the highly publicized health hazards of asbestos, the Environmental Protection Agency determined in 1973 that asbestos must be banned from use in any building materials, thereby eliminating its presence of asbestos in buildings constructed after 1973. As a natural carryover, concern developed about the effect of asbestos materials in existing buildings on the inhabitants and workers in those buildings. This prompted the EPA to develop a series of regulations detailing how asbestos was to be removed and how it could be disturbed in the day-to-day workings of buildings.

The establishment of the EPA requirements on limiting asbestos exposure to workers became a political football, and it created hysteria among occupants of buildings containing asbestos. This, in turn, forced the involvement of both state and local governments, which further investigated the hazards of asbestos and developed their own laws to protect the public from those hazards. Various states and cities developed laws governing the removal and disturbance of asbestos. One of the most detailed and inclusive laws was Local Law 76, developed by the city of New York.

As a result of the pressure created by the federal, state, and local governments to limit asbestos exposure in existing buildings, insurance companies and financial institutions began to pressure the real estate industry to eliminate asbestos from buildings, thereby limiting their liabilities as well as curtailing the potential decrease in the value of these properties. In addition to the requirements of the insurance companies and financial institutions, there was tremendous pressure from major tenants, who would not occupy spaces that contained asbestos, prompting building owners to take drastic measures and remove asbestos en masse from their buildings.

EFFECT OF ASBESTOS
ON THE REAL ESTATE INDUSTRY

The legal requirements and public and financial pressure heaped onto owners of property where asbestos-containing material was present prompted the development of a new industry, including asbestos removal contractors, asbestos consultants, and asbestos testing laboratories. Meanwhile, building owners and managers were faced with the following realizations:

1. Determining the extent and condition of asbestos in their buildings would cost the owners tremendous sums.
2. If they decided that the best approach to the situation would be to remove all asbestos as spaces became available, the owners would also incur great costs—as much as $20 to $30 per square foot for removal of asbestos-containing fireproofing, and subsequent replacement with a non-asbestos-containing insulation. This is a significant number, considering the fact that the usual figure for building a tenant space is in the same vicinity. Furthermore, removal of asbestos-containing materials from mechanical equipment rooms, steam lines, plumbing lines, and other building systems also had to be considered, albeit at a lower cost than removal of asbestos-containing fireproofing.

Public Reaction to the Asbestos Issue

In general, the public hysteria forced many building owners to remove asbestos rather than try to manage it in-place. In many cases, office workers questioned their management as to whether asbestos was present in the building. These tenants were in turn forced to inquire of building management, and, if so, what their intentions for removing it were.

One of the major laws passed during this period was Local Law 76, which was approved by the city of New York. This law had the most far-reaching effect on the real estate industry in terms of cost of removal and the ability to finance buildings with asbestos.

Local Law 76 was approved by the city council on December 2, 1985. Its purpose was to safeguard the public by requiring that renovation or demolition projects that disturbed asbestos are conducted in accordance with procedures established pursuant to its provisions, and that workers who handle materials containing asbestos receive appropriate training and certification. The law provides a method by which the New York City Department of Buildings and the New York City Department of Environmental Protection can ensure that appropriate measures are taken to remove or stabilize asbestos by requiring a separate asbestos inspection report whenever a renovation or alteration is filed through the building notice application procedure (through the Department of Buildings) to obtain a work permit. However, if a building has asbestos, it is sufficient for the owner to indicate this. If the building does not have asbestos, one is required to hire an asbestos investigator to verify the truth of this statement, thereby placing a burden on owners who do not have asbestos in their buildings.

DEP Program to Control Asbestos

The Department of Environmental Protection was ordered to come up with a program in order to ensure that asbestos control would be put in force by December 3, 1986. It involved the following:

1. Developing a training and certification program for asbestos workers, supervisors, and asbestos investigators.
2. Bringing authority for the DEP to develop regulations to protect the public and workers near an asbestos project.
3. A tie-in with the building department's permit plan approval process for alterations and demolition. Prior to commencing a project, the applicant must determine whether activity could disturb asbestos and take appropriate measures, including notifying the proper city agency (in New York, the Department of Environmental Protection).
4. Strong enforcement provisions, including civil penalties—a minimum of $1,000 for most violations, and issuance of stop-work orders.

During this process, it became evident to the building industry that the development of the various parts of the program, as indicated above, would not be accomplished in the mandated time frame. The DEP also did not consider the consequences this law would have to the general public, financial institutions, potential tenants, and building owners in the real estate industry. The DEP continually indicated that it was not requiring anything not already mandated under OSHA and EPA requirements concerning asbestos. What the department failed to realize is that the hysteria created by asbestos had affected the real estate industry in the following ways:

1. Financial institutions, in many cases, refuse to finance buildings with asbestos-containing materials present unless those materials are to be removed.
2. Major tenants, including banks and other financial institutions, often require asbestos-free space when signing new leases.
3. Potential buyers of buildings containing asbestos have either turned away or asked that the price of the building be discounted, so the asbestos can be removed.
4. Because of the uncertainties involved in asbestos exposure and the potential long-term liability, many owners are unable to procure insurance coverage for asbestos.
5. Many contractors are only able to procure up to $500,000 coverage, and only on a claims-made basis, which means that claims must be made in the same year that the insurance policy takes effect. Therefore, if a claim is made five years from that time, the insurance coverage would not be applicable. To avoid this, building management should request that the contractor provide an occurrence insurance policy. Although this type of coverage is difficult to acquire, it does offer the best protection for all parties. The occurrence policy continues "ad infinitum"; therefore, if a claim is made 20 years from the date of occurrence, the insurance carrier will cover the claim. This is significant because, as previously discussed, diseases caused by asbestos exposure usually have a long latency period. There *are* insurance carriers willing to provide this coverage.

When the law became effective, owners of commercial properties felt compelled to remove asbestos that in many cases was stabilized and therefore harmless to the public. The other problem was where to dispose of such large quantities of asbestos. At the time of this writing, there is only one dumpsite within the city limits, and the limit is 80 cubic yards of asbestos per day. The city has not come up with any additional sites for disposal of asbestos-containing materials. The real estate industry has been informed that there are sites in northern New York, Pennsylvania, Maine, West Virginia, and Kentucky; one can only imagine what the trucking costs would be to transport asbestos-containing materials to these sites from New York City.

It is believed that out of the 300 million square feet of commercial buildings in New York, approximately 100 million square feet contain asbestos in one form or another. As the pressure to remove asbestos escalates, it will be difficult to acquire the services of licensed or certified contractors, workers, and investigators to monitor and remove asbestos.

RECENT STUDIES BY THE FEDERAL GOVERNMENT AND NEW YORK CITY

Both the federal and local governments have dramatically changed their views toward asbestos management. Initially, the main idea was to remove asbestos. This created hysteria in the industry because tenants, institutions, and owners developed a wholesale removal program in order to avoid potential health hazards and liability issues. However, this attitude has been modified on the federal level by the results of the *Environmental Protection Agency Report to Congress on Asbestos-Containing Materials in Public Buildings*.

According to the study, which addresses the extent and condition of asbestos in approximately 3.6 million public and commercial buildings, about 20 percent, or 733,000 buildings, contain friable asbestos material, and most of the significantly damaged asbestos was found in nonpublic building areas such as mechanical areas and boiler rooms. The study also points out that the presence of asbestos, by itself, does not necessarily pose a human health risk. Asbestos hazards occur when the material is damaged or disturbed, releasing fibers that can be inhaled. Most importantly, the study states that no safe threshold has been established for asbestos.

An interesting footnote to the study is that the results "appeared" to indicate no difference between fiber concentration in building air and outdoor air levels. It was further indicated that perhaps the disturbance created by mass removal may cause a greater health hazard than leaving it in place and managing it properly.

THE AHERA PROGRAM

In October 1986, the federal government released the Asbestos Hazard Emergency Response Act (AHERA). The purpose of this program was to develop an approach of managing asbestos in schools. However, based on the report to Congress, this approach is not presently being applied to office buildings until further studies are made. The general outline of the approach is nonetheless interesting because general step-by-step provisions are set forth for handling and managing in-place asbestos. The provisions consist of the following:

1. Inspection.
2. Reinspection.
3. Sampling and analysis.
4. Management plan (including a description of response actions).
5. Response actions.
6. Requirements for training and periodic surveillance.
7. Air sampling requirements.
8. Use of accredited persons to inspect buildings for asbestos-containing materials (ACM), developing management plans, and designing and conducting response actions.
9. Recordkeeping.

Furthermore, on the local level, New York City has recently completed its study of in-place asbestos in some 900 buildings in 14 categories. The preliminary findings indicated that in tall buildings, the majority of asbestos-containing material was located in mechanical areas and machine rooms, and exposure to the general public and occupants of the building was thus limited. The study further found that only 30 to 38 percent of the buildings contained surface asbestos material—which means that it was sprayed, troweled, or otherwise applied onto surfaces such as structural members, ceilings, and walls—of which only 1 to 4 percent was in poor condition and warranted removal.

As a result of these findings, the city has now taken an attitude that closely parallels that of the EPA, which is to reduce wholesale removal of asbestos, since this could create a larger exposure hazard. A management approach should thus handle the asbestos problem by implementing a program that covers the following areas:

1. A building inspection survey to determine the type, amount, and condition of asbestos in the building.

2. Worker training certification to ensure that building personnel are trained in awareness of asbestos-containing materials and the handling of asbestos on a limited basis.
3. An operations and maintenance program that is tailored for each property. It includes worker training and protection, work practices for in-place asbestos, and recordkeeping procedures.
4. Assessment and collection of information—an analysis of bulk samples and air samples collected during assessment survey.
5. A management plan detailing all aspects of building management policies and procedures on asbestos abatement including recordkeeping and a chain of command.
6. Response actions to determine what response—removal, encapsulation, or enclosure—is required in a given situation.
7. Reinspection, usually on a yearly basis, to determine whether the condition of materials throughout the building has changed, and, if so, what the response should be.
8. Respiratory protection training to ensure that all personnel involved in the asbestos abatement program are trained in the use and care of respiratory protection.

New York City has introduced a new proposed law entitled Intro 453, formerly known as Intro 1164, which deals with the management of in-place asbestos. This law addresses the program indicated above and recognizes that disturbance and removal of asbestos may, in some cases, create more of a hazard than managing the material in place. This proposed law is before the city council at the time of this writing and should be enacted shortly.

The city believes that the overall program can be implemented in stages, and the two main areas for immediate consideration are (1) the initial building inspection survey and (2) a training program for maintenance workers and contractors that are most likely to come in contact with asbestos. These programs are not required by law at the present time. However, in the interim, owners or managers should use a professional approach to managing asbestos, setting up some consistent corporate policies of dealing with it during demolition or renovation projects, as well as on a continual basis, with normal operation of the building.

The first step in developing a corporate policy is to set up a professional team to evaluate all of these issues, addressing the health hazards, requirements of law, and the protection of employees, tenants, and contractors, thereby ultimately reducing the owner's liability.

The professional team should consist of a representative from management, an asbestos consultant, an attorney familiar with environmental litigation, and a state- and federally certified asbestos abatement contractor. This team helps to create policies and procedures that will consider all the issues of the asbestos problem. All owners have rushed out to make random surveys of their buildings and have not considered all aspects of the issue. A better approach is to develop a corporate program that starts with an inspection survey plan, which establishes general guidelines for investigators to follow while conducting an asbestos inspection. The purpose of this plan is twofold:

1. To ensure uniform response to the presence of asbestos within the owner's various buildings.
2. To provide necessary documentation for compliance with all government regulations.

This will demonstrate that the owner's measures exceed those required by law. However, when the plan is established, it should have flexibility to change with additions, revisions, and amendments of all federal, state, and local laws. It should establish, identify, and assess the condition of asbestos in the buildings. Assessment of the condition of asbestos-containing materials in the building is paramount. The investigator must identify areas that contain friable asbestos, which means that the asbestos-containing materials can be crumbled, pulverized, or reduced by hand pressure. The condition of asbestos should help the investigator to develop response actions. The final results of the inspection will be documented in the investigator's survey report.

The survey plan generally requires the investigator to obtain building specifications and plans. Bulk or air samples of asbestos can be located on these plans, and photographs of representative and unusual sites, accompanied by the investigator's affidavit, should be included. Inspection forms should be completed for all areas surveyed, as well as a chain-of-custody log, which establishes the chain of custody for both air and bulk samples on file. If litigation occurs, results of the survey will be properly documented and serve as proof that the building owner or manager is trying to provide a building environment that is safe for all occupants.

Once the survey is completed, the investigator should prepare a report outlining the appropriate actions to be taken. These may range from removal to encapsulation or enclosure, in the case of friable asbestos, to the development of an operations and maintenance (O&M) manual and plan for the management of material that is not friable or delaminated.

Conditions requiring removal, encapsulation, or enclosure should be prioritized by the level of severity. Removal of severely damaged material would be the first area of concern, and next would be material that, because of its accessibility, is susceptible to friability or has already shown signs of damage but is not an imminent hazard. Furthermore, lease expirations and subsequent vacant tenant space provide the opportunity to remove asbestos there, as well as that which may be exposed by demolition. By removing this material, the building owner can offer a space that is more attractive to prospective tenants. All removals, including encapsulation and enclosure, should be completed by a certified asbestos abatement contractor, with air monitoring performed by the asbestos consultant—an industrial hygienist. The consultant provides daily logs of air monitoring for air clearance, and a final air clearance when the abatement project is completed. As part of the corporate asbestos abatement program, management should have at least three licensed and certified asbestos abatement contractors available to complete asbestos removals and at least two industrial hygienists or consultants to perform air monitoring and project management, each having completed qualification forms providing information on company employees, financial standing, insurance coverage, and licensing. This information should be retained on file at the corporate management office.

As documentation and recordkeeping are essential to any asbestos abatement program, separate files must also be maintained in the corporate management office for each asbestos removal project, including copies of the following items:

1. Federal, state, and local notifications detailing dates of work and amount of ACM to be removed, as well as names of the asbestos abatement contractor, third-party monitoring firm, asbestos handler, and disposal site.
2. Bulk sample analysis confirming ACM content.
3. Scope of work—detailed specifications and description of the project as developed by an industrial hygienist.
4. Air sample analysis, including final air clearance.
5. Description of reinsulation materials used, where applicable.
6. Dumpsite contract providing a detailed listing of the name of the building generating the asbestos, the removal contractor, the amount of material, the dates of pick-up and delivery of

material, the hauler's name and licensing, the landfill name and location, dump ticket number, and signature for receipt of material by the landfill.

7. Certificates of insurance for abatement contractor and air monitoring firm.

The procedures in the O&M manual and plan should cover ways of training employers to work in and around nonfriable asbestos, as well as to deal with asbestos on an emergency basis, such as a steam leak. At the present time, there are no approved certified programs for maintenance worker training, but the state of New York requires operations and maintenance training for a minimum of 12 hours. However, the program is not complete, and there are no approved training schools available. The city of New York is requiring training of electricians and carpenters who are working as part of an asbestos removal project as restricted handlers. The city is also currently studying the issue of certified programs for operations and maintenance people. Therefore, a member of a maintenance staff should be sent to a more extensive program, such as the New York state certified handler's course until such programs are solidified for operation and maintenance workers.

It is advisable to develop a service contract with a certified asbestos removal contractor for 24-hour, 7-day-a-week service, as many emergency situations may arise where the fiber release or potential fiber release is beyond that which can be handled by the building staff. The asbestos removal contractors have personnel and equipment readily available to handle an emergency asbestos project—10 feet of ACM or more—whereas the building staff is more likely to handle a steam leak or other situation requiring the removal of less than 5 feet of ACM.

Aside from training, the O&M manual should also detail corporate procedure with standardized documentation for the owner's or manager's entire portfolio. Tenants should receive a notification letter outlining the presence of asbestos in the building. All contractors, before completing any work for the owner, manager, or tenant, should be required to obtain approval in the form of a signed consent form from the building manager. This will prevent exposure to asbestos in tenant spaces without the knowledge of building management; allow building management to review inspection survey plans to determine whether work will disturb ACM; and, if so, will provide a procedure for contacting an asbestos removal contractor to clean the area prior to commencement of the work. A sample tenant notification letter is shown in Exhibit 14–1.

EXHIBIT 14–1
Sample Tenant Notification Letter

Dear Tenant:

As you may be aware, asbestos was commonly used by the construction industry prior to the early 1970s because of its proven insulation and fire-proofing capabilities. Recently there has been considerable national publicity on the presence of asbestos in buildings and the promulgation of regulations and guidelines relating to its handling.

At this time we would like to advise you that we have voluntarily chosen to conduct an inspection to determine whether there is any asbestos at _____, and have gone far beyond any requirements by city, state, or federal governments. The inspection was conducted by an independent facility, air samples were taken, and bulk sampling analysis was performed. A building representative is available to discuss the inspection.

To summarize, the report stated that, as in almost all buildings built prior to 1971, asbestos-containing material was found in the building. Air sampling tests revealed very low levels of asbestos in the air—well below any permissible exposure level set by city, state, or federal agencies.

According to government reports, the mere presence of stabilized asbestos does not warrant its removal. However, care must be taken to avoid unnecessary disturbance or release of asbestos. Because even minor repairs (including improvements or installations such as hanging light fixtures, electrical work, or installing air conditioners or phones) may affect the asbestos-containing material above the ceilings or behind the wall, compliance with certain newly enacted and proposed city, state, and federal regulations may be required. Management has broadened its services, including the appointment of an asbestos program coordinator, to help you.

In this regard, it is important, both to protect yourself from unknowingly violating statutes and to ensure the comfort and safety of all building occupants, that you avail yourself of these services, in addition to complying with all building procedures already in existence.

As you know, existing building rules provide that before you, your employees, or independent contractors undertake any kind of work, alteration, or repair on your premises, landlord approval must be obtained through the building manager. This is especially important with regard to work involving removal, destruction, or renovation of pipes, ceiling tiles, or walls. The building manager will be available to assist you. We have also set new guidelines for both minor and major work with which you must comply. These guidelines are enumerated in the building alteration consent form. Compliance is crucial to help maximize the comfort and protection of all concerned, including workmen and building occupants. The building manager can be reached during regular business hours at _____.

The landlord's prime concern is the safety and well-being of building occupants. We will be working with you to help achieve this goal. If you have any questions, we are at your service.

THE BUILDING MANAGEMENT

Standard contracts with asbestos provisions should be developed between the contractor and management, including insurance requirements and work performance standards, according to city, state, and federal requirements, as well as considerations for worker and tenant safety. After the corporate building management plan and policy are developed, a specific building management plan can be tailored for each property in the owner's or manager's portfolio, addressing the specific conditions of an individual building. The asbestos management team should address unusual and unforeseen circumstances on an individual basis to discuss the best solution to the problem.

Under the O&M manual and plan all areas of each building should be resurveyed on a periodic basis. The frequency of resurvey is based on condition and accessibility of ACM. It may include not only a visual survey, but also random air sampling to ensure that air levels remain below those prescribed by state, city, and federal regulations.

Each aspect of the O&M manual and plan should be reviewed by the attorney, as part of the asbestos management team. To ensure that all of the appropriate steps are documented, the wording of these procedures must be such that the owner is protected in the event of any further litigation.

The asbestos issue is very critical, not only in terms of health of the building owners, employees, and tenants, but also of cost to the owner. However, if one addresses it in an intelligent, organized manner, one can deal with it. Based on the EPA's study and on other studies currently being made, it seems evident that on a long-term basis, everyone will be required to have an established building management plan. Any program must be flexible enough to be adjusted at the time definite asbestos management programs are mandated by both the federal and local governments.

New York City presently is developing a management plan that generally follows the outline as indicated above. However, any plan will have to be adjusted, based on future regulations that may develop within one's area.

RECENT SCIENTIFIC STUDIES

Recently a number of studies have come out, including one from Harvard University, and a widely reported study that appeared January 19, 1990, in *Science* (a highly regarded peer review journal published by the American Association for the Advancement of Science), entitled "Asbestos: Scientific Developments and Implication for Public Policy."

This study concluded that the asbestos panic in the United States must be curtailed. Five eminent scientists concluded that the hundreds of billions of dollars that could be spent in the next 30 years on asbestos removal projects would be a waste, because the risk from exposure to asbestos in buildings is miniscule.

This report concluded the following:

1. Measured concentrations of asbestos in building air, even when the buildings contained damaged ACM, are comparable to levels in outdoor air—a point surely relevant to assessing the health risk of asbestos in buildings.
2. Asbestos-related diseases have been linked with exposure in factories and shipyards. The levels of asbestos concentrations in these areas were 100 or more fibers per cubic centimeter of air. In contrast, surveys of asbestos in schools and public buildings show that the mean airborne concentrations are several thousand times lower.
3. The type of asbestos fiber found predominantly in buildings is chrysotile and current epidemiology data suggest that exposure to chrysotile at current occupational standards does not increase the risks of asbestos-associated diseases.
4. According to estimates of risk, the number of probable deaths per million from long-term smoking, home accidents, motor vehicle accidents, drowning, aircraft accidents, and so forth are several hundreds—maybe thousands—of times greater than from exposure to asbestos.
5. These data support the concept that low-level exposure to asbestos is not a health hazard in buildings and schools.
6. The removal of previously damaged or encapsulated asbestos can lead to increases in airborne concentration of fibers in buildings, sometimes for months afterward, and can result in problems with safe removal and disposal.
7. Asbestos abatement has also led to the exposure of a large cohort of relatively young asbestos removal workers.
8. For dealing with exposure to maintenance workers and service workers in buildings with severely damaged ACM, worker education and building maintenance will prove far more effective than removal as risk prevention measures.

As one can see, the majority of recent scientific studies seem to indicate that usual levels of airborne asbestos in office buildings are quite low, and, therefore, an alternative to the wholesale removal of asbestos, which increases airborne levels substantially, is the in-place management of asbestos, whenever possible.

CHAPTER 15

MODERNIZING AND RETROFITTING ELEVATORS

William O. Lippman, Jr.
Calvin Brast
Armor Elevator Company, Inc.

The retrofit or modernization process of an elevator or group of elevators may be started by a simple statement from the route maintenance mechanic that the equipment should be replaced, or it may be started because of economic reasons. Whatever the reason, work that is done must be well-planned and -defined to prevent future disappointment.

In this chapter, we will discuss the many parts of an elevator and the various phases of the retrofit or modernization. A successful project includes a review of all mechanical, electrical, and aesthetic components to determine the action required, and it must consider the following items:

1. Excessive elevator downtime and lack of available parts.
2. Safety reasons—possible injury exposure to employees and public.
   - Stopping accuracy cannot be achieved or maintained.
   - Severe releveling after floor stops.
   - Equipment is unsafe to operate.
3. Code requirement—life safety.
   - Handicap laws must be met.
   - Fire-fighting controls must be installed.
   - Emergency power operation may be required.
   - Hospital emergency operation.

- Mandatory code updates.
- Other local code requirements.
4. Increased maintenance costs.
   - Repairs.
   - Added maintenance time.
5. Building occupancy changes.
   - Major tenant.
   - Type of building function.
6. Tenant requirements.
   - Restore to equivalent of new building for competitive reasons.
   - Complaints about service—waiting times, noise, or ride quality.
   - Congested lobby traffic.
7. Economic reasons.
   - Short- and long-term plans.
   - Immediate sale or purchase.
   - Capital or expense.

Modernization planning should be carefully thought out. Older buildings that are brought up to a high quality level can offer distinct advantages over new buildings, including the following:

1. Prestigious location.
2. Convenient parking.
3. Unique architectural appearance.
4. Historical site.
5. Accessibility to public transportation.
6. Proximity to closely related functions or businesses.

As one considers these advantages, the owner's future plans should be a factor in the type of retrofit planned. Improving the sales price of building or property in the short or long term will be a factor in determining the extent of retention, replacement, or repair of the various components comprising an elevator system. A completely modernized elevator system should provide a minimum of 15 years of good performance.

The demand for improved service in existing buildings has created considerable interest in modernizing elevator systems. Waiting times at the main or upper floor lobbies are a major source of tenant complaints. The increased use of computers and higher rental rates has caused tenants to increase population density from the original configuration or design parameters, which can increase the building occupancy to a level where demands on the elevators cannot be efficiently handled by older systems. New technology offers dramatic improvements in the capabilities of the group control system. Microprocessors have allowed many additional inputs to be weighed in the system's decision-making process and in allocating elevators to respond to a call. This technology, when applied to existing elevator groups, again allows the system to operate within acceptable parameters. However, if a building is seriously under-elevatored, a modernization cannot alone overcome this design error.

MODULARITY OF DESIGN

When planning any system, the modularity of design should be considered. The system should be designed so that the retrofit can be completed in stages, if necessary. Ineffective traffic handling traceable to the existing group control or signal logic system does not necessarily mean that the elevator door operators, for example, should be replaced. Most major systems outlined hereafter should work well by themselves and be compatible with each other. Even if the planned retrofit includes all components except rails and machines, the new equipment should still allow for future replacement of major components. Components such as car station, which are added during the retrofit, should be compatible with control equipment and not proprietary so they do not limit future modernization efforts.

Any partial retrofit should retain major components that are fully compatible to the next phase of a modernization. This will permit the phases of modernization to be done over a longer time period and minimize up-front costs. This practice also allows the flexibility of using one supplier for one phase of modernization, such as door equipment, and later changing to another supplier for the next phase.

There are many products on the market today that allow such flexibility, but the items that should come from a single supplier are the signal and motion control logic systems. These systems are closely interwoven and, if procured from different sources, they may be incompatible. Portions may have to be duplicated or specially designed to work together. An example is installing a system overlay on an elevator that later will be fully modernized. If the overlay supplier were not used for the added motion control, the overlay portion would need to be replaced, and the original investment in the overlay would be lost. In the purchase of an overlay, the ability to reuse the hardware for motion control updates should be the prime consideration.

Mechanical components, on the other hand, are usually stand-alone items. For example, roller guides can be changed without other equipment changes, and door operators are a self-contained package that allows changing of the master operator, door tracks, hangers, or interlocks without changing other equipment.

Equipment compatibility should be thoroughly analyzed before any retrofit work is done, and a long-range plan established. This can be done without making any financial commitments. If ownership of the building is short-range, a well-planned retrofit will help to establish a price for prospective buyers.

Exhibit 15–1 shows an approach to modernization and the way in which the various major components relate to each other. The diagram demonstrates that various processes can be performed individually. The items marked with an asterisk are shown connected to the parts of the equipment that they affect.

CRITERIA FOR GOOD ELEVATOR SERVICE

The lobby response time and transportation, or handling, capacity of the system in a five-minute period of time are two important measurements of elevator service. Lobby response time is the time interval between elevators' leaving the main lobby with the intended load. The lobby response time for various types of buildings should be in the ranges as indicated in Exhibit 15–2.

The transportation capacity of the system is the percentage of the building population that can be transported in a five-minute period of time. Transportation capacity for various types of buildings should be within the parameters shown in Exhibit 15–3.

The average waiting time of passengers at various floors throughout the building is usually considered to be approximately 60 percent of the lobby response time. The response time for a car to cancel a call is not the average waiting time. When a call is established, the response time starts, but as other passengers arrive in the corridor where a call has been placed, the time for late passengers is less than the time of the first person. Thus, the average waiting time is less than the system response to the call.

To measure the system response time, a traffic analyzer should be connected to the existing system and all established calls logged

EXHIBIT 15–1
Modernization Block Diagram

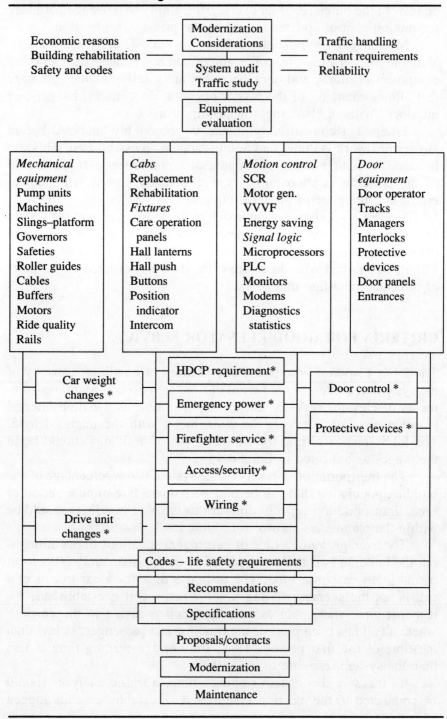

Modernization Considerations

Economic reasons — Building rehabilitation — Safety and codes —

— Traffic handling — Tenant requirements — Reliability

System audit
Traffic study

Equipment evaluation

Mechanical equipment	*Cabs*	*Motion control*	*Door equipment*
Pump units	Replacement	SCR	Door operator
Machines	Rehabilitation	Motor gen.	Tracks
Slings–platform	*Fixtures*	VVVF	Managers
Governors	Care operation	Energy saving	Interlocks
Safeties	panels	*Signal logic*	Protective
Roller guides	Hall lanterns	Microprocessors	devices
Cables	Hall push	PLC	Door panels
Buffers	Buttons	Monitors	Entrances
Motors	Position	Modems	
Ride quality	indicator	Diagnostics	
Rails	Intercom	statistics	

Car weight changes *

HDCP requirement*

Emergency power *

Firefighter service *

Access/security*

Wiring *

Door control *

Protective devices *

Drive unit changes *

Codes – life safety requirements

Recommendations

Specifications

Proposals/contracts

Modernization

Maintenance

EXHIBIT 15–2
Lobby Response Time

	Interval (in seconds)	
Quality	Incoming	Two-way
Excellent	20–25	25–32
Good	25–32	32–40
Satisfactory	32–40	40–50

for the length of time they are established. This recording should be done over a specific time frame during the normal day and not diluted by slack periods such as weekends or nights. Including a building's off-hours will not give an accurate analysis of performance during the regular work days.

Traffic handling during peak periods can be accomplished by actually counting passengers to be transported and the number of times that the elevators leave the lobby floor. This manual count can be used to calculate the percentage of the population that is transported during a unit of time and the average departure interval. The combination of the response time and lobby traffic gives the information necessary to compare the present service to the standards for modern elevator service. Most new microprocessor-based systems have traffic statistic recordings and a monitor display or printout that allows for easy, routine checks of system-response time.

This analysis also requires the building to be occupied to normal expected occupancy for accuracy. If the building has fewer occupants,

EXHIBIT 15–3
Transportation Capacity

Type of building	Working hours	Transportation capacity	
		Excellent	Good
Offices			
One company	Common	15–20%	13–16%
One company	Flexible	14–18	12–15
Diversified	Common	13–16	11–14
Diversified	Flexible	12–14	10–12
Hospitals			
Visitors		12–16	10–14
Personnel		15–20	12–16
Hotels		14–20	12–15

the response time should be estimated for expected full capacity. To calculate the expected response time, the following list comprises the minimum information required:

1. Speed of elevators.
2. Capacity of elevators.
3. Number of elevators in the group.
4. Floors served and building designation of floors.
5. Net rentable space per floor for all floors, and anticipated or planned average space per person.
6. Travel distance between floors.
7. Type of doors—center-parting or slide, two-speed or single.
8. Opening width of doors.
9. Type of existing control.
10. Type of occupancy planned—single, diversified, insurance, government, and so forth.
11. Actual personnel count on each occupied floor.
12. Other facilities and floor location—a restaurant, private club, retail space, garage, and so on.

With this information, performance can be calculated and compared to the current performance of the system and to standards.

Traffic analysis of an existing system compared to the calculated performance of a microprocessor-run system will show the dramatic improvements that can be achieved therewith. When traffic handling is a reason for considering a retrofit, a traffic analysis is requisite to writing the specification. It will show actual traffic problems so an informed decision can be made. Building occupancy or use may have changed so much over the years that rearrangement of floors served or addition of landings or elevators may be required to solve the problem.

When analyzing current traffic statistics, the performance of the existing elevators must be considered. Excessive performance time can also cause poor traffic handling. Exhibit 15–4 shows a sample performance and quality audit form.

The existing system may not be adjusted for optimum performance or may be unable to perform to modern standards. Acceptable standards of performance for a one-floor run for center-opening doors of a 42-inch opening should be approximately 9 seconds, and for two-speed side-opening doors of the same width, under 10.5 seconds. Performance time is measured in seconds from the start of door

EXHIBIT 15-4
Building Elevator Quality Audit

BLDG. NAME _____ DATE _____

BLDG. ADDRESS _____

BLDG. MANAGEMENT COMPANY _____

TYPE OF EQUIPMENT _____ SPEED _____ FPM (APPROX.)

MFR. OF EQUIPMENT _____ CAPACITY _____

TYPE OF DOOR SS _____ C/O _____ 2-SPEED _____ DOOR OPENING WIDTH _____

OPERATING TIME IN SECONDS

ELEVATOR #	DOOR OPENING TIME	DOOR CLOSING TIME	DOOR TIME (LONG)	DOOR TIME (SHORT)	BRAKE-TO-BRAKE		PERFORMANCE	
					1-FLOOR RUN	2-FLOOR RUN	1-FLOOR RUN	2-FLOOR RUN

305

EXHIBIT 15-4 (continued)

AESTHETIC AND QUALITY CHARACTERISTICS

ELEVATOR #	CAB APPEARANCE	FIXTURE APPEARANCE	DOOR NOISE	RIDE QUALITY	STOPPING ACCURACY	NUMBER OF STOPS	COMMENTS

USE (1)EXCELLENT (2)GOOD (3)AVERAGE (4)POOR (5) BAD

GENERAL COMMENTS _____

_____

_____

INFORMATION GIVEN TO _____ SIGNATURE _____

PERFORMANCE—ACTUAL TIME OF START OF DOOR CLOSE TO DOOR THREE-FOURTHS OPEN AT NEXT CONTIGUOUS STOP (AVERAGE DISTANCE 12 FEET).

BRAKE TO BRAKE—ACTUAL TIME FROM START OF CAR MOTION TO STOP OF CAR MOTION.

close to three-fourths open between two contiguous floors of average floor height. Factors such as door opening distances, door speed, door weight, types of doors, and motion control adjustment affect performance time. Code limitation on door close force and kinetic energy require slower closing speeds than for opening, where only the door operator mechanics and electrical control are the limiting factors. Because the speed is reduced during closing, the distance traveled by the doors is a factor. Single-speed side-opening doors will take longer to open and close than center-opening doors for the same size opening.

Exhibit 15–5 shows approximate closing time of various types of doors.

Door-opening speed should be set for a minimum average speed of two feet per second over the opening area, as there is neither danger of striking a passenger nor limitation on door forces in the open direction.

EXHIBIT 15–5
Closing Time in Seconds

Entrance width (inches)	Code distance feet	Single-slide doors		Two-speed doors		Center-opening doors		Center-opening doors	
		B/E*	S/S**	B/E*	S/S**	B/E	S/S	B/E	S/S
32	2.34	2.7 (1.1)	2.8 (1.0)						
36	2.67	3.2 (1.0)	3.5 (0.9)	2.6 (1.3)	2.8 (1.2)	1.7 (1.1)	2.0 (0.9)		
42	3.17	3.7 (1.0)	4.0 (0.9)	3.1 (1.2)	3.4 (1.1)	2.1 (1.0)	2.3 (0.9)		
48	3.67			3.8 (1.1)	4.2 (1.0)	2.6 (0.9)	2.8 (0.8)		
54	4.17					2.8 (0.9)	3.1 (0.8)	2.4 (1.1)	2.6 (1.0)
60	4.67							2.8 (1.0)	3.1 (0.9)
72	5.67							3.7 (0.9)	4.1 (0.8)

*B/E = Baked Enamel Finish (8 lb./sq.ft.)
**S/S = Stainless or Formica Clad (10 lb./sq.ft.)
Minimum door closing time in seconds, based on code distance. Maximum average door closing speed, in feet per second. (Based on 7-foot high doors; with 1 1/4 inch thick panels; slowdown control time of 0.5 seconds added.)

When considering a modernization, only extreme complications require complete replacement of the entrance frames. It is expensive and requires additional downtime and extensive work, including building modifications.

When analyzing door operation and motion control and comparing them to acceptable standards for their individual operations, the extent of improvement utilizing the microprocessor signal logic can be determined. These analyses must be considered realistically, without assuming that changing to a microprocessor is the answer to all problems. When the traffic and performance information is gathered, the system as a whole can be evaluated. Each piece of equipment should be listed and reviewed for retention or replacement in accordance with long- or short-range plans; from this list, specifications can be written. The reason for either decision should be clearly defined to avoid unpleasant surprises after the specifications are written and proposals received. Questionable items should be listed and priced separately. Reused equipment, however, may detract from the improvements offered by new microprocessor signal and motion control.

CODE REFERENCES

In the United States, the American Society of Mechanical Engineers and the American National Standards Institute have developed a set of rules known as the ASME/ANSI A17.1 Code. This code has established minimum requirements for various mechanical and industrial products. A set of rules is not a code unless it is adopted by a state, county, municipality, or other enforcing authority as law. The version of the ANSI rules to be applied is defined in the statute that adopts it as law for a local regulating authority. Some authorities establish their own set of modifications, which provide a myriad of rules used throughout the United States, as each state or local government determines what rules to apply to its area of authority.

The Southern Building Code (SBC), Uniform Building Code (UBC), and Building Officials and Code Administrators (BOCA) are all model building codes that are used by various areas for minimum building requirements. Each of these codes has certain standards that must be met for permits and approvals. An example of such a requirement is that of earthquake provisions; the model building code states that equipment must meet an applicable earthquake zone requirement. The ANSI A17.1 rules provide the minimum requirement for equipment design to meet the building requirement for earthquake provisions. Model building codes also provide the requirements for laboratory certification of some safety-related devices. These testing laboratories are Underwriters Laboratories (UL), the Canadian Standards Association (CSA), or other regional laboratories. In some countries, a standard code is applied to the entire country, which eliminates the problem of conflicting rules. Regardless of where a project is undertaken, the applicable code or rules must be known so equipment can be made to comply with them. When retrofitting, certain equipment requires that the entire system be brought into compliance with the codes. This fact must be known when the specifications are finalized so all the costs of the project are known and no difficulties will be encountered when trying to obtain final approval from the inspecting authority.

To define the technical approach to retrofitting elevators, Exhibit 15–6 shows the various types of elevators and the building parameters that establish elevator requirements.

TYPES OF ELEVATORS

Hydraulic Elevators

Hydraulic elevators are elevators that operate with a liquid in a closed system where the liquid is recycled. They utilize a plunger in a cylinder; the plunger is located directly below the elevator platform in most cases. Some early versions utilized cables and sheaves in combination with plungers and cylinders; many years ago, hydraulic elevators utilizing the building water supply were installed. The water from the building water main was used to push the elevator up and then discharged into a drain system to lower the elevator. Water systems cannot be retrofitted. Later versions of hydraulic elevators utilize oil in a closed system that has a motor and a pump to push the oil into the cylinder for upward movement. The elevator is lowered by opening a valve to allow the oil to return to a storage tank. Approximately two-thirds of all elevators installed in the United States today are oil hydraulic elevators. Modern versions of oil hydraulics are generally limited to a speed of 200 feet per minute and six stops. There are higher-rise hydraulic systems, but they are not used as frequently as the lower-rise systems because of the speed limitation.

EXHIBIT 15–6
Elevator Type versus Speed

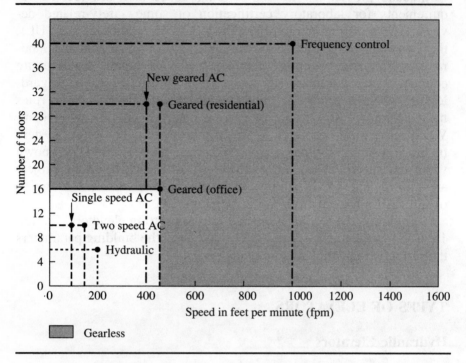

These are the various types of hydraulic elevators available today:

1. *Direct plunger.* The plunger is fastened directly under the car and the plunger and cylinder extend downward a distance approximately equal to the travel of elevators (see Exhibit 15–7a).
2. *Indirect plunger.* The plunger is located at some position other than that described in (1) to reduce the hole depth required for the cylinder.
3. *Telescopic plunger.* The plunger assembly consists of various sizes of plungers within each other; this reduces the overall length of the cylinder when fully retracted but still provides the plunger length required when fully extended. This configuration usually eliminates or considerably reduces the hole size that is required with a direct plunger. These plungers can have either a direct or indirect mounting arrangement (see Exhibit 15-7b).

4. *Roped hydraulic.* A combination of sheaves and steel ropes allow for reduced travel of the indirect plunger and eliminate the requirement of a cylinder hole below the elevator. The roping is usually 2:1 so that the plunger is required to travel only half of the elevator travel distance, making it possible to install the complete jack assembly in the hoistway. This arrangement is more acceptable for higher travel than direct plunger hydraulics. The ANSI A17.1 code has recently been modified to accept roped hydraulic elevators as an approved type.

EXHIBIT 15–7
Hydraulic Elevators with (a) Direct Plunger and (b) Telescopic Plunger

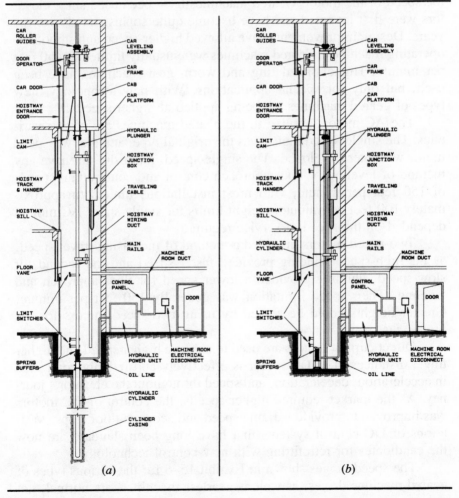

(a) *(b)*

Geared Elevators

A geared elevator uses a geared machine with a ring gear and a worm gear of various ratios (see Exhibit 15–8a). The worm gear is driven with either an alternating current motor or direct current motor. The ring gear is fastened to a shaft assembly with the output traction sheave. AC motors utilize the alternating current power as it is supplied to the building. They rotate at constant revolutions per minute (rpm), depending on their design. The motors are connected to the AC line, and their rpm value and the gear ratio of the machine determine the output speed of the geared machine and thus the elevator's speed. Direct current motors convert the AC power to DC, which is varied to control the speed of the motor. Geared machines have been used since elevators were first invented and have become quite sophisticated over the years. Design improvements have allowed higher-speed and smoother-operating machines. Geared machines were usually limited to 450 feet per minute. Higher-speed ring and worm gear machines have been used, but only for special applications. With new technology, new types of geared machines are being applied at higher speeds.

The AC motors applied to the geared machines are of two varieties: The single-speed motor was the original type, and the two-speed motor was later developed. The single-speed motor did not have any method of leveling or floor approach control and could attain speeds of 150 feet per minute, with most installations limited to approximately 100 feet per minute. Height limits for single-speed AC motors depended on the speed of service required.

Two-speed motors provided a method of increasing travel speed, as the high-speed winding provided faster speed and the second, or slow-speed, winding provided a lower speed for floor approach and leveling. Their speed limitation was generally 150 feet per minute. Greater heights could be served by using two-speed motors for the higher car speeds.

Direct current motors are used to achieve higher speed and higher travel distances. The DC motor is effectively and reliably controlled in acceleration, deceleration, and speed throughout the elevator's journey. As the market required higher speeds, the control of DC motors was improved to provide variable speed and accurate floor stops. Variations of DC control systems that have long been standard are now the candidates for retrofitting with new control technology.

The speed ranges shown in Exhibit 15–6 for the various types of geared machine drives, as well as gearless machines, are normal, not

EXHIBIT 15–8
(a) Geared Traction and (b) Gearless Traction Elevators

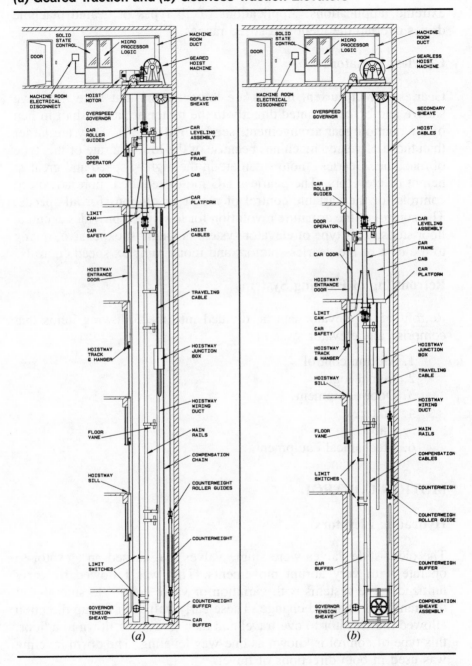

(a)

(b)

extreme, applications. Applications of all types of geared machine drives overlap the identified speed ranges.

Gearless Elevators

Gearless direct current motors are large motors that have the drive sheave and brake mounted directly to the motor armature shaft in lieu of a reduction gear arrangement (see Exhibit 15-8*b*). They are larger than those of geared machines because of the low rpm rate of this type of machine. Gearless motors can attain the highest speed and greatest height of elevators. The gearless DC motor required more advanced controls for the variable control of motor revolutions for all speeds. The control of the armature revolution for low speed provides accurate floor stops. This type of elevator system is the most expensive, owing to the cost of the gearless motors and more complex speed controls.

Retrofitting of Existing Systems

Retrofit of an elevator can be divided into the following items that comprise any elevator system:

1. Motion control.
2. Signal logic.
3. Door equipment.
4. Fixtures.
5. Cab.
6. Mechanical equipment.

MOTION CONTROL

Hydraulic Elevators

The older-style valves were single valves that caused an elevator to operate with very abrupt movements. This was followed by early unitized valve systems with variation of valve control to smooth out the transition of speed change. These early valves in the up direction allowed the elevator to overtravel and then level back down to a floor; this type of control is known as one-way leveling. The down leveling was used in both directions of travel.

Modern valves are integrated valve units with separate leveling controls for each direction of travel. The control of these valves is very smooth from acceleration through the deceleration and stopping phases. Some new valves are electronically controlled and operated by a feedback system that provides constant speed control. Replacement of existing valve systems with newer types of valves should be considered when smoothness, reliability, and more precise floor stops are required. Newer valve systems usually reduce floor-to-floor time with the improved leveling control. Replacing the total power unit is usually less expensive than replacing the valves only. The repiping and reworking of storage tank connections are usually labor-intensive and offset the cost of a complete tank and valve assembly. New storage tanks offer isolation, smoother and quieter operating pumps, and, when combined with new piping techniques, dramatically improve a hydraulic elevator system's motion control.

The hydraulic jack plunger and cylinder can be retained in place. Older jack assemblies can be fitted with new packing assemblies to reduce friction and improve the operation of the elevator. The new type of packing usually reduces oil leakage between the plunger and seal.

The cylinder and plunger assembly can be replaced with new assemblies if they have developed plunger scoring, an underground leak, or both. Soil conditions for various geographical areas directly determine the hydraulic cylinder life. The installation procedures used, such as cylinder wrapping, coating, or outside sealed casing, also determine the possibility of corrosion and potential failure of the cylinder. A telescopic assembly can be used as a replacement, but indirect plunger and roped hydraulic systems cannot, unless the total elevator assembly is redesigned and replaced. The indirect and roped hydraulic systems require additional shaft space or reduced platform and cab size for the jack assembly. The structural load on the building will change and will require recalculation and new support areas.

Hydraulic elevator speeds cannot be increased by valve or jack assembly replacements without checking for required overtravel at both the top and bottom of the shaftway, as well as a motor horsepower increase. Speed increase can be considered if the shaft dimensions allow it, and if the power unit, consisting of the pump and motor, is changed. The pipe size to the cylinder also must be checked.

Geared Machines

Single-Speed Alternating Current Motors
The control of single-speed alternating current motors has been dramatically improved in recent years. This offers an economical

approach to correct uncontrolled and inaccurate floor stops. AC motors originally operated by shutting off power to the motor and sliding to a stop, resulting in most cases with the final stop being load-dependent. Releveling was not possible once the stop was made. Today, variable-frequency drives offer complete control of most AC motors and provide releveling capabilities.

Reuse of the existing AC motor and geared machine, with conversion to variable frequency drive, is often effective. Since most AC elevators were installed in residential buildings, electronic floor-stopping accuracy offered by variable frequency drives significantly reduces the risk of tripping injury caused by inaccurate floor stops. Maintenance cost of brake lining replacement is reduced, as the brake is only used to hold the elevator at the floor. Motion control and new solid-state logic will improve the reliability of the elevator system by reducing or eliminating failures associated with electromechanical relays and control methods.

Two-Speed Alternating Current Motors

Two-speed AC motors provided the ability to run at higher speeds on one winding and then switch to the low-speed winding for floor approach. The low-speed winding reduces the floor approach speed and this provides better stopping accuracy. Leveling is done on the slow-speed winding. Although the lower speed may still be reasonably fast, it does provide better stopping accuracy. The winding ratios of two-speed alternating current motors vary from 2:1 at lower speeds to 8:1 at high speeds. Advanced control of two-speed AC motors has been available for some period of time.

One type of control allows the high-speed winding of the motor to be phase-controlled for driving; the low-speed winding is used for direct current control for acceleration, deceleration, and floor approach. Variable-frequency control is another option available to control two-speed motors. Utilizing either of these two AC motion control drives has allowed new geared elevators with AC motors to be applied throughout the full speed range of geared machines.

The main concern when replacing a control using the phase control system involves the existing wire, feeder, and disconnect sizes. The DC injection into the windings for rpm reduction requires increased current through the supply lines. Total power consumption of this system is higher than that for both the variable-frequency control and standard two-speed application.

Frequency control reduces the line current and does not require line size increases on existing elevators. Both systems allow the reuse of existing motors; however, these were not specifically designed for the new drives, and they may be noisy at various times in the drive cycle. The machine room location may be critical in noise transmission; when selecting either one of these controls, one must consider noise control design. Some systems do provide quiet operation.

Direct Current Motors

Direct current motors were used more extensively in the United States to meet leveling requirements for control and stopping accuracy; initial AC design technology could not meet the requirements. Use of motor generator sets provided variable voltage control until static converter drives were developed. The term *static converter* is applied to silicon-controlled rectifier (SCR) drives. Silicon-controlled rectifiers eliminate the need for a motor generator set and are more efficient. They are the most advanced method of motor generator replacement.

When using either electronically controlled motor generator sets or silicon-controlled rectifier drives, tachometers provide feedback that gives precise speed control. Computerized speed curve patterns are closely followed to provide better performance and comfortable motion. Acceleration and deceleration patterns are optimized for comfort and minimum time, accurate floor stops, and smoothly controlled releveling.

Electronic control of motor generator sets requires recalculating the size of the existing ones. Generator sets were downsized because of elevator's intermittent duty requirements. When generators must respond to precisely computed curves for electronically controlled performance, they may need to produce higher currents than original design allows, and severe commutator arcing will occur. Performance will be sacrificed if undersized sets are used. Reuse of properly sized generators can reduce the wiring changes required to connect the new controls; reuse of wiring is dependent on location of both old and new equipment and condition and type of existing wire.

Machine room space requirements for control replacement with motor generator sets generally remain the same, and heat release is only slightly changed. If the generator sets are too small, and if they are later required to perform at increased output, the heat release will be increased. The alternative to increasing power consumption is a corresponding reduction in elevator performance, which counteracts the retrofit process. Some installations that have inadequate ventilation will require changes in the cooling system to provide a better environment for solid-state signal logic or solid-state devices in the motion control system.

Silicon-controlled rectifier drives eliminate the motor generator set and the associated maintenance of these units. They are highly efficient and reduce power consumption by approximately one-third when compared to generator drive systems. Existing generator space may be recovered for other uses. The hoist motors are usually properly sized and good performance can be achieved. Power lines for the existing motor generator sets are usually adequate. Using silicon controlled rectifier drives reduces power consumption that can change a hot machine room to a relatively comfortable one that may not require additional cooling.

Silicon-controlled rectifier drives have been criticized because they produce both electromagnetic interference and audible noise. This noise has varying frequencies, however, and tenants' main objection to it occurs when turning the SCR on and off. Proper application of line filters and chokes can reduce the noise level below that caused by generator sets. Location of the machine room and its proximity to occupied space should be considered. The system design must be emphasized when using silicon-controlled rectifier drives.

Direct Current Gearless Machines

All gearless machines used for high-speed elevators have been DC-powered for many years. New technology has introduced the AC gearless machine.

Gearless machines have been one of the most durable products of the elevator industry. Reuse of existing DC gearless machines is almost always recommended. The application of motor generators and silicon-controlled rectifier drives is the same for DC gearless motors and DC geared machines.

Gearless machines have higher armature currents than geared motors, and wire sizing for the motor generator sets should be verified on all installations.

POWER

Comparison of Power Consumption

Each type of motion control has different consumption requirements. In most situations, energy-saving changes or devices improve the performance of elevator operations.

The following items can reduce energy consumption:

1. Hydraulic elevators.
   Power factor correction.
   Reduced-voltage starting.
   Wye-Delta starting.
   Energy-efficient motors.
2. Single-speed AC geared elevators.
   Energy-efficient motors.
   Reduced-voltage starting.
   Frequency control.
3. Two-speed AC geared elevators.
   Phase control.
   Frequency control.
   Reduced-voltage starting and acceleration.
4. DC variable voltage, geared and gearless.
   Power factor corrections on MG sets.
   SCR drives.
   Proper application of equipment (geared versus gearless).

The following table compares power consumption of the various types of elevators (the highest power demand unit has a maximum value of ten). The power required to move the elevator at a given speed or load does not change; power needs are reduced through improved efficiency of the motion control system and design of controls.

Type of elevator	Relative power consumption
Hydraulic	10
Alternating current	
Two-speed	8
DC injection	7.5
Single-speed	7.5
Direct current	
Geared MG set	7.5
Gearless MG set	6.5
Geared SCR	5
Gearless SCR	4
Variable frequency AC	3.5

Heat-producing power resistors have been eliminated with the use of electronic control, thus reducing the amount of heat to be removed from machine room. The resulting reduction in heat, ventilation, and air conditioning provides additional savings. Although these savings at today's power rates do not pay back the entire cost of retrofitting, they do save a sizeable sum in operating costs. For total building power planning, the American Society of Heating, Refrigeration, and Air Conditioning Engineers has developed a set of standards called the ASHRAE 100 Series Standards:

100.1—Low-rise residential.

100.2—High-rise residential.

100.3—Commercial.

100.4—Industrial.

100.5—Institutional.

100.6—Public assembly buildings.

Emergency Power

Emergency power usually is provided in new buildings but may not be available in existing ones. In some areas emergency power is required to be added to existing buildings. However, whether a building has an emergency system or not, the new signal logic system should include an emergency power mode. The cost to add an automatic selection system is minimal when it is included in the new signal logic. When emergency power supply is later furnished, the signal logic will be ready for use.

The emergency power system should be an automatic selection system with a manual override. Such a system provides automatic transportation of passengers to a selected floor if the main power system fails. When building power fails, the building engineering personnel usually have many other problems to worry about and may not be immediately available to manipulate switches to bring elevators down. Automatic selection will handle this chore immediately and each elevator can be properly moved.

The amount of power available from the standby generator determines the number of elevators that can simultaneously operate. Its capacity should be checked, and power regulation should be compatible with the type of motion control system proposed. One elevator serving all floors is the minimum recommended to be on standby power. Buildings that have more than one bank of elevators should have adequate emergency power to run one elevator in each bank.

Direct Current Power

Commercial three-phase AC power, in adequate supply, is acceptable for use with all modern motion control systems. Older buildings that still use DC power can be modernized without changing the main power supply. Existing direct current–to–direct current (DC/DC) motor generator sets or new sets of the same type can be used. If new DC/DC motor generator sets are used, they should allow the drive motor of the generator set to be replaced with an AC drive motor when the building is converted to AC power. If the DC supply is reused, the new system may require a limited supply of three-phase AC power for operation of the signal logic, door operators, and other devices that may be replaced. When DC/DC generators are reused, they should be checked for proper size. A retrofit must allow for reinsulation and refurbishment of any existing or reused MG sets. These units have been in service for many years and should be thoroughly checked for insulation breakdown and commutator wear before they are reused.

SIGNAL LOGIC

Signal logic is the part of the control system that receives all demand inputs and makes decisions to activate the appropriate motion control devices. This is the control area that has involved most of the latest technology improvements in the industry. The old manually operated elevators relied on human operators to make decisions. Automatic elevators using relay logic appeared in the 1940s and 1950s. Since they appeared, the sophistication of the systems has steadily increased by using many smaller multicontact relays and solid state devices.

Solid-state components were first used in relay logic in the early 1970s, and full solid-state logic followed soon after. In the late 1970s and early 1980s, the microprocessor was introduced, and it offered a complete new technological approach to elevator signal logic and capability.

Various types of microprocessor-based systems have been developed, starting from the simple commercial programmable controller to the more complex systems developed by elevator manufacturers. Programmable controllers with their additional features and ease of change hastened the change from relay logic to microprocessor systems.

Programmable logic controls offer the reliability of solid state with relay flexibility. Application of programmable logic devices is neither difficult nor time-consuming. It does not require a large investment from the elevator company, as the investment has been made by the programmable controller manufacturers to provide the basic program. The logic is basically the same as previous relay control systems used and should not be confused with sophisticated new elevator software logic algorithms for microprocessor use that have taken years to develop.

Some early microprocessor signal logic systems were updated solid-state or relay logic systems that were elevator-dedicated, utilizing commercially available microprocessor hardware systems. Added to the normal output requirements for the motion control were diagnostic and monitor display capabilities. The emphasis was placed on conversion to microprocessors and the new display ability rather than on advanced algorithms that improve elevator system performance.

Microprocessor systems should have nonvolatile memory so that reprogramming is never necessary. *Nonvolatile* means that the programming remains if power is lost for any length of time or that the system is designed so that nothing can enter the memory to disrupt it; removal of the memory chips should not void the memory. These precautions will allow the memory to be duplicated for the building for which it was programmed; the original manufacturer will not be needed for replacement programs. These precautions remove the proprietary aspect and allow other companies with qualified mechanics to service the equipment. If the system is working properly at the time of building acceptance, future programming should only be needed when building changes affect elevator requirements.

Signal Logic for Different Types of Systems

Hydraulic Elevators
Hydraulic elevator control systems are usually designed for single or two-car operation, owing to the low rise nature of the buildings in which they are installed. This type of system does not require a sophisticated microprocessor algorithm. Solid state for reliability is the important factor. Simple programmable controls are ideal for this type of signal logic. For hydraulic elevators, the cost of maintenance must also be considered. Using solid state or boards may raise the cost as most of the systems are on one or two boards. Simple programmable controls keep individual board cost down and make boards

readily replaceable. Training mechanics is less expensive and easier on programmable controls; and hydraulic elevators are generally in buildings in remote areas, so mechanics must be able to correctly perform repairs on these systems on the first try.

Retrofit of the existing relay system in large buildings with new technology is important for increased reliability. The replacement system should contain all required diagnostic lights or test instruments. If it utilizes removable diagnostic equipment, it should be available as part of the system's initial purchase price. Full instructions for using this equipment should be included in the final documents given to the owner. Advanced single-board systems with proprietary diagnostics may reduce the number of maintenance companies capable of maintaining the job and may increase the monthly maintenance costs.

Dependable performance is achieved with a good signal logic system. Any hydraulic signal system over 15 years old is a good candidate for replacement. Signal replacement should also be coordinated with any required mechanical updates and changes.

Single-Speed Alternating Current Systems

Single-speed alternating current systems are usually single or two-car systems. The height and speed limitations of these elevators mean that rarely more than two cars operate together. The same signal logic applied to hydraulic elevators would be recommended. As with hydraulic elevators, one must make sure that all diagnostic equipment is part of the retrofit package. Advanced algorithms are not necessary for these systems, as they will not substantially improve traffic handling. New motion control is more important for reliable operation, floor accuracy, and the overall improvement.

Two-Speed Alternating Current Systems

Older two-speed AC elevators requiring retrofit are also generally associated with single or duplex systems. These systems use the same concepts as single-speed AC and hydraulics. Some of the older systems did have more than two elevators, and the application of the previously described motion control with updated microprocessor signal logic can be a great improvement.

Direct Current Geared or Gearless

Direct current motion control systems are used for higher-rise, higher-speed elevators and are usually found in multicar banks of elevators or simplex and duplex installations where AC control could not meet the building's requirements. Commercial office buildings and hospitals, for example, require this type of performance.

Multicar systems utilizing a microprocessor system can improve traffic handling capability. A building that is marginally elevatored can be updated with good elevator service. Old relay logic systems had a "bus stop" approach; an elevator passing in the direction of the call would respond. The ability to respond was only negated if the load switches were activated. Elevators were delayed at terminals but, once released, would respond to all calls in the direction of travel.

During the 1960s and 1970s, before microprocessors were introduced, systems were designed with elevator zone control. Zone control was a method of assigning an elevator to a specified area, or zone, of a building. A zone comprised a selected number of floors. Zoning was an important step in improving elevator traffic handling capability. However, the use of electrical/mechanical relays in the systems limited their overall capability.

Microprocessor systems and programmable controls that convert relay logic still perform the same function as the relay logic; however, added inputs increase their effectiveness. Microprocessors allow numerous inputs and sophisticated algorithms providing better traffic and handling capabilities. The decision process can take into account many facets of the traffic demands and make decisions in micro- or milliseconds. Microprocessors work on a call assignment principle to prevent bunching of elevators.

The prime objective of a microprocessor signal system is improved handling of traffic. Microprocessor systems that are structured properly have vast amounts of computation and programming power and can provide many more features to make the system more efficient. Special operations such as fire fighter service, hospital emergency services, VIP service, shuttle service, riot control, access control, swing car service, remote monitoring, lobby monitoring, keyboard control, statistical data for traffic, statistical data for faults, modems for off-site diagnostics, system display, convention service, or interface to building systems are available with little additional hardware in the control cabinet. These can be programmed when software is compiled for the job or a field selected from the base software. Some systems include special features in the base and only peripheral hardware is needed to place the program in operation. A selected system should have adequate memory and computer power to run any combination of these programs.

Programs with the features for various peak traffic, parking assignments, and other traffic features provide a system that can serve a building's needs now and in the future.

When reviewing building requirements, all possible needs should be discussed to make sure that necessary features are included. Time used for careful selection and understanding at this part of the modernization planning will be well-spent. Microprocessor systems offer the flexibility of adding features with software programming and minimum hardware modification.

Overlays

Microprocessors have had such an effect on traffic handling that the use of this technology in conjunction with the old motion control devices can improve existing systems without extensive modernization. An overlay is a system in which elevator group decisions are done by a microprocessor that is integrated into or replaces the existing relay logic group controller.

If traffic handling capability is the main difficulty, and if the existing individual elevator motion control is still in good condition, an overlay may solve the problem. Overlays do not address problems with mechanical selectors, door equipment, ride problems or control, or floor-stop accuracy. Only traffic-call assignments and responses are handled in a more efficient manner. The length of time for which the overlay is to serve the building should be considered. Any system that will need other control work in a few years precludes consideration of an overlay. Overlays are for larger groups of elevators and should not be used on simplex or duplex systems.

Overlays can be applied as a temporary control when modernizing groups of elevators. One elevator can be removed, the complete control system modernized, and the new control connected to the overlay group control. This type of system allows elevators with their original group control overlays and the fully modernized elevators to be in direct communication during the modernization process. The problem of communication between the old group and new group systems has been eliminated. Traffic handling is improved through the overlay, and the effect on service of one car out for modernization is minimized.

This system should be designed so that the entire group of elevators and statistical and diagnostic equipment is retained for the final system. The overlay cost then is not a total loss, and the only nonrecoverable costs are in the installation cost association with the moderization overlay control. This approach may be well worth the cost because tenant inconvenience is reduced, and dual system operation is eliminated.

Overlays are helpful when properly planned and the results understood. They are not a low-cost fix for all system problems. An overlay purchaser must clearly understand what is being done and should not expect solutions to motion control or mechanical problems.

Advanced Features of Microprocessor Signal Logic

The computation and memory capabilities of a microprocessor have introduced built-in traffic analyzers, fault logging, and operational displays. Most systems display car position, direction, and calls; door position and motions; elevator operational status; corridor calls; call assignments; system status; and other data. This information provides a detailed picture of events in the system. Other displays of traffic statistics and fault logs provide historical data to analyze how the system has been operating. This information and specialized functions, such as controlled access, can be displayed on monitors in the lobby or other remote locations. During the last decade, the ability to monitor elevator systems through telephone lines has brought system monitoring to a new level.

The ability to remotely request and receive operational data allows building management to watch the system for elevators out of service and other problems that may delay service. Making a hard-copy printout at a remote location provides a record of the statistics. Monthly statistical reports can be kept to monitor the system's level of performance. Effects of tenant changes can be readily seen and adjustments made.

Microprocessor signal logic has also expanded the ability to control access to a building. The term *controlled access* is used when elevators are used as a part of a security system. Building security is a total system and involves many other aspects of control. The elevators, through various operational modes or switching, can be programmed to allow access only when certain preprogrammed conditions are met. Various types of key switches, stand-alone push-button systems, or access codes can be interfaced to the microprocessor logic.

Locked-out floor calls or car calls can be readily seen on the monitor displays, and, when calls to the locked-out floors are registered, security personnel can easily monitor this for appropriate action.

The ability to log all of the described information and interface with building computer systems allows building management to keep its own records for security purposes, or for traffic control. Commands from other building areas can be sent to the elevator system through the building computer to establish special programs to allow the system to be ready before the actual need arises.

Artificial Intelligence

Artificial intelligence will be the phrase for the future in signal logic. AI will allow the system to utilize its history to anticipate future requirements by gathering historical data to analyze traffic patterns. However, this technology is quite new in its application to elevator systems, and its effectiveness has yet to be determined.

Patterns of elevator passengers are affected by many factors, exact predictions are often not possible.

With today's changing technology, knowing whether a system can be updated without complete replacement is important. The algorithm contained in the signal logic should be capable of expansion to include additional features; however, it should also be able to respond in real time rather than in sequential order.

OTHER MAJOR PARTS OF THE ELEVATOR

Door Equipment

Doors on elevators cause more shutdowns and injuries than any other component. Reliable operation of door equipment is vital. Quiet operation is secondary to dependability but important for tenant satisfaction. Door equipment consists of the following items:

- Master door operator.
- Door tracks.
- Hangers.
- Interlocks or door drives.
- Closers.
- Clutch or interface between car and hoistway doors.

- Door panels.
- Entrance frames.

When the decision has been made to upgrade the elevator system, door equipment should also be reviewed. Door operation must be checked for performance time; their physical appearance and noise they make are critical issues as well. Noisy doors or poor aesthetic appearance present the image of old, deteriorated equipment, regardless of how well the motion control or signal logic systems might work.

Entrance frames and sills can usually be reused in place; the frames can be sanded, bonded, and repainted in place. Reusing or cladding the frame eliminates the need to repair or refinish the wall area around the frame. Code requirements for entrance size should be confirmed; when extensive modernization is performed, codes often require the entire elevator system to be brought up to date, and this may involve frame sizes.

Door panels must also conform to applicable codes. For example, depressions of panels on the face of the doors may be deeper than allowed. Door panels must be in good condition, so that when they are painted or refinished, their appearance is aesthetically pleasing. Glass inserts on doors are no longer acceptable. Insulation of the door is important, as asbestos insulation may have been used. If it was used, special precautions and a licensed contractor are required for removing equipment mounted to the doors and remounting equipment or replacing panels. Today, codes require all door panels to be labeled for fire rating.

The tracks and hangers that support the door panels should be reused, if possible. When door operators are changed, the tracks and hangers may be reusable. A solid bar track that has been kept clean and has a smooth top surface usually does not require replacement. Only the track rollers may need to be replaced to provide smoothly moving, quiet door panels. Steel tracks with resilient rollers provide quieter door movement and should be used when replacing tracks and hangers. If this combination is currently installed, only the defective rollers need replacement.

The master door operator provides the control and speed of panel movement. Closing speed is code-limited, as is kinetic energy and force. The opening speed can be varied to achieve improved performance times. Door reversal (in case of obstruction) should be quick and quiet. Door operators that have been in use for a long time probably have worn linkages and controls that do not reverse the doors as demanded for modern performance. Replacement of the master door operator should include a solid-state control that can provide the required sophisticated speed control. Replacement of the interlocks, door closers, door drives, and clutch interface are all part of the door package that should be reviewed for replacement. These are interrelated parts and are usually replaced, but they are not always included in the master door operator replacement.

Door safety and protective devices are items critical to passenger protection. Replacement of mechanical retractable edges with new solid-state electronic edges is recommended. The noise of the movable parts and damage to the projected edges is eliminated, and the electronic control projects a sensitive field beyond the door edge, so reversal of the door is accomplished without physical contact.

Photo electric eyes and mechanical safety edges are an alternative and can reduce door contact of transferring passengers or objects.

Door closing time reduction after the entrance has been cleared helps reduce overall waiting time and should be part of the control logic.

A close evaluation of the existing door equipment and replacement of only necessary items keeps retrofit costs down and provides the quality desired for future use. This is not an area to overlook to save costs; equipment should be changed if it is suspect for *any* reason, including obsolescence and marginal ability to maintain it.

Fixtures

Fixtures as discussed here consist of the following items:

- Car operating panels (main and auxiliary).
- Phone boxes.
- Car position indicators.
- Hall position indicators.
- Hall lanterns.
- Hall push buttons.
- Code-required devices.
- Lobby and other display panels and devices.

The main items seen by the elevator passengers are these fixtures. When modernization is in process and the elevators are out of service for a period of time, tenants experience some degree of inconvenience. Once an elevator is returned to service with new fixtures as a sign of physical change, tenants realize a change has taken place.

Smoothly operating, trouble-free elevators are often taken for granted. Poor aesthetics and noisy elevators are a subject of many complaints and demonstrate the building's age and management's or owners' attitudes.

Good fixtures that are well-coordinated and functional can be reused if they are compatible to the new control. Outdated or deteriorated fixtures should be replaced.

Existing hall fixture mounting boxes may be reused if located at proper height and if new cover plates are installed. Building work is reduced if new electrical boxes are not required. Regulations for handicapped persons require one riser of hall push buttons at a specified height. Lowering the hall buttons can require some architectural changes if the original fixtures were recessed or incorporated into the elevator lobby decor.

Car operating panels meeting handicap code requirements must have safety devices located at a specific height from the floor. The required location is, in most cases, lower than that of the original fixtures. Simply relocating car operating panels may not meet requirements for serving the handicapped. Safety buttons and switches may not be located in the car station as required. A new car operating panel that covers the larger portion of the front return improves the elevator's appearance by covering old holes or openings. The panel cover can be hinged and large enough to cover the entire cab return panel. The requirements for communication devices—intercoms or telephones—can be met by incorporating them into the car operating panel. Surface-mounted fixtures require minimum alterations to existing lobby finishes and eliminate costly or mismatched final finishes. Surface-mounted fixtures that are aesthetically pleasing can be installed over the existing boxes also. Position indicators using new technology displays can be part of the new car operating panel as well.

Code requirements must be considered for location, communication and other required devices in the car operating panel. The types of operating features also affect the devices required. All basic operational devices must be confined to a specific area and may require panels wider than available space on the front return, necessitating locating the car operating panel in the side wall.

Two car operating panels are preferred over single panels to reduce passenger loading time by allowing better access for several entering passengers when ample door width is available. All center-opening door installations of 10 stops or more should have dual car operating panels.

Lobby fixtures that previously had position indicators and control switches are normally replaced with a lobby monitor and keyboard. This provides a better display of the system, as well as keyboard commands that previously would have required many key switches. When commands are given, the display confirms the system's response. Fireman's service is still activated by key operation; however, the activation should be displayed on the monitor. Either a display or hall position indicator is required for fireman's service in most areas.

Hall lanterns at all landings can normally be reused. A decision about replacing covers and lenses for aesthetic reasons is required. Double-stroking the gong to meet provisions for handicapped people is part of the control logic. The existing gongs and bulbs can be reused in some systems. Companies address these components in various ways, but lanterns do not have to be changed when a system is updated, except for aesthetic and handicap reasons.

Fixture changes visibly improve any elevator system. The costs for replacement fixtures is a small percentage of the overall cost of modernization.

Cabs

Modernization of cabs can range from small changes to total cab replacement. Architectural changes to fit with a building decor change are usually the most expensive changes.

If a cab shell can be retained, the elevator modernization can be completed before the cab work is done. The main concern (besides cost) is the physical weight change of the cab. Traction elevators compensate for the total car weight—the cab weight plus a percentage of the capacity. When cab weight is changed, the counterbalance must be checked and rebalanced by adding or removing weights. Weight changes of over 5 percent require new structural and reaction calculations. Weight changes also affect traction relation, groove pressure, and sheave shaft load of machines. The total load applied to the safeties and safety factor of the cables may also be affected. Extensive changes to mechanical equipment may be required if weight is excessive. Proposed weight changes should be carefully coordinated to stay within the capabilities of the original equipment.

Cabs that are to be replaced should be selected and approved before any elevators are removed for modernization. Time constraints could delay the work in progress and extend the downtime of the elevators if the actual delivery date of the cab is not considered. Tentative approvals can result in considerable (and inconvenient) schedule changes.

RIDE QUALITY

Ride quality is as important as any other phase of modernization. Although control changes can improve elevator performance and landing control, other factors affect ride quality. Although every aspect of ride quality (and problems detracting therefrom) should be examined, realignment of the rails is often the principal area of concern. A properly aligned rail system is the real heart of a smooth ride. It is extremely difficult, and sometimes impossible, to correct on an existing installation. Alignment is also difficult to maintain if bracket sizing, location, and rail sizing were not correct on the original installation. Rails and brackets that meet code-required factors of safety and deflection may not be adequate for a quality ride on high-speed elevators. Building settling and compression over time causes alignment problems. Adequately spaced stiff brackets and larger-sized rails with slip clips on the brackets help keep rails aligned. Minor rail adjustments can be made by fixing other items that are independent of the building structure.

In higher-rise buildings with fixed cast or forged clips, rails should be checked to be sure brackets and mountings have not been forced out of alignment. Installing new sliding clips can relieve compression. An adjustable blocking arrangement should be provided below the rails to limit movement during clip replacement. Additional brackets can be added if distance between brackets is too long. Code limitations for bracket spacing have usually been followed, but if smaller rails were originally installed, additional brackets can help. All brackets and rail splice plates should be checked for tightness and signs of stress or movement. It is wise to check and review all these issues because the cost/value relationship and the fact that it may not be possible to achieve perfect results may influence the final decision regarding rail alignment.

Car balance is critical in allowing roller guide assemblies to operate. Out-of-balance cars apply heavy forces on guide shoes or rollers, causing noise and excessive wear. During retrofitting of an elevator, the relocation of cable hitches or traveling cable suspension could make a difference. Balancing weight, shifting components, or both can be done if necessary to bring the car sling, platform, and cab into balance.

Roller guides to replace slide guides are usually recommended. Roller guides are quieter at high speeds and eliminate the need for lubricating rails, as well as the associated problems of keeping oil and grease off the car and pit area. Size of the rollers should be determined from space available for mounting them and the speed involved. Roller guides should be designed so that the rollers remain in constant contact with the rails. Proper location, alignment, size, design, and compatibility with existing equipment (such as safeties) are all contributing factors in roller-guide operation. Alignment and concentricity of roller-guide wheels require special attention.

Isolation of platforms and cabs from the car sling assembly on traction elevators can provide a quieter ride. The platform should be suspended from rigid contact with the frame. Movement at the top of the cab should be restricted. These restrictions should allow the cab to float without being forced to move by the structural car frame movement. Connection between the fixed frame members and the cab should be flexible and nonmetallic to prevent transmission of noise into the cab assembly. In retrofits, new platform and isolation assemblies may be required. When new cabs are installed, the platform replacement should be considered if it is nonisolated or if the existing isolation is not effective. If cabs are in good condition and are reused, isolation is more difficult and expensive to obtain, as it may require cab removal, reworking, and reinstallation. Isolation of the total car sling may be more appropriate when a nonisolated platform and slings are retained.

Instruments for checking the noise, acceleration, and lateral motion of the car are now available. These readings can provide information about the frequency and reason for vibration. Corrective action can then be applied to the source of the problem. After the cause of these problems has been determined, issues concerning the method of correction, elevator downtime, and cost involved should be discussed. In some instances, minimal work provides adequate results. Most of these items stand alone and can be individually addressed without a total rework.

REUSE OF MACHINES

Geared machines can usually be rehabilitated by gear adjustment and bearing replacement if they are the cause of uneven or rough starts and stops. In severe cases the gear may require replacement because of wear that adjustment cannot correct or safety factors that are reduced. Traction sheaves may require regrooving if traction is lost or if one or more ropes are lower in the groove than others. Regrooving the sheave will depend on the amount of sheave material remaining after the procedure. Safety factors of material strength must be maintained. Before regrooving a sheave its hardness should be checked, as this is sometimes the reason for sheave wear. The relationship of hardness between the cables and sheave groove area partly determines available traction. If sheaves are regrooved when they are not hard enough, the new grooves will wear at a faster rate than normal. Proper sheave hardness, the correct type of hoist cable, and groove pressure should be originally designed so that the cables wear rather than the sheave. Correct application should not cause the sheaves to require reworking.

The combination of worn sheaves and gear work may be so severe that replacing the machines is more economical. Replacements will ensure the best long-range cure, as the new machine will have all the required design criteria to handle the capacity of the elevators.

Replacement of gaskets, brake linings, and brake pins are usually minor items and not a cause for machine replacement. New controls require positive brake operation and should not be overlooked when evaluating the machine for required work on modernization.

Gearless machines that are properly sized for the applied capacity and speed should not require replacement. Armatures can be turned and undercut if necessary, field coils checked for internal winding breakdown and reinsulated, brake linings and pins replaced and the sheave checked for wear. Once these items are checked and corrected, machines can be expected to perform like new. Most gearless machines are welded or bolted to building steel without isolation between the machine and steel. To isolate an existing machine can be expensive, difficult, and sometimes impossible. Existing machine beams and deflector beams may require moving or replacing to isolate the machine, but it may not be necessary with properly designed controls.

Most of the other mechanical equipment such as safeties, governors, car slings, and so forth can usually be retained if it has been properly lubricated and maintained. Some tests or recalibration may be required to verify the condition and operation. Today's controls and signal logic make some of the other mechanical equipment unnecessary. All mechanical components should be evaluated to determine the extent of wear, as well as possible future use. No component should be automatically accepted because it does not appear to be a cause of a current problem. Safety is of utmost concern, and all components must function properly when needed, whether they are used for normal operation or emergency purposes.

Cables for hoisting, compensation, and governor should be covered under a full maintenance contract. Having all necessary work performed under the contract can save money that the maintenance company has been reserving for the future replacement.

RETROFIT SCHEDULE AND COMMUNICATION

Once retrofitting has been decided upon and the extent of work determined, a schedule should be planned. It should allow for contract negotiation, lead times, and project work time, which will be determined by the amount of work to be performed. Downtime should be kept to a minimum. All schedules should include building work required for the new equipment to be furnished and restoration of any surfaces where original equipment was located. New or modified machine rooms or supports may be required if equipment is changed; this could lead to additional downtime if actual elevator work has to be stopped to allow for building alterations. Heating, ventilation, and air conditioning work may be required, as some new equipment may not perform reliably in the current environment. Modern codes often differ from those in effect when the building was erected and may require additional machine room space. The schedule must include all work to coordinate with subcontractors and to clearly define elevator downtime. The work process should be discussed among all parties involved to determine the best way to accomplish the task with minimum tenant inconvenience. Once a schedule is set, the building owner or manager should discuss it with the tenants in detail in order to avoid inconvenience or considerable schedule rearrangement. The schedule and approximate costs indicate the time and amounts of progress made for budgeting the job.

Tenants who are well-informed and involved can help to control their employee concerns during the retrofit program. If all are aware of the events to take place, they will be more receptive of changes or inconveniences that occur. Ongoing updates in building bulletins or signs will help tenants follow progress. When the first phase of a project is completed, newly retrofitted elevators should not be put into tenant use until they are thoroughly completed and checked. The project will be judged on the performance and reliability of the first completed work. If this results in problems, tenants will believe that the new or modified system is not any better than the old equipment. Incomplete work that requires shutting down partially complete elevators will also cause the same opinion. Tenants only know that an elevator is out without caring why. An out-of-service elevator adds to their inconvenience. If the project goes smoothly and the new elevators perform flawlessly, hearing positive comments is highly unlikely because tenants expect such work to be done properly the first time around.

Schedules should be realistic. Any schedules that are planned and not followed appear to be ineffective. Schedules not met will lead to conflicts because explaining why the work has not progressed as planned is difficult.

If the project scope changes after the initial plans are formed, the extent of project and schedule changes should be communicated to the tenants. Changes made in the early stages may have less effect on labor costs. Equipment modification or coordination can be done to minimize equipment cost and delivery problems. Starting work without proper equipment or a firm delivery date may result in project shutdowns and out-of-service elevators. Progress will not be seen and cannot be reported, which causes complaints and questions. Requiring that all new equipment be delivered to the site before work commences may be necessary. Prior delivery is important in short-duration projects.

Removal of existing equipment from the building and delivery of new equipment to the building should be part of the schedule. Storage areas should be assigned. Work should be coordinated to minimize use of the lobby for storage if no loading area is available. Time frames should be established to allow building management to keep tenants informed of disruption. The equipment should be staged, and as much equipment as possible moved at one time. Equipment should not be moved in or out one piece at a time unless it is through freight or service entrances that do not affect tenants. In busy buildings located in congested areas, consideration should be given to off-hours deliveries and removals.

Well-planned, well-communicated schedules are usually accepted. As much detail as possible should be included on the schedule to help check adherence thereto.

Work in the elevator shaft is performed by elevator mechanics; in some cases, the wiring is done by electricians. Making shaftways comply with codes and refinishing of exterior hoistway surfaces should be done by the owners or general contractors. When writing a specification that requires work besides that for the elevators, the work to be done should be clearly and definitively detailed. If someone is hired to draft a specification, he is being paid to define the work to be done, thereby placing all bids on the same level, minimizing requests for additional work later. A good specification details all elevator work and other work, including which party is to do the work. Contract for the other work directly instead of placing it in the elevator contract is usually less expensive. Regardless of where the work is or who does the work, it should not be left undefined.

SUMMARY

We have discussed the need for modernization, the technical aspects, and some project details. These are general guidelines to assist in planning and implementing a retrofit or modernization of an elevator system. Equipment, work methods, and regulations are not the same everywhere. Planning a particular project may require consultation with elevator specialists, company personnel, or perhaps a person in one's own organization who is familiar with elevators. Regardless of who is consulted, the total elevator system of a building should be reviewed. Determining long- or short-range goals affect the entire modernization plan. An accurate scope and specification results in proposals that are comprehensive and competitive. Surprises during the project are eliminated, and work can be done on time. Tenant inconveniences are minimized, and end results are achieved with minimum disruption and confusion.

PART 4

MANAGING OFFICE BUILDINGS

CHAPTER 16

MANAGING THE OFFICE BUILDING IN A CHANGING MARKET

Mazhar Raslan
IT Properties Management, Inc.

Real estate markets follow a cyclical behavior. When demand exceeds supply, rents and building values increase; when supply exceeds demand, rents and values decrease.

Factors affecting supply side include availability of money to finance new construction, availability of land, and local politics regulating development. Demand is also dependent on many factors, including the health of the local economy, local government policies on improving the business environment, and the market's ability to compete with other markets near and distant.

In many office markets today supply exceeds demand; therefore, there is aggressive competition among building owners and developers. To keep existing tenants and to attract new ones, owners and managers must revise their strategies, improve their marketing techniques, upgrade their building quality, and lower their operating costs. To accomplish these objectives, building owners must hire the best available talent.

Owners of office buildings are struggling to trim operating expenses and property taxes that are eroding profit margins. High vacancy levels are forcing owners to commit more funds to already costly marketing efforts, to hire more leasing people, and to host more sales events to attract tenants. A survey by the Building Owners and Managers Association (BOMA) in early 1989 showed that the average net operating income for office buildings dropped 4.1 percent in 1987, after decreasing by 2.2 percent in 1986.

During the early 1980s in the Northeast region of the country, building owners enjoyed a booming market. They could negotiate favorable rents, and escalations grew faster than operating expenses. But more recently, rents have flattened out, and in some cities declined, while taxes and expenses have continued to increase. In Manhattan's financial district, some tenants who negotiated leases in the early 1980s have annual rent obligations of up to $65 per square foot. A new lease signed today will command a rent of $35 to $40 per square foot.

According to BOMA, in 1987 taxes and insurance represented 32 percent of the total operating costs, utilities 22 percent, repairs 17 percent, cleaning 13 percent, administration 10 percent, and security and building maintenance, 6 percent. Many building owners have implemented strategies to reverse this trend toward increased operating expenses. For example, managers are using watt-saver lighting and

EXHIBIT 16–1

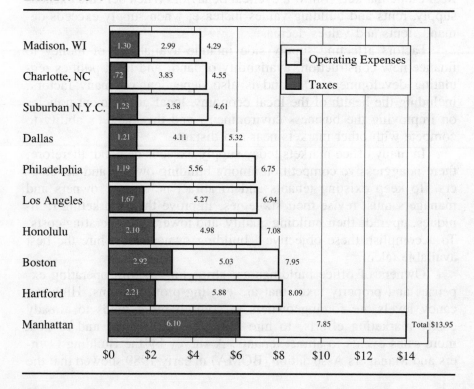

City	Taxes	Operating Expenses	Total
Madison, WI	1.30	2.99	4.29
Charlotte, NC	.72	3.83	4.55
Suburban N.Y.C.	1.23	3.38	4.61
Dallas	1.21	4.11	5.32
Philadelphia	1.19	5.56	6.75
Los Angeles	1.67	5.27	6.94
Honolulu	2.10	4.98	7.08
Boston	2.92	5.03	7.95
Hartford	2.21	5.88	8.09
Manhattan	6.10	7.85	Total $13.95

$0 $2 $4 $6 $8 $10 $12 $14

are insulating windows to cut utility costs. Administration and maintenance costs are being altered by the use of computerized management systems, which are replacing laborers to operate lights, heating systems, and air conditioning maintenance schedules.

Although a building must remain competitive in the marketplace, costs cannot be cut at the expense of building quality.

THE DALLAS TOWER* — A CASE STUDY

Building a Team of Professionals

The Tower is a modern building designed by one of America's most reputable architects and developed and managed by Delpro, one of America's largest and best developers. In January 1989 I was given the assignment to cut operating costs for the Tower in Dallas from $11 million to $10 million and to do so while improving quality.

My first step in assuming this challenge was to familiarize myself with the building and the operating people. I met Ron, the property manager of the Tower and one of Delpro's top property managers in the Dallas area. I also called on a number of prominent property managers in Dallas to interview them for project consulting assignments. I met the senior executives of City Development, Delpro's prime competitors in downtown Dallas, and toured a number of their buildings. City Development has a very impressive management approach, but they also respect Delpro's turf and vice versa. However, the executives agreed to be of assistance if they could.

Back in New York I met with Kelly, the head of the property management department in a prestigious real estate company. He knew the property very well and agreed that its expenses were very high.

We went over the expenses line by line and agreed on a strategy: all major contracts would be rebid under new conditions and specifications, and the best consultants would be hired to report on the quality of the elevator system maintenance, heating ventilation and air conditioning (HVAC), and security. Kelly and I agreed that operating expenses could be decreased by 10 percent without jeopardizing services or quality.

---

* This study is factual; however, the names of individuals, cities, and companies are fictitious.

Building a team of professionals was crucial for establishing my credibility with Delpro so they would accept my leadership in this task and for proving my abilities to John, the Tower's owner's representative, so that I could depend on his support. The team provided a forum for ideas and creative solutions.

Rebidding Contracts

Cleaning
The Tower consists of over 1.6 million cleanable square feet and was being cleaned by a staff of 150 people on a cost-plus basis. I worked with Kelly to research the merits of a cost-plus versus a cost-per-square-foot contract.

Before I took the assignment, Delpro had already rebid the contract on a cost-plus basis and was waiting for my approval to sign the new contract. I told John that my recommendation would be to inform Delpro that we do not accept a cost-plus cleaning contract. Delpro's specifications would have to be rewritten to provide a tighter, more efficient performance control and then the contract should again be rebid. There were two reasons for these recommendations.

First, the current cleaning contract provided no incentive to save money: the more the contractor spent the higher the fees received. Second, 80 percent of buildings are bid on a per-square-foot basis, and according to experienced professionals, cleaning costs increase every time cleaning contracts are rebid on a cost-plus basis.

After John independently confirmed my recommendations with several experienced real estate consultants, he agreed that we should inform Delpro of our intent to change.

When I met with Ron, his two assistants, and his superior officer, Jay, to discuss rebidding the contract, I was clearly outnumbered but well prepared. They repeated their opinion that a cost-plus contract is more cost efficient and provides better quality control. After much discussion, I was still unable to change their minds, so I asked to tour the building with the cleaning crew.

Gary, Ron's assistant at the lobby, introduced me to the cleaning project manager and the account executive, and we toured the building. Such hands-on visits are vital to providing effective management of a project. Reading reports on a project does not give you the same information as watching and talking with the workers does.

For obvious reasons, the representatives of the cleaning contractor were trying to back Delpro's opinion on the cost-plus contract. As they talked about their administrative efficiency, we opened the service closet and found one worker sleeping on the job. This provided me with an example of the owner bearing the cost and not the contractor.

After reporting my findings to John, I informed Ron that the ownership had decided to rebid the cleaning contract on a cost-per-square-foot basis. I asked him to provide us with a list of qualified bidders and a draft of a modified contract and specifications. Although Delpro was not convinced that there would be a cost savings and was not familiar with that form of contract, they were prepared to go along with our decision and to learn fast.

In the next 20 days, the contract and specifications were completely reworked. They were written tighter to control the contractor's performance. In the previous contract the contractor was provided with cleaning equipment. We asked that the contractors offer a price to purchase the equipment in their bids.

We had agreed that I would be present at the bid opening for all bids exceeding $200,000. The cleaning contractors were being scheduled one hour apart, which some people felt might favor some contractors by giving them an extended period of time to present their bids. Ron felt such a favoritism claim was unwarranted, stating that the one-hour schedule would allow for a better review of the bids and an opportunity to ask questions. However, we agreed that to eliminate any doubt and rumors, we would open the bids, verify that all the important information is provided, and then analyze them together once they all completed their submissions. The meetings would be scheduled in 15-minute intervals.

The day bids were submitted the cleaning contractors all arrived at the same time. We admitted them one after another, opened the sealed envelopes, and read the important figures aloud while we took notes. Twenty minutes later all three contractors had completed their submissions.

The existing contractor knew the building very well but for some reason did not bid low enough to keep the job; in fact, he was the highest bidder. His price was $0.0557 per square foot per month, while the lowest bidder, an equally qualified contractor, bid $0.04093 per square foot per month (which was 26.52 percent lower).

In retrospect, the weak point in the bid was defining the cleanable square feet. The existing contractor had calculated this area to be 1,533,042 square feet. Delpro's calculations later showed 1,683,000 of cleanable square feet. This calculation should be made by Delpro and by each contractor prior to bid submissions.

ABC was awarded the contract. After adjustments for items included in the cleaning expense line of the budget, the cleaning cost was projected to be $928,836 for the year, compared with the previously budgeted cost of $1,240,000 for the same year and actual costs of $1,311,752 for the previous year.

Elevators

The Tower has 50 elevators and 2 escalators. Six of the elevator cabs are 80 square feet and have 9-foot ceilings. They travel 60 floors nonstop, linking the two lobbies at the ground floor and the 60th floor.

To review elevator maintenance, we hired Tim, an experienced consultant in this area. Tim explained to Ron what he intended to review and the areas of the building he needed access to.

I met Tim at the Tower to discuss his progress. Tim felt he was getting excellent collaboration from Delpro and the elevator maintenance contractor. He reported that the elevators were well maintained. He had found a number of deficiencies, but he explained that typically he finds twice as many deficiencies. Tim was very impressed with the maintenance work. He pointed out how concerned the contractor was with order and cleanliness. For example, an adhesive mat had been placed in the equipment room behind the door to attract grease and dirt from the shoes of the mechanics to protect the carpets in the hallways. Also, the electrical and mechanical parts were properly labeled, as built drawings were visibly placed and protected with a plastic transparent cover. In addition, grease-soaked mats had been placed over the cables in order to protect them from rust formation and to keep them well lubricated.

The deficiences in the equipment room included a missing sheave guard (which protects the tape that instructs the elevator when to slow, stop, and recognize calls), a damaged cotter pin in the brake hinge pin, and a hoist machine–bearing developing noise. There were deficiencies in the cab operation also. Some cabs exhibited "spotting," which means that the stop procedure is not gradual, and others experienced nudging malfunction. (Nudging occurs when elevator doors start to close slowly after a certain prescribed delay, overriding the automatic door closing mechanism. This feature is designed as a fire precaution override.)

When I met with Ron to discuss Tim's findings, I congratulated him on the contractor's work, but restated our intention to rebid the elevator maintenance contract.

The existing elevator maintenance contractor was more quick-witted than the cleaning contractor; he realized that the fat days were over and brought his annual price down from $683,544 in 1988 to $368,279. There were four other bidders; however, the present contractor was the lowest, and, because he was providing excellent service, we decided to renew his contract for three years. A three-year contract is typical, because if some expensive elevator part is replaced, the cost is amortized over a longer period. Such a contract works like an insurance policy.

Before changing contractors, a survey must be conducted to identify if defective parts have been replaced, to review the condition of as-built drawings, and to review prior service quality.

Reviewing Security

Walt was hired as a security consultant. He was not popular with Delpro, due partly to a personality conflict with Ron but, most importantly, because he filed a negative report regarding the Tower's state of security. His conclusion was that the Tower was providing below average security. Peter, who heads our leasing operations, confirmed that the Tower has a poor security image and that many tenants were complaining to us about weak security in the building and the garage.

During his investigation, Walt interviewed the building's security personnel and analyzed their character and qualifications one by one. He then met with the security officers of the Tower's three major tenants, all of whom reported inadequate security and lack of liaison with the building's security officers. Walt also met with the chief of police, the head of the FBI, and other knowledgeable security officers in Dallas. The reports indicated that crime in Dallas was on the rise as a result of increased drug trafficking.

John had also felt that security in the building was weak; he was concerned that action be taken to improve security before a major incident occurred.

John, Walt, and I met to review Walt's recommendations. Walt believed that security should not only exist, but should be visible to deter criminals. He recommended that a highly qualified lead guard with strong character and demeanor be stationed visibly in the lobby, while retaining access to the same equipment and information available at the emergency station. This building security manager would communicate with other tenant guards and the city police. He would come to recognize all building occupants and would be alert to the building's traffic relative to security.

Walt also reported that deliveries were not being sufficiently controlled. Delivery people should not be allowed to use passenger elevators. Therefore, Walt recommended that a guard be stationed at the building's loading dock to log all deliveries in and out and to provide the delivery person with a pass that would be signed by the tenant. As the delivery person entered the building he would be required to use the service elevator, which should be operated by an attendant.

Walt also recommended that the roving guard in the garage be replaced, as that guard's skills were not acceptable.

John was impressed with Walt's work and wanted to implement his recommendations.

We also discussed offering security escort for employees who work late hours and are afraid of being attacked while walking to the garage. There were many dimensions to this issue. If we announce that escort security is provided and an incident occurs, a major liability case may be filed against us. The logistics of physically escorting workers individually may be too costly. How many hours a day should this service be offered?

We then reviewed the building's security hardware. Walt recommended adding two closed-circuit cameras in the main lobby to cover hidden areas in front of elevator banks, enabling the lead guard to view these blind areas on his screens. Another improvement recommendation was to replace the building's 48 key door controls with card readers, which allow a digital readout of names of persons and hours when they access the space. This provides a higher security since keys can be stolen or lost but a card can be immediately cancelled and access denied.

We immediately drafted a new security contract and specifications and installed the closed-circuit cameras. Ron had prior approval to build a granite circular counter in the lobby for the concierge. We decided that this would be an ideal location for the lead guard.

The selection of a qualified security contractor is determined by more than the price factor. It also is important, but often difficult, to evaluate the quality of people who will serve as guards and the quality and experience of the company in recruiting, training, and keeping excellent guards.

Evaluating the qualities of the lead guard requires an interviewer who knows at least as much as the lead guard. Because Walt was an expert in this area, he conducted the interview. He asked each contractor how guards were recruited and trained and how long their guards remained with the company. He asked them about their emergency procedures, their job performance monitoring procedures, and their experience in providing security escort. Each interview lasted about an hour.

The contractors' responses made it clear who was the most qualified for the job. Managers must remember that the use of professional consultants in such situations is invaluable. They shed light on what could be a process full of nuances. In addition, contractors who are interviewed by such professionals are careful in their performance and pricing.

Reviewing Fire and Life Safety Procedures

Fire and life safety was another area of major concern. A few months prior to my assignment to the Tower project, another major downtown building caught fire while the owners were removing asbestos. It gave the building a bad reputation in terms of life safety, and a number of tenants relocated, some of whom moved to the Tower.

Walt reviewed the fire and life safety procedures at the Tower and found a number of deficiencies.

> The security guards were not trained as qualified life safety officers. In case of an emergency after normal working hours, the guards would have to notify the building manager who may not be at the building.
>
> The fire marshal's inspection of the building was overdue.
>
> The list of floor wardens was outdated.

Ron and I discussed these deficiencies and agreed with Walt's recommendations. He indicated that Delpro had produced a videotape showing tenants how to evacuate the building.

Reviewing the HVAC System

Tom was hired as our HVAC consultant. Tom's approach was to let the engineers know that he respected them. As a result, he had the full cooperation of the engineers, which is very important in a consulting task.

After Tom inspected the building's HVAC system, he reported that the 12 engineers were doing an excellent job, that the rooms were clean, and that the equipment was well maintained. He reported that the most important deficiency was that the control systems were outdated and needed to be more fully automated.

For this reason, the engineers had no choice but to manage the system using their experience and judgment on when to start and stop the system. This resulted in inefficient energy utilization and uncomfortable conditions for the tenants. Tom's recommendation was to upgrade the energy management system and to initiate feasibility/payback study. Utilization of a computerized system with a payback potential of 1.2 years was recommended. The $120,000 cost would save $100,000 annually and would better serve the tenants.

Reviewing the Structure

A review of the roof indicated that exterior cleaning scaffold tracks were improperly installed. Expansion joints were not properly cared for, resulting in cracking of concrete supports and parts of the roof. In addition, it was determined that certain portions of the exterior facade could not be reached with the existing scaffold structure. It was recommended that a structural engineer prepare guidelines for remedial action.

Also, some equipment used at the machine shop could be a fire hazard (e.g., oxygen tanks for welding) and a liability if injury is caused to workers. It was recommended that an inventory be made and some equipment be sold.

Presenting the Findings

John asked me to present our findings to the partners. Since the partners would not be interested in reading hundreds of pages of technical jargon, I decided to use diagrams, which showed the systems overlaid on the building's background, to point out the deficiencies. These diagrams were supplemented by an executive summary, which clearly stated the owner's objectives, and by a summary of various reports.

John was pleased with the clear and concise nature of the reports, diagrams, and the style of the presentation. When I confidently delivered my message to the partners, my recommendations were accepted.

SUMMARY

To successfully manage the office building in a changing market, the manager must remember several things. First, lean times mean lean management. All expenses must be evaluated and contracts rebid to ensure that operations are being handled in a cost-effective manner. When reviewing expenses, safety concerns, and structural quality, it is necessary to have a professional team working with you. Many people know 50 percent about a certain matter, but their solutions are average. To achieve excellence, the person should know 90 percent to 99 percent of that speciality—they should be the top talent. When times are lean and the market is competitive, the only answer is to seek the help of top and honest talent.

QUALITY CONTROL REPORT

As stated earlier, our primary object is to maintain or improve quality.

In this report, we will concentrate on the major items while minor findings can be found in the respective consultants' reports.

Deficiencies shown as (D-1) . . . (D-n) hereunder refer to Exhibits 16-2, 16-3, and 16-4.

A. Elevator Maintenance

Our consultant found XYZ to be very competent and providing excellent service.

Deficiencies found in the building's 50 elevators and 2 escalators are being repaired by XYZ and should be completed by June 30, 1991.

Excessive sway was found among a few of the six sky lobby elevators and one high rise elevator (Deficiency: D-1). This is due to improper installation of the rails by the manufacturer during building construction. XYZ will be conducting tests to identify the elevators with the most sway and propose corrective action. The cost of such repairs, however, is not in their contract. Our interviews with the property manager revealed that there were no tenant complaints on this matter, and our consultants mentioned that this does not pose a safety hazard.

Minor deficiencies include:

- (D-2) Photo electric lights missing (needed for passenger safety).
- (D-3) Nudging malfunction (needed for fire safety).

EXHIBIT 16–2

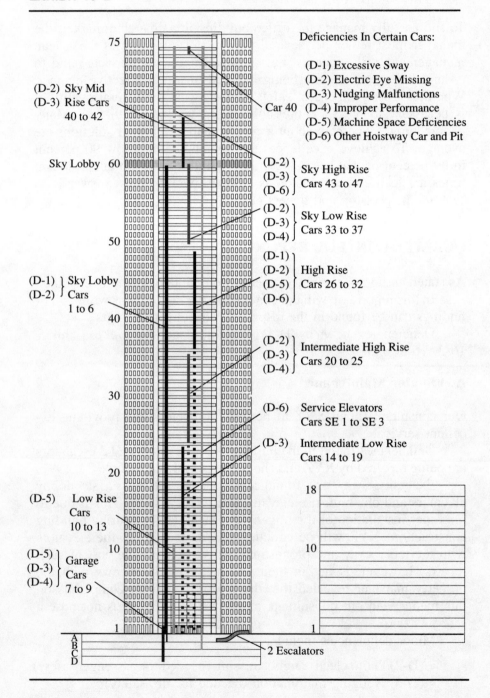

Deficiencies In Certain Cars:

(D-1) Excessive Sway
(D-2) Electric Eye Missing
(D-3) Nudging Malfunctions
(D-4) Improper Performance
(D-5) Machine Space Deficiencies
(D-6) Other Hoistway Car and Pit

(D-2) Sky Mid
(D-3) Rise Cars
40 to 42

Car 40

Sky Lobby 60

(D-2)
(D-3) Sky High Rise
(D-6) Cars 43 to 47

(D-2)
(D-3) Sky Low Rise
(D-4) Cars 33 to 37

(D-1)
(D-2) High Rise
(D-5) Cars 26 to 32
(D-6)

(D-1) Sky Lobby
(D-2) Cars
        1 to 6

(D-2)
(D-3) Intermediate High Rise
(D-4) Cars 20 to 25

(D-6) Service Elevators
       Cars SE 1 to SE 3

(D-3) Intermediate Low Rise
       Cars 14 to 19

(D-5) Low Rise
       Cars
       10 to 13

(D-5)
(D-3) Garage
(D-4) Cars
        7 to 9

2 Escalators

EXHIBIT 16–3

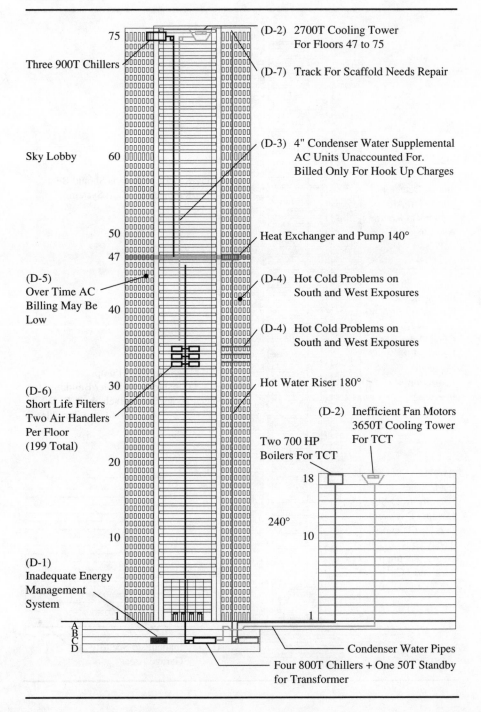

Three 900T Chillers

Sky Lobby

(D-5)
Over Time AC
Billing May Be
Low

(D-6)
Short Life Filters
Two Air Handlers
Per Floor
(199 Total)

(D-1)
Inadequate Energy
Management
System

(D-2) 2700T Cooling Tower
For Floors 47 to 75

(D-7) Track For Scaffold Needs Repair

(D-3) 4" Condenser Water Supplemental
AC Units Unaccounted For.
Billed Only For Hook Up Charges

Heat Exchanger and Pump 140°

(D-4) Hot Cold Problems on
South and West Exposures

(D-4) Hot Cold Problems on
South and West Exposures

Hot Water Riser 180°

(D-2) Inefficient Fan Motors
3650T Cooling Tower
For TCT

Two 700 HP
Boilers For TCT

240°

Condenser Water Pipes

Four 800T Chillers + One 50T Standby
for Transformer

EXHIBIT 16–4

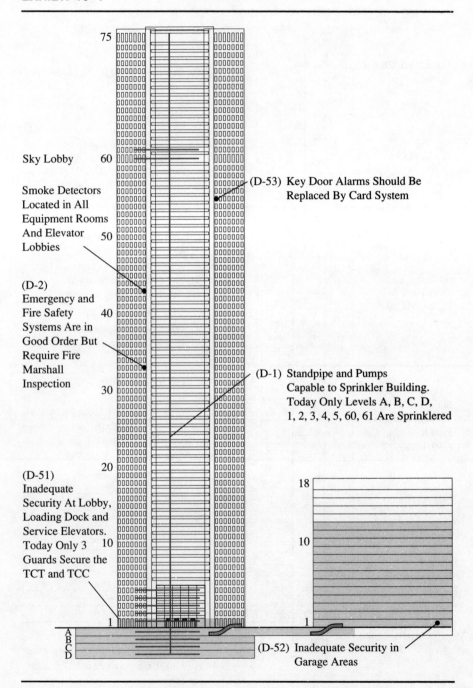

75

Sky Lobby   60

Smoke Detectors
Located in All
Equipment Rooms
And Elevator   50
Lobbies

(D-2)
Emergency and
Fire Safety   40
Systems Are in
Good Order But
Require Fire
Marshall
Inspection   30

(D-53) Key Door Alarms Should Be
       Replaced By Card System

(D-1) Standpipe and Pumps
      Capable to Sprinkler Building.
      Today Only Levels A, B, C, D,
      1, 2, 3, 4, 5, 60, 61 Are Sprinklered

20

(D-51)
Inadequate
Security At Lobby,
Loading Dock and
Service Elevators.
Today Only 3   10
Guards Secure the
TCT and TCC

18

10

1

A
B
C
D

(D-52) Inadequate Security in
       Garage Areas

- (D-4) Showing "spotting" (improper slow-stop procedure).
- (D-5) Other machine space deficiencies, some selector tape sheave guards missing (needed to protect selector tape which informs the elevator when to slow, stop and recognize calls). Some seals were experiencing more leaks than others.
- (D-6) Other hoistway, car and pit deficiencies.

B. Heating Ventilation and Air Conditioning (HVAC)

The engineers of the Tower were found to be doing a good to excellent job maintaining the building systems. However, the problem lies in that these systems were not upgraded to enhance efficiency, comfort to certain tenants nor provide appropriate extra billing to tenants.

D-1: The energy management system (EMS) is in need of upgrading. The building's mechanical systems are being started and stopped through experience and do not take into consideration the exterior/interior temperatures and humidity levels. This is resulting in inefficiency in electric consumption as well as hot/cold complaints by the tenants (D-4). Delpro has acknowledged this deficiency. They have assigned a proposal for upgrading the system (enclosed). The pay back is 1.2 years and would result in annual utilities savings of close to $100,000. We recommend such upgrading.

D-2: Cooling towers could run more efficiently with 2-speed motors. A feasibility/payback study should be explored to determine savings versus installation costs.

D-3: A 150 Ton 4" condenser water pipes for supplemental AC could become inadequate. They currently serve only floors 36 to 75. This is prompting some tenants to use domestic water going to waste in order to satisfy their supplemental AC needs. Tenants are being billed connection fees only, which may be insufficient to account for all costs of providing condenser water. No inventory exists today on supplemental A/C connections.

Our consultant mentioned that existing cooling tower capacity could deliver additional condenser water for supplemental systems of 360 Tons from the Center and 270 Tons from the Tower. Delpro will review these and other alternatives with the mechanical engineers of the building.

D-4:   Hot/cold complains surge on Mondays and especially if unseasonal exterior conditions exist. This could be a problem of improper balancing, air flow distribution, or system control which could be resolved with the EMS upgrade. This matter is being reviewed by Delpro and they will report on their findings.

D-5:   Overtime A/C billing of $50 per floor per hour may be low. A study should be done to determine the cost of such extra service, otherwise tenants not requiring this service are subsidizing such costs. If the market cannot support an increase of such charges, then we should explore the feasibility of adding a smaller 450 Ton chiller for added efficiency of after hour use and flexibility during normal hours use.

D-6:   The type of filters used today are being replaced every three months. A feasibility study should be made to see if longer life filters could be used which may reduce labor and material costs.

C. Emergency & Life Safety

Emergency and life safety systems are in good condition. Two deficiencies could be noted in this summary.

(D-1)   The Tower's mechanical engineers informed us through Delpro that the sprinkler system's standpipe and pumps are capable of sprinklering the entire building. However, when the Tower was built in 1982, the code did not require full sprinkler system installation. Only levels A, B, C, D, 1, 2, 3, 4, 5, 60, and 61 are sprinklered today. It may be feasible to sprinkler floors where tenant work will be done in the future.

(D-2)   Emergency and life safety systems are in good order. However, an inspection by the fire marshal is necessary since the last inspection was made two years ago.

An update of the list of floor wardens should be made. The guard in the Emergency control room should be a trained Fire Safety Director in the absence of the property manager and his assistants.

D. Security

Although the security aspects of this review are the most subjective, we could certainly note that security in the Tower and garage are below what the owners and tenants would like to see in the face of increased crime in Dallas.

It was revealed that in 1988 there was a pistol attack at a law firm. The response of the guards was that they were changing shifts and could not respond.

There was an attack on a woman in the garage and attempted kidnapping. Overall our existing security contractor reported 66 incidents in 1989 and 10 incidents from January 10 to April 7, 1990, while the Dallas police department reported 30 incidents in the Tower and center as compared with 150 in the central business district. The Tower cannot afford a reputation of lax security or a major security incident which will affect its marketability to tenants or its reputation.

Today, the Tower and garage security is provided by one guard at the security office, one roving guard in the Tower and one roving guard in the garage on a 24-hour basis.

Following are the major deficiencies and minimum security recommended by our consultant.

(D-51) A lead guard with adequate experience should be visible during working hours at the lobby level and should monitor close circuit cameras installed to provide coverage of elevator, other lobby and "A" level hallways. The existing roving guard will assist him in his duties.

A second guard should be stationed during working hours in the loading dock to screen all deliveries and messengers prior to entering the building. This duty is now performed by a cleaning person. Two cleaning persons should be stationed in the service elevators logging in and out delivery people who have been already screened by the loading dock guard. Exit of the cleaning people should be enforced through the lobby and not through the loading dock area.

(D-52) A more comprehensive review should be done to enhance security in the garage areas.

(D-53) The tenant key pad alarm controls (48 exist today) should be gradually upgraded to card access mechanism. This enables the security staff to record time and name of persons entering the premises. A minimum of one per floor could also monitor the movement of the night roving guard.

CHAPTER 17

TYPICAL ESCALATIONS AND ADDITIONAL RENT INCLUDED IN COMMERCIAL LEASES

Steven W. Ford
Cushman & Wakefield, Inc.

Since World War II, owners of commercial real estate have been faced with the challenge of preserving their profit margins included in rental income. The owners look to protect their equity position during the ownership period, keeping in mind that increased rentals will not only pay for increased expenses but will also preserve the purchasing power of the equity dollar. The owners also hope that the asset will appreciate in value over time by achieving higher rentals.

This chapter focuses on the theoretical components of rent, and in particular on escalations and other additional rent typically included in commercial leases. The chapter also attempts to provide the reader with an understanding of the most frequently used escalations and other additional rent provisions, indicating their intended purposes.

In theory, an owner attempts to lease space at a rental rate that will cover the building's expenses for real estate taxes, operating expenses, financing costs, and anticipated capital expenses with enough left over for a contribution to owner equity. The base rental will be increased through the use of various escalations and other additional rent clauses that allow the owner to recapture increased expenses over the lease term. In practice, however, the owner rents for whatever the market will bear. A building owner is always subject to competition from neighboring buildings and is affected by the general economic condition of the marketplace; therefore, the owner's pricing is influenced by the pricing of competitors.

In a strong market, when the business community is vibrant and rentable space is scarce, rent will be established at a premium rate. The law of supply and demand prevails. Those with long-term ownership plans, however, try to be reasonable even in a tight market since they recognize the value of future lease renewals by good tenants. In a soft market, the converse is true: Owners give greater concessions and accept less rent.

HISTORICAL PERSPECTIVE

Before the different types of escalation and other additional rent are explained, one must consider the history of the escalation clauses that permit the owner to increase a tenant's rent during the lease term.

- *Pre-1950s.* Before 1950, there were virtually no escalation clauses in commercial leases. Leases tended to be short, with one, two, or three years being the usual term. Therefore, as leases expired (usually every three years), new leases would be negotiated at a higher rental, indicative of the owner's higher costs. Tenancies also tended to be smaller than they are today. At that time, a tenant who occupied 10,000 to 15,000 square feet was large, and a 50,000 square-foot user was considered to be extremely large. The size of the space and the short lease term generally did not encourage a large investment by the tenant for construction improvements to the leased premises. Consequently, improvements to the space were minimal.
- *Late 1950s and early 1960s.* As tenants became larger users of space and improvements became more frequent, tenants began to require longer lease terms in order to justify the greater initial installation costs. In the late 1950s and early 1960s, 20-year lease terms with options to renew for two additional 10-year periods were not unusual. The rent rates were usually fixed for the initial 20-year lease term, with no escalation provisions or with limitations on escalation recoveries.
- *The 1960s and early 1970s.* In the 1960s and early 1970s, the economy experienced rapid inflation and owners were faced with escalating operating expenses. Because of the long-term, fixed-rental nature of the leases of many larger tenants, owners were unable to recapture these increased costs. Reacting to these economic influences, owners began to request escalation clauses, the first of which was real estate tax escalation. The owner wanted to recapture increases

in the property's real estate tax expenses, as well as increases in operating expenses, from the tenants. Among the first was a clause that provided for reimbursement of the owner's cost over a base-year amount to be paid in the year following the one in which the expense had been incurred. This is commonly called *operating expense escalation.*

Initially, tenants were reluctant to agree to lease escalation clauses. They were generally skeptical, thinking it was merely a method for the owner to generate more revenue or to charge more rent. Many leases were written with a limitation, or cap, on the amount of escalation that could be charged to the tenant, an arrangement satisfactory to both parties in times of low inflation.

• *The 1970s.* During this period, prices began to skyrocket. The oil embargo of 1973 caused dramatic increases in utility expenses. Labor increases were also significant. Owners were strapped; they could not recapture their increased expenditures because of long-term leases and the limitations included in the escalation clauses. The increased rents did not keep pace with the increased expenses, which caused an erosion of owner equity. The general economy slipped into a recession and many owners were forced to declare bankruptcy. The years from 1973 to 1975 proved disastrous for real estate investors as well as lending institutions.

Building owners began to react to these economic influences by insisting on escalation clauses that would protect their equity. The limitations on escalation clauses were removed when the leases rolled over. In an attempt to deal with the recapture of operating expenses in a simpler fashion, formula clauses of different types were introduced in several markets. These clauses utilized a published index as the basis for estimating operating expenses and thus eliminated the detailed accounting procedures required for the pass-through methods previously in effect.

In the late 1970s, owners also began to include consumer price index escalation, providing for equity adjustments. Because the other escalations were intended to recover increased costs only, owners were looking to protect the purchasing power of their equity dollars. This escalation was based on a government-published index; therefore, it was simple for the tenants to verify the escalation calculation.

• *The porter's wage escalation.* An early example of an escalation based on published information was the porters' wage escalation, introduced in the New York market in the early 1960s. This escalation was based on the change in labor rates for the employees of a specific union in New York City. The concept originally provided for the tenant to pay one cent per square foot for each one percent increase in the hourly wage for a porter on an annual basis. The theory justifying this escalation clause was that the percentage increases in wages paid to porters closely tracked the percentage increases in operating expenses for the owner. The typical operating expenses for a building in New York at that time were approximately $1 per square foot.

The porters' wage escalation was a simple clause for owners and tenants to understand, and, because it was based on a published union contract, the escalation calculation was simple to verify. The owners relieved themselves of the administrative burden of tenant audits, and the tenants felt more comfortable with the escalation billing. As the market strengthened and operating costs exceeded $1 per square foot, owners began to ask for multiples of one cent for each one percent increase in porters' wages. By the middle to late 1960s, the New York market began to see the penny-for-penny formula for the porters' wage escalation: The tenant would be billed one cent per square foot for each one cent increase in porters' wages. In the late 1960s, combined wage and benefit clauses began to appear as porters negotiated better benefits as part of their compensation package. The increases in wages and benefits began to be passed on to the tenants on a penny per square foot for each penny increase in wages plus the cost of the benefits converted to an hourly basis, based on 2,080 hours per year, the assumption being that the porter worked 40 hours per week, 52 weeks per year.

In the late 1970s, the rental market in New York strengthened. In reaction to a stronger market, owners began to add utility cost escalation. Utility cost escalation protected owners from the large increases in utility expenses they had experienced in the early 1970s, which they had been unable to recover. This escalation allowed the owners to collect these increases from the tenants on a pro-rated basis.

• *The 1980s.* As the real estate market continued to strengthen in the early 1980s, New York owners introduced multiples of the penny-for-penny concept. Porters' wages and benefits were calculated on an actual hours-worked basis, not on the basis of 2,080 hours. It was recognized that a porter did not actually work 2,080 hours per year, because vacation, sick days, and so forth were elements of owner cost for a porter. This reduced the number of hours worked to approximately 1,600, which, when divided into the total annual cost of each benefit, resulted in an increase in the hourly rate and protected owners against future reductions in hours worked by a porter.

In other markets, the most frequently used escalation clauses were real estate tax, operating expense, and consumer price index. As a matter of fact, finding other formula clauses such as the porters' wage or separate utility cost escalation outside New York City is quite unusual.

As the length and size of leases increased, owners looked to incorporate escalation clauses to allow for recapture of increases in their operating costs.

From a historical perspective, owners initially focused on relieving a particular problem—hence, the establishment of real estate tax escalation and operating expense escalation. Over time, owners have endeavored to make leases more flexible in an attempt to protect themselves against adverse economic influences.

For this reason, leases that permit the owner to switch from porters' wage coupled with utility cost escalation to operating expense escalation at any time during the lease term are not unusual. Most gross leases provide for real estate tax escalation. Escalation provisions are owners' reactions to economic influences in the real estate industry.

OPERATING EXPENSE ESCALATION

Concept

Operating expense escalation is the simplest form of escalation and the easiest to understand. The concept behind the calculation is to merely pass through the increase in operating expenses of the property that has occurred since the period when the tenant first occupied the premises.

Theoretically, the owner has included in the base rental all costs associated with the property on a pro rata basis as of the date the lease commenced. These costs would include capitalized acquisition and construction expenses, debt service, depreciation, ground rent expense, operating expenses, taxes, and other financial expenses associated with the building. The owner's intention is to protect the equity in the property by passing through to the tenant the increase in costs of operating and maintaining the property over what such costs were when the tenant's lease commenced. Many building owners utilize pass-through operating expense escalation because it is the most direct reflection of an increase in the owner's cost of operating and maintaining the property and is therefore the easiest escalation to "sell" to tenants.

From the owner's perspective, operating expense escalation has the following advantages and disadvantages.

Advantages

- A direct relationship exists between the escalation and the owner's cost of operating and maintaining the property.
- The operating expenses included in the schedule are usually easy to verify.
- The method of computing operating expense escalation is easy to understand and trace.
- The base year information is usually easy to predict, and, if not, a "base stop" can be utilized to safeguard against large comparison-year spreads.

Disadvantages

- The escalation is based on the operating history of a single building rather than on statistical averages. As a result, a poorly managed or inefficient building may cause the tenant to suffer inordinately high escalations compared to other buildings.
- Items included in the operating expense schedule may be subject to interpretation, which in turn may lead to differences of opinion between landlord and tenant and may eventually lead to costly arbitration or litigation between the parties. This often happens when the landlord charges for costly repairs that the tenant disputes.
- An owner may be hesitant to spend capital dollars in an effort to decrease operating expenses, since it would decrease the additional rent recovered from the tenants.

Method of Computation

Billing the operating expense escalation consists of two steps. The first step involves preparing a schedule of operating expenses, which is usually done by an independent auditor. This schedule lists all of the expenses of a given building that are deemed to be operating expenses in conformance with the leases.

The following items are usually *excluded* from an operating expense schedule:

- Administrative wages and salaries (wages and salaries of property management and ownership personnel not permanently assigned to the building).
- Renting commissions.
- Franchise taxes or income taxes of the landlord.
- Taxes on the land and building (these items are usually billed in a separate real estate tax escalation).
- Cost of painting, decorating, and otherwise altering individual tenant spaces, including "take-back" spaces.
- Interest and amortization costs of a mortgage and any refinancing costs.
- Ground rents.
- Depreciation.
- Costs or expenses for which the landlord is separately reimbursed, except for escalation recoveries (for example, insurance claims, overtime elevator or air conditioning services, and so on).
- Capital improvement expenses except (1) those that are expensed under generally applied real estate practice or are deferred expenses and (2) those that are required by law (such as retrofitting fire alarm and sprinkler systems).

The second step consists of the actual calculation of the escalation. The operating expense schedule is compared to the lease to determine whether there are any special exclusions for a given tenant. Items that can be excluded are deducted from the expense schedule; the method of calculation is as follows:

Billing year operating expenses

Minus: Base year operating expense

Equals: Increase in operating expenses

Multiplied by: Tenant's proportionate share of building

Equals: Operating expense escalation for billing year for that particular tenant space

Operating expense escalations can be billed annually or monthly on the basis of actual figures or with estimates computed with the landlord. Usually, estimated escalation charges are billed at the beginning of the year based on the current year's operating budget. The base year operating costs may be the actual costs of operating the building in the year the tenant occupied the premises, or they may consist of an arbitrary amount negotiated between the landlord and the tenant, known as a base stop. In the case of a base stop, the subsequent billing years may be subject to "grossing-up," predicated on the percentage of occupancy of the total building or complex. This would involve adjusting the bill up or down, depending on the occupancy of the premises. For example, if the base stop of $5 per square foot is predicated on 95 percent occupancy and the weighted average occupancy for the billing year is 85 percent, the expenses, which vary with occupancy for the billing year, would be adjusted accordingly.

The $5 per square foot amount is used as an example only. In practice, only the operating expenses that are sensitive to occupancy (for example, cleaning, repairs and maintenance, and supplies) are adjusted. Careful consideration must be given to the specific wording of the lease clause.

REAL ESTATE TAX ESCALATION

Concept

Real estate tax escalation is intended to protect against the erosion of the owner's equity in much the same way that the operating expense escalation does. The difference is that real estate tax escalation only recovers funds spent for real estate taxes. Usually, real estate tax escalation is billed separately from operating expense escalation because the tax year may be a different fiscal period than most owners' operating years. Consequently, the real estate tax escalation is geared toward recovering the funds as quickly as they are disbursed. Landlords must pay real estate taxes, and tenants must invariably pay the landlords for their pro rata share of the increase.

If a building receives tax benefits, the tenants of the building will benefit by lower real estate tax recoveries of the landlord. A tenant may also benefit by lower escalations in buildings in which the landlord aggressively pursues lower property assessments through certiorari or other legal proceedings. However, most of the landlord's costs in obtaining the revised assessment via these proceedings can be recovered from the tenants on a pro rata basis.

Method of Calculation

Real estate tax escalation is usually billed during the same periods in which it is paid. In most cities it is billed on a semiannual basis in July and January, although it is sometimes billed to tenants on a quarterly or annual basis, or very infrequently, on a monthly basis. Base stops may also be used in the same manner as outlined in the operating expense escalation section. The calculation of real estate (R/E) tax escalations is as follows:

Billing year R/E taxes
Minus: Base year R/E taxes
Equals: Increase in R/E taxes
Multiplied by: Tenant's proportionate share of building
Equals: R/E tax escalation for billing year for tenant's space

PORTERS' WAGE INDEX ESCALATION

Concept

The concept of the porters' wage escalation is also to protect against the erosion of the owner's equity. In this instance, however, the means by which the owner's equity is protected bears no direct relationship to actual increases in the operating expenses of the building. Rather, a formula based on the increase in industry-wide union labor rates for a particular segment of the work force is used.

Many building owners employ a porters' wage index escalation because it can be billed utilizing an index based on the wages of porters belonging to building service unions. The other major attraction for owners is the fact that historically, the porters' wage index escalation generates significantly more revenue for the owner than the operating expense escalation does.

The porters' wage escalation has many variations. Originally, its formula was calculated by multiplying the tenant's square footage by the percentage increase in the wages paid to porters over the tenant's base year (penny per percent). This formula was used because the percentage increases in wages typically closely tracked the average increase in operating costs of major office buildings.

As time went on, landlords switched the formula from penny per percent to penny per penny, which calculated the escalation by multiplying the tenant's square footage by an amount equal to one cent for each one-cent increase in hourly wages paid to porters over the tenant's base year hourly wage rate. This increased the escalation income over the previous calculation method.

The porters' wage escalation was expanded to include fringe benefits. These include mandatory overtime, social security, workman's compensation, unemployment insurance, disability insurance, pension fund, welfare fund, education training and safety fund, vacation, sick pay, holidays, birthday, and any other benefit stated in the union contract. In addition to the development of fringe benefits, a recent trend to use the actual hours the average porter works instead of 2,080 hours has also developed. This adjustment results in a higher cost per hour for billing purposes.

From the landlord's perspective, the porters' wage index escalation has the following advantages and disadvantages:

Advantages
- The escalation is billed monthly, allowing for the tenant's expense to be paid out evenly over a 12-month period.
- The escalation is based on a statistical average rather than on the operating history of a single building, thereby avoiding the cost of tenant audits.
- The rate of increase is usually predictable from year to year for budgeting purposes.
- Tenants have difficulty disputing a porters' wage index escalation because most leases state that fringe benefits include *all* items covered in the basic union contract.
- The landlord has an incentive to spend capital dollars to decrease operating expenses or to operate the building in a more cost-effective manner without detriment to his or her recovery of additional rent.

Disadvantages
- The lease clauses are not standard; therefore, hourly wage rates vary greatly from building to building unless an industry-wide labor agreement rate is used.

Method of Computation

The porters' wage index escalation is computed in two steps. The first is the formulation of the escalation schedule. Porters' wage index escalations today usually include fringe benefits in addition to the base hourly wage rate. Once the fringe benefits schedule has been computed, the escalation is calculated as follows:

Billing year wage rate

Minus: Base year wage rate

Equals: Increase in wage rate

Multiplied by: Tenant's square footage

Equals: Escalation computed

Multiplied by: 1.0, 1.25, or 1.5

(depending on what ratio is stated in lease)

Equals: Porters' wage escalation per square foot of tenant space

One takes the increase in the wage rate index for the comparison year over the wage rate index in the base year and multiplies the increase by the square footage of the premises. Depending upon how the lease is negotiated, that number is then multiplied by 1, 1.25, or 1.5. These are known as penny per penny, penny and a quarter per penny, or penny and a half per penny porters' wage escalations. In a penny per percent escalation, the tenant's square footage is multiplied by the percentage increase in the wage rate.

CPI ESCALATION

Concept

The consumer price index (CPI) escalation protects against the erosion of the owner's equity by increasing the rent based on an inflation factor that is published in government statistics. Various indices can be used; the most frequently used is the consumer price index for all urban wage earners for the geographical region in which the building is located.

Building owners may utilize the CPI escalation with the operating expense or the porters' wage index escalations. During periods of high inflation, owners use one of these combinations to help prevent losses in purchasing power greater than the amounts recovered by the owner with the other escalations. In cases where the CPI escalation is used with other escalations, caps or ceilings on the amount of the CPI escalation may be provided in the lease.

From the owner's perspective, the CPI escalation has the following advantages and disadvantages:

Advantages
- The escalation is billed monthly, allowing for the tenant's expense to be paid out evenly over a 12-month period.
- The rate of increase is usually predictable from year to year.
- The rate of increase is favorable in periods of high inflation for the general economy.
- The method of computation allows the landlord to multiply the percentage increase in the CPI by the amount of the tenant's rent. With rents in the $35 to $45 per square foot range at the time of this writing, the escalation is becoming significant. The most expensive escalation for tenants with these high rents is now 100 percent CPI escalation.

Disadvantages
- The rate of increase is unfavorable in periods of low inflation for the general economy.

Method of Computation

The CPI escalation is normally calculated by multiplying the percentage increase in the consumer price index of the comparison year over the base year by the tenant's annual base rent:

> Billing year CPI
> Minus: Base year CPI
> Equals: Increase in CPI
> Divided by: Base year CPI
> Equals: Percentage increase in CPI
> Multiplied by: Tenant's annual base rent
> Equals: CPI escalation for tenant's space

This example uses 100 percent CPI. For 50 percent CPI, one-half of the escalation would be computed.

UTILITY COST ESCALATION

The utility cost escalation protects against the erosion of the owner's equity by passing through the increased cost of utilities for a given building. This escalation is often used with other escalations such as real estate tax and porters' wage escalations. The utility escalation, or fuel escalation, relates only to the cost of common-area electricity and other utilities and not to tenant-area electrical costs. This is only true in New York, where submetering or electric rent inclusion is used; in other parts of the country, rent includes electricity without adjustments.

The building owner uses utility cost escalation with another (usually porters' wage) escalation because it protects against the erosion of his or her equity from large increases in the cost of utilities. This escalation is less prevalent today because of the recent decrease in the price of petroleum and gas, with the resulting stabilization of utility rates.

The utility cost escalation is calculated in virtually the same manner as operating expense escalations. The billings may be monthly or annual.

Billing year utility costs (40 percent electric plus steam) (representing common-area expenses)
Minus: Base year utility costs
Equals: Increase in utility cost
Multiplied by: Tenant's percentage share
Equals: Utility cost escalation

ELECTRICITY

Owners of commercial property have three basic options in providing electricity to their tenants.

Direct Metering

The tenant purchases electricity directly from the utility company and is connected to the public utility's power lines at the point of entry or on each floor with a separate meter.

Advantages
- Accurate metering of tenant usage of light and miscellaneous power.
- Landlord is not involved in associated adjustments, billings, and collection.
- No electric survey required.

- Promotes energy conservation by tenant.
- Billing is directly from utility company, not by landlord.

Disadvantages
- Additional capital to implement and install meters.
- Additional space allocation for distribution equipment and risers, which reduce the rentable area of the building.
- Reduced system flexibility for future tenant alterations.

Submetering

The tenant purchases electricity through the landlord's meters, generally located in an electrical closet servicing that floor.

Advantages
- Accurate metering of tenant consumption.
- No surveys required.
- Less costly to install than direct metering.
- Promotes energy conservation by the tenant.

Disadvantages
- Must be approved by public service commission to install submeters.
- Cost of implementing meters.
- Cost of maintaining meters.
- Improperly installed meters may measure other tenants' usage.
- Multi-tenant floors require additional facilities, thereby reducing space.
- Public areas paid through other escalation clauses.
- Utility company rate classification is negotiable—uninformed tenant may not receive greatest benefits.

Rent Inclusion

The tenant purchases electricity by estimated usage. The amount has usually been agreed upon and is subject to survey and future adjustments.

Advantages
- No cost for meter installation involved.

- Single building meter or meters; no additional equipment or area required.
- Most flexible billing method for the landlord.

Disadvantages
- Least accurate method of billing tenants.
- Requires initial survey and subsequent surveys, with the possibility of tenants' sharing costs.
- Change in tenant use, rate, or fuel adjustment requires constant monitoring and accounting adjustments.
- More susceptible to errors, which result in tenant disputes.
- Owner is penalized if rate structure is tilted against large users.

SUMMARY

The escalations presented in this chapter are typical of additional rent clauses that may be encountered during lease negotiations.

The escalation lease clauses are drafted by the landlord's attorney and addressed at length during lease negotiations. The first step in knowing where to look for escalation lease wording to protect the landlord is in understanding the concepts behind the escalation and how it is calculated.

I hope that this chapter has provided some insight into that process.

CHAPTER 18

THE ACCOUNTING AND TAX ASPECTS OF PROPERTY MANAGEMENT

Knute P. Kurtz
Coopers & Lybrand
Brad P. Keller
Coopers & Lybrand

OVERVIEW OF ACCOUNTING AND TAX CONSIDERATIONS

The financial records maintained by a property manager are the building blocks upon which all other financial and tax documents depend. If transactions are not properly recorded in the books and records, the owner will be unable to obtain an accurate evaluation of the performance of the property. The property manager must therefore not only be able to effectively market the property, coordinate maintenance, and fulfill tenants' needs, but also be able to keep an accurate record of the financial affairs of the property.

The property manager is responsible for, among other matters, collecting rentals and paying expenses related to a particular property. The accounting and tax aspects of property management arise from recording these activities and reporting financial results regarding a particular property.

This chapter is organized into two primary topics: (1) accounting aspects of property management and (2) tax aspects of property management. Although these topics overlap, each has particular nuances that warrant special elaboration.

This discussion necessarily disregards the legal form adopted by the entity that owns the property. The legal form adopted by any individual real estate entity is determined by numerous considerations, among which are tax considerations, preferred method of financing, and the amount of risk any individual investor wishes to bear. Each of the different legal entities entitled to own and operate commercial real estate has income taxation and debt financing advantages unique to its legal structure. A detailed discussion of these income tax and financing implications is far beyond the scope of this chapter. Therefore, this chapter will focus on the accounting issues pertinent to office building management and, from a tax standpoint, ad valorem real property taxation and certain income taxation issues germane to any form of legal ownership.

One should note that we have assumed that the building has been substantially completed, that it is held available for occupancy, and that the owner's present intention is to retain ownership of the property. The final assumption is important because a lease that transfers substantially all of the benefits and risks of ownership must be accounted for as the sale or financing of an asset by the owner.[1] All other leases are accounted for as operating leases, the pure rental of property. The first two assumptions are also important because information on the accounting and income taxation principles applicable to the development of commercial real estate is so voluminous that each topic requires its own separate publications.

ACCOUNTING ASPECTS OF PROPERTY MANAGEMENT

Generally Accepted Accounting Principles (GAAP)

GAAP requires financial reporting to follow an accrual rather than a cash basis. The accrual system is based on the premise that the timing of cash flows is not necessarily relevant to measuring when revenue is actually earned. Therefore, under GAAP, revenue is recognized when it is earned rather than when it is collected. The same accrual system is applicable to the time that expenses are recognized. Expenses are recognized and reported when they are incurred rather than when they

---

[1] Statement of Financial Accounting Standard No. 13, ¶7.

are actually paid. This concept of accrual basis accounting will be developed with specific examples later in this chapter. Although the property manager's function with regard to accounting may seem to involve merely collecting rents and paying operating expenses, certain aspects of commercial office building operations can be complex.

Basic Books and Records

The primary books and records utilized by the property manager in recording the transactions of a commercial office building are a cash receipts journal, a cash disbursements journal, and a general ledger. These records may be supplemented by other accounting journals and ledgers, depending upon the complexities of the property's operations.

The cash receipts journal is used to record all recurring sources of cash related to the property, such as the receipt of rentals or other fees paid by tenants. The journal usually includes the date the cash is received, from whom it is received, and the nature and amount of the receipt. Totals from the cash receipts journal are transferred to the general ledger at the end of an accounting period.

The cash disbursements journal is used to record all cash payments made by the property manager for the property. This journal typically contains the date of payment, check number, payee, and the nature and amount of payment. Totals from this journal are also posted in the general ledger at the end of an accounting period.

The general ledger is the accounting record that is both the culmination of all other accounting activity and the permanent record of all activity in the various balance sheet and income and expense accounts. See Exhibit 18–2 at the end of this chapter for a depiction of a typical chart of accounts that comprises the general ledger accounts for the management of a typical commercial office building.

Accounting for Operating Leases

The proper accounting procedure for operating leases is to report rent as income over the lease term as it becomes receivable according to the terms of the lease.[2] Rent is reported in this manner because it is not truly earned until the property is made available to the tenant in accordance with the terms of the lease. Therefore, any prepayment of rent is

---

[2] Statement of Financial Accounting Standard No. 13, ¶196.

not exactly revenue at the time it is received by the owner. At the time it is collected, prepaid rent is revenue, an asset, and a liability of the business. This may best be explained by an example:

> A tenant prepays three months rent, which totals an amount of $1,500 ($500 per month). In the month it is paid, the owner has received $500 of revenue, representing rent for the current month. However, the owner is now obligated to permit the tenant to remain in the facility without paying additional rent for two additional months. Thus, the owner's cash account will increase by $1,500. The owner has also incurred a $1,000 liability for prepaid rent and should recognize rental revenue of $500. The additional $1,000 will be reported as $500 of revenue in each of the two successive months, with appropriate $500 adjustments being made to the prepaid rent liability account. Simply stated, until the owner has made the facility available for each of the two successive months, she has not yet earned the monthly rent.

Accounting for Operating Expenses

Most office buildings incur similar types of operating expenses: common area and general maintenance, utilities, property taxes, janitorial expenses, and the like. In addition, most owners require tenants to contribute to operational expenses. Accordingly, revenue is received by the owner in excess of the base rent. These direct rental operating expenses are generally reported as current period expenses. However, if they cover more than the current period, they are to be treated as prepaid expenses and must be allocated to future periods in a rational and systematic manner.

An owner's operating expenses can be allocated to tenants by two basic methods: the net lease and the full-service lease. Whenever operating expenses are paid to the lessor, they continue to be treated as revenue. However, in net leases, where the tenant pays these costs directly to the vendor, the amounts are not included as revenue to the owner.

Net Lease Accounting
In a net lease, the tenant pays a base rent amount and a set percentage of all actual operating expenses. This percentage can represent the percent of square footage occupied by the tenant or can be generated by utilizing historical usage information (as in the case of utilities). Because these expenses are paid by the tenant to the owner in the period in which they are incurred, they are treated as revenue by the

owner for the period in which they are to be paid by the tenant. As such, they represent a receivable until paid.

Full-Service Lease Accounting

This is perhaps the most common form of office building lease. A full-service lease requires the owner to make a specified contribution, sometimes called a *rent stop,* to operating expenses. This contribution may be made in aggregate or may involve a set contribution on an expense-by-expense basis. Having a separate basis or rent stop for every individual operating expense is not advisable and is seldom practiced. However, separate bases are often used for real estate taxes, insurance, and utilities.

Utilizing separate contributions as opposed to an aggregate contribution can be advantageous to an owner. If an owner agrees to contribute $2,500 per month to operating expenses, that amount (assuming that at least this sum is actually incurred) will be paid by the owner every month regardless of fluctuations of any individual expense item.

In Exhibit 18–1 the owner has agreed to rent stops for each of the individual expense items that aggregate $2, 500.00.

The owner directly benefits from passing along the increase in taxes and reducing the total amount of his contribution from the savings in utilities expense. Thus, by using separate rent stops, savings may be retained by the owner while increases are passed on to the tenant.

The owner's contribution to operating expenses does no more than reduce the amount of revenue received in that period for rent. The owner's contribution is set off against the payment received by the tenant for the current period; the net amount is reported as revenue from that particular lease.

EXHIBIT 18–1
Rent Stops for Individual Expense Items

	Year 1 Actual Expenses	Contributions Owner	Tenant	Year 2 Actual Expenses	Contributions Owner	Tenant
Taxes	$2,000	$1,500	$500	$2,500	$1,500	$1,000
Insurance	300	250	50	300	250	50
Utilities	750	750	–0–	600	600	–0–
Total	$3,050	$2,500	$550	$3,350	$2,350	$1,500

Property Taxes as a Separate Basis. The previous discussion demonstrates how an owner may pass along an increase in property taxes to her tenants through the use of a full-service lease. The issue that must be addressed is whether passing along a property tax increase in all instances where it is identified as a separate basis for owner contribution is permissible. This point is important because the tax base year used is usually the last tax assessment, even if the assessment substantially predates the lease term.

A tenant is generally not responsible for increases in property taxes unless an express provision to the contrary exists.[3]

Property tax increases can occur for the following reasons:

- Increase in tax rate.
- Increase in assessed value.
- Changes in the property tax statute.

In addition, these items can increase the assessed value:

- Inflation.
- Owner improvements.
- Tenant improvements.

Although most leases provide for rent escalation if property taxes increase, such an increase may not be able to be passed along to the tenant if the language is too specific.[4]

The most troublesome property tax increases are those resulting from improvements in the property itself. If the tenant has caused the improvements to be made, the courts have had little difficulty permitting the increase to be passed along to the tenant, pursuant to a rent escalation provision.[5] However, the courts have not always permitted property tax increases to be passed along if the increased tax is the result of owner improvements to the property that are extraordinary in nature.[6]

---

[3] *See, generally,* 86 ALR2d 670; 48 ALR3d 297.

[4] *Los Angeles Land & Water Co. v. Consumer Rock & Gravel Co.,* 3 Cal2d 77, 43 P2d 281 (1935), where lease provision provided for rent escalation based upon an increase in "assessed value," tenant only responsible for that portion of increase resulting from the increased assessment.

[5] *Marine Bank v. S S. Kresgee Co.,* 283 F2d 119 (CA7, 1960).

[6] *Gold Medal Stamp Co. v. Carver,* 270 NE2d 834 (Mass 1971), Tenant not responsible for increase in property taxes resulting from increase in assessed value due to extraordinary permanent improvements by owner; *Bryant Park Bldg., Inc. v. Acunto,* 133 Misc. 225, 231 NYS 451 (1928), tax increase resulting from nine story addition to buiding would not be passed along to tenant under rent escalation clause.

"Grossing Up" Operating Expenses. Grossing up operating expenses is absolutely essential when using full-service leases. Because a full-service lease requires the tenant to pay operating expenses in excess of a base amount, the base amount must be a truly representative benchmark of those expenses. If a building is not yet fully occupied or has recently undergone substantial renovations, the operating expenses incurred in the future will differ greatly from existing base year calculations. Therefore, the base-year or base amount must be increased, or *grossed up,* to reflect what the operating costs would be if the building were fully occupied. To illustrate this point, assume that a tenant occupies 10 percent of an office building that is presently only 50 percent occupied. Utility costs are presently 20 cents per square foot. If the building is fully occupied, the utility costs will increase to 30 cents per square foot. The building's total utility costs will then increase from $50,000 to $150,000. If the tenant's utility cost is calculated at 20 cents per square foot, the owner will sustain an additional $5,000 (10 cents × 50,000) in utility expenses.

The reverse is true if the operating expense (such as janitorial expense) decreases on a marginal basis as occupancy rises. Then the tenant would be overassessed for expenses—a windfall for the owner.

Grossing up relates *only* to variable—not fixed—costs. Maintenance and utility expenses are variable costs because they increase or decrease with occupancy. Although tenant improvements may affect real estate taxes, taxes do not fluctuate with occupancy. To avoid unfair profits for the owner, only fixed costs should be grossed up.

Grossing up is inappropriate for net leases. If a tenant pays a fixed percentage of all actual expenses, there is no base year or amount to adjust. If actual expenses are increased and passed along to tenants, the entire increase would give the owner undeserved profit.

Accounting for Lease Incentives

Owners' offering incentives or concessions to prospective tenants in order to induce occupancy is not unusual. These incentives generally include paying moving expenses for a tenant, reimbursing him for unamortized leasehold improvements in his current space, and assuming alternative obligations under an existing lease.

In general, incentives reduce rental revenue over the term of the lease and should be recognized on a straightline basis by the owner.[7]

---

[7]Statement of Financial Accounting Standard Technical Bulletin No. 88–1, ¶6.

When these reductions should be recognized is determined primarily by the continuing value of those concessions. Incentives that have no continuing value, such as payments for moving expenses or un-amortized leasehold improvements, should be recognized as current expenses.[8] If an owner assumes the tenant's obligation under a pre-existing lease, any loss suffered by the owner should be estimated, based on the total remaining costs reduced by the expected benefits from a sublease of the assumed lease.[9]

To illustrate, assume that in conjunction with an operating lease for four years, an owner assumes a tenant's existing lease obligation that has three years remaining. The old lease payment was $1,200 per year and the new lease payment is $1,600 per year. If we also assume that the owner can sublease the old property for $800 per year, then her loss on its lease will be $1,200 over its remaining term or a $400 yearly revenue reduction.[10] The journal entries for this incentive would appear as shown in Exhibit 18–3.

Accounting for Costs Incurred to Rent Real Estate

In addition to the initial costs incurred to promote and advertise an office building while it is being developed and completed, numerous other costs are incurred by an owner that relate to rental efforts. Costs and expenses to promote, advertise, and encourage occupancy should be capitalized if they were incurred in order to obtain tenants under operating leases, and if they can reasonably be expected to be recovered from future rental payments.[11]

Capitalized expenses that directly relate to revenue from a specific lease are to be amortized over the term of that lease. If relating a capitalized expense to a specific lease is not possible, the expense should be amortized over the period of time in which it is expected that the operation as a whole will derive a benefit.[12]

Other costs are incurred as part of the rental effort that are not directly attributable to marketing and promotional efforts and therefore do not meet the criteria for deferral. Office overhead expenses such as utilities, general office supplies, janitorial services, and the like

---

[8] Statement of Financial Accounting Standard Technical Bulletin No. 88–1, ¶8.
[9] Id.
[10] Statement of Financial Accounting Standard Technical Bulletin No. 88–1, ¶9.
[11] Statement of Financial Accounting Standard No. 67, ¶20.
[12] Id.

EXHIBIT 18–3
Journal Entries for Lease Incentives

	Debit	Credit
Lessor Accounting		
At inception:		
Incentive to lessee	$1,200	
Liability on sublease assumed		$1,200
To record deferred cost and liability related to loss on assumption of remaining lease		
Recurring journal entries in years 1 through 3:		
Liability on sublease assumed ($1,200–3 years)	$ 400	
Sublease expense	$ 800	
Cash		$1,200
To record cash payment for rent and amortization of the liability and deferred asset on the assumed lease		
Cash	$ 800	
Sublease revenue		$ 800
To record cash received from sublease of the property		
Recurring journal entries in years 1 through 4:		
Cash	$1,600	
Rental revenue		$1,300
Incentive to lessee (1,200/4 years)		$ 300
To record cash received on new lease and amortization of incentive over new lease term		

are not capitalizable and should be expensed in the period in which they are incurred.

Accounting for Subleases

Subleasing activity generally falls into two different categories: true sublease and substituted lessee. In a true sublease, the existing tenant, usually subject to the approval of the owner, subleases his or her existing space. In this situation, the original lessee remains responsible for all lease payments to the owner. Accordingly, no change is made in the accounting treatment for the lease from the property manager's perspective.[13]

---

[13] Statement of Financial Accounting Standard No. 13, ¶36.

The second category of subleasing activity involves the substitution of a new tenant for the current lessee. This can occur by releasing the existing space and having the new lessee assume the existing lease. It may also come about by the cancellation of the existing lease, which is then replaced by a new lease with the new tenant. In either case, the accounting treatment is the same. Any unamortized capital costs associated with the old lease must be expensed as costs in the current period, and expenses associated with the new lease should be amortized and expensed in the manner described in the lease incentive accounting section.[14]

Accounting for Leases Between Related Parties

Owners often lease space to a subsidiary or affiliate. When this occurs, whether the relationship between the parties should affect the accounting treatment given to the lease must be considered.

One must remember that, for the purpose of this section, we assume that no issue concerning the lease's classification as an operating versus a capital lease exists. Although leases to affiliates often convey the risks and benefits of ownership and are therefore capital in nature, a discussion of the accounting and tax treatment of such a capital lease exceeds the scope of this chapter.[15]

When dealing with related-party leases, one must first consider whether the lease bears any relation to economic reality. Transactions between related parties are presumed to have been negotiated at less than arm's length; accordingly, the economic substance of the lease transaction as opposed to the legal form should control the accounting treatment.[16] This rule's purpose is to prevent parent companies and their affiliates from possibly distorting the economic realities of transactions in their financial statements.

For example, if an owner leases to an affiliate at substantially higher-than-market rent and provides the affiliate with none of the lease incentives given to other tenants, the owner cannot report the lease as an arm's-length transaction. The realities of the lease transaction as disclosed by the economic substance of the lease control the accounting treatment. Because of these rules, owners generally should treat a lease with an affiliate as any other lease transaction, unless the

---

[14] Statement of Financial Accounting Standard No. 13, ¶37.

[15] See, generally, Statement of Financial Accounting Standard No. 13, ¶¶7 and 8.

[16] Statement of Financial Accounting Standard No. 13, ¶29.

full significance of the economic substance of the lease (and its effect on the owner's financial statements) has been thoroughly evaluated.

Accounting for Tenant Defaults

No matter how carefully you screen and evaluate tenants, some eventually default on the terms of a lease. Unfortunately, in the past decade, tenant defaults have increased at a dramatic, if not alarming, rate. However, preparing for what has become almost the inevitable will reduce not only your loss exposure, but your blood pressure as well.

The effective drafting of leases circumvents the general rule that a tenant is not responsible to an owner for additional rent after the termination of a lease. Most commercial leases now contain a survivability clause or covenant that does not relieve the tenant of her financial responsibility to the owner after termination. However, you should always confer with your attorney before terminating a lease to ensure adherence with your particular state's laws.

When a tenancy is terminated, all unamortized expenses must be recognized in the current period. Losses caused by missed monthly rental payments are recognized for each period in which the payment was due. More complex situations may arise if an owner attempts to mitigate damages by finding a new tenant for the property. Not all states require mitigation, but prudence would dictate finding a new tenant, as opposed to relying upon legal process as an effective way to recover rents.

If the space vacated by the defaulting tenant is released at a lower rate, the loss represented by that difference should be recognized over the remaining period of the original lease. If the new tenant pays a higher rental rate than the defaulting tenant did the excess rent may have to be credited against any amount owed by the defaulting tenant.

Although permitting a defaulting tenant to benefit from breaching a lease seems preposterous, some courts have required that the defaulting tenant be given such a credit.[17] If a court requires this approach, monthly adjustments to the outstanding amount owed by the defaulting tenant must be made. His receivable account would be reduced each month by the amount of rent actually received above the amount of rent payments that would have been received if the old

---

[17] *Truitt v. Evangel Temple, Inc.*, 486 A2d 1169 (Col. App. 1984); *Dalamagas v. Fazzina*, 36 Conn. Supp. 523, 414 A2d 494 (Conn. 1979).

lease were still in effect. This adjustment would have to be made for the remaining period of the old lease.

Only the *net* excess rent should be considered in determining any amount to be credited. Lease incentives and costs incurred to obtain the new tenant should be amortized and offset against rental revenue, as well as current period expenses, before the amount of any "credit" is determined. Using the net revenue figure ensures that the owner can recapture all of the expenses associated with the new lease and prevents the defaulting tenant from profiting further.

A more rational approach is taken by courts that do not require that a credit be given. This prevents a defaulting tenant from receiving profits from a property manager's successful leasing efforts.[18] In this case, making adjustments to the outstanding amount owed by the defaulting tenant is unnecessary, and the rent revenue is accounted for in the normal fashion.

Accounting for Management Fees

There are numerous methods for determining how a property manager should be compensated for his or her efforts. This determination is affected by the extent of the services to be provided by the property manager as well as by the size of the project. For accounting purposes, property manager compensation generally falls into two categories — a fixed monthly amount and an amount based on an percentage of rents.

Not surprisingly, the fixed monthly amount is the easiest to account for. The monthly management fee is reported as a charge against the total revenue of the project for each period in which it is paid. Escalation provisions, whether tied to time or occupancy, simply increase the expense for management fees recognized in the current period. Determining and reporting management fees as a percentage of rents proves, however, to be more problematic. If a property manager is to be paid a percentage of rents, he or she must clearly understand what that payment is to be a percentage of; merely stating that the fee is a percentage of the gross or net revenues is insufficient.

Although property mangement fees as a percentage of the gross revenues are easily tracked and calculated, they provide little incentive to the property manager to control costs. In addition, if revenue

---

[18]*N.J. Industrial Properties, Inc. v. Y.C. & V.L., Inc.,* 100 N.J. 432, 495 A2d 1320 (N.J. 1985); *D. H. Overmeyer Co. v. Blakely Floor Covering, Inc.,* 266 S.2d 925 (La App 1972). See also 50 ALR4th 369.

margins are small, they discourage the owner from retaining sufficient amounts of revenue for capital improvements. Accordingly, net revenue is a preferable basis for payment.

Adopting net revenue as a basis is not, however, without pitfalls of its own. When the property management agreement does not discuss how net revenue will be determined, it will be calculated in accordance with generally accepted accounting principles (GAAP). However, when a provision specifies that certain items should be applied to gross revenues in arriving at a net revenue amount, it limits rather than enlarges the net revenue calculation under GAAP.[19] Accordingly, if a property management agreement stated that all charges paid or payable for the accountable year were to be used as deductions from gross revenues, uncollectible rents and other normal charges against gross revenue were not permitted to reduce the basis from which the property manager was to be paid.[20] Therefore, the specific language of each property management agreement controls the manner in which charges to gross revenue are made. Skillful drafting is critical to ensure that expenses incurred but not yet paid are handled in an appropriate fashion.

THE AD VALOREM PROPERTY TAX

Commercial property ownership and financing can be skillfully handled to accommodate the tax needs of almost every investor. The result is a complex web of legal forms of ownership that are best served by different types of financing. Accordingly, a thorough analysis of the income taxation considerations of commercial property ownership is beyond the scope of this work. We shall therefore focus only on the ad valorem property tax.

The ad valorem property tax is usually imposed by state, county, and local authorities and consists of a tax either on real estate or on real and personal property, depending on the jurisdiction. The formulas and methods used to calculate ad valorem taxation are often complex and vary significantly by jurisdiction. However, all formulas share one primary basis—the value of the property subject to taxation.

Most methods of ad valorem taxation operate in the same general manner. The assessed value of the property is determined by taking

---

[19] *Tower Corp. v. Morris,* 153 SW2d 654 (Texas Civ. App. 1941).
[20] Id.

some percentage of its fair market value. A millage rate is then applied to the assessed value in order to determine the amount of ad valorem tax. The percentage figures applied to the fair market value and the millage rate are usually the result of legislative enactment and vary by jurisdiction. Once established, they are generally not subject to challenge on a property-by-property basis.

The same, however, is not true of the fair market value of the property. A property's fair market value is a subjective determination and is frequently the subject of controversy and litigation. Thus, although an overall ad valorem tax system may be fair, its application to specific properties and property tax owners may not, because of overvaluation of individual properties.

No property owner enjoys taking the position that his property is worth less than its appraised value. Unfortunately, the market dynamics in the 1980s that resulted in the devaluation of real property have become a harsh reality in many sections of the country. When this occurs, one step a prudent owner can take to improve her position is to challenge a property's ad valorem tax.

An owner should follow four basic steps when challenging a property's ad valorem tax:

- Property appraisal.
- Negotiation with taxing authority.
- Administrative appeal.
- Judicial appeal.

Having the appropriate professionals assist at various stages of this process is obviously important. The property appraisal is the most vital component of the entire process and can be supervised by the property manager.

The scope, objective, and purpose of the appraisal must be discussed with and understood by the appraiser. Without this understanding at the outset, the appraiser's final report will probably not supply the information needed to challenge the ad valorem tax. This report must be well-reasoned and describe in detail the market research performed, the valuation methods utilized, and the rationale for the final valuation analysis and conclusion. The length of the report depends upon the object of the appraisal. If the purpose of the appraisal is to provide the information necessary to make the decision whether the potential tax savings justify an ad valorem tax challenge, a brief report would be satisfactory. However, after the decision has been made to actually challenge the assessment, a full narrative is in order.

Negotiating with the taxing authority or resorting to a formal administrative appeal of an assessment, may be performed at two different times—at the time of a periodic assessment or when the property changes hands. In fact the acquisition of property often presents the best opportunity to review and analyze whether an ad valorem tax should be challenged, because an appraisal (or at least a careful study) of the property's fair market value has already been performed. Generally, the administrative appeal process must be exhausted before turning to the courts to challenge an assessment. Before seeking judicial relief, the owner should work closely with legal counsel and the appraiser in order to assess the case and determine whether the challenge will be cost-effective.

CONCLUSION

Although the accounting issues applicable to office building management are not complex, the accounting system and process utilized by a property manager require an enhanced focus on detail and accuracy, without which the accounting records maintained by the property manager serve little or no purpose. However, an accurate and current set of books provides an owner with the ability to assess the value and performance of his or her investment.

EXHIBIT 18–2
Property Management Chart of Accounts

Income Statement

Revenues
Recovery
Straight-line rentals
Central parking revenue
Central parking (expenses)
Miscellaneous income
Work-order profit
Other income
Total revenue

Operating Expenses
Electricity
Water and sewer
Waste removal
Utilities
Repair and maintenance
   Electrical
   Plumbing
   HVAC
   Elevators and escalators
   Structural and roof
   Furniture, fixtures, and
      equipment
   Grounds
   Painting and carpeting
   Other
Cleaning
   Labor
   Contract Cleaning
   Supplies
   Windows
   Carpets and drapes
   Other
General building
   Labor

Supplies
Uniforms
Pest control
Gardening and landscaping
Operating equipment
Other
Leasing commissions
Building monitors
Exterior patrol
Security
Management fee
Leasing administration
Administration labor
Office supplies
Telephone
Licenses and fees
Advertising
Marketing and promotion
Professional services
Other expenses
Total operating expenses

Fixed Expenses
Real estate taxes
   Building
   Corner lot
   Insurance
   Total fixed expenses

Net Income Before Debt Service
Interest Expense
   Garage
   Mortgage
Depreciation
Common expense amortization

EXHIBIT 18–2 *(continued)*

Leasing/marketing cost
  amortization
Deferred cost amortization
Other amortization
Operating profit and loss
Investment income

Cash Flow Adjustments
Accounts receivable
Straight-line rentals
Depreciation expense
Prepaid real estate taxes
  Building
  Building (pmts)
  Corner lot
  Corner lot (pmts)

Mortgage principal payments
Commission expense amortization
Garage expense mortgage principal
  payments
Prepaid insurance amortization
Prepaid insurance payments
Other adjustments
Capital expenditures
Tenant finish
Lease commission payments
Cash balances
Beginning cash
Add (deduct)
  Cash distributions
  Cash contributions
Ending cash

EXHIBIT 18–2 *(continued)*

Property Management Balance Sheet

Assets
Cash Assets
Cash depository and invest
Cash disbursement
Cash—venture
Cash received from bender
Cash sent to bender
Cash received from owners
Cash sent to owners
Petty cash
Payroll clearing
Cash
Accounts receivable
Non-income receivable
Accounts receivable
    Partners
    Escalations
    Allowance for doubtful accounts
    Other
Notes receivable
Prepaid items
    Insurance
    Taxes
    Expenses
Total other assets

Fixed Assets
Land improvements
Land
Building
Furniture, fixtures, and equipment
Accumulated depreciation
    Site
    Building
    Furniture, fixtures, and equipment
Capital appropriations—tenant
    finish
Accumulated depreciation—tenant
    finish
Capital appropriation—lease
    commissions
Lease commissions—current year
Capital appropriations—other
Other fixed assets
Organizational expense

Deferred charges and commissions
Accumulated amortization
Accumulated amortization—deferred
    leasing costs
Accumulated deferred development
    costs
Total net fixed assets
Other assets
Other—deposits
Deferred free rent
Total other assets
Total assets

Liabilities
Current liabilities
Accounts payable
Accounts payable—venture
Deferred lease commission payable
Other payable
Equity advances to owners
Accounts payable
Accrued—other
Tenant deposit
Accrued expenses
Prepaid rent
Total current liabilities

Other Liabilities
Mortagages payable
Notes payable
Accounts payable fixed assets
Total other liabilities
Accounts payable retainage
Accrued interest
Total liabilities

Equity
Partners' capital—contribution
Partners' capital—distribution
Prior year profit and loss
Current year profit and loss
Accumulated profit and loss
Total liability and equity

CHAPTER 19

INSURANCE ASPECTS OF PROPERTY MANAGEMENT

Kenneth N. Ryan
Willis Corroon P.L.C.

OVERVIEW OF PREMISES LIABILITY EXPOSURES

The ownership, use, occupancy and/or possession, and control of land gives rise to legal duties and correspondingly to premise liability exposures. Tort liabilities arise when an unjustified or negligent breach of a legal duty causes damage or injury to the person or property of another. Such a duty is owed either by the owner to the tenant, by the owner or tenant (if the landlord has leased the entire building to a single tenant) to third parties, or by the tenant to the owner.

The owner/tenant has a common law duty to third parties on or off the premises. A breach of that duty may occur through ordinary negligence, intentional interference, or by strict liability. If the owner/tenant creates or allows a condition to exist on the premises that causes injuries or property damage to another, the owner/tenant will be liable. This duty may also arise due to the owner's/tenant's failure to obey specific laws or ordinances designed to protect third parties.

The owner/tenant may owe a different duty to different persons. For example, the *business invitee* (a person invited for business reasons beneficial to the invitor to be on the premises) can expect the owner/tenant to provide reasonable care to avoid accidents and to inspect the property to discover and eliminate any hazards. If the invitee is a child, the owner/tenant will owe a higher duty of care. The owner/tenant may also owe a duty of care to a trespasser (a person on the premises, without legal right or invitation of the owner/tenant). if the trespasser is a child, an even higher degree of care might be required. The duty owed varies by judicial jurisdiction and the circumstances surrounding each situation.

The terms and conditions in the lease agreement govern much of the landlord's liability exposure. The landlord owes the tenant a reasonable duty of care, which requires that the landlord (or property manager) maintain the premises in a safe condition. The landlord also may be liable to the tenant for intentional interference as well as strict liability.

The property owner or manager may also injure another by breach of contract, which is a civil violation of an agreement for which the wronged party may seek monetary damages. In addition, if the property owner or manager violates the law, he or she will be subject to a fine or imprisonment.

The tenant also has a duty to the landlord under the terms of the lease. If the property is damaged or destroyed by the negligence of the tenant, the tenant will be liable.

Tenants also owe other tenants a reasonable duty of care. Damage or injury to the tenant or the tenant's property may result in breach of this duty.

COMMERCIAL GENERAL LIABILITY

A commercial general liability (CGL) policy provides the property owner or manager with protection against legal liability imposed by tort and breach of contract. Various provisions in this policy restrict coverage. The entire policy must be read carefully to determine rights, duties, and coverages.

Throughout this policy the words "you" and "your" refer to the named insured shown in the declarations. The words "we," "us," and "our" refer to the company providing this insurance. The word "insured" means any person or organization qualifying as such under Section II. Other words and phrases that appear in quotation marks have special meaning and are defined in Section V.

Policy Language

I. Coverages
   A. Bodily Injury and Property Damage Liability

1. Insuring Agreement.
    a. We will pay those sums that the insured becomes legally obligated to pay as damages because of "bodily injury" or "property damage" to which this insurance applies. No other obligation or liability to pay sums or perform acts or services is covered unless explicitly provided for under Supplementary Payments—Coverages A and B. This insurance applies only to "bodily injury" or "property damage" that occurs during the policy period. The "bodily injury" or "property damage" must be caused by an "occurrence." The "occurrence" must take place in the "coverage territory." We will have the right and duty to defend any "suit" seeking those damages. But:
        (1) The amount we will pay for damages is limited as described in Section III—Limits of Insurance.
        (2) We may investigate and settle any claim or "suit" at our discretion; and
        (3) Our right and duty to defend end when we have used up the applicable limit of insurance in the payment of judgments or settlements under Coverages A or B or medical expenses under Coverage C.
    b. Damages because of "bodily injury" include damages claimed by any person or organization for care, loss of services, or death resulting at any time from the "bodily injury."
    c. "Property damage" that is loss of use of tangible property that is not physically injured shall be deemed to occur at the time of the "occurrence" that caused it.

Comments on Coverage A

Carriers will pay those sums (not all sums) that the insured is legally obligated to pay in damages because of bodily injury or property damage to others. The insurer has *no other obligation* to the insured except as provided in supplementary payments. The damage must be within the policy period, caused by an occurrence, and within the coverage territory.

The carrier has the right and duty to defend subject to limits of insurance, the right to investigate and settle at their discretion, the limits of the obligation (these obligations include defending alternative dispute resolution proceedings, such as arbitration, pretrial, and mediation).

The property owner has coverage for claims involving loss of use. This is important if there are tenants in the building.

Policy Language

2. Exclusions (Coverage A). This insurance does not apply to:

  a. "Bodily injury" or "property damage" expected or intended from the standpoint of the insured. This exclusion does not apply to "bodily injury" resulting from the use of reasonable force to protect persons or property.

  b. "Bodily injury" or "property damage" for which the insured is obligated to pay damages by reason of the assumption of liability in a contract or agreement. This exclusion does not apply to liability for damages:

   (1) Assumed in a contract or agreement that is an "insured contract"; or

   (2) That the insured would have in the absence of the contract or agreement.

  c. "Bodily injury" or "property damage" of which any insured may be held liable by reason of:

   (1) Causing or contributing to the intoxication of any person;

   (2) The furnishing of alcoholic beverages to a person under the legal drinking age or under the influence of alcohol; or

   (3) Any statute, ordinance, or regulation relating to the sale, gift, distribution, selling, serving, or furnishing of alcoholic beverages.

  This exclusion applies only if you are in the business of manufacturing, distributing, selling, serving, or furnishing alcoholic beverages.

  d. Any obligation of the insured under a worker's compensation, disability benefits, or unemployment compensation law or any similar law.

  e. "Bodily injury" to:

(1) An employee of the insured arising out of and in the course of employment by the insured; or

(2) The spouse, child, parent, brother, or sister of that employee as a consequence of paragraph e.(1).

This exclusion applies:

(1) Whether the insured may be liable as an employer or in any other capacity; and

(2) To any obligation to share damages with or repay someone else who must pay damages because of the injury.

This exclusion does not apply to liability assumed by the insured under an "insured contract."

f. "Bodily injury" or "property damage" arising out of the actual, alleged, or threatened discharge, dispersal, release, or escape of pollutants:

(1) At or from premises you own, rent, or occupy;

(2) At or from any site or location used by or for you or others for the handling, storage, disposal, processing, or treatment of waste;

(3) Which are at any time transported, handled, stored, treated, disposed of, or processed as waste by or for you or any person or organization for whom you may be legally responsible; or

(4) At or from any site or location on which you or any contractors or subcontractors working directly or indirectly on your behalf are performing operations:

(a) If the pollutants are brought on or to the site or location in connection with such operations; or

(b) If the operations are to test for, monitor, clean up, remove, contain, treat, detoxify, or neutralize the pollutants.

g. Any loss, cost, or expense arising out of any governmental direction or request that you test for, monitor, clean up, remove, contain, treat, detoxify, or neutralize pollutants. "Pollutants" means any solid, liquid, gaseous, or thermal irritant or contaminant, including smoke, vapor, soot, fumes, acids, alkalis, chemicals, and waste. Waste includes materials to be recycled, reconditioned, or reclaimed.

h. "Bodily injury" or "property damage" arising out of the ownership, maintenance, use, or entrustment to others of any aircraft, "auto," or watercraft owned or operated by or rented or loaned to any insured. Use includes operation and "loading or unloading."

This exclusion does not apply to:

(1) A watercraft while ashore on premises you own or rent;

(2) A watercraft you do not own that is:

   (a) Less than 26 feet long; and

   (b) Not being used to carry persons or property for a charge;

(3) Parking an "auto" on, or on the ways next to, premises you own or rent, provided the "auto" is not owned by or rented or loaned to you or the insured;

(4) Liability assumed under any "insured contract" for the ownership, maintenance, or use of aircraft or watercraft; or

(5) "Bodily injury" or "property damage" arising out of the operation of any of the equipment listed in paragraph f.(2) or f.(3) of the definition of "mobile equipment" (Section V.8).

i. "Bodily injury" or "property damage" arising out of:

(1) The transportation of "mobile equipment" by an "auto" owned or operated by or rented or loaned to any insured; or

(2) The use of "mobile equipment" in, or while in practice or preparation for, a prearranged racing, speed, or demolition contest or in any stunting activity.

j. "Bodily injury" or "property damage" due to war, whether or not declared, or any act or condition incident to war. War includes civil war, insurrection, rebellion, or revolution. This exclusion applies only to liability assumed under a contract or agreement.

k. "Property damage" to:

(1) Property you own, rent, or occupy;

(2) Premises you sell, give away, or abandon, if the "property damage" arises out of those premises;

(3) Property loaned to you;

(4) Personal property in your care, custody, or control;

(5) That particular part of real property on which you or any contractors or subcontractors working directly or indirectly on your behalf are performing operations, if the "property damage" arises out of those operations; or

(6) That particular part of any property that must be restored, repaired, or replaced because "your work" was incorrectly performed on it.

Paragraph (2) of this exclusion does not apply if the premises are "your work" and were never occupied, rented, or held for rental by you.

Paragraph (3), (4), (5), and (6) of this exclusion do not apply to liability assumed under a sidetrack agreement.

Paragraph (6) of this exclusion does not apply to "property damage" included in the "products—completed operations hazard."

l. "Property damage" to "your product" arising out of it or any part of it.

m. "Property damage" to "your work" arising out of it or any part of it and included in the "products—completed operations hazard."

This exclusion does not apply if the damaged work or the work out of which the damage arises was performed on your behalf by a subcontractor.

n. "Property damage" to "impaired property" or property that has not been physically injured, arising out of:

(1) A defect, deficiency, inadequacy, or dangerous condition in "your product" or "your work"; or

(2) A delay or failure by you or anyone acting on your behalf to perform a contract or agreement in accordance with its terms.

This exclusion does not apply to the loss of use of other property arising out of sudden and accidental physical injury to "your product" or "your work" after it has been put to its intended use.

o. Damages claimed for any loss, cost, or expense incurred by you or others for the loss of use, withdrawal, recall, inspection, repair, replacement, adjustment, removal, or disposal of:

(1) "Your product";

(2) "Your work"; or

(3) "Impaired property"

if such product, work, or property is withdrawn or recalled from the market or from use by a person or an organization because of a known or suspected defect, deficiency, or inadequate or dangerous condition in it.

Exclusions c. through o. do not apply to damage by fire to premises rented to you. A separate limit of insurance applies to this coverage as described in Section III—Limits of Insurance.

Comments on Exclusion for Coverage A

These exclusions represent the limitations imposed by the carrier on coverage.

a. There is no coverage for intentional acts of the insured (court cases). Cases should be reviewed by an attorney if any question arises.

b. There is no coverage for contractual liability unless the contract is an "insured contract" (see Section V—Definitions).

c. The property owner should have the liquor liability exclusion removed by endorsement, particularly if the tenant is serving liquor in insured premises.

d. There is no coverage where worker's compensation or similar coverage is involved.

e. There is no coverage for an injury to employees whether it occurs in or out of their course of employment. This liability should be covered under worker's compensation or similar coverage.

f. and g. This exclusion is referred to as the "absolute pollution exclusion." Certain off-premises exposure may be inferred, but an insured should obtain specific protection by obtaining an endorsement (CG 04 22) if the underwriter is willing. There is no coverage even though the insured may be ordered by the government to remedy a pollution condition.

h. The new CGL has included "entrustment" of such vehicles to others to avoid any possibility of coverage. The perils excluded can be specifically covered by other policies dealing with aircraft, auto, or watercraft. Mobile equipment, however, is covered.

i. This exclusion is commonly referred to as the "war" exclusion. Private carriers consider war or war-related losses as not insurable by them.

j. and k. These relate to "completed operations exposures." Losses arising out of the products-completed operations hazard are subject to a products-completed operations aggregate limit, which is separate and distinct from the general aggregate limit. For this reason, it is important to distinguish products and completed operations losses from premises and operation losses. The products hazard uses the term "your product." The completed operations hazard uses the term "your work." Under the product hazard, two conditions must be met:

1. The damage (bodily or property) from the insured's product must occur away from the premises of the named insured.

2. The product must be in the physical possession of someone other than the named insured. The term "your product" does not include real property or goods or products that are merely rented to others, because this is coverage afforded under the premises and operations hazard.

These exclusions clearly do not provide coverage for "property damage" to "your product." This exempts the insurer from having to pay for repairs or replacement of an improperly designed or defective product.

The completed operations hazard covers only bodily injury or property damage occurring away from the insured premises and arising out of the insured's work that has been completed or abandoned. If the loss occurs while operations are in progress, it will be a premises and operations loss.

No coverage is provided where property is sold and damage

occurs because of a latent defect where the property causes the loss.

l. This exclusion is referred to as the injury to work performed exclusion. No insurer will pay for replacing, repairing, or otherwise redoing faulty work of the named insured.

m. and n. To understand this coverage the definition of impaired property should be reviewed. These exclusions are applicable generally to manufacturers and/or contractors. The premises owner or manager should be concerned if the tenant (manufacturer) fails to have proper coverage and, as a result of a loss, cannot make rent payments.

Policy Language

B. Personal and Advertising Injury Liability

  1. Insuring Agreement.

    a. We will pay those sums that the insured becomes legally obligated to pay as damages because of "personal injury" or "advertising injury" to which this insurance applies. No other obligation or liability to pay sums or perform acts or services is covered unless explicitly provided for under Supplementary Payments—Coverages A and B. We will have the right and duty to defend any "suit" seeking those damages. But:

      (1) The amount we will pay for damages is limited as described in Section III—Limits of Insurance;

      (2) We may investigate and settle any claim or "suit" at our discretion; and

      (3) Our right and duty to defend end when we have used up the applicable limit of insurance in the payment of judgments or settlements under Coverage A or B or medical expenses under Coverage C.

    b. This insurance applies to "personal injury" only if caused by an offense:

      (1) Committed in the "coverage territory" during the policy period; and

(2) Arising out of the conduct of your business, excluding advertising, publishing, broadcasting, or telecasting done by or for you.

c. This insurance applies to "advertising injury" only if caused by an offense committed:

(1) In the "coverage territory" during the policy period; and

(2) In the course of advertising your goods, products, or services.

Comments on Coverage B

This coverage could be important to the property owner or manager who has to advertise the premises for tenants. This is intended for businesses that buy advertising but are not in the advertising business.

The definitions of "personal injury" and "advertising injury" must be reviewed. Under personal injury, bodily injury is excluded. The allegation that injury was personal should be made to provide coverage. Personal injury does include coverage for liability arising from invasion of a person's right to private occupancy of a room, dwelling, or premises if the offense is committed by or on behalf of the owner, landlord, or lessor.

Policy Language

2. Exclusions (Coverage B). This insurance does not apply to:

a. "Personal injury" or "advertising injury":

(1) Arising out of oral or written publication of material, if done by or at the direction of the insured with knowledge of its falsity;

(2) Arising out of oral or written publication of material whose first publication took place before the beginning of the policy period;

(3) Arising out of the willful violation of a penal statute or ordinance committed by or with the consent of the insured; or

(4) For which the insured has assumed liability in a contract or agreement. This exclusion

does not apply to liability for damages that the insured would have in the absence of the contract or agreement.

b. "Advertising injury" arising out of:

(1) Breach of contract, other than misappropriation of advertising ideas under an implied contract;

(2) The failure of goods, products, or services to conform with advertised quality of performance;

(3) The wrong description of the price of goods, products, or services, or;

(4) An offense committed by an insured whose business is advertising, broadcasting, publishing, or telecasting.

Comments on Exclusions for Coverage B

The most important exclusion to property owners or managers is in paragraph a.(4). Real estate leases often include the term "personal injury" rather than "bodily injury." If this is not changed, the insured could be without insurance if the landlord seeks indemnification from the tenant because of a suit alleging wrongful eviction or other intentional acts.

Policy Language

C. Medical Payments

1. Insuring Agreement.

a. We will pay medical expenses as described below for "bodily injury" caused by an accident:

(1) On premises you own or rent;

(2) On ways next to premises you own or rent; or

(3) Because of your operations

provided that:

(1) The accident takes place in the "coverage territory" and during the policy period;

       (2) The expenses are incurred and reported to us within one year of the date of accident; and

       (3) The injured person submits to examination, at our expense, by physicians of our choice as often as we reasonably require.

    b. We will make these payments regardless of fault. These payments will not exceed the applicable limit of insurance. We will pay reasonable expenses for:

       (1) First aid at the time of an accident;

       (2) Necessary medical, surgical, x-ray, and dental services, including prosthetic devices; and

       (3) Necessary ambulance, hospital, professional nursing, and funeral services.

Comments on Coverage C

Premises medical payments coverage is not a form of liability insurance, because the negligence of the insured is not a condition precedent to payment. This coverage is very helpful to the property owner or manager. Payments can be made for medical expenses to persons who suffer injury by accident on premises that the insured owns or rents, on ways next to such premises, or because of the insured's operations.

Policy Language

   2. Exclusions (Coverage C). We will not pay expenses for "bodily injury":

    a. To any insured.

    b. To a person hired to do work for or on behalf of any insured or a tenant of any insured.

    c. To a person injured on that part of premises you own or rent that the person normally occupies.

    d. To a person, whether or not an employee of any insured, if benefits for the "bodily injury" are payable or must be provided under a worker's compensation or disability benefits law or a similar law.

    e. To a person injured while taking part in athletics.

    f. Included within the "products—completed operations hazard."

    g. Excluded under Coverage A.

    h. Due to war, whether or not declared, or any act or condition incident to war. War includes civil war, insurrection, rebellion, or revolution.

Comments on Exclusions for Coverage C

The exclusions are self-explanatory, except for the exclusion in paragraph b, which would exclude any contractor working for the insured or a tenant of an insured.

Policy Language

    D. Supplementary Payments—Coverages A and B.

    1. We will pay, with respect to any claim or "suit" we defend:

      a. All expenses we incur.

      b. Up to $250 for cost of bail bonds required because of accidents or traffic law violations arising out of the use of any vehicle to which the bodily injury liability coverage applies. We do not have to furnish these bonds.

      c. The cost of bonds to release attachments, but only for bond amounts within the applicable limit of insurance. We do not have to furnish these bonds.

      d. All reasonable expenses incurred by the insured at our request to assist us in the investigation or defense of the claim or "suit," including actual loss of earnings up to $100 a day because of time off from work.

      e. All costs taxed against the insured in the "suit."

      f. Prejudgment interest awarded against the insured on that part of the judgment we pay. If we make an offer to pay the applicable limit of insurance, we will not pay any prejudgment interest based on that period of time after the offer.

    g. All interest on the full amount of any judgment that accrues after entry of the judgment and before we have paid, offered to pay, or deposited in court the part of the judgment that is within the applicable limit of insurance.

  2. These payments will not reduce the limits of insurance.

Comments on Coverage D

The most important provision in the supplementary payments section is paragraph 2.

Paragraph C will also provide cost of bonds to release attachments, which may be placed against the insured's property as a result of pending litigation. The insurer has *no* obligation to provide the bonds.

Policy Language

II. Who is an Insured
  A. An insured is classified as follows:
    1. If you are designated in the declarations as:
      a. An individual, you and your spouse are insureds, but only with respect to the conduct of a business of which you are the sole owner.
      b. A partnership or joint venture, you are an insured. Your members, your partners, and their spouses are also insureds, but only with respect to the conduct of your business.
      c. An organization other than a partnership or joint venture, you are an insured. Your executive officers and directors are insureds, but only with respect to their duties as your officers or directors. Your stockholders are also insureds, but only with respect to their liability as stockholders.
    2. Each of the following is also an insured:
      a. Your employees, other than your executive officers, but only for acts within the scope of their employment by you. However, none of these employees is an insured for:

(1) "Bodily injury" or "personal injury" to you or to a co-employee while in the course of his or her employment; or

(2) "Bodily injury" or "personal injury" arising out of his or her providing or failing to provide professional health care services; or

(3) "Property damage" to property owned or occupied by or rented or loaned to that employee, any of your other employees, or any of your partners or members (if you are a partnership or joint venture).

b. Any person (other than your employee) or any organization while acting as your real estate manager.

c. Any person or organization having proper temporary custody of your property if you die, but only:

(1) With respect to liability arising out of the maintenance or use of that property; and

(2) Until your legal representative has been appointed.

d. Your legal representative if you die, but only with respect to duties as such. That representative will have all your rights and duties under this coverage part.

3. With respect to "mobile equipment" registered in your name under any motor vehicle registration law, any person is an insured while driving such equipment along a public highway with your permission. Any other person or organization responsible for the conduct of such person is also an insured, but only with respect to liability arising out of the operation of the equipment, and only if no other insurance of any kind is available to that person or organization for this liability. However, no person or organization is an insured with respect to:

a. "Bodily injury" to a co-employee of the person driving the equipment; or

b. "Property damage" to property owned by, rented to, in the charge of, or occupied by you or the employer of any person who is an insured under this provision.

4. Any organization you newly acquire or form, other than a partnership or joint venture, and over which you maintain ownership or majority interest, will be deemed to be a named insured if there is no other similar insurance available to that organization. However:

    a. Coverage under this provision is afforded only until the 90th day after you acquire or form the organization or the end of the policy period, whichever is earlier;

    b. Coverage A does not apply to "bodily injury" or "property damage" that occurred before you acquired or formed the organization; and

    c. Coverage B does not apply to "personal injury" or "advertising injury" arising out of an offense committed before you acquired or formed the organization.

  B. No person or organization is an insured with respect to the conduct of any current or past partnership or joint venture that is not shown as a named insured in the Declarations.

Comments on Section II

Paragraph 2.b. is particularly significant to the property owner or manager. Insured status is afforded to these people, but only while managing your real estate.

Paragraph 3 is also important. This additional provision provides coverage with respect to "mobile equipment" for persons other than those who are insured. The additional persons are only covered during "operation" of the equipment and only if no other insurance of any kind is available.

Paragraph 4 provides named insured status to any organization, newly acquired or formed (except partnership or joint venture). The insurer reiterates its problem with partnerships and joint ventures by denying insured status for any current or past such relationship. If coverage is to be afforded by the insurer, then such partnership and/or joint venture must be so designated in the current policy. This can be very important if past coverage is to continue. There may be an additional charge for this coverage.

Policy Language

III. Limits of Insurance

  A. The limits of insurance are outlined as follows.

    1. The limits of insurance shown in the declarations and the rules below fix the most we will pay regardless of the number of:

      a. Insureds;

       b. Claims made or "suits" brought; or

       c. Persons or organizations making claims or bringing "suits."

   2. The general aggregate limit is the most we will pay for the sum of:

       a. Medical expenses under Coverage C; and

       b. Damages under Coverage A and Coverage B, except damages because of injury and damage included in the "products—completed operations hazard."

   3. The products—completed operations aggregate limit is the most we will pay under Coverage A for damages because of injury and damage included in the "products—completed operations hazard."

   4. Subject to paragraph 2, the personal and advertising injury limit is the most we will pay under Coverage B for the sum of all damages because of all "personal injury" and all "advertising injury" sustained by any one person or organization.

   5. Subject to paragraph 2 or 3, whichever applies, the each occurrence limit is the most we will pay for the sum of:

       a. Damages under Coverage A; and

       b. Medical expenses under Coverage C.

   6. Subject to paragraph 5, the fire damage limit is the most we will pay under Coverage A for damages because of "property damage" to premises rented to you arising out of any one fire.

   7. Subject to paragraph 5, the medical expense limit is the most we will pay under Coverage C for all medical expenses because of "bodily injury" sustained by any one person.

B. The limits of this coverage apply separately to each consecutive annual period and to any remaining period of less than 12 months, starting with the beginning of the policy period shown in the declarations, unless the policy period is extended after issuance for an additional period of less than 12 months. In that case, the additional period will be deemed part of the last preceding period for purposes of determining the limits of insurance.

Comments on Section III

The declarations page of the policy shows the monetary limits of insurance available to an insured but clearly governed by the rules set forth in Section III of the policy.

The general aggregate limit is the most the insurer will pay during the policy period for the sum of damages under Coverages A and B, other than injury and damages included within the products—completed operations hazard, and medical expenses under Coverage C. There is a separate aggregate limit for damages within the products—completed operations hazard.

Paragraph 4 provides for a personal and advertising limit under Coverage B for the sum of all damages sustained by any one person or organization.

Paragraph 5 also stipulates a per occurrence limit that can limit the amount of damages the insurer will pay.

Policy Language

IV. Commercial General Liability Conditions

    A. Bankruptcy.

        1. Bankruptcy or insolvency of the insured or of the insured's estate will not relieve us of our obligations under this coverage part.

    B. Duties in the event of occurrence, claim, or suit.

        1. You must see to it that we are notified promptly of an "occurrence" that may result in a claim. Notice should include:

            a. How, when, and where the "occurrence" took place; and

            b. The names and addresses of any injured persons and witnesses.

        2. If a claim is made or a "suit" is brought against any insured, you must see to it that we receive prompt written notice of the claim or "suit."

        3. You and any other involved insured must:

            a. Immediately send us copies of any demands, notices, summonses, or legal papers received in connection with the claim or "suit";

    b. Authorize us to obtain records and other information;

    c. Cooperate with us in the investigation, settlement, or defense of the claim or "suit"; and

    d. Assist us, upon our request, in the enforcement of any right against any person or organization that may be liable to the insured because of injury or damage to which this insurance may also apply.

  4. No insureds will, except at their own cost, voluntarily make a payment, assume any obligation, or incur any expense, other than for first aid, without our consent.

C. Legal action against us.

  1. No person or organization has a right under this coverage part to:

    a. Join us as a party or otherwise bring us into a "suit" asking for damages from an insured; or

    b. Sue us on this coverage part unless all of its terms have been fully complied with.

  2. A person or organization may sue us to recover on an agreed settlement or on a final judgment against an insured obtained after an actual trial; however, we will not be liable for damages that are not payable under the terms of this coverage part or that are in excess of the applicable limit of insurance. An agreed settlement means a settlement and release of liability signed by us, the insured, and the claimant or the claimant's legal representative.

D. Other Insurance.

  1. If other valid and collectible insurance is available to the insured for a loss we cover under Coverage A or B of this coverage part, our obligations are limited to:

    a. Primary insurance.

      (1) This insurance is primary except when paragraph b applies. If this insurance is primary, our obligations are not affected unless any of the other insurance is also primary. In that case, we will share with all the other insurance by the method described in paragraph C.

    b. Excess insurance.

      (1) This insurance is excess over any of the other

insurance, whether primary, excess, contingent, or on any other basis:

    (a) That is fire, extended coverage, builder's risk, installation risk, or similar coverage for "your work";

    (b) That is fire insurance of premises rented to you; or

    (c) If the loss arises out of the maintenance or use of aircraft, autos, or watercraft to the extent not subject to exclusion h of Coverage A.

(2) When this insurance is excess, we will have no duty under Coverage A or B to defend any claim or "suit" that any other insurer has a duty to defend. If no other insurer defends, we will undertake to do so, but we will be entitled to the insured's rights against all those other insurers.

(3) When this insurance is excess over other insurance, we will pay only our share of the amount of the loss, if any, that exceeds the sum of:

    (a) The total amount that all such other insurance would pay for the loss in the absence of this insurance; and

    (b) The total of all deductible and self-insured amounts under all that other insurance.

(4) We will share the remaining loss, if any, with any other insurance that is not described in this excess insurance provision and was not bought specifically to apply in excess of the limits of insurance shown in the declarations of this coverage part.

c. Method of Sharing.

(1) If all of the other insurance permits contribution by equal shares, we will follow this method also. Under this approach each insurer contributes equal amounts until it has paid its applicable limit of insurance or none of the loss remains, whichever comes first.

(2) If any of the other insurance does not permit contribution by equal shares, we will contribute by limits. Under this method, each insurer's share is based on the ratio of its applicable limit of insurance

to the total applicable limits of insurance of all insurers.

Comments on Section IV

Conditions have been defined as all the qualifications that the insurer attaches to its provisions. Some conditions set forth the insured's rights, duties, or obligation to the insurer, while others govern the insurer's rights and duties.

According to paragraph B, the insured has duties to promptly give notice of an occurrence, including details. If a suit is filed, the insured must give notice of it. The insured also must cooperate and assist in enforcing rights (e.g., subrogation) against any responsible parties. The insured cannot (except as a volunteer) bind the carrier by payment or assumption of an obligation.

Paragraph C provides the conditions for suits against the insured. The insured must comply with these conditions.

According to Paragraph D, Coverages A & B may be limited if there is other valid and collectible insurance available to the insured. The CGL policy provides primary insurance unless the other insurance is also primary. If both are primary then both pay equal shares up to their applicable limits. If both are primary but one does not allow equal shares, the method is to contribute on a limits-ratio basis. The CGL policy is excess over fire, extended coverages, builder's risk, installation risk, or similar coverage (for "your work"), and for fire insurance for premises rented to you. The intent is to make fire legal liability coverage of this policy excess over direct property insurance to the building.

Policy Language

V. Definitions.

A. The following terms and their accompanying definitions appear in this policy.

1. "Advertising injury" means injury arising out of one or more of the following offenses:

a. Oral or written publication of material that slanders or libels a person or organization or disparages a person's or organization's goods, products, or services;

    b. Oral or written publication of material that violates a person's right of privacy;

    c. Misappropriation of advertising ideas or style of doing business; or

    d. Infringement of copyright, title, or slogan.

2. "Auto" means a land motor vehicle, trailer, or semitrailer designed for travel on public roads, including any attached machinery or equipment. But "auto" does not include "mobile equipment."

3. "Bodily injury" means bodily injury, sickness, or disease sustained by a person, including death resulting from any of these at any time.

4. "Coverage territory" means:

    a. The United States of America (including its territories and possessions), Puerto Rico, and Canada;

    b. International waters or airspace, provided the injury or damage does not occur in the course of travel or transportation to or from any place not included in paragraph 4.a.; or

    c. All parts of the world if:

        (1) The injury or damage arises out of:

            (a) Goods or products made or sold by you in the territory described in paragraph 4.a.; or

            (b) The activities of a person whose home is in the territory described in paragraph 4.a. above, but is away for a short time on your business; and

        (2) The insured's responsibility to pay damages is determined in a "suit" on the merits, in the territory described in paragraph 4.a. or in a statement we agree to.

5. "Impaired property" means tangible property, other than "your property" or "your work," that cannot be used or is less useful because:

    a. It incorporates "your product" or "your work" that is known or thought to be defective, deficient, inadequate, or dangerous; or

    b. You have failed to fulfill the terms of a contract or agreement

but that can be restored to use by:

    a. The repair, replacement, adjustment, or removal of "your product" or "your work"; or

    b. Your fulfilling the terms of the contract or agreement.

6. "Insured contract" means:

    a. A lease of premises;

    b. A sidetrack agreement;

    c. An easement or license agreement in connection with vehicle or pedestrian private railroad crossings at grade;

    d. Any other easement agreement, except in connection with construction or demolition operations on or within 50 feet of a railroad;

    e. An indemnification of a municipality as required by ordinance, except in connection with work for a municipality;

    f. An elevator maintenance agreement; or

    g. That part of any other contract or agreement pertaining to your business under which you assume the tort liability of another to pay damages because of bodily injury or property damage to a third person or organization, if the contract or agreement is made prior to the "bodily injury" or "property damage." Tort liability means a liability that would be imposed by law in the absence of any contract or agreement.

7. An "insured contract" does not include that part of any contract or agreement:

    a. That indemnifies an architect, engineer, or surveyor for injury or damage arising out of:

        (1) Preparing, approving, or failing to prepare or approve maps, drawings, opinions, reports, surveys, change orders, designs, or specifications; or

        (2) Giving directions or instructions, or failing to give them, if that is the primary cause of the injury or damage;

    b. Under which the insured, if an architect, engineer, or surveyor, assumes liability for injury or damage arising out of the insured's rendering or failing to render professional services, including those listed in paragraph 7.a. and supervisory, inspection, or engineering services; or

   c. That indemnifies any person or organization for damage by fire to premises rented or loaned to you.

8. "Loading or unloading" means the handling of property:

   a. After it is moved from the place where it is accepted for movement into or onto an aircraft, watercraft, or "auto";

   b. While it is in or on an aircraft, watercraft, or "auto"; or

   c. While it is being moved from an aircraft, watercraft, or "auto" to the place where it is finally delivered;

9. "Loading or unloading" does not include the movement of property by means of a mechanical device, other than a hand truck, that is not attached to the aircraft, watercraft or "auto."

10. "Mobile equipment" means any of the following types of land vehicles, including any attached machinery or equipment:

   a. Bulldozers, farm machinery, forklifts, and other vehicles designed for use principally off public roads;

   b. Vehicles maintained for use solely on or next to premises you own or rent;

   c. Vehicles that travel on crawler treads;

   d. Vehicles, whether self-propelled or not, maintained primarily to provide mobility to permanently mounted:

     (1) Power cranes, shovels, loaders, diggers, or drills; or

     (2) Road construction or resurfacing equipment such as graders, scrapers, or rollers;

   e. Vehicles not described in paragraphs 10.a., 11.b., 10.c., or 10.d. that are not self-propelled and are maintained primarily to provide mobility to permanently attached equipment of the following types:

     (1) Air compressors, pumps, and generators, including spraying, welding, building, cleaning, geophysi-

cal exploration, lighting, and well servicing equipment; or

(2) Cherry pickers and similar devices used to raise or lower workers;

f. Vehicles not described in paragraphs 10.a., 10.b., 10.c., or 10.d. maintained primarily for purposes other than the transportation of persons or cargo.

11. Self-propelled vehicles with the following types of permanently attached equipment are not "mobile equipment" but will be considered "autos":

a. Equipment designed primarily for:

(1) Snow removal;

(2) Road maintenance, but not construction or resurfacing; or

(3) Street cleaning;

b. Cherry pickers and similar devices mounted on automobile or truck chassis and used to raise or lower workers; and

c. Air compressors, pumps, and generators, including spraying, welding, building cleaning, geophysical exploration, lighting, and well servicing equipment.

12. "Occurrence" means an accident, including continuous or repeated exposure to substantially the same general harmful conditions.

13. "Personal injury" means injury, other than "bodily injury," arising out of one or more of the following offenses:

a. False arrest, detention, or imprisonment;

b. Malicious prosecution;

c. Wrongful entry into, or eviction of a person from, a room, dwelling, or premises that the person occupies;

d. Oral or written publication of material that slanders or libels a person or organization or disparages a person's or organization's goods, products, or services; or

e. Oral or written publication of material that violates a person's right of privacy.

14. "Products—completed operations hazard" means:

a. All "bodily injury" and "property damage" occurring

away from premises you own or rent and arising out of "your work" except:

(1) Products that are still in your physical possession; or

(2) Work that has not yet been completed or abandoned.

b. "Your work" will be deemed completed at the earliest of the following times:

(1) When all the work called for in your contract has been completed;

(2) When all the work to be done at the site has been completed, if your contract calls for work at more than one site; or

(3) When that part of the work done at a job site has been put to its intended use by any person or organization other than another contractor or subcontractor working on the same project.

c. Work that may need service, maintenance, correction, repair, or replacement, but which is otherwise complete, will be treated as completed.

d. This hazard does not include "bodily injury" or "property damage" arising out of:

(1) The transportation of property, unless the injury or damage arises out of a condition in or on a vehicle created by the "loading or unloading" of it;

(2) The existence of tools, uninstalled equipment, or abandoned or unused materials; or

(3) Products or operations for which the classification in this coverage part or in our manual of rules includes products or completed operations.

15. "Property damage" means:

a. Physical injury to tangible property, including all resulting loss of use of that property; or   ·

b. Loss of use of tangible property that is not physically injured.

16. "Suit" means a civil proceeding in which damages because of "bodily injury," "property damage," "personal injury," or "advertising injury" to which this insurance applies are

alleged. "Suit" includes an arbitration proceeding alleging such damages to which you must submit or submit with our consent.

17. "Your product" means:

    a. Any goods or products, other than real property, manufactured, sold, handled, distributed, or disposed of by:

      (1) You;

      (2) Others trading under your name; or

      (3) A person or organization whose business or assets you have acquired; and

    b. Containers (other than vehicles), materials, parts, or equipment furnished in connection with such goods or products.

"Your product" includes warranties or representations made at any time with respect to the fitness, quality, durability, or performance of any of the items included in paragraphs 17.a. and 17.b. "Your product" does not include vending machines or other property rented to or located for the use of others but not sold.

18. "Your work" means:

    a. Work or operations performed by you or on your behalf; and

    b. Materials, parts, or equipment furnished in connection with such work or operations.

"Your work" includes warranties or representations made at any time with respect to the fitness, quality, durability, or performance of any of the items included in paragraphs 17.a. and 17.b.

Comments on Section V

Paragraphs 6 and 7 clearly set forth what an "insured contract" is and further clarifies coverage for contracts identified in this section. This definition should be read in conjunction with Section II, exclusion b.(2).

Paragraph 12 defines "occurrence." This definition does *not* apply to bodily injury or property damage expected or intended from the standpoint of the insured. It should also be emphasized that although bodily injury and property damage usually result immediately upon contact with someone or something, the phrase "continuous or repeated exposure" eliminates the necessity of proving the exact moment at which damage is sustained.

OCCURRENCE VERSUS CLAIMS-MADE POLICY

There are two different types of commercial general liability policies, occurrence and claims-made.

In an *occurrence policy* (which we have just reviewed), the bodily injury or property damage must occur during the policy period. As an example, if someone is injured by the insured today, and the occurrence policy is in effect today, it will apply whether the claim is made this year or some later year.

In a *claims-made policy,* the claim against the insured must be made *during the policy period*. The clear intent was to eliminate long tail (reporting of claims after policy period) business. This limitation may eliminate coverage for the insured.

Other claims-made policy features include the retroactive dates and the extended reporting period option. The retroactive date provision of the claims-made policy states: "This insurance does not apply to bodily injury or property damage which occurred before the retroactive date, if any, shown in the declarations." The date must be agreed to by the insurer as submitted by the insured.

If the claim is made during the policy period and the bodily injury or property damage occurred after the retroactive dates, then the extended reporting period may be applicable (if purchased). The basic tail actually provides you with two separate periods of different length. One period runs for 5 years from the end of the policy period. The 60-day tail applies to all other claims that were *not* reported to the insurer before 60 days after the end of the policy period. There is no additional premium for this coverage. The 5-year or supplemental tail will have an additional charge.

Even though there may be some premium difference in favor of the claims-made policy, the purchase of an occurrence policy is recommended.

CHAPTER 20

INSURANCE COVERAGE FOR DIRECT DAMAGE AND CONSEQUENTIAL LOSS

James H. Costner
Willis Corroon P.L.C.

Physical damage to or destruction of an office building will result in the following financial consequences:

1. The cost to repair or rebuild.
2. Expenses to expedite repairs.
3. Operating profits interrupted or reduced.
4. Normal operating expenses and fixed costs that continue.
5. Extra expenses to continue, as nearly as practicable, normal operations of the business and to restore income and yield to normal.
6. Expenses for professional services to assist with preparing documentation to file a claim.

Insurance is available to protect against all these financial consequences of risk. Most of the property insurance written in the United States uses policy forms published by the Insurance Services Office (ISO). Other companies develop proprietary forms using the ISO forms as a template.

ISO follows a modular approach to assembling property insurance coverages. Six modules are assembled, on an "a la carte" basis, to describe the property insured, the perils insured against, property and perils excluded from coverage, and various clauses describing how loss amounts will be calculated and paid.

All property insurance policies can be analyzed by answering the following questions:

1. What property is insured?
2. What property is excluded?
3. What perils are covered?
4. What perils are excluded?
5. How is the loss payment calculated?

ISO's basic form is called the Building and Personal Property Coverage Form (CP 00 10).

What Property Is Insured by CP 00 10?

All covered property must be located at the address of the premises described on the policy itself. When the policy covers buildings, the following are included automatically: completed additions; fixtures; machinery; equipment; outdoor fixtures; fire extinguishing equipment; outdoor furniture; floor coverings; appliances used for refrigerating, ventilating, cooking, diswashing, or laundering; additions under construction, alterations, and repairs; and materials, equipment, supplies, and temporary structures within 100 feet of the described premises. When the policy covers business personal property, the following are included automatically: furniture and fixtures; machinery and equipment; stock (a special definition applies); all other business personal property; the insured's interest as a tenant in improvements and betterments consisting of fixtures, alterations, installations, or additions to buildings or structures; and personal property of others in the care, custody, or control of the insured while located in or on the building described on the policy or within 100 feet of the building.

What Property Is Excluded by CP 00 10?

The following property is excluded from coverage:

- Accounts, bills, currency, deeds, evidences of debt, money, notes, or securities. All these items are insurable for damage or destruction, but not for loss of use, under various crime insurance policies that are available from ISO or others. Separate insurance is required for loss due to employee dishonesty and for loss caused by theft through the use of a computer.

- Animals. This exclusion can be eliminated if the owners of an office building have animals on display or held as stock.
- Automobiles held for sale. Automobile physical damage insurance policies are available from ISO.
- Bridges, roadways, walks, patios, or other paved surfaces. An office development may have a significant portion of its capital assets committed to construction in these categories. Further, such properties are susceptible to large damage from perils such as flood or earthquake. This exclusion can be removed for an additional premium.
- Contraband, or property in the course of illegal transportation or trade. Insurance on contraband is considered contrary to public policy and, therefore, illegal.
- The cost of excavations, grading, backfilling, or filling. Capital improvements in these categories are susceptible to great damage resulting from perils such as flood or earthquake. Coverage can be provided for an additional premium.
- Foundations of buildings, structures, machinery, or boilers if their foundations are below the lowest basement floor or the surface of the ground, if there is no basement. This exclusion can be removed from the policy.
- Land, water, growing crops, or lawns. It has never been the intent of insurance companies to cover damage to land or pollution clean-up expenses. Excluding coverage on land clarifies that intent. Lawns, however, are susceptible to damage by fire-fighting equipment. In large office developments where lawns represent a significant exposure, the exclusion on lawns can be eliminated.
- Personal property while airborne or waterborne. Full coverage is available on property in transit via special transportation insurance policies. Consequential loss usually is not covered; however, via negotiation with the insurance company, it can be added.
- Pilings, piers, wharves, or docks. Property owners who have significant exposures to the loss of capital assets in these categories can have this exclusion eliminated.
- Retaining walls that are not a part of the building described in the declarations. This exclusion can be eliminated for an additional premium.
- Underground pipes, flues, or drains. As with foundations and

paved surfaces, these categories of assets can be insured by deleting this exclusion.

- The cost to research, replace, or restore the information on valuable papers and records, including electronically encrypted records. Special insurance is available to cover the restoration of accounts receivable records, uncollectible accounts if the records cannot be restored, other valuable papers, and electronic data processing media including proprietary software.

- Vehicles or self-propelled machines (including aircraft or watercraft). This exclusion does not apply to inventory. Vehicle insurance is available through other policy forms. Vehicles used exclusively in or on the insured's property can be covered by agreement with the underwriter.

- Grain, hay, straw, or other crops. This exclusion is not a problem for most office developments.

- Fences, radio or television antennas (including their lead-in wiring, masts, or towers), signs not attached to buildings, and trees, shrubs, or plants. This exclusion can be removed from the policy by declaration of values of properties in these categories to be insured and by payment of an additional premium.

In addition, swimming pools, diving towers, diving platforms, crop silos and their contents, and property stored in open yards are not excluded from coverage automatically, but they may be excluded at the discretion of the underwriter. Underwriters also may want to exclude awnings or canopies from coverage.

What Perils Are Covered?

ISO publishes three progressively broader forms that define perils insured against. A *peril* is a condition or circumstance, such as fire or windstorm, that causes damage to or destruction of covered property. One of the following forms must be attached to every policy:

- BASIC FORM (CP 10 10) covers fire (in the United States, fire following a nuclear incident or fire following an earthquake is covered by policies covering the peril of fire), lightning, explosion, windstorm, hail, sudden and accidental smoke damage, contact by aircraft or vehicles, riot or civil commotion, vandalism, sprinkler leakage, sinkhole collapse, and volcano eruption.

- BROAD FORM (CP 10 20) covers, in addition to all the basic form perils, glass breakage; falling objects; weight of ice, sleet, or snow; and water seepage, leakage, or freezing.
- SPECIAL FORM (CP 10 30) covers "risks of direct physical loss not excluded." The exclusions are listed and described in the next section.

What Perils Are Excluded by CP 10 30?

The following perils are excluded from coverage by CP 10 30:

- The enforcement of any ordinance or law regulating the construction, use, or repair of any property or requiring the tearing down of any property, including the cost of removing its debris. Various jurisdictions have statutes requiring that a building not meeting current codes be upgraded if the building is damaged beyond a certain percentage specified in the law. For example, an office building may have to be retrofitted with automatic sprinklers before it can be reoccupied. In certain circumstances, the undamaged portion of a damaged building will have to be demolished and torn away. Building ordinance coverage is available to cover the additional costs of restoration and for the consequential loss (business interruption and/or extra expense). Particular care must be exercised to make sure building ordinance coverage applies to direct damage and consequential loss. Remember, ISO follows an "a la carte" approach.
- Earth movement. This exclusion includes earthquake, landslide, sinking, rising, shifting, volcanic eruption, and explosion or effusion. When purchasing earthquake insurance, care must be taken to assure that the coverage purchased replaces all the perils excluded by CP 10 30. Some policies cover earthquake only.
- Governmental action. This exclusion was added to all policies because negligent zoning practices of certain municipalities on the West Coast were held to be nonexcluded perils. Insurance companies were being forced by the courts to pay for damages caused by earthquakes on policies that excluded earthquake damage because negligent zoning had contributed to the damages. The purpose of this exclusion is to clarify the intent of

the insurers that they do not cover any loss caused solely by negligent zoning practices.

- Nuclear reaction, radiation, or radioactive contamination. An endorsement is available to add back some coverage for this exclusion. The endorsement covers, "loss by sudden and accidental radioactive contamination, including resultant radiation damage, provided such radioactive contamination arises out of material on the insured's premises, provided at the time of such loss, there is neither a nuclear reactor capable of sustaining nuclear fission in a self-supporting chain reaction nor any new or used nuclear fuel which is intended for or which has been used in such a nuclear reactor." If any tenant stores or uses radioactive materials, the building owner needs to purchase the radioactive contamination endorsement to cover direct and consequential damages to his or her own property.

- Interruption of utility services. Coverage is available under endorsements from ISO to cover physical damage and consequential loss (business interruption and extra expense) caused by the interruption of any utility service (on an a la carte basis) caused by damage to property of the utility caused by a peril not excluded. A separate endorsement is required to cover damages and expenses resulting from interruption of utility services caused by damages to transmission lines. Broader utility interruption insurance is available from the Chubb Group of Insurance Companies and from the Factory Mutual Companies.

- War, which is considered an uninsurable, catastrophic peril.

- Water, including flood, surface water, waves, tides, tidal waves, overflow, spray, mudslide, sewer back-up, and underground hydrostatic pressure. As with earthquake, when flood insurance is purchased, it is important to make sure the coverage purchased replaces the perils excluded in CP 10 30.

- Electric arcing. Coverage is available under boiler and machinery insurance policies.

- Delay, loss of use, or loss of market. Income interrupted or reduced and increased expenses for operations or restoration of the business to normal are insurable under consequential loss forms.

- Smoke, vapor, or gas from agricultural smudging or industrial operations. This is considered an uninsurable pollution exposure.

- Wear and tear, rust, corrosion, fungus, decay, deterioration, hidden or latent defects. All these perils are considered conditions that will occur in the normal course of events. Hence, they are not "risks."

- Mechanical breakdown, including rupture or bursting caused by centrifugal force, or explosion of steam boilers, steam pipes, steam engines, or steam turbines. These exclusions apply to all property covered under this policy and not just to machinery or boilers. Coverage for damages caused by machinery breakdown or boiler explosion is available under boiler and machinery insurance policies.

- Smog and release of contaminants or pollutants; settling, cracking, shrinking, or expansion; dampness or dryness; extremes of temperature; marring or scratching; insects, birds, rodents, or other animals. All these situations are considered controllable by the insured. Therefore, losses if any, are avoidable and preventable. Hence, they are not considered insurable "risks."

- Gradual water seepage or leakage. Water damage caused by leakages lasting less than 14 days are covered. Water leaks or flows caused by freezing in unattended, unheated buildings are excluded.

- Dishonest or criminal acts by the insured, partners, employees, and directors. Acts of sabotage or deliberate destruction by employees is not excluded. Employee theft is insurable under fidelity bonds.

- Voluntary parting with any property, if induced to do so by any fraudulent scheme, trick, device, or false pretense. Theft of physical assets, including money, can be covered by special crime insurance policies.

- Damages caused by rain, snow, ice, or sleet to personal property in the open. These are not considered insurable "risks."

- Collapse. Collapse insurance can be provided by eliminating this exclusion or by purchasing a special policy that would include collapse coverage.

How Is the Loss Payment Calculated?

The basic policy provides coverage on an actual cash value basis. *Actual cash value* means the depreciated value of the asset. Replacement cost coverage (replacement without deduction for depreciation) is available by declaring replacement cost values, paying the additional premium due, and checking the appropriate box on the form.

Time element insurance, also known as consequential loss insurance in many parts of the world, includes business interruption insurance, extra expense insurance, loss of rental income insurance, and loss of leasehold interest insurance.

1. Business interruption insurance covers: (1) loss or reduction of pretax operating profits, (2) repayment of normal operating expenses that necessarily continue during a shutdown, and (3) expenses paid to reduce the amount of loss under items 1 and 2, but only to the extent the loss is reduced. Business Interruption insurance does *not* include the amount of increase in normal operating expenses resulting from insured loss, nor does it cover extra expenses incurred to continue normal operations of a business.
2. Extra expense insurance covers expenses incurred to continue or resume normal operations following restoration of insured damages.
3. Rental income insurance covers the amount of rent not collected because of insured damage to an asset minus the amount of operating expenses that do not continue during the time a building is uninhabitable. Rental income insurance is substituted for business interruption insurance when the only income subject to interruption is rental receipts.
4. Leasehold interest insurance covers the difference between existing favorable lease expenses because of damages caused by an insured peril (low rent) and the market value of replacement property if the favorable lease is cancelled. The cancellation must result from damage to or destruction of the leased property. Coverage applies to property the insured leases from a third party for business operations.

Damage to or destruction of an office building or complex will almost always result in business interruption and extra expense loss. ISO companies provide coverage on the Business Income Coverage Form (CP 00 30).

What Consequential Loss Is Insured Under Form CP 00 30?

A general policy covers net income reduced or interrupted, fixed costs and expenses that "necessarily" continue, extra expenses incurred to avoid or minimize the suspension of business, and expenses incurred to expedite the repair of insured damages. This form does not cover expenses for purchased professional services necessarily incurred to prepare documentation to file a claim. In the event of a large and complex claim, claims preparation expenses can be material; therefore, consideration should be given to adding special language providing coverage for these purchased professional services.

How Long Will the Policy Pay?

The policy pays from the time the direct physical damage loss occurs until restoration should be completed. The policy requires completion with reasonable speed. Unless endorsed, the period of restoration does not include any increased period required due to the enforcement of any law that regulates the construction, use, or repair of the property or that requires the tearing down of any property (this coverage is available under the Building Ordinance Coverage Endorsement). The form covers 30 days following the period of restoration to return business operations to normal. If more than 30 days' coverage is required, coverage is available for an additional premium.

Highly Protected Risks

Owners of very large schedules of fully sprinklered properties to be insured are almost always eligible for insurance from underwriters of highly protected risks (HPR). HPR underwriters provide broader coverage. Generally, their forms are easier to read and understand. Typically, the rates charged by HPR underwriters are lower than rates charged by ISO companies. HPR underwriters include the Factory Mutual Companies (Allendale Mutual, Arkwright Mutual, and Protection Mutual), Industrial Risk Insurers, Kemper Insurance Companies, Wausau Insurance Companies, American International Insurance Companies, the Chubb Group of Insurance Companies, and St. Paul Insurance Companies. Those to whom the HPR option is available will certainly want to consider purchasing their insurance from one of these insurers.

Coinsurance

All the ISO policies described in this chapter contain a "coinsurance clause," which requires the purchase of a minimum amount of insurance, usually 80 percent, of the value of the property being insured. In the event of a coinsurance deficiency, the loss payment will be calculated according to the following formula:

$$\frac{\text{Amount of insurance purchased}}{\text{Amount of insurance required}} \times \text{Loss} = \text{Payment}$$

The coinsurance clause can be nullified by activating the optional agreed value clause. On the request of the insured, accompanied by an acceptable schedule of values insured, the insurance company will agree to suspend the coinsurance clause until the next value statement is due. Most practitioners believe the agreed value clause should always be activated.

Recommendations

To provide the best coverage for direct damage and consequential loss, these recommendations should be followed.

1. Buy the broadest possible insurance coverage with the narrowest possible exclusions. The higher premiums for broader coverages can be offset by increasing the per occurrence deductible. An uninsured exposure or peril represents a 100 percent deductible for that risk.
2. Use a combination business interruption (or loss of rents) and extra expense policy to cover consequential losses.
3. Use the broadest possible definition of "covered property." Do not accept property exclusions related to paved surfaces, foundations, footings, antenna, trees, lawns, or shrubs.
4. Consider coverage for direct damage and for consequential loss caused by interruption of utility services.
5. For consequential loss insurance, include pretax operating profits, normal expenses that continue including payroll expenses, and any increase in the cost of doing business in the defined loss.
6. For consequential loss insurance, designate the defined period to cover the period of time during which the business is affected by the damage to or destruction of the insured property. The time following the period during which physical damages are repaired or restored can be insured under so-called "lag" insurance. It provides an additional period of time during which insurance payments continue for the pur-

pose of restoring business operations, income, and yield to normal.

7. Delete or nullify all coinsurance clauses by the use of agreed amount endorsements.

8. Add special language to cover actual expenses incurred for professional services (accounting, legal, appraisal, salvaging, etc.) purchased to accumulate data and to prepare documentation necessary to file a claim.

CHAPTER 21

MAINTENANCE AND ENERGY ASPECTS OF PROPERTY MANAGEMENT

Michael J. McCambridge
Robert D. Castro
Rockefeller Center Management Corp.

Maintenance and energy management, both of which require a large amount of data and analysis, should be discussed jointly for a number of reasons. The foremost reason, however, is that both require a complete understanding by those who operate buildings so that property can be managed efficiently. Operating personnel must also clearly understand the overall philosophy of ownership, including financial policies of a particular property. Maintenance and energy management are expensive activities requiring continuous analysis, coupled with cost management methods. Although the actual percentages may vary according to type of building, region, and year, repair and maintenance costs account for 20 to 30 percent of normal annual operating costs (without real estate taxes). Energy costs can easily account for another 25 to 35 percent.

A building's maintenance and energy programs are primarily controlled by the initial design (quality and flexibility) and to a great extent by the manager, who operates the physical plant. For example, if the building is located in a major commercial or industrial market, the property was probably designed with operating costs in mind and is managed by a property management company or an experienced in-house staff. Staff members are trained in a broad range of disciplines such as engineering design and operations, energy management, cost accounting, and purchasing. Such expertise is usually an unaffordable luxury in small, isolated buildings, or even in a smaller complex of buildings. Even if such facilities were large enough to justify both a building manager and operating engineers, the maintenance and energy programs would be only a part of their overall total responsibilities. In the smallest buildings, the property manager is likely to have limited experience, and the physical plant operator might be an inexperienced janitor. Managers and operators in the smaller buildings are more likely to have had to rely on their practical experience rather than on any formalized training and licensing. Since the proliferation of personal computers in the early 1980s, smaller facilities have had the opportunity to use management tools and techniques that were previously unaffordable and therefore available only to the larger organizations.

Both maintenance and energy management require the processing of large quantities of data on a repetitive basis, which is now easily accomplished with computers and standardized software packages for any size building. Maintenance and energy management require a coordinated (but not necessarily integrated) financial reporting and cost management system, and both rely on a skilled operator who must understand management's policies and objectives.

Throughout this chapter I discuss the various types of buildings and the effect that the owner or developer has on both the initial design and the resulting maintenance and energy aspects of the property.

Building owners can be categorized into three groups: speculator, developer, and corporate. Each group approaches design—and ultimately repairs and maintenance—from a different business viewpoint.

The speculator intends to dispose of his property in the near future and will minimize both initial construction cost capital and operating tools at the expense of annual operating costs. At the other end of the spectrum is the owner- or corporate-occupied building; this type of developer develops a long-term, first class investment. As a result, both the physical and economic lives of the building and its components are considered when formulating the initial design and the resultant energy and maintenance programs. In the owner-occupied building energy conservation measures and equipment selection that will be economical in the long term will be undertaken even though they may be initially uneconomical. The developer is interested in a quality building that is well-maintained and competitive in today's corporate marketplace. In terms of operating expenses, of which repairs and maintenance are a significant part, the owner will spend the proper amount of money on preventive and corrective maintenance. However, he will defer maintenance but minimize it and the associated risks.

The type of owner, the marketplace, and the decisions made during the design and construction process are key factors in determining maintenance and energy management programs.

MAINTENANCE

The subject of maintenance falls into three main categories:

- Preventive
- Corrective
- Deferred

Preventive maintenance is performed to prevent serious long-range problems. Examples of preventive maintenance are greasing bearings and replacing filters.

Corrective maintenance is required when items must be repaired immediately in order to maintain the physical plant or operational integrity, as in the case of a physical breakdown.

Deferred maintenance can be either preventive or corrective maintenance work that is deferred until absolutely necessary.

The speculator, developer, and corporate owner each approach maintenance and its associated staffing requirements differently. The design, the selection of major equipment, the construction means—in essence, the overall quality—dictates the resultant level of maintenance.

The speculator tries to minimize initial capital costs for maintenance and will defer repair work as long as possible. In most cases, the more one defers, the more one pays for corrective work and experiences risk or discomfort at some point in the future.

The speculator can pay in immediate repair costs or in ancillary damages that may be caused by deferred repair. One should understand that work sometimes gets deferred because of dollars and cents, and not because of physical or scheduling issues.

Each approach to development and property management requires a different operating budget; yet all owners share the task of making sure their buildings operate efficiently and effectively at minimum cost.

Initially and annually, each owner must perform the following tasks:

1. Define the work to be done.
2. Categorize all tasks in terms of deferred, preventive, or corrective work.
3. Implement the plan accordingly.

What Constitutes Maintenance

There are six main categories that make up maintenance: (1) administration, (2) facilities, (3) protection, (4) elevators, (5) engineering, and (6) building maintenance. Maintenance (R&M) constitutes as much as 25 to 35 percent of a building's annual normal operating expenses (exclusive of real estate taxes). The percentage breakdown for each of the six major categories for one building could be quite different from any other building's percentages.

To provide for further detail for cost analysis and control, each of the six major categories can be further broken down by type of expense, such as payroll, fringe benefits, materials, and contracted services.

In-House Versus Contracted Maintenance

Different owners have different operating budgets. Each owner will approach the solution to dealing with repairs and maintenance work in a different way. Just as there's the quality developer, there's the quality maintenance company. The question is whether the owner should do the maintenance in-house, consider an outside service company, or combine both options, and what factors influence this decision.

This decision is often determined automatically according to how the building was designed and when it was built. If it was built as a speculative building, the owner does not spend a lot of money to buy quality equipment and therefore does not require top-of-the-line service companies to maintain that equipment. One does not purchase and install a second-level elevator and ask a major supplier to come in and maintain it. This just does not make practical and economic sense. The quality of the main components of a building certainly determines the amount spent on annual repairs and maintenance.

The speculator tends to minimize on-site staff, preferring to contract outside for most of the required repairs and maintenance services. The developer provides a reduced, efficient, on-site operating staff to give immediate and professional service to maintenance and repair problems and uses service contracts for only a portion of the work and major pieces of equipment. The corporate owner usually provides a 24-hour, on-site, over-staffed crew capable of responding to problems and repairing necessary items, with outside contracts to service and repair major pieces of equipment, such as elevators, refrigeration machines, and the like.

Experience shows that a quality building costs more per square foot to maintain than a speculative building. These annual ranges of additional costs could vary as much as 50 percent. If repair and maintenance costs are approximately 30 percent of the annual operating costs, the degree of variance could be as much as 15 percent from the speculative to the corporate building.

To a great extent, the selection of in-house vs. outside contracted maintenance is dependent upon the size of the building, the owner, and his commitment to physical, on-site labor. If the speculative developer can get away with it, in some cases there will be no maintenance personnel on-site, or the individual will be responsible for a number of buildings. The work will therefore be handled by outside contractors.

In an unskilled labor market, service and preventive maintenance work will be contracted to skilled services and skilled workers. New York City is unique in that it is fortunate enough to have a large, generally skilled labor force of engineers and other workers who provide most in-house maintenance work and also perform most preventive maintenance on a regularly scheduled basis. In any case, elevator maintenance and repair, general and window cleaning, and servicing of significant mechanical and electrical work are subcontracted to skilled professionals experienced in these areas.

Your contracted agreements, however, must allow you to reevaluate your costs by going out into the marketplace to ensure competitive subcontractor pricing.

The Maintenance Management System

Whether your maintenance is performed by in-house or out-of-house personnel, you must have a system that allows you to track the work done by the maintenance people, as well as costs accrued. How? By automating. Everyone acknowledges that automated systems are appropriate. The question is how to devise an automated system that can run the gamut from the major corporate developer to the owner who is running a small facility in suburbia.

The major corporate headquarters—the more sophisticated buildings of half a million square feet or more—have automated systems. A wide range of automated systems are available, from time-shared mainframe systems to simple PC-based systems. Some systems allow the preventive maintenance work to be assigned on a more practical, non–assembly-line basis.

ENERGY

The Energy Managers

We will not attempt to offer advice on how to deal with the technical aspects of energy management; we will leave that to the technicians. Rather, we would like to offer a few suggestions on how to manage the energy managers so they will give you the best results in your facility. We have tried to minimize the use of energy jargon in this discussion, and where technical terms have been used it is with the intent of describing how an energy principle works within the overall discipline of cost management.

The energy manager is generally thought of as an engineering type who is constantly calculating, throttling, and recalculating a building's utilities. Actually, many people and organizations are energy managers and each plays that role in a different way. The building owner is the primary energy manager; he is the most influential in establishing the overall energy management program. The building owner defines it as soon as he sets the basic criteria for the planning and construction of the building. The owner ensures a certain interpretation of that criteria when he hires the design professionals to plan the building, selects the construction team to build it, and hires the operators to manage it, all with the objective of meeting his economic requirements.

The architect and engineer translate the owner's functional criteria into a set of construction plans and specifications, and prescribe and witness the performance tests at project completion. In addition to planning and overseeing construction, they may be called in at various times during the life of the building to make modifications. The engineer might even be retained on an ongoing basis to help the building's operating personnel understand the basic design and operate the new building systems.

Service and maintenance organizations also act as energy managers because they perform the boiler and refrigeration machine efficiency tests and make equipment adjustments or replacements. Utility companies reluctantly became energy managers when they began imposing brownouts on their customers. Over the past two decades utility companies have participated in and even initiated more anticipatory conservation programs, especially for electrical demand reduction. Some utility companies offer incentives such as special rates for curtailable service or for customer-supplied supplementary power, and rebates for installation of more efficient equipment by their customers. Finally, the utilities have become much more willing in recent years to provide usage and metering data to customers. The data allow the customer to evaluate energy conservation steps, including peak load shedding.

The tenants of the building, however, are the major energy managers. They determine lighting design and consumption and choose room temperatures by controlling thermostats. The tenants decide whether office computers and other equipment should be kept online to be immediately available when desired.

The overall use of power is a major asset that must be monitored and controlled. Either an engineer or an electrical contractor should keep "score" of the use of building power. Monitoring the use of power and energy ensures against overextended usage of power supply and potential major downtimes. Power supply should be divided into base-building and tenant usage. Any variations to the supply or usage must be monitored and recorded to ensure against overloading of the system or individual system components.

When tenants request more power than allocated by lease terms, the owner should consider some method of compensation. Eventually all of the spare power will be consumed, and additional capacity will be required from the local utility company. Many owners have established escrow accounts, funded by payment for additional power, as their financial source for additional future power supplies.

The facility manager has the task of bringing the energy managers together as a team and directing each member toward specific energy management programs and targets.

The Energy Audit

Before an energy management program is initiated, the targets and their dollar value have to be identified. Such a program does not necessarily require a great deal of technical skill and effort. Too often, the audit becomes an end in itself, with many labor-hours spent with recording instruments, laboratory analyses of equipment efficiency, and computerized reports with multipage executive summaries. With 12 months' worth of utility bills as a starting point, a walk-through of the building, and some common sense reasoning, an annual energy profile similar to that shown in Exhibits 21-1 and 21-2 can readily be prepared as a basic starting point.

Energy Measurement

Although the utility industry has become increasingly responsive to customer needs in recent years, there is still very little information on a utility bill that is of direct use to the customer. The main reason is that the bill does not show how the energy was used, but shows on-ly what the total usage was. If the building is large and in an area where costs are high, (for example, a high-rise office building in New York), a one-month electricity bill will cover a demand load measured in

EXHIBIT 21–1
Monthly Electricity Profile

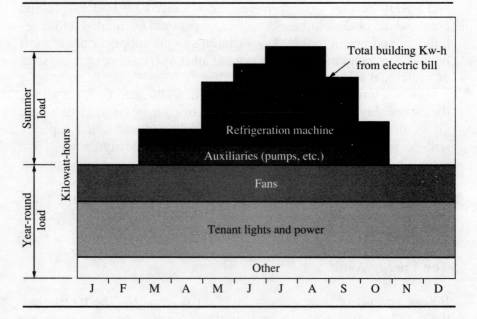

EXHIBIT 21–2
Annual Electricity Costs

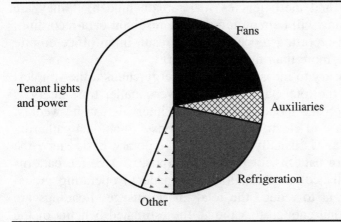

thousands of kilowatts (energy usage in megawatt-hours) and can cost well over a million dollars. If plus or minus 5 percent is given as an acceptable tolerance for budget control—and most operators would consider that to be an optimistic tolerance—that would translate into $100,000 worth of drift for that one-month bill. Even in smaller buildings the numbers can quickly become unmanageable if standard utility company billing data is used exclusively. To underscore the point, consider that the previously noted million-dollar bill is exactly the same in appearance as, and contains only two more pieces of data, than the one presented to the average New Yorker receiving service during the same period for his studio apartment.

When billing data are used exclusively, their significance is often unclear. The units of energy that were consumed can be compared to last month's bill only in an approximate manner. The number of days in the two billing periods may have been different. The weather may have been different. A manager who tries to compare the bill to that of the corresponding month of the previous year may find that the operating hours or even the occupancy itself has changed enough to preclude direct comparison. Nevertheless, the manager must decide under these circumstances whether or not the information on the bill is sufficiently detailed for the effectiveness of his program to be judged. If not, the manager must define manageable chunks of energy and then find a way to measure those chunks in an effective manner.

The key word is *effective,* and it is here that the manager's judgment is critical. If the chunks are still too big and too few measurements are made, waste and inefficiencies will remain hidden; if they are too small, too many will be required and the resultant data-recording, -processing, and -reporting procedures will result in an office empire dedicated to little more than measuring energy.

If it is necessary to measure smaller energy chunks, the simplest way is to record the total building usage over smaller time intervals than is reported on the monthly bill. These intervals can be weekly, daily, or in the case of electricity, hourly or less. Such data gathering over short intervals is usually done on a temporary basis since the purpose is to learn patterns for planning purposes. Once the patterns have been established, modifications are made to operating procedures or equipment to reduce the total energy usage. Readings are continued only long enough to validate the estimated benefits of the modification.

Interval metering of electricity is an exception, however, and is often done on a continuous basis. The peak demand charge in the electricity bill, which accounts for about one-half of the total cost, is for the maximum rate of electrical energy usage during a short (usually half an hour) time interval. In such a case measurements are continuously made through an automation system, not just to record but to actively limit the peak demand.

Another way of partitioning the energy load is to break it down by function. Ideally, the building's energy distribution systems should be configured so that discrete load centers, such as the refrigeration plant, perimeter heating system, and elevators—items commonly described as base building—could be individually metered. Unfortunately, that rarely happens in the real world. With the exception of tenants, whose electricity is sometimes submetered by lease agreement, economic constraints during design and construction do not normally permit a building's mechanical or electrical distribution systems to be configured for separation and metering of loads by function. Reasonably accurate approximations are possible, however. Even though the arrangement of a distribution system may require some compromises in the metering, it may nevertheless be feasible to install primary meters and subtractive submeters that will permit a reasonable measure of the desired loads.

Energy retrofits are sometimes implemented for which the before and after usage cannot be compared. The reasons given are often that

(1) the saving in the retrofit was too small to be noticed in the utility company's bill for the entire building, and (2) it would have been uneconomical to install the local metering at the process itself. This situation is occasionally unavoidable, but it should not become the rule.

Economics

The energy management program is driven primarily by the financial policies of the building's owner and his contractual agreements. For example, if tenant electricity usage is submetered and the tenant reimburses the owner for all direct costs of that electricity (perhaps with a markup), there is little incentive for the owner to minimize that electricity usage. On the other hand, if electricity and steam usage are included as part of the rent, then it behooves the owner to modulate those utilities as much as possible.

The problem may be compounded when leases provide that the tenant utility usage should be submetered and paid for by the tenant, but that the cost of the remaining base building utility expenses be shared by all tenants in addition to the rent. Such lease arrangements tend to make an owner complacent during periods of full occupancy because the leases permit him to pass off the utility costs and the underlying energy management problems to the tenants. On the other hand, when the real estate market tightens and building occupancy rates drop, the higher total cost to tenants reduces the building's marketability. That which had previously been an area of little concern can quickly turn into a major liability. It certainly behooves an owner to control the energy usage at all times during the building's life. Such energy control is not only economical, but ensures the owner's reputation and competitive position in the marketplace.

Conservation Measures

Whenever energy conservation is mentioned, the discussion sooner or later turns toward the more spectacular and esoteric conservation measures such as cogeneration of energy, reclamation of heat, ice storage, and the use of well water for cooling. The current national concern with air and water pollution and related environmental issues has generated broad interest in passive conservation measures such as solar heating, wind power, and even geothermal energy.

Although these measures are certainly feasible, the dispropor-
tionate emphasis on them tends to mask the more mundane but potentially more economically beneficial measures that are possible in
the average office building. The bottom-line benefits of any one conservation measure are often difficult to identify, even to those who are
familiar with the planning and implementation of the measure. Sometimes a measure is implemented simply to demonstrate the owner's
support of environmental concerns (installing solar collectors on the
roof, for example). Sometimes modifications are implemented on the
basis of unrealistically optimistic energy cost savings. It quickly becomes evident that the energy windfall will not materialize, resulting
in dissatisfaction with the modifications.

The most effective conservation measures are often those that
would be dismissed as mundane or even simplistic. Measures that
fall within this category include outdoor air cooling (i.e., economizer
cycle), simple start-stop control of equipment, night temperature set-
back, and reduced lighting levels. Presumably, these measures were
implemented during the first energy crunch. Although these measures
may very well have been in place at one time, chances are (in most
buildings) that one or more of them have since been abandoned, or
modified to the point where they warrant reconsideration.

Some operating procedures that were once simple tend to become
complex without measurable justification. Computerized operating
programs are a case in point. Before the proliferation of microcomputers, the starting and stopping of equipment was performed by
time clocks. Once the calculating powers of microcomputers became
economical, equipment start-stop commands were controlled through
more complex methods, such as scheduling them with outdoor air temperature, or anticipated occupancy levels. Although these programs
may be interesting from a theoretical point of view, it is questionable
whether the more complex procedures have resulted in sufficient savings in the utility bill to justify the design and maintenance measures.
One might argue that it is not necessary to demonstrate a significant
energy savings because once the building automation system is purchased, the additional cost of adding this one feature is negligible.
Although this reasoning may be correct in a literal sense, it tends to
redirect the focus from more basic targets.

A simple but effective way of achieving appreciable energy savings is to concentrate on the major energy consumers—especially
those that operate over long periods of time. Lighting and motors

are two prime targets. As previously noted, lighting accounts for half of the total electricity bill for a typical office building. Fan motors provide an opportunity for effective energy conservation measures, because they operate throughout the year whenever the building is occupied. Because of their conspicuous size and location, the large refrigeration machines in a building's central plant are commonly thought of as the major energy users of the building's air conditioning system. Most often, however, the supply and return fans servicing the air conditioning systems are the real energy consumers. Because these motors operate over extended periods of time, a relatively small increase in efficiency can result in significant energy savings throughout the year.

Sometimes a net energy savings can be achieved by increasing energy usage in one area in exchange for an even greater reduction in another. One example of this type of trade-off is the reduction of the chilled water supply temperature from the refrigeration plant so that the supply air temperature, and consequently the supply air volume from the air conditioning systems, can also be reduced. Although more energy is spent at the refrigeration machine, the energy saved by the fans often compensates for the expense. If the operating engineers are unaware of the direction in which the energy balance favors their building, they may adjust water and air temperatures in a manner that will increase total energy usage.

It is not wise to incorporate a conservation measure into a building's operating program merely because the measure *seems* reasonable and *appears* likely to save a certain amount of energy. In the first place, energy savings calculations are notoriously optimistic. Virtually all published engineering data are oriented toward the calculation of peak loads. The design process is a conservative one, making use of both explicit and implicit safety factors throughout the process. As a result, the actual peak load energy usage is always less than the calculated peak. When the calculation process is put into reverse, the safety factors are rarely completely eliminated and the result is often a calculated savings that will exceed the actual one. When the calculation is performed by someone with a vested interest in the outcome, an energy equipment manufacturer or contractor, for example, the projections are even more suspect. During the last energy crunch, more than one building owner reported that if all the conservation measures that every energy merchant had tried to sell them were implemented, and if the savings claimed by each merchant proved to be true, their buildings would have started to generate energy and they would have been forced to become utility companies.

The best way to check projected energy savings is to see how those savings compare to the load centers defined in the energy audit. As an example, use the profile illustrated in Exhibits 21–1 and 21–2. If the addition of solar film is estimated to save x kilowatts annually, the validity of that estimate can be verified by comparing it to the "refrigeration machine" portion of the profile.

If the amount of energy saved from a conservation measure cannot be measured, or cannot be at least reasonably inferred, the cost benefit of modification is questionable even if the modification is economically reasonable. Sometimes a conservation measure might not be acceptable even though the dollar savings of the measure are unquestioned. For example, load shedding of air conditioning fans in a building that markets itself as a first class commercial building would damage its marketing image far more than the savings would be worth if the air conditioning fans were shut off for fifteen-minute periods on a hot summer day in order to reduce the peak electricity charge from its local utility company.

Because limiting electric demand is such a common conservation measure, it deserves more than just a passing reference. Demand limiting is not an energy conservation measure in the strict sense of the word. The energy that is actually saved is usually negligible; it is avoiding the peak demand charge that is important. The common picture of a daily electricity profile for an office building can be compared to the Swiss Alps. Each day's usage rises to an almost instantaneous peak, then immediately drops off to repeat roughly the same pattern the following day. The profile is expected to start at a relatively low level at 8 A.M., rise to a peak at about 3 P.M., and drop off toward the 5 P.M. close of business. This picture is based on the common notion that because the hottest part of the day is between 2 and 4 P.M., the refrigeration plant must be working at its maximum during that period of the day. Consequently, the building's electricity usage must certainly be at its peak. There is no doubt that many buildings, most frequently buildings of lighter mass, follow such a pattern. However, this is not true of all buildings.

Some buildings, usually those with heavy facade materials or with a large floor-area-to-envelope ratio, have a completely different profile. As a result, they do not lend themselves to peak demand shaving. See Exhibit 21-3 for an example of such a case. The profile in this

EXHIBIT 21-3
Electric Demand Profile

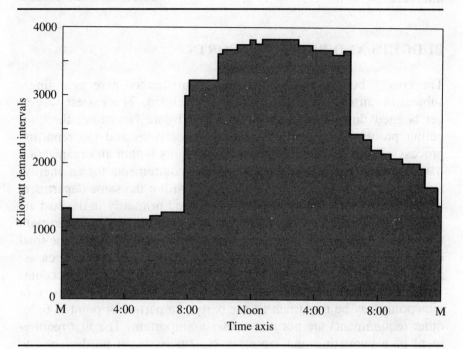

type of building is such that the demand rises from 8 A.M. when the
refrigeration plant is started and occupants begin to enter the building, until about 10 A.M., when both the building and tenant loads
begin to stabilize. The peak electricity demand rises sharply between
8 and 10 A.M., because the refrigeration plant is not only removing
heat directly from the conditioned spaces the occupants have just entered, but is also removing heat that has built up in the structure
throughout the previous night. The thermal inertia of the building
tends to dampen any additional electrical power demands until quit-
ting time. If the building in question is a high-rise building, the peak
demand is not likely to occur during late afternoon at all. Rather,
peak demand is at lunch time, because of the increased elevator load.
Variations in demand during this six- to eight-hour period are relatively small, less than 5 percent of the monthly peak. In buildings
such as this, an energy study may not find demand limiting to be a
worthwhile effort, since the building itself may have its own built-
in load-leveling mechanisms. If so, the studies should concentrate on

the reduction of energy-using equipment that operates during long intervals.

BUDGETS AND BUDGET REPORTS

The energy budget and budget reports are treated here as a single subject because they are so closely interrelated. The easiest way to get bogged down in a mass of paper and data is to have the budgeting process designed around one set of rules and the reporting process around another. Different departments within an organization have different perspectives and different requirements for an energy-reporting system. Often, different people within the same department have different needs. Some will be interested primarily in the cost aspects of the energy program, whereas others will be concerned with the usage. As for costs, the area of concern in some cases is the total cost of the entire utility bill and the total energy usage; in other cases, however, the area of concern is in the net costs, once the cost accounting adjustments have been made. But just because one perspective or viewpoint may be important to one party at a particular point in time, other requirements are not necessarily unimportant. The first requirement of a budgeting and reporting system is that it be designed to serve the needs of all the users within the organization. Everyone should be concerned about both cost and consumption.

The second requirement is that the reporting system should use exactly the same methods that were used to calculate the budget in the first place. In other words, the budgeting and reporting system should be a cyclical process in which the information in this year's reports can easily be updated into next year's budgets. Next year's budgets can in turn be translated into the following year's reports, and so on. I will use the budgeting process as the starting point for discussion of this cycle. Budgets can be prepared in any one of many ways.

One Extreme—Budget by Fiat

By this I mean a procedure whereby an arbitrary limit is established for energy usage or demand for a particular period. These limits may be based on a rough idea of the factors that affected previous performance or may simply be arbitrary. The property manager might dictate that gas usage, for example, should be 5 percent less than it was last year. As crude as this system may be, it does have advantages. In the first place, it is easy to administer and raises absolutely no question about what is expected from the operating staff. On the other hand, because it is so arbitrary, there is no way of comparing the accuracy of the budget with the effectiveness of the operation over the course of the year. This type of budgeting approach probably has its greatest applicability in smaller facilities where the cost of a more sophisticated approach is not justified.

The Other Extreme—Budget by Theoretical Model

A theoretical model is a computer program that calculates the energy effects of all of the building's major energy components. The building's physical characteristics, including walls, windows, and mechanical and electrical equipment, are entered into the program. The program then calculates the energy usage patterns of the building during its operating hours over the course of a year. The simpler models may calculate only the peak summer and winter loads and then extrapolate those peak loads for the balance of the year. Other more sophisticated models might do an independent set of calculations for each of the 8,760 hours in each year. Regardless of the degree of complexity of the program in question, all programs have as their objective the calculation of the total energy usage throughout a typical year and will provide breakdowns as to where and how that energy is used.

The advantage of the budget by theoretical model is its versatility. Such a model can be used to evaluate the sensitivity of changes in energy usage. One can observe the contemplated physical or operational changes in the building such as possible energy conservation retrofits, or even simple projected changes in use and occupancy patterns. The disadvantages of the load-modeling approach are obvious. Load models are extremely complicated and require skilled personnel just to enter data into the program when the model is first constructed. A load model also requires trained personnel to operate the system and to prepare the forecasts necessary for a budget. Even then, before the first budget is prepared, the model must be correlated with actual usage records in order to validate the system's ability to serve as a reliable forecasting device. This validation procedure can be a major time-consuming process.

Computerized models prove to be practical in relatively few

applications but are most useful in the initial design of the building. They are used by a consulting engineer not only to determine the peak loads of a building in order for the building's equipment to be sized, but also as a tool to help decide which of several energy alternatives would be most effective. It follows, then, that if such a program were used during initial building design it would be worthwhile to take advantage of it and use it again during the life of the building. Used in this manner, the computerized load model would become an appendix to the operating manuals and other documents that provide instruction on how the building's systems should be operated and maintained.

The Compromise Method—Budget by Historical Average

This method is somewhere between the two methods previously described as far as complexity is concerned. Just how simple or complex the procedure need be depends on the building and the required accuracy. At the simple end of the scale, the arithmetic average monthly usage over the past two or three years is computed and projected into the next year. More accurate, but correspondingly more complex, averaging methods using statistical techniques are also available. Such methods use a computer-based program that will compare, for example, steam usage (the dependent variable) against weather (the independent variable). When historic data for both the dependent and independent variables are entered, the program, using regression analysis techniques, will calculate the degree to which steam usage is affected by weather. The result is a program that is capable not only of preparing energy budgets based on historical performance and anticipated weather conditions, but also of preparing reports during the year, that compare the actual usage and budgeted usage to the usage that would have been budgeted had the actual weather been known.

In its most basic form, this type of budgeting can be built with a spreadsheet program. Monthly energy usage can be entered into a spreadsheet along with monthly weather data, for example. Nowadays, spreadsheet programs come equipped with statistical analysis packages that will perform linear regressions against one or more variables. This approach should be considered only when the usage period is large, the number of buildings and utilities are few, and the amount of data to be handled is small. When the amount of data to be handled becomes significant, the statistical analysis program must be completely automated. Both the data-processing and data-gathering procedures must be automated. In such a system, meters would automatically feed consumption data into a database together with daily weather data. Once the data-gathering and data-processing portions of the operation have been automated, doing regressions on very small time periods becomes practical. It also becomes practical to perform sensitivity analyses on small periods of time, and weekend usage can be compared to weekday usage. Even Saturday to Sunday usage could be compared if operating patterns differed.

Although the statistical method has not yet become popular without the commercial building sector, it has been used widely in industrial facilities, where energy usage is often directly proportional to production output. I expect that with proliferation of microcomputers in building automation systems, reduced cost of data gathering, and storage on large data bases, the statistical form of budgeting and reporting will become more common in the future.

Although this technique is certainly more complex than the budgeting-by-fiat method described earlier, it is much simpler than the modeling procedures, which require an engineering background. Most business people have a working knowledge of statistical techniques. The spreadsheet programs that contain the regression packages previously mentioned were designed primarily for use by business people. The disadvantage of this type of approach is that fully automated programs are not available and must be custom-made. The market for this type of program is in its infancy, however, and is expected to grow as building automation systems become more common.

CHAPTER 22

DEVELOPING AND IMPLEMENTING AN AUTOMATED SYSTEM

Patrick Lynskey
Applied Systems and Technologies Inc.

Most people agree that society in general and the business community in particular have benefited from the application of computer and software technologies. However, many loudly complain that, having become dependent on these evolving technologies, they now find themselves entangled in a web of incompatible and redundant elements, and that they are often faced with numerous complex and intimidating responsibilities. Properly engineered and applied, automated technologies can dramatically reduce the costs associated with operating and managing your facility. On the other hand, improperly engineered and applied technologies will have the same dramatic effect—in the opposite direction.

Every building development and management project has unique characteristics upon which its feasibility is based. All projects, however, share a set of common requirements. This chapter will focus on these common denominators. More specifically, it will provide a blueprint for developing and implementing a practical approach for the application of automated building technologies.

THE INTELLIGENT BUILDING CONCEPT

In order to determine what technologies qualify as candidates in your building plan, it will be helpful to explore the elements of the "Intelligent Building" concept.

All investors and owners are faced with fixed and variable costs associated with building and managing a facility. A majority of the fixed costs are incurred during the construction phase, whereas the variable costs tend to come with ongoing operations and maintenance. The Intelligent Building concept is designed to reduce these construction and administration costs compared with traditional methods. How?

A predominant feature of the Intelligent Building is the uniform jack, or plug, into which any device (e.g., phone, terminal, sensor, relay, alarm) can be connected. The building is to be saturated with jacks to provide ready access to the wiring network embedded in the infrastructure. Somewhere within the building a central control room will be established where these wires terminate. All subsystem processors will reside here and be cross-connected with their devices at the other end of the wires. Connectivity is administered using a "cable management" system and an electronic switching device. In theory, here's how it's supposed to work:

1. A tenant moves into an office bringing a telephone, computer terminal, and fax machine.
2. After rearranging the furniture, the tenant plugs each device into one of several conveniently located wall jacks.
3. He notes the unique number on the faceplate of each jack and borrows his neighbor's phone to call the control room.
4. He tells the control room administrator that the phone is plugged into "jack 1," the terminal to "jack 2," and the fax machine to "jack 3."
5. The control room administrator updates the cable management database with the information. This automatically triggers an electronic cross-connect via a switching system to establish a device connection: jacks 1 and 3 are now connected with the PBX and jack 2 with the mainframe.

PBXs, computers, environmental controls, and security and fire safety devices can all be installed in your building using a unified system architecture. Construction costs can be reduced by eliminating wiring redundancies that typically occur with the installation of the various subsystems. In some cases, building-wide conduit can be eliminated, because a few of the new wiring backbones are based on low-voltage telephone wire. Intelligent Building vendors are also quick to point out that administrative and management costs can be significantly reduced, particularly those associated with the time it takes to move, rearrange, add, and eliminate devices as tenants come and go or redesign their floor plans. Some vendors have gone so far as to say that by complementing the architecture with raised flooring, a building's overall height can be reduced or, conversely, more floors can be crammed into the same building dimensions.

Is there a practical way to implement the Intelligent Building concept? In order to answer that, a few additional considerations must be mentioned. First, most of the various subsystem manufacturers have a master plan for marketing their entire product line, and most have built their Intelligent Building architectures around proprietary connectivity standards. Although each manufacturer may guarantee end-to-end compatibility of its own products, these proprietary standards often prevent one from connecting elements from different manufacturers. Second, the idea of the centralized control room assumes that investors and owners will accept building-wide administrative and management responsibilities for the entire tenant population. A third consideration is the assumption that investors and owners can and will establish global connectivity standards with which tenants will readily comply.

You are a candidate for a practical application of the Intelligent Building concept if (1) you will commit millions of dollars to a single vendor; (2) you will hire, train, and oversee the high-tech staff required to administer the system; and (3) you can fill up your building with tenants willing to live in it. It would be hard to convince a reasonable person to do these things.

ADAPTATIONS OF THE CONCEPT

What can be salvaged from the Intelligent Building concept? If the architecture can be "opened up" and tenant services scaled back, then the whole concept has practical application and one can benefit from the cost reductions alluded to earlier.

Tenant Services

In order to develop a cost-effective strategy, you should consider two important aspects of your tenant services relationship. First, you should not accept responsibility for providing tenants with office services connectivity. This shouldn't be a problem, especially since this is what tenants are used to. Now you won't have to impose strict building

Standards, and you won't incur the construction expense of saturating the facility with "conveniently" located wall jacks. Second, you should not integrate tenants' office services into the building's wiring platform as a matter of standard practice. You can still offer fee-based tenant services (e.g., moves, changes, additions, and deletions of devices) without the headache of dealing with high-tech compatibility, administrative, and management issues. And if by chance a tenant's devices happen to be compatible with building-wide, in-place wiring standards, then you have the option of integrating the tenant's services. You'll avert the staff costs alluded to earlier and minimize wire "pollution" throughout the facility.

Eliminating these two feature significantly streamlines the design of the architecture and still reduces costs. What we have left is a blueprint for construction, operations, and maintenance rather than a global, end-to-end, all-things-to-all-people megamonster.

Openness and Connectivity

Now all we have to do is "open up" the connectivity standards and we'll have a real winner. But again, we need to set the stage before these terms can have any practical meaning. Both openness and connectivity are attributes of the building's wiring platform. This platform is the common denominator for all the systems incorporated in the Intelligent Building concept. Every device hanging on the platform (phone, terminal, sensor, relay, etc.) must be wired for power (24/48 V), signaling (4–20 mA or 0–5 V), and control (relay or DDC). These services can be integrated within the platform to establish connectivity between a processor and its devices. Connectivity is defined as the ability of a device to send a signal from one end of a wire to the other in such a fashion that the wire's attributes and characteristics remain transparent to the process. In English, it's the "two paper cups on a string" scenario. If we isolate the "string" and observe that its architectural topology resembles a spiderweb, then we have something more true to life. Nevertheless, what we're concerned with is whether or not it passes a clean signal and can be built cost-effectively.

An open system is the opposite of a proprietary one, and is defined as a system as having the ability to connect a hodge-podge of various devices and processes to the spiderweb. As we saw earlier, all devices must be provided with power, signaling, and control services whether they are hanging on an Intelligent Building wiring platform or connected in the conventional manner. This is where the uniform jack comes into play. The standard RJ45 telephone company jack is an eight-pin connector, one piece of which is crimped to the device and the other to the building's wire, that establishes the physical connection of devices with their processors. It looks just like your modular phone jack at home except that it has eight rather than four pins. These connectors are used as an alternative to hard wiring devices to systems and can be used on every device mentioned in this chapter.

Wiring Platform Installation

We have now established the foundation for implementing automated technologies within your facility, namely, the backbone wiring platform. We stated earlier that construction costs could be significantly reduced during the platform's installation. Since the platform consists mainly of low-voltage telephone wire, you can install it without conduit and thus avoid the associated labor and material costs. Additionally, if you intend to place device-driven subsystems within the facility (e.g., environmental monitoring and control, security and access, or fire safety systems) you will be able to eliminate substantial wiring redundancies and save even more money. In my own experience, the design, engineering, and implementation of Intelligent Building schemes throughout a variety of facility types resulted in construction costs 20 to 30 percent lower than the costs associated with conventional methods.

SPECIFIC APPLICATIONS

We will now address specific applications of automated technologies to significantly reduce the variable costs associated with managing a facility. The single largest area of potential savings is in the energy consumption costs required to operate environmental systems. Next largest are the costs for ongoing preventive maintenance and other related activities. These expenses are not determined by building and systems design alone, but rather are for the most part dependent on the methods and procedures of system operation as well as on the quality and timeliness of maintenance. I cannot emphasize enough just how significant these factors will be in determining whether or not you succeed in minimizing operations and maintenance expenses.

We will not discuss systems whose costs of operations can be minimally impacted through variations in operating strategies, such as security and access or fire safety systems. We will instead focus on two categories of computer-based systems that can affect the bulk of your variable costs: (1) environmental monitoring and control systems and (2) maintenance management systems. Properly used, these applications can lower annual expenses by 30 percent or more. In terms of investment performance, one can achieve ROI and payback at about 30 percent and 36 months, respectively.

Environmental Monitoring and Control Systems

Energy management systems (EMS) exploded on the scene during the mid-1970s in response to the tremendous price increases in the world oil market. The need to reduce energy consumption ensured the rapid acceptance of EMS systems by the facility management industry. Overnight, what was once considered an unnecessary and impractical expense became one of the best investment alternatives around. Where else could an investment be completely paid back in 24 to 36 months? ROIs of 30 percent or more became common. In fact, one had to be careful in presenting technology business cases with such high returns, because they raised the eyebrows of bankers and financial managers who weren't used to seeing such investment performance. Once EMS systems proved themselves to be sound investments, the market took off.

Evolution of EMS Systems
When EMS systems first appeared, they were not much more than glorified timeclocks. Most of them knew the day of the week and the time of the day, but little else. They were designed to turn relays on and off at the beginning and end of the occupancy period, saving energy by denying it to nonessential devices after the building emptied. It soon became apparent that there were times during occupancy when some devices could be shut down for brief periods if other devices could compensate for them and maintain a balanced environment. *Time-based duty cycling* was developed and soon proved instrumental in significantly reducing total energy consumption.

But there were side effects. The engineer couldn't readily see the impact of a cycling pattern on temperature and humidity conditions throughout the building. And if one were not careful, the environmental systems could fall behind, and the building occupants would suffer for the rest of the day. This was called "losing the building," and it was serious enough to cause engineers to lose their jobs. A mechanism was needed whereby an engineer could quickly evaluate the environmental impact of various cycling patterns in order to determine which one best suited his particular building's needs, without losing the building (or his job) in the process.

Sensors and monitoring logic were added to the systems so that engineers could quickly see the environmental impact of their adjustments to cycling patterns. An engineer could now react to a bad pattern before the system fell behind.

However, building engineers were at first reluctant to accept automated control systems. Their reluctance was attributed largely to the "man versus machine" syndrome and to the relatively unproven performance history of EMS systems. As a result, the evolution of EMS systems during the early 1980s was slow.

By 1985, people had grown accustomed to the high price of oil. Its effects had finally rippled throughout the infrastructure of the nation's economy, everyone stopped complaining, and eventually complacency won out over panic. The oil crisis simply wasn't newsworthy anymore. And EMS systems weren't the hot items they had once been.

Fundamentals within the EMS marketplace had to change in order to sustain momentum in the sale of systems. Building owners and managers were no longer beating down doors, standing in queues, or calculating their monthly losses while eagerly anticipating the arrival of their long-awaited machines. In an effort to increase market share and in the face of a downturn in demand, manufacturers began active marketing campaigns. The ensuing competition fueled the second stage of EMS evolution and was characterized by the addition of interactive logic to EMS systems.

Previously, manual intervention by the building engineer was required in the adjustment and fine-tuning process. This function was ripe for automation. *Event-initiated control* was introduced to link the monitoring and control functions and an interactive logic was established between them. Time-based duty cycling was ousted in favor of sensor-driven control techniques. By establishing comfort indices and appropriate environmental targets *(setpoints),* the system could now schedule device runtimes using feedback from sensors dispersed throughout the facility. The logic worked something like this:

```
IF the day of the week is WEEKDAY or WEEKEND
   AND If the time of day is   > 0000 hrs and < 0600 hrs
                          or
                    > 0600 hrs and < 1259 hrs
THEN execute   WEEKDAY-NIGHT-CONTROL-SET
                    or
               WEEKDAY-DAY-CONTROL-SET
ELSE execute   WEEKEND-NIGHT-CONTROL-SET
                    or
               WEEKEND-DAY-CONTROL-SET
```

This degree of automation was new to many operating engineers, and only the more progressive embraced it at first. But it eventually caught on because it addressed an important concern of owners and managers—namely, how to balance strategies for reducing energy consumption with the comfort needs of building occupants. Event-initiated control logic accomplished this, so engineers once again adapted to changing conditions. And the ROIs and paybacks continued to top those of more conventional investments.

Although the process of determining cycles and patterns had become highly sophisticated, the underlying techniques were for the most part simple on/off commands. However, large mechanical devices are not designed to withstand frequent and sporadic starts and stops. This fact led to the third major evolution trend in EMS systems, *variable control logic*. Simply stated, this is the process of gradually throttling the output of a device throughout a range of its operating capacity (0 to 100 percent) over a specific time interval. The resulting savings in energy consumption are based on the "merry-go-round" principle. We all know how this works. It takes a lot of energy to get something moving but considerably less to maintain momentum. So once you get a fan blade spinning at a targeted rate, you can cut back on the energy to its motor and just "slap at it" occasionally to keep the rate up. Although the principle is simple, there are a lot of variables that must be evaluated before a desired performance can be achieved. The EMS processor crunches a lot of sensor data through one or more algorithms to determine a desired performance level. It then sends a set of commands to a variable speed controller ("slapping" mechanism), which in turn smoothly adjusts the output of the particular device (motor) over a specific time interval. The algorithm continues to process data and makes adjustments on an ongoing basis, creating a *modulating control sequence*.

Unfortunately, most devices are not equipped to operate according to the merry-go-round principle; they push just as hard to maintain momentum as they do to get started. Variable control logic saves extraordinary sums of money because a significant amount of energy can be denied a mechanical device without affecting output at higher operating ranges (70 to 100 percent). Paybacks on variable controllers are typically less than 24 months.

Choosing an EMS System

Any EMS system under consideration must incorporate the features we've just discussed: calendar and clock, time-based duty cycling, event-initiated control, and variable control logic. In addition, the system must have a "window" through which the engineer can manage and supervise the following general functions: monitoring, alarming, diagnostics, control, and data collection. The window is typically a personal computer with a color monitor, preferably an IBM or IBM-compatible.

The single most important criterion in choosing your system and vendor is the quality of the engineering support, especially the services made available after the sale. Conditions rarely remain static for long, and if your building engineering staff can't adjust the EMS system in response to factors such as tenant demands or changes in utility tariffs, then sooner or later they'll shut it down. Moreover, as investor and owner, you will probably concur with their decision at that point. More systems die on the plant floor because of inadequate support and the accompanying loss of trust than all other reasons combined. It's unfortunate but true that the EMS marketing effort has slowly but surely moved away from a commitment to "total systems support before *and after* the sale" in favor of a "total systems support before the sale" approach. I emphasize this based on my experience in dusting off and reactivating EMS systems over the last ten years.

The EMS system's various devices (sensors, relays, etc.) can be easily connected to the building-wide wiring platform. Physically mark the places where they are to be installed and pull the platform wire (four pairs) as close as possible to each point. Then take a short piece of wire and screw down one end to the device and crimp the male portion of the RJ45 connector to the loose end.

Maintenance Management Systems

Like EMS systems, maintenance management systems can significantly reduce the variable costs associated with managing your facility. Whereas equipment operating methods and procedures primarily affect energy consumption expenses, maintenance practices affect the costs associated with labor, spare parts, and tenant services. Properly applied, computer-based applications can be ideally suited to address these concerns.

Maintenance philosophies are based on a fundamental issue of economics: how to allocate resources (labor and materials) to needs (maintenance/service requirements) in consideration of budgetary restraints. Of these resources, labor consumes the lion's share of every operating budget. So it comes as no surprise that the greatest effect on expenses can be made by focusing on this element.

Your resident engineering staff is responsible for several types of maintenance activities. These typically include preventive maintenance, breakdown and emergency maintenance, fee-based project work, custodial tasks, grounds activities, and tenant trouble calls. You must determine and maintain an optimum staffing level that balances available with required staff hours and establishes a responsive state of readiness. In addition, spare parts and tools must be readily accessible to support the total maintenance effort. Once these issues are properly addressed and resolved, you can expect to get more work from each person on any given day. You can also expect to find that overtime requirements will be substantially reduced. In other words, you can run your maintenance operation with a smaller staff without a degradation in the timeliness and quality of maintenance activities. And this translates directly into dollars saved at the plant floor level.

Workload Balancing

So, how do you balance the workload? First you must calculate a staffing level. Isolate routine maintenance activities that can be "prescheduled." Typically, these are preventive maintenance, custodial, and grounds tasks. Determine the annual staff hours for each of these activities. The sum becomes your baseline. To this, you then add a "fudge factor" to account for unscheduled events such as equipment breakdowns, emergencies, and tenant trouble calls. A second fudge factor can be applied as a safety net if you are not completely confident in your baseline calculation. You now have developed an "estimated annual labor requirements" model. To determine your staffing level, make a second pass at your baseline calculation to segregate the maintenance tasks by trade, craft, or skill type. Now total up the labor-hours associated with each to derive an "estimated annual labor by craft requirements" model. If you figure that you can expect to get five productive work hours per eight-hour day, then dividing each of the estimated labor requirements figures by the annualized productive hours will give you a staffing level.

The next step in the workload balancing procedure is to create a matrix or grid, whose north/south border contains row after row of equipment needing maintenance and whose east/west border contains 52 columns representing the weeks in a year. Each cell within the matrix has a unique, two-coordinate name (e.g., Chiller #1/Week 15). Within this square is placed one or more maintenance tasks, each to include the labor-hours required, labor-hour standard(s), and the craft type. Since most if not all tasks have a repetitive performance frequency (weekly, monthly, etc.), you can hop across the columns to post the annual schedule. After completing this process for all maintenance-worthy equipment, you can determine the weekly required staff hours by craft, by totaling each column. Now list your weekly available staff hours by craft underneath these figures and net them out. It will quickly become apparent whether or not your workload is balanced. You will probably need to make at least three passes at the matrix before it is properly balanced. Remember, the net must be in your favor to reflect the fudge factored labor needs relating to unscheduled events.

This workload balancing process must be developed for each of the various scheduled maintenance categories. The procedure just illustrated relates to preventive maintenance. The other categories (custodial and grounds) are balanced the same way, except that the grids' north/south borders will contain zones or areas rather than equipment.

Once the workload is balanced, generating weekly work orders is simple: just move down the appropriate weekly column and create the orders as you go. Whether or not there is sufficient available staff to address unscheduled events can be easily determined.

Unfortunately, this method of scheduling may be inappropriate for some tasks, particularly preventive maintenance. Some tasks may need to be scheduled in consideration of either the date the work was last done or "elapsed clicks" (runtime). These alternative scheduling requirements play havoc with a balanced staffing model since they often creep across the weekly columns in an unpredictable fashion and throw off all the carefully calculated totals. In frustration you wind up trashing the schedule, increasing your staff, and facing each day as it comes. Here's where you'll start to see overtime expenses take a sharp upturn.

So what do you do? You already know the answer. If there ever was an ideal application for computer automation, maintenance scheduling would be it. The computer deals with all techniques of task scheduling and isn't bothered in the least by scenarios that frustrate a human scheduler. Furthermore, it gives the engineer a window to peek in when scheduling unplanned events (especially fee-based services). You no longer need to haphazardly increase your staff or authorize unnecessary overtime. Additionally, the effects of any proposed adjustments to the overall staffing level can be justified as a result of comparing required and available labor-hours. The savings in labor dollars will be significant enough to pay for the technologies in a year or two. Last and by far not least is the positive impact that the timeliness and quality of maintenance will have on the useful life of major building equipment.

I would like to mention an interesting side note at this point. It's a management concept that I have frequently encountered in working with our Japanese friends in plants and facilities across America. They call it "Genba Genbutsu", and freely translated it means: "Get off your butt, manage on your feet, put your feet out on the plant floor and your hands on the problem. Experience the problem firsthand and then evaluate the options before marshaling your resources. Act decisively, promptly, and thoroughly to correct the problem now. Then develop and implement an improvement plan to prevent the problem from ever occurring again." Personally, I like the idea. You can't spend your time pencil-whipping problems and still maintain an effective maintenance operation. But automated technologies love pencil-whipping tasks, and once you implement them, your engineering staff can "Genba" to further reduce your ongoing operations and maintenance expenses.

Workforce Readiness
The leading cause of lost productive work hours is the time taken to prepare to do the work. Have you ever heard the words, "If only I had the proper tools then I could do the job" or "If only I had the proper parts, then I could finish the job"? I won't elaborate on the

implications of these issues other than to say that with the proper tools and parts one is fortunate to get five productive work hours in any eight-hour day. Consider the following case study.

There is a popular resort in the heart of the Blue Ridge mountains of central Virginia. The houses, condos, inns, restaurants, and shops are located on the mountain top, but the engineering shop with its five-man staff is—you guessed it—in the valley. The nearest village is 20 mountainous miles away and the nearest city is approximately 40. My own analysis of the situation revealed that on a daily basis at least one labor-day was spent on trips to town to buy spare maintenance parts. It also wasn't uncommon that a man would be dispatched all the way up the mountain only to return for the proper part or tools. A round trip, including the troubleshooting time, could take an hour. It's apparent that a combined total of five round trips among the remaining four men would result in the loss of another labor-day . . . every day! Losing two out of five labor-days represents a 40 percent loss of productive work time. And because the preventive maintenance and tenant requests workload hadn't changed the staff was forced to put in overtime to beat down the backlog. This scenario is exaggerated, but it makes a point—namely, that the state of readiness of your staff will have a significant impact on your maintenance budget. Now, how can you establish a practical, elevated state of readiness?

It all comes down to coordinating the availability of spare parts and tools with the maintenance task schedule. First, let's talk about spare parts inventory from a financial perspective. Items sitting on a warehouse shelf aren't the most productive assets on your balance sheet. But they're assets nevertheless; they're cash transformed into materials. They don't produce interest, dividends, or capital gains income in the usual sense. As an asset, inventory typically produces a negative return in the short run (lost income earning opportunities, cost of financing) and a positive return in the long run (resale value at markup). Your inventory management savvy will become the principal factor contributing to the level of your overall return, for a couple of reasons. First, you're not in the retail business and so you won't be reselling very much inventory at a markup. Second, buying maintenance parts and putting them in a warehouse is like buying a new car: it loses significant resale value as soon as you drive it off the lot. So the part's conversion value, if it is liquidated, will often contribute to the negative aspect of the return.

So how do you produce a positive return in the long run? First and foremost, you must optimize the quantities of items shelved in your spare parts locations. This lowers your inventory baseline value as well as the associated carrying costs (negative short-term returns). We all know how percentages work: the "combined" return on inventory will continue to rise as the value of the baseline falls (assuming that the positive value of the return remains constant). So, the solution is to keep your inventory to the minimum needed and turn it over three or four times a year.

How do you optimize inventory levels in a maintenance operation? First, inventory must be organized in a practical and efficient manner. Consider the following example. A major international airport in the northeastern United States contracted out the tasks associated with operating and maintaining the cargo and baggage handling process. The airport authority *required* that the successful bidder purchase from them all the maintenance spare parts currently stocked in the inventory stores. The airport's estimated valuation of these parts was considerable. Instead of allowing each bidder to take a physical count to verify the purchase valuation, the airport authority stated that the award winner would be entitled to a dollar for dollar refund if the contractor's own physical inventory valuation was less than the airport's estimate. In addition, the airport authority agreed to rebate, via formula, the "fat" value (the difference between pre-existing and proposed carrying levels). If the contractor demonstrated within 12 months of start-up that, through sound management and scheduling practices, an overall lower level of inventory could be carried without negatively affecting the integrity of airport operations, then further rebate would be forthcoming. Needless to say, the process was immediately automated and the contractor succeeded in receiving from the airport authority a refund far greater than the cost of automation. Once again, an exaggerated example makes a point: optimizing inventory levels will produce significant returns regardless of the particular application.

To establish an inventory baseline, first determine the spare parts required to perform regularly scheduled maintenance activities. This calculation can be incorporated within the matrix used in the workload balancing procedure. You can then calculate the baseline inventory quantities that will be consumed throughout the year. So, how do you optimize the baseline to avoid carrying an unnecessarily fat inventory? It's a relatively simple but laborious process and one well suited for automation.

Suppose that you've classified each spare part as (A) absolutely critical, (B) support of critical, or (C) noncritical. Suppose further that you've established turnover rates for the three levels: (A) one turn a year, (B) two turns a year, and (C) three turns a year. Finally, suppose that you have determined the minimum reorder and/or safety stock levels and standard reorder quantities. You can then determine the types and quantities of parts in each category required annually to support the maintenance operation. Then take all quantities in category A and add the minimum reorder and/or safety levels to establish stock levels. Take category B's quantities and divide by two (for two turns a year) and divide category C's quantities by three, and to these add the appropriate reorder/safety levels. You've now optimized the inventory baseline. Estimate the miscellaneous parts, quantities, turns, and criticalities needed to take care of unscheduled events (tenant trouble calls especially) and you'll now have a lean and mean, totally optimized inventory. Again, if there ever was an ideal application for computer automation, maintenance inventory management would be it.

Let's back up and tie this discussion to our earlier question: "how do you produce a positive return on inventory in a maintenance operation?" The answer is that you can't, without first optimizing it. The positive returns on your inventory investment will result from *not* sending your staff "up the mountain" unprepared and *not* having someone standing at a supply house counter doing nothing. These are practical problems, so I've given you a practical plan for automation. With properly applied automation, you can coordinate the availability of spare parts and tools with the maintenance task schedule. And once you've done this, you can harvest all of the byproduct data and feed it through job cost models and other accountability processes to stay on top of things both financially and operationally. Your savings in staff size, overtime, and carrying costs is your interest, dividend, and gain on the investment. Your management savvy will widen the spread between the short-term negative and long-term positive returns. All in all, an investment in automation makes good, solid business sense.

SUMMARY

In this chapter we have discussed the development and implementation of automated systems in facilities that you, as owners and investors, are likely to build and/or operate. We've looked at the financial implications in order to make a cost-justified case for the use of these systems. The case is based on the effects of properly applied technologies on fixed and variable cost scenarios. By incorporating our variation of the Intelligent Building concept, you can anticipate construction costs in the capital budget 20 to 30 percent lower than the costs of providing the same services using conventional methods. And by automating the operations and maintenance functions (EMS and Maintenance Scheduling systems) you can achieve a further reduction in your ongoing operating budget, also in the neighborhood of 20 to 30 percent.

We explored the functional aspects of these systems from a practical perspective without getting into too much technical jargon, focusing instead on the redundancies of traditional methods, the attributes and characteristics to look for in automated systems, and the philosophies behind the technologies. Now it's up to you to put these ideas to use.

It is appropriate at this point to impart some advice which, if heeded, will substantially reduce the aggravation and frustration of dealing with integrated building technologies. First, take whatever measures are necessary to acquire experienced project management who will accept *entire* responsibility for the technology plan from inception through ongoing support. Second, beware of any single manufacturer claiming to have all the answers. The best solution, and the one most likely to produce the financial and functional gains discussed in this chapter, will more often result from mixing and matching the products of a few vendors who have demonstrated financial stability and market staying power. Third, introduce and incorporate the technological considerations in the early planning phases of each building project. Finally, if you establish an intimate relationship with the pertinent job costing and accountability information, you'll be able to bring your projects in on time, at budget, and at performance.

INDEX